ISBN 978-1-5285-0244-3
PIBN 10139819

English
Français
Deutsche
Italiano
Español
Português

www.forgottenbooks.com

Mythology Photography **Fiction**
Fishing Christianity **Art** Cooking
Essays Buddhism Freemasonry
Medicine **Biology** Music **Ancient**
Egypt Evolution Carpentry Physics
Dance Geology **Mathematics** Fitness
Shakespeare **Folklore** Yoga Marketing
Confidence Immortality Biographies
Poetry **Psychology** Witchcraft
Electronics Chemistry History **Law**
Accounting **Philosophy** Anthropology
Alchemy Drama Quantum Mechanics
Atheism Sexual Health **Ancient History**
Entrepreneurship Languages Sport
Paleontology Needlework Islam
Metaphysics Investment Archaeology
Parenting Statistics Criminology
Motivational

ANNUAL REPORT

OF THE

STATE SUPERINTENDENT

OF THE

STATE OF WISCONSIN,

FOR THE

SCHOOL YEAR ENDING AUGUST 31, 1880.

WILLIAM C. WHITFORD,
State Superintendent.

MADISON, WIS.:

DAVID ATWOOD, STATE PRINTER.

1881.

OFFICE OF THE STATE SUPERINTENDENT,

MADISON, WIS., December 10, 1880.

To His Excellency, WILLIAM E. SMITH,

Governor of Wisconsin:

SIR — I have the honor of submitting, through you, to the Legislature, the thirty-second Annual Report of the Department of Public Instruction, which covers the school year ending August 31, 1880.

I am, sir, very respectfully,

Your obedient servant,

WILLIAM C. WHITFORD,

State Superintendent.

CONTENTS.

Contents.

ANNUAL REPORT

OF THE

STATE SUPERINTENDENT

OF

WISCONSIN.

OFFICE OF STATE SUPERINTENDENT,
MADISON, December 10, 1880.

To the Legislature of Wisconsin:

GENTLEMEN: — In compliance with law, I have the honor of submitting to you my third Annual Report, which is the thirty-second issued by this Department, and covers the school year ending August 31, 1880.

I have arranged the items herewith furnished, under the following heads: First, Statistical Summaries; second, Official Labors; third, Observations on the Present Condition of the Public Schools; fourth, Accompanying Documents; and fifth, Statistical Tables.

The returns given in the summaries and the tables are unusually complete and reliable. They have been collected with considerable labor, and supply interesting facts on many points which have never before been presented to the Legislature. A careful examination of these returns will tend to strengthen the confidence of the people in our educational operations, in all of which there has been marked stability the past year; and in some, very satisfactory improvements.

I — ST. SUP.

STATISTICAL SUMMARIES.

The statistics are here frequently classified, as in the tables at the close of the work, so as to present separately the conditions of the public schools in the sixty-two organized counties and in the twenty-seven independent cities.

I. NUMBER OF SCHOOL-DISTRICTS.

	1879.	1880.	*Increase.*
In the counties	5,568	5,573	5
In the cities	31	31	..
Totals	5,599	5,604	5

II. NUMBER OF SCHOOL-DISTRICTS REPORTING.

	1879.	1880.	*Decrease.*
In the counties	5,542	5,530	12
In the cities	31	31	....
Totals	5,573	5,561	12

III. NUMBER OF MEMBERS OF SCHOOL-DISTRICT BOARDS.

	1879.	1880.	*Increase.*
In the counties	16,704	16,719	15
In the cities	190	190	....
Totals	16,894	16,909	15

IV. NUMBER OF PUBLIC SCHOOLS.

	1879.	1880.	*Increase.*
In the counties	5,765	5,797	32
In the cities	167	187	20
Totals	5,932	5,984	52

V. NUMBER OF UNGRADED SCHOOLS.

	1879.	1880.	*Increase.*
In the counties	5,475	5,507	32
In the cities	24	26	2
Totals	5,499	5,533	34

Statistical Summaries.

VI. NUMBER OF GRADED SCHOOLS.

	1879.	1880.	*Increase.*
In the counties, with two departments...........	166	165	dec. 1
In the cities, with two departments	42	36	dec. 6
In the counties, with three departments	52	54	2
In the cities, with three departments...........	27	33	6
In the counties, with four or more departments..	72	75	3
In the cities, with four or more departments.....	74	88	14
Totals	433	451	18

VII. NUMBER OF HIGH SCHOOLS.

	1879.	1880.	*Increase.*
In the counties, under Free High School law....	68	74	6
In the cities, under Free High School law.......	20	21	1
In the counties, not under Free High School law.	9	10	1
In the cities, not under Free High School law...	5	5	....
Totals ....,.....	102	110	8

VIII. NUMBER OF PRIVATE SCHOOLS.

	1879.	1880.	*Decrease.*
In the counties	384	351	33
In the cities............................	134	138	inc. 4
Totals	518	489	29

IX. TOTAL NUMBER OF PUBLIC AND PRIVATE SCHOOLS.

	1879.	1880.	*Increase.*
In the counties	6,129	6,128	dec. 1
In the cities.........	301	325	24
Totals.....................................	6,430	6,453	23

X. NUMBER OF TEACHERS REQUIRED FOR THE PUBLIC SCHOOLS.

	1879.	1880.	*Increase.*
In the counties	6,075	6,133	58
In the cities	769	828	59
Totals...................................	6,844	6,961	117

Statistical Summaries.

XI. NUMBER OF TEACHERS EMPLOYED IN THE PUBLIC SCHOOLS.

	1879.	1880.	Increase.
In the counties, males	2,718	2,781	63
In the cities, males	119	137	18
In the counties, females	6,381	6,525	144
In the cities, females	657	672	15
Totals	9,875	10,115	240

XII. NUMBER OF TEACHERS EMPLOYED IN THE PRIVATE SCHOOLS.

	1879.	1880.	Decrease.
In the counties	464	411	53
In the cities	395	393	2
Totals	859	804	55

XIII. TOTAL NUMBER OF TEACHERS EMPLOYED IN BOTH PUBLIC AND PRIVATE SCHOOLS.

	1879	1880.	Increase.
In the counties	9,563	9,717	154
In the cities	1,171	1,202	31
Totals	10,734	10,919	185

XIV. NUMBER OF PUBLIC SCHOOL-HOUSES.

	1879.	1880.	Increase.
In the counties	5,453	5,497	44
In the cities	173	170	dec. 3
Totals	5,626	5,667	41

XV. NUMBER OF PUPILS SCHOOL-HOUSES WILL ACCOMMODATE.

	1879.	1880.	Increase.
In the counties	311,039	315,728	4,689
In the cities	46,147	45,405	dec. 742
Totals	357,186	361,133	3,947

XVI. NUMBER OF CHILDREN OF SCHOOL AGE.

	1879.	1880.	Decrease.
In the counties, males	199,285	198,734	551
In the cities, males	46,792	47,349	inc. 557
In the counties, females	187,763	187,554	209
In the cities, females	49,613	49,592	21
Totals	483,453	483,229	224

Statistical Summaries.

XVII. NUMBER OF CHILDREN OF SCHOOL AGE IN DISTRICTS MAINTAIN-
ING LEGAL SCHOOL.

	1879.	1880.	*Decrease*
In the counties	384,964	383,283	1,681
In the cities	96,405	96,941	inc. 536
Totals	481,369	480,224	1,145

XVIII. CLASSIFICATION OF CHILDREN OF SCHOOL AGE FOR THE PAST
YEAR.

	Four to Seven.	*Seven to Fifteen.*	*Fifteen to Twenty.*
In the counties	88,174	183,054	115,060
In the cities	24,001	46,522	26,418
Totals	112,175	229,576	141,478

XIX. NUMBER OF CHILDREN ATTENDING PUBLIC SCHOOLS.

	1879.	1880.	*Increase.*
In the counties, under 4 years of age	1,459	482	dec. 977
In the cities, under 4 years of age	......	1	1
In the counties, over 20 years of age	402	1,285	883
In the cities, over 20 years of age	71	65	dec. 6
In the counties, between 4 and 20 years of age	244,078	251,224	7,146
In the cities, between 4 and 20 years of age	45,276	46,201	925
Totals	291,286	299,258	7,972

The increase in the attendance of the children between *four* and *twenty*
years of age, was 8,071, during the past year.

XX. CLASSIFICATION OF CHILDREN OF SCHOOL AGE ATTENDING PUBLIC
SCHOOLS THE PAST YEAR.

	Four to Seven.	*Seven to Fifteen.*	*Fifteen to Twenty.*
In the counties	49,235	149,723	54,665
In the cities	11,989	20,679	3,750
Totals	61,224	170,402	58,415

XXI. NUMBER OF CHILDREN ATTENDING PRIVATE SCHOOLS ONLY.

	1879.	1880.	*Increase.*
In the counties	10,647	9,659	dec. 988
In the cities	15,200	16,279	1,079
Totals	25,847	25,938	91

Statistical Summaries.

XXII. CLASSIFICATION OF CHILDREN OF SCHOOL AGE REPORTED AS
ATTENDING PRIVATE SCHOOLS.

	Four to Seven.	Seven to Fifteen.	Fifteen to Twenty.
In the counties	1,685	5,647	...
In the cities	2,352	7,863	868
Totals...........	4,037	13,510	868

XXIII. ATTENDANCE OF CHILDREN BETWEEN SEVEN AND FIFTEEN
YEARS OF AGE AT PUBLIC AND PRIVATE SCHOOLS THE PAST YEAR.

Total number in the State	229,576
Number in attendance at public schools....................	170,402
Number in attendance at private schools.......................	13,510
Total number in attendance	183,912

XXIV. TOTAL NUMBER OF PUPILS ATTENDING SCHOOLS OF ALL GRADES.

DESCRIPTION.	1879.	1880.	Increase.
Public Schools	291,286	299,258	7,972
Private Schools	25,847	25,938	91
State Normal Schools....	1,803	1,880	77
State University	449	481	32
State Charitable and Reformatory Schools...	915	948	33
Other Benevolent Institutions, estimated	700	700	....
Academies	297	1,803	1,006
Denominational Colleges....................	1,253	1,775	522
Theological Seminaries, estimated for 1879...	325	331	6
Business Colleges, estimated for 1879........	900	955	55
Totals..................................	323,775	333,569	9,794

XXV. PERCENTAGE OF ATTENDANCE OF CHILDREN.

	1879.	1880.	Increase.
In the counties, at public schools	63.	65.	2.
In the cities, at public schools	47.	47.17	0.17
In both the counties and cities, at public schools...	59.8	61.8	2.
In the counties, at private schools...........	2.7	2.5	dec.0.2
In the cities, at private schools	15.7	16.6	0.9
In both the counties and cities, at private schools....	5.37	5.38	0.01
At other schools of all grades	1.59	1.72	.13
At all the schools of the State.	66.97	69.04	2.07

Statistical Summaries.

XXVI. PERCENTAGE OF ATTENDANCE OF CHILDREN BETWEEN SEVEN
AND FIFTEEN YEARS OF AGE.

	At Public Schools.	At Private Schools.
In the counties	81.7	.3
In the cities	44.4	16.9
In both the counties and cities...............	74.2	5.9
In both the counties and cities, at both public and private schools....	80.1	

XXVII. PERCENTAGE OF ATTENDANCE OF CHILDREN ON NUMBER
ENROLLED.

In the counties, at public schools................................	63.5
In the cities, at public schools..................................	79.8
In both the counties and cities, at public schools	66
In the counties, at private schools...............................	26.1
In the cities, at private schools.................................	62.7
In both the counties and cities, at private schools	49.1
In both the counties and cities, at both public and private schools....	64.6

Last year, the percentage in the public schools of the cities, was *seventynine.* That of the counties was not given.

XXVIII. AGGREGATE NUMBER OF DAYS PUBLIC SCHOOLS HAVE BEEN
TAUGHT BY QUALIFIED TEACHERS.

	1879.	1880.	*Increase.*
In the counties	855,357	899,154	43,797
In the cities............................	5,273½	5,181	dec. 92½
Totals...................................	860,630½	904,335	43,704½

XXIX. AGGREGATE NUMBER OF DAYS PRIVATE SCHOOLS HAVE BEEN
TAUGHT.

	1879.	1880.	*Increase.*
In the counties	45,696	47,876	2,180
In the cities	25,393	24,978	dec. 415
Totals...................................	71,089	72,854	1,765

XXX. AVERAGE NUMBER OF MONTHS BOTH PUBLIC AND PRIVATE SCHOOLS
HAVE BEEN TAUGHT.

	1879.	1880.	*Increase.*
In the counties, the public schools.........	7.68	8.14	.46
In the cities, the public schools	9.76	9.59	dec. .17
In the counties, the private schools....	5.59	6.82	1.23
In the cities, the private schools............	9.47	9.05	dec. .42

Statistical Summaries.

XXXI. KINDS, CONDITIONS, AND VALUATION OF PUBLIC SCHOOL-HOUSES.

DESCRIPTION.	1879.	1880.	Increase.
In the counties, number built the past year	60	191	131
In the cities, No. built the past year	5	6	1
In the counties, number built of stone or brick	710	745	35
In the cities, number built of stone or brick	102	107	5
In the counties, number in good condition	4,209	4,295	86
In the cities, number in good condition	160	165	5
In the counties, number properly ventilated	3,694	3,561	dec. 133
In the cities, number properly ventilated................. ...	77	85	8
In the cities, number yet required.	14	18	4
In the counties, number with sites well enclosed.............	1,823	1,894	71
In the cities, number with sites well enclosed...	133	133	....
In the counties, number with sites containing less than one acre. ..	3,750	3,782	32
In the cities, number with sites containing more than one lot	143	145	2
In the counties, highest valuation of school-house and site........	$45,000 00	$40,000 00	dec.$5,000 00
In the cities, highest valuation of school-house and site	50,000 00	52,000 00	2,000 00
In the counties, cash valuation of school-houses	2,936,245 81	2,992,134 62	55,888 81
In the cities, cash valuation of school-houses	1,382,200 00	1,441,600 00	59,400 00
In both counties and cities, cash valuation of school-houses	4,319,445 81	4,433,734 62	114,288 81
In the counties, cash valuation of sites	288,495 95	298,795 04	10,299 09
In the cities, cash valuation of sites	405,025 00	403,625 00	dec. 1,400 00
In both counties and cities, cash valuation of sites...............	693,520 95	702,420 04	8,899 09
In the counties, cash valuation of apparatus, etc	140,112 30	141,348 58	1,236 28
In the cities, cash valuation of apparatus, etc....................	16,900 00	20,175 00	3,275 00
In both counties and cities, cash valuation of apparatus, etc........	157,012 30	161,523 58	4,511 28
In the counties, cash valuation of public school property.........	3,364,854 06	3,432,278 24	67,424 18
In the cities, cash valuation of public school property..........	1,805,125 00	1,871,020 00	65,895 00
In both counties and cities, cash valuation of public school property.	5,169,979 06	5,303,298 24	133,318 18

Statistical Summaries.

XXXII. SCHOOL ROOMS AND SCHOOL APPURTENANCES.

	1879.	1880.	*Increase.*
In the cities, No. of school rooms occupied	715	725	10
In the counties, No. of school-houses with blackboards	....	5,161	......
In the cities, No. of school rooms with blackboard ..	709	715	6
In the counties, No. of public schools with map of Wisconsin...	....	2,116	......
In the counties, No. of public schools with map of United States....................	....	2,541	......
In the counties, No. of public schools with Webster's Dictionary	....	4,631	......
In the cities, No. of school rooms with charts........	477	483	6
In the cities, No. of school rooms with outline maps.	297	339	42
In the cities, No. of school rooms with globes.......	188	288	100
In the cities, No. of school rooms with other apparatus	144	187	43
In the cities, No. of school-houses with outhouses for the sexes	167	154	dec. 13
In the cities, No. of school-houses with outhouses in good condition	160	153	dec 7

XXXIII. TEXT-BOOKS IN SCHOOL-DISTRICTS.

	1879.	1880.	*Increase.*
In the counties, No. having adopted text-books......	2,992	3,234	242
In the cities, No. having adopted text-books...	31	31	......
In the counties, No. using only text-books adopted ...	2,106	2,470	364
In the cities, No. using only text-books adopted	23	23	......
In the counties, No. purchasing text-books..........	1,606	1,851	245
In the cities, No. purchasing text-books.............	6	6	......
In the counties, No. loaning text-books to pupils ...	437	619	182
In the cities, No. loaning text-books to pupils	3	3	......
In the counties, No. selling text-books to pupils	1,070	1,253	183
In the cities, No. selling text-books to pupils	4	4	......

XXXIV. NUMBER OF SCHOOLS HAVING ADOPTED COURSES OF STUDY.

In the counties, 537; in the cities, 183.

Of those in the counties, 294, and of those in the cities, 157, are the regular graded schools.

Statistical Summaries.

XXXV. TEACHERS' WAGES.

DESCRIPTION.	1879	1880.	Decrease
In the counties, average per month, males....	$37 75	$37 14	$0 61
In the counties, average per month, females..	25 72	24 91	81
In the cities, average per year, males	838 51	829 32	9 19
In the cities, average per year, females	841 89	836 35	5 54
In the cities, average per month, males	85 90	85 74	16
In the cities, average per month, females.....	35 03	35 06	inc. 03
In the counties, highest per month	166 60	160 00	6 60
In the cities, highest per year, males.	2,800 00	2,200 00	....
In the cities, highest per year, females.......	1,200 00	1,200 00	....

XXXVI. TEACHERS' CERTIFICATES GRANTED TO APPLICANTS.

DESCRIPTION.	1879.	1880.	Decrease.
In the counties, No. of third grade, to males....	2,299	2,025	274
In the counties, No. of third grade, to females..	5,521	5,602	inc. 81
In the cities, No. of third grade, to males..	22	29	inc. 7
In the cities, No. of third grade, to females....	237	235	2
In the counties, No. of second grade, to males..	270	356	inc. 86
In the counties, No. of second grade, to females	399	380	19
In the cities, No. of second grade, to males.....	10	20	inc. 10
In the cities, No. of second grade, to females...	57	68	inc. 11
In the counties, No. of first grade, to males	160	148	12
In the counties, No. of first grade, to females...	56	68	inc. 12
In the cities, No. of first grade, to males.......	23	25	inc. 2
In the cities, No. of first grade, to females.....	18	17	1
State certificates granted to males, five years ...	12	16	inc. 4
State certificates granted to females, five years ..	30	25	5
State certificates granted to males, unlimited...	12	37	inc. 25
State certificates granted to females, unlimited..	28	34	inc. 6
Whole No. of third grade granted.	8,079	7,891	188
Whole No. of second grade granted	736	824	inc. 88
Whole No. of first grade granted	257	258	inc. 1
Whole No. of State certificates granted	82	112	inc. 30
Aggregate No. of certificates granted...	9,154	9,085	69

XXXVII. NORMAL SCHOOL TEACHERS THE PAST YEAR.

In the counties, number of graduates of Normal Schools, teaching... 169

In the cities, number of graduates of Normal Schools, teaching...... 128

In the counties, number not graduates having attended Normal Schools 1,211

In the cities, number not graduates having attended Normal Schools . 50

Whole number of teachers from the Normal Schools................ 1,558

Statistical Summaries.

XXXVIII. TEACHERS' CERTIFICATES REFUSED TO APPLICANTS THE PAST YEAR.

	To males.	To females.
In the counties, for third grade...........	1,017	3,157
In the cities, for third grade......................... .	6	54
In the counties, for second grade.......................	67	88
In the cities, for second grade	....	3
In the counties, for first grade	27	21
Whole number refused	1,117	3,323
Aggregate number refused to both sexes		4,559

XXXIX. DISTRICT AND TOWN LIBRARIES.

DESCRIPTION.	1879.	1880.	Decrease.
In the counties, No. of town libraries	37	26	11
In the counties, No of school-district libraries...........................	273	273	....
In the cities, No. of school-district libraries...................... ...	18	19	inc. 1
In the counties, No. of volumes in the libraries.....	16,762	15,850	912
In the cities, No. of volumes in the libraries..	4,360	5,482	inc. 1,122
In the counties, No. of volumes added the past year	2,195	1,549	646
In the cities. No. of volumes added the past year......................	282	363	inc. 81
In the counties, amount expended for libraries.........................	$1,831 94	$1,287 46	$544 48
In the cities, amount expended for libraries	404 00	401 00	3 00
In the counties, cash value of all the libraries................	15,710 15	13,141 98	2,568 17
In the cities, cash value of all the libraries	4,690 00	5,620 00	inc. 930 00
Total value of the libraries in the counties and cities...............	20,400 15	18,761 98	1,638 17

XL. NUMBER OF SCHOOLS VISITED BY COUNTY SUPERINTENDENTS.

	1879.	1880.	Decrease.
In the counties	4,963	4,916	47

XLI. APPORTIONMENT OF SCHOOL FUND INCOME.

	1879.	1880.	Increase.
Amount apportioned...............	$183,270 64	$191,917 60	$10,646 96
On number of children	477,028	479,741	2,713
Rate per child, in cents	38	40	2

Statistical Summaries.

XLII. AGGREGATE OF RECEIPTS FOR PUBLIC SCHOOLS.

BY TAXES AND INCOMES.	Counties.	Cities.	Totals.
Amount on hand August 3, 1879....	$359,395 27	$106,884 11	$466,279 38
Taxes levied for building and repairs	130,850 23	11,444 84	142,295 07
Taxes levied for teachers' wages...	889,918 38	24,310 00	914,228 38
Taxes levied for apparatus and libraries	10,184 01	350 00	10,534 01
Taxes levied at annual meetings ..	84,168 61	331,535 97	415,704 58
Taxes levied by county supervisors.	164,881 60	84,657 67	249,539 27
Income from public school fund...	146,808 35	37,600 71	184,409 06
Income from all other sources......	289,597 67	25,213 16	314,810 83
Totals............	$2,075,804 12	$631,996 46	$2,697,800 58

XLIII. COMPARATIVE AGGREGATE OF RECEIPTS.

	1879.	1880.	Decrease.
In the counties	$2,033,953 80	$2,075,804 12	Inc. $41,850 32
In the cities..............	722,927 33	621,996 46	100,930 87
Totals	$2,756,881 13	$2,697,800 58	$59,080 55

XLIV. AGGREGATE OF DISBURSEMENTS FOR PUBLIC SCHOOLS.

DESCRIPTION.	Counties.	Cities.	Totals.
For building and repairs...........	$149,970 26	$48,027 96	$197,998 22
For services of male teachers.......	492,132 43	114,735 90	606,868 33
For services of female teachers.....	690,585 31	271,238 68	961,823 99
For apparatus and libraries	11,920 20	1,759 52	13,679 72
For old indebtedness..............	58,686 31	10,868 96	69,555 27
For furniture, registers, etc.........	28,017 41	6,147 12	34,164 53
For all other purposes	195,541 83	81,439 99	276,981 82
Amount on hand August 31, 1880 ...	447,634 61	190,609 35	638,243 96
Amount paid out the past year......	$1,626,853 75	$534,218 13	$2,161,071 88
Amount paid out and on hand......	2,074,488 36	724,827 48	2,799,315 84

XLV.— COMPARATIVE AGGREGATE OF DISBURSEMENTS.

	1879.	1880.	Increase.
In the counties..................	$2,029,499 08	$2,074,488 36	$44,989 28
In the cities........	717,390 28	724,827 48	7,437 20
Totals.....................	$2,746,889 36	$2,799,315 84	$52,426 48

Statistical Summaries.

XLVI.—AMOUNT EXPENDED IN PUBLIC SCHOOLS FOR EACH CHILD.

	1879.	1880.	*Increase.*
In the counties, for each child of school age......	$4 25	$4 23	dec. $0 02
In the cities, for each child of school age........	5 38	5 48	10
In both the counties and cities, for each child of school age.......	4 45	4 48	03
In the counties, for each pupil in school.........	6 68	6 51	dec. 17
In the cities, for each pupil in school...........	11 21	11 51	30
In both counties and cities, for each pupil in school	7 44	7 24	dec. 20

XLVII.—TOTAL EXPENDITURES FOR PUBLIC EDUCATION.

DESCRIPTION.	1879.	1880.	Increase.
Disbursements for public schools....	$2,152,783 15	$2,166,568 43	$13,785 28
Salaries of county superintendents...	31,044 00	46,700 00	15,656 00
Salaries of city superintendents	10,630 00	12,955 00	2,325 00
Incidental expenses of superintendents	10,000 00	10,045 21	45 21
Salaries in office of State Superintendent..........	6,300 00	6,300 00	....
Incidental expenses of this office	2,047 81	2,505 90	458 09
Expenditures for teachers' institutes..	6,930 53	7,000 00	69 47
Expenditures for State University....	94,346 82	97,060 04	2,713 22
Expenditures for State Normal Schools	72,708 07	74,015 33	1,307 26
Expenditures for charitable and reformatory schools.................	123,011 45	182,476 71	59,465 26
Total amounts.....	$2,509,801 83	$2,605,626 62	$95,824 79

XLVIII. EDUCATIONAL FUNDS.

The amount of these productive funds for 1879 and 1880, is stated, in the report of the Secretary of State for this year, as follows:

FUNDS.	1879.	1880.	Increase.
School fund....	$2,713,992 55	$2,747,843 62	$33,851 07
University fund	224,891 61	226,460 78	1,569 17
Agricultural College fund..........	264,719 24	267,330 86	2,611 62
Normal School fund..............	1,053,877 77	1,070,674 11	16,796 34
Totals...	$4,257,481 17	$4,312,309 37	$54,828 20

XLIX. INCOMES OF EDUCATIONAL FUNDS.

The income from the several productive funds is also stated, in the report of the Secretary of State, as follows:

Incomes.	1879.	1880.	Increase.
School Fund Income	$188,702 98	$193,155 90	$4,452 92
University Fund Income.........	66,750 97	64,799 03	dec. 1,951 94
Agricultural College Fund Income	16,199 29	15,472 98	dec. 726 31
Normal School Fund Income	81,588 32	81,956 66	368 34
Totals	$353,241 56	$355,384 57	$2,143 01

L. UNPRODUCTIVE EDUCATIONAL FUNDS.

The following table is taken from the last report of the Commissioners of Public Lands, and shows the amount of the unproductive capital of the several funds, in the form of unsold lands and of cash in the State Treasury:

FUNDS.	Value of Lands.	Cash in Treasury.	Aggregate, 1880.	Aggregate, 1879.
School....................	$247,268 50	$31,581 70	$278,850 20	$265,201 84
University	11,526 25	19,085 38	30,611 63	17,705 21
Agricultural College	30,449 00	22,811 34	53,260 34	69,307 63
Normal School......... ...	577,956 54	31,131 51	609,088 05	625,131 95
Totals	$867,200 29	$104,609 93	$971,810 22	$977,346 63

LI. RECEIPTS AND EXPENDITURES OF PRIVATE SCHOOLS.

The effort has been made the past year, the first of the kind in this State, to obtain statistics upon this subject, with the view of ascertaining the aggregate cost of education in both the public and the unincorporated private schools. The returns are not altogether satisfactory.

RECEIPTS.

	Counties.	Cities.	Totals.
From tuition	$17,770 37	$5,107 00	$22,877 37
From donations	12,114 30	600 00	12,714 30
From all other sources................	13,224 67	2,915 00	16,139 67
Totals........	$43,109 34	$8,622 00	$51,731 34

Statistical Summaries.

EXPENDITURES.

	Counties.	Cities.	Totals.
For teachers' wages....................	$35,977 47	$7,361 00	$43,338 47
For buildings and repairs.............	5,871 67	20,235 00	26,106 67
For all other purposes	2,405 39	751 00	8,156 39
T..tals..........................	$44,254 53	$28,347 00	$72,601 53

LII. NORMAL SCHOOL STATISTICS.

The following statistics are taken from the annual report of the president of the Board of Normal Regents, extracts of which are found among the documents appended to my Annual Report. They embrace the items reported from the four State Normal Schools.

DESCRIPTION.	1879.	1880.	Increase.
Number of teachers employed..........	55	55	....
Number of pupils in Model Department.	685	796	111
Number of pupils in Normal Department	1,018	1,084	66
Total number of pupils in both Departm'ts	1,703	1,880	177
No of graduates in Elementary Course..	73	65	dec. 8
No. of graduates in Advanced Course....	31	13	dec. 18
Whole number of graduates........	104	78	dec. 26
Aggregate salaries of teachers..........	$55,631 75	$57,869 00	$2,237 25
Expenses for building and repairs	3,178 51	6,276 63	3,098 12
Expenses for apparatus and cabinets.....	1,694 76	838 16	dec. 856 60
Expenses for incidentals	9,193 58	9,031 54	dec 162 04
Aggregate expenditures	69,698 60	74,015 33	4,316 73
Receipts from tuition....................	9,480 69	8,889 20	dec. 591 49
Receipts from other sources	3,589 43	3,683 40	93 97
Aggregate receipts from all sources......	13,070 12	12,572 60	dec. 497 52
Aggregate income and receipts..........	81,588 32	81,956 66	368 34

Of the 1,084 students in the Normal Departments the past year, only 28 did not declare their intention to teach.

Through the courtesy of the presidents of these schools, I am able to present the following interesting facts connected with the operation of the schools, from the dates of their establishment to the close of the last academic year, in June, 1880. The Platteville school was opened in 1866; the Whitewater, in 1868; the Oshkosh, in 1871; and the River Falls, in 1875.

Statistical Summaries.

FROM THE ESTABLISHMENT OF THE SCHOOLS.	PLATTE-VILLE.		WHITE-WATER.		OSH-KOSH.		RIVER FALLS.		Totals
	Male.	Female.	Male.	Female.	Male.	Female.	Male.	Female.	
Total number of different pupils in Model Departments........	1,036	959	285	260	395	438	329	465	4,167
Total number of different pupils in Normal Departments.	574	684	596	969	588	907	106	195	4,619
Total number of different pupils in all Deparments..	1,610	1,643	881	1,229	903	1,249	430	660	8,605
Total number of graduates in the Elementary Course.	35	45	30	69	85	51	9	14	288
Total number of graduates in the Advanced Course. .	62	58	34	60	12	12	3	3	244

The occupation of the graduates in both the Elementary and Advanced Courses of these schools, is reported to be the past year as follows:

DESCRIPTION.	Platteville.	Whitewater.	Oshkosh.	River Falls.	Totals.
Teaching..........................	99	132	64	21	316
Students.	11	19	38	5	73
Superintendents of schools...........	4	......	......	......	4
Graduates in 1880	9	22	29	7	67
In other occupations.....	30	20	5	1	56
Married	19	21	2	1	43
Deceased	2	1	1	1	5

The returns from the county and city superintendents the past year, show that 297 graduates of Normal Schools were employed at that time in the public schools; and that 1,261 other teachers so employed, had attended Normal Schools, though they had not graduated at these Schools.

Statistical Summaries.

LIII. STATE UNIVERSITY.

DESCRIPTION.	1879.	1880.	Increase.
No. of instructors.	31	37	6
No. of students in Preparatory classes	120	105	dec. 15
No. of students not in Regular classes	79	93	14
No. of students in Freshman class.	66	83	17
No. of students in Sophomore class.	64	63	dec. 1
No. of students in Junior class.. ...	34	48	14
No. of students in Senior class.....	38	37	dec. 1
No. of students in Law class.......	48	52	4
Whole No. of students in all classes	449	481	32
No. of graduates at last commencement........................	60	71	11
Who'e No. of graduates.	576	647	71
No. volumes in library............	9,000	10,000	1,000
Cash valuation of site	$50,000 00	$50,000 00	....
Cash valuation of land, not including site	44,273 71	41,000 00	dec. $3,273 71
Cash valuation of buildings.......	300,000 00	300,000 00	....
Cash valuation of apparatus, etc....	50,000 00	50,000 00	... .
Amount of endowment and other funds	489,610 85	449,091 64	dec. 40,519 21
Amount of income from these funds	30,307 13	29,727 12	dec. 580 01
Amount of income from tuition and incidental fees..................	4,008 15	4,381 30	373 15
Whole amount of income..........	82,544 42	80,106 24	dec. 2,438 18
Amount paid for instruction......	40,206 77	49,502 40	9,295 63
Amount paid for build'g and repairs	27,045 07	25,136 14	dec. 2,908 93
Amount paid for incidental expens's	27,094 98	29,421 50	2,326 52
Whole amount of expenses........	94,346 82	97,060 04	2,713 12

LIV. COLLEGES AND UNIVERSITIES.

Reports from all the institutions of collegiate character, State, unsectarian, and denominational, have been received; and their statistics will be found in Table XXV.

DESCRIPTION.	1879.	1880.	Increase.
No. of institutions reporting.	8	16	8
No. of instructors, reported........	99	153	54
No. of students in Preparatory classes	977	1,021	44
No. students not in Regular classes.	171	230	59
No. of students in Freshman class.	177	257	80
No. of students in Sophomore class.	164	175	11

II — ST. SUP.

Statistical Summaries.

LIV. COLLEGES AND UNIVERSITIES — Continued.

DESCRIPTION.	1879.	1880.	Increase.
No. of students in Junior class....	110	178	67
No. of students in Senior class	81	129	48
Whole No. of students in all classes	1,742	2,211	469
No. of graduates at last commencement......	105	169	64
Whole No. of graduates...........	1,619	2,177	558
No. of acres of land owned by the institutions....................	35,309	33,202½	dec. 2,106¼
Cash valuation of lands........ ...	$219,423 71	$320,150 00	$100,726 29
Cash valuation of buildings.......	581,500 00	665,000 00	83,500 00
Cash valuation of apparatus, cabinets, etc....	....	82,050 00	....
Amount of endowment and other funds	754,259 00	842,221 95	87,962 95
Income from these funds	....	54,756 45	....
Income from tuition and incidental fees	64,895 08	77,549 99	12,654 90
Income from all other sources	32,989 17	57,664 50	24,675 33
Whole amount of income from all sources.................... ...	127,191 88	140,052 67	12,861 29
Amount paid for instruction.......	88,870 67	93,295 88	4,425 21
Amount paid for building and repairs...............	....	89,824 41	....
Amount paid for incidental expenses	38,336 95	41,074 75	2,737 80
Whole amount of expenses for all items....................	194,357 67	217,323 06	22,965 39

LV. NUMBER OF TEACHERS HOLDING STATE CERTIFICATES.

From the reports of the County and City Superintendents, are gathered the following items, which show the number of teachers holding State Certificates and employed in the public schools the past year:

In the counties 121

In the cities 31

     Total.. 152

LVI. AVERAGE EXPERIENCE OF TEACHERS IN THE CITIES.

Average time in years male teachers remain in school............ ..... 4.2

Average time in years female teachers remain in school............. 4.5

Average experience in years of male teachers in school............. 8.5

Average experience in years of female teachers in school 5.5

Statistical Summaries.

LVII. OTHER PRIVATE INSTITUTIONS THE PAST YEAR.

DESCRIPTION.	Theological Seminaries.	Academies.	Business Colleges.
No. of institutions reporting...........	5	17	6
No. of instructors reported......... ...	24	101	21
No. of students in Regular classes	154	526	955
No. of students in Preparatory and other classes	177	667	....
Whole No. of students	331	1,303	955
No. of graduates the past year.........	39	36	39
Whole No. of graduates...............	560	235	599
No. of volumes in library	16,996	9,075	810
No. of scholarships used	....	12	387
No. of acres of land owned...........	708	482¾	....
Cash valuation of lands	$114,000 00	$88,594 00	....
Cash valuation of buildings	105,000 00	263,500 00	....
Cash valuation of apparatus, etc	....	10,900 00	$8,350 00
Amount of endowment and other funds	72,000 00	53,000 00	....
Income from these funds..........	8,200 00	....	....
Income from tuition and incidental fees	....	49,282 35	14,096 50
Whole amount of income	14,000 00	70,082 35	....
Amount paid for instruction	4,000 00	20,470 00	700 00
Amount paid for buildings and repairs	200 00	6,905 00	....
Amount paid for incidental expenses ..	50 00	11,887 20	3,598 68
Whole amount paid for all items	....	43,717 20	5,298 68

LVIII. FREE HIGH SCHOOLS.

DESCRIPTION.	1879.	1880.	Increase.
No. of schools reporting	88	91	8
No. of male teachers employed.......	106	111	5
No. of female teachers employed......	90	96	6
Whole No of teachers employed	196	207	11
No. of pupils registered..............	6,693	6,730	37
Average daily attendance of pupils ...	53	48.9	dec. 4.1
No. of days schools were kept.... ..	15,735	16,003	268
No. of pupils in common branches only	2,891	2,535	dec. 356
No. of pupils in algebra or geometry..	2,714	2,449	dec. 265
No. of pupils in natural sciences	2,917	3,065	148
No. of pupils in modern languages....	1,104	1,023	dec. 81
No of pupils in ancient languages....	1,186	1,128	dec. 58
No of male graduates in 1880.........	....	114	....
No. of female graduates in 1880	....	237	....
Total No. of male graduates..........	501	615	114
Total No. of female graduates........	850	1,087	237
Whole No. of graduates..............	1,351	1,702	351
Amount received for tuition	$9,087 90	$9,862 05	$774 15
Amount of aid received from States ..	25,000 00	25,000 00	....
Salaries paid principals..............	....	78,023 83	....
Whole amount paid for instruction....	119,098 15	116,683 53	dec. 2,414 62

Statistical Summaries.

LIX. TEACHERS' INSTITUTES.

DESCRIPTION.	1879.	1880.	Decrease.
Number of institutes held by the State.............	64	64	... .
Number of institutes in the spring series	13	11	2
Number in the summer and fall series	51	53	inc. 2
In counties and superintendent districts............	57	57	....
Number of one week in duration..................	24	15	9
Number of two weeks in duration.................	39	49	inc. 10
Whole number of weeks in session	106	113	inc. 7
Number of conductors employed...................	46	28	18
Number of male teachers enrolled.............	1,405	1,134	271
Number of female teachers enrolled..............	3,721	3,309	412
Whole number of teachers enrolled................	5,126	4,443	683
Whole number of teachers required in the counties	5,842	6,018	inc. 176
Number of teachers holding first grade certificate .	201	188	13
Number of teachers holding second grade certificate.	697	555	142
Number of teachers holding third grade certificate.	2,947	2,697	250
Average age of members of institutes, in years	21.9	21.3	0.6
Average experience of members in teaching, in m'ths	22.2	22 9	inc. 0.7
Number of members not having taught............	1,063	1,061	2
Number having previously attended institutes......	3,288	2,983	305
Number instructed in colleges or universities......	497	382	115
Number instructed in academies	413	305	108
Number instructed in Normal Schools.............	535	521	14
Number instructed in common schools only........	1,362	1,178	184
Number instructed in high schools................	2,123	1,987	136
Number of institutes not held by the State..........	7	8	inc. 1
Number of members enrolled in them	483	478	5

LX. PROGRESS OF SCHOOLS IN PAST TEN YEARS.

	1870.	1880.	*Increase.*
Number of school-districts in counties.................	4,764	5,573	809
Number of independent cities.	17	27	10
Number of children of school age......................	412,481	483,229	70,748
Number of children attending public schools.....	267,391	299,258	31,867
Number of children attending private schools.......	15,618	25,938	10,320
Number of students attending academies and colleges.....	2,727	3,559	832
Number of inmates in benevolent institutions....	1,110	1,648	548

Statistical Summaries.

LX. PROGRESS OF SCHOOLS IN PAST TEN YEARS — Continued.

	1870.	1880.	*Increase.*
Average length of time public schools are maintained, in days	154	162.5	8.5
Number of teachers required to teach the schools........	5,661	6,961	1,301
Number of teachers employed in the schools.............	9,304	10,115	811
Average wages of male teachers in the counties, per month.	$41 77	$37 14	dec. $4 63
Average wages of female teachers in the counties, per month.	27 40	24 91	dec. 2 49
Average salary of male teachers in the cities, per year....	1,001 00	829 32	dec. 171 68
Average salary of female teachers in the cities, per year....	370 00	336 35	dec. 33 65
Whole number of certificates issued to male teachers.....	2,396	2,656	260
Whole number of certificates issued to female teachers...	5,138	6,429	1,291
Aggregate number issued to teachers	7,534	9,085	1,551
Number of graded schools....	332	451	119
Number of school-houses	4,965	5,667	702
Cash valuation of school-houses	$3,295,729 00	$4,433,734 62	$1,138,005 62
Cash valuation of sites.......	472,055 00	702,420 04	230,365 04
Cash valuation of apparatus..	72,629 00	161,523 58	88,894 58
Cash valuation of school property	3,840,052 00	5,303,298 24	1,463,246 24
Receipts for public school purposes	2,578,492 93	2,697,800 58	119,307 65
Expenditures for public school purposes	2,006,820 66	2,161,071 88	154,251 22
Amount expended for each child of school age	4 86	4 48	dec. 0 38
Amount expended for each pupil attending school......	7 49	7 24	dec 0 25
Number of days school taught by qualified teachers.......	795,895	904,335	108,440

Official Labors.

LX. PROGRESS OF SCHOOLS IN PAST TEN YEARS — Continued.

	1870.	1880.	*Increase.*
Number of pupils school-houses will accommodate..	296,369	361,133	64,764
Amount of school fund income apportioned	$159,271 38	$191,917 60	$32,646 22
Amount of income for State University	41,313 53	80,106 24	38,792 71
Amount of income for State Normal Schools	52,121 91	81,956 66	29,834 75
Number of teachers institutes	44	64	20
Number of students in State University	234	481	247
Number of pupils in State Normal Schools...........	762	1,880	1,118
Number of teachers attending institutes held by the State..	1,834	4,443	2,609

OFFICIAL LABORS.

I. COLLECTION OF STATISTICS.

This year a vigorous effort has been made in my office to collect not only the usual but additional returns from the schools of all grades. This has been performed with the view of satisfying the demands, created in great part by the General Government in taking the recent Federal Census, that the State should furnish fuller and more accurate statistics of its educational operations. I am under many obligations to the county and city superintendents, and to the district and town clerks, for their prompt and efficient work in preparing their reports in compliance with the special as well as the ordinary requirements laid upon them. A comprehensive review of the information obtained from these and other sources, is presented, in the most condensed form possible, in the preceding Statistical Summaries.

Official Labors.

II. THE SCHOOL CODE.

I stated in my Annual Report last year that the demand of district officers for copies of the School Code, would require the issue of another edition of this work, "thoroughly revised and somewhat enlarged." Accordingly, fifteen hundred copies of it were printed this year, with all the amendments to the school laws passed since the revision of the general statutes in 1878, and with such changes in the comments as the new provisions require and the experience of the office has suggested. This supply will meet the applications of district clerks for the next two years.

III. MAP OF WISCONSIN.

By the 10th of December this year, one hundred and fifty-one copies of Nicodemus and Conover's Map of the State, purchased by the Legislature in February, 1879, have been sold to the school boards, teachers, and public officers. There remain on hand five hundred and forty-nine copies. I have used the means in my power, such as correspondence, the publication of items in the Wisconsin Journal of Education, and the distribution of circulars, to invite the attention of people throughout the State to this valuable work. The names and boundaries of the counties formed since the map was published, are neatly placed upon each copy sold. The demand for it seemed to increase in the last part of the year.

IV. WEBSTER'S UNABRIDGED DICTIONARY.

The last Legislature authorized, on the 19th of February, the State Superintendent "to purchase, on behalf of the State, six hundred copies of the latest edition of Webster's Unabridged Dictionary, at a cost, delivered at his office, not to exceed seven dollars per copy." This work when so procured, it was directed, should be "furnished to any school-district, or to any school or distinct department thereof, in any city or village," "on receipt of an affidavit of the district clerk, or the school superintendent of such village or city, that such school or department has not yet been supplied, or that the dictionary furnished to said school has

Official Labors.

been lost, or is unfit for use, and on payment in advance of the cost price to said Superintendent for any so to be replaced." By the 2d day of March last, the six hundred copies were purchased of the publishers at seven dollars apiece, delivered at my office, — the lowest price at which the Dictionary could be obtained. Immediately the work began of filling the applications which had accumulated in the office. By the 10th of December, when my present Annual Report is dated, two hundred sixty-seven copies have been distributed on first supply to school-districts, and one hundred eighty-seven sold on re-supply, at the price paid by the State. The money realized by this sale, $1,309, has been handed to the State Treasurer, whose receipt for this amount is on file in my office. The remainder of the copies, one hundred forty-six, will barely suffice to meet the demands which will be received by the time the Legislature authorizes the purchase of another supply for the coming year.

V. STATE CERTIFICATES.

Two sessions for the examination of the applicants for Teachers' State Certificates, have been convened this year at Madison. The first was special, having been called the first two days in January last, in accordance with the petition of eleven teachers who participated in the Annual Examination held in August, 1879. It was in charge of the Board of Examiners appointed last year. Certificates were granted to the following persons: The limited (five years), to Ira C. Adams, of Viroqua; Amzi W. Burton, of Madison; H. M. Rulifson, of Darien; Albert Edward Schaub, of Madison; and Winfield Scott Sweet, of Richland Center; the unlimited (life), to John Fred Hirsch, of Milwaukee; and Phillip H. Perkins, of Madison.

The regular Annual Examination was held for four days in the second week in August last. It was conducted by the Board of Examiners for this year, Prof. Geo. W. Peckham, of Milwaukee; Supt. James T. Lunn, of Ironton, Sauk county; and Prof. Jesse B. Thayer, of River Falls. Of the thirteen applicants present, four were awarded the unlimited certificate, viz.: Edwin Auerswald, of

Official Labors.

Marinette; J. B. Estee, of Milton Junction; Miss Mary Lantry, of Manitowoc; and Miss Harriet A. Salisbury, of Whitewater.

The following recommendations of the Board of Examiners have been accepted, and will be enforced at the next session of the applicants in August, 1881.

1. Zoology introduced as a study, united with Botany in Elementary Biology.

2. Text-books named in connection with the branches above those required for the first grade county certificate, with notification that their contents or the equivalent thereof shall be expected at examination.

3. Instead of promiscuous recommendations, obtained no examiner knows how, a blank be prepared with questions searching into the applicant's professional and personal worth to hold a State Certificate; and such blank be sent to persons acquainted with the applicants, with the request to fill and return to the State Superintendent; and such answers have an important bearing upon the success of the applicants.

4. The regulations under the law be so changed that the three members of the Board, provided with all the questions on the list, shall submit, on the same days, such questions at three separate places in the State; and at the close of the examination each shall express to the others his quota of answers for marking. Within two weeks thereafter the Board shall meet at Madison and decide upon the applications.

In pursuance of the provisions found in section 405 of the Revised Statutes, I have countersigned, the past year, the certificates of thirty-six graduates in the Elementary Course of the State Normal Schools, thus converting them into limited Teacher's State Certificates; and the diplomas of twenty-three graduates in the Advanced Course of these schools, thus making them unlimited State Certificates. During the three years of my administration, I have countersigned one hundred forty-three certificates and diplomas, granted by the Normal Schools to ninety-five ladies and forty-eight gentlemen. I have no means of knowing how many graduates of these schools now hold State Certificates, in consequence of

Official Labors.

the act of countersigning by my predecessors, as they preserved no record of this work. I shall endeavor, next year, to ascertain who were granted these privileges prior to 1878, and shall publish in my next Annual Report their names in connection with those entered by myself on the record book of the office.

Since March 21, 1878, the State Superintendent has had the authority to countersign the diploma of any graduate of the State University, who has, after graduation, successfully taught a public school in Wisconsin for sixteen school months, and who furnishes suitable testimonials as to moral character, learning, and ability to teach. This diploma so countersigned becomes in effect an unlimited State Certificate. Since this law has been in force, I have placed my signature to forty-seven such diplomas, and to eleven of them the past year. Twenty-eight of the diplomas were held by ladies, and nineteen by gentlemen. A list of these I will also publish in my next Annual Report.

The Legislature in March last granted also this favor, on the same conditions, to the graduates of any other "incorporated college or university located in the State of Wisconsin, whose courses of study are fully and fairly equivalent to the corresponding courses of study in the State University." In compliance with the provisions then enacted, I have countersigned, in the past nine months, the diplomas of thirty-one graduates of Beloit College, Lawrence University, Milton College, and Ripon College,— the only institutions whose courses of study are deemed by me as answering the terms of the law, and whose graduates have applied for my signature. Of those holding diplomas thus countersigned, fourteen are ladies and nineteen are gentlemen.

In performing the responsible duties devolving upon me in conferring upon teachers the privileges which belong to a State Certificate, I have uniformly attempted to ascertain with due care the qualifications of each applicant.

VI. ADOPTION OF TEXT BOOKS.

The duties of school boards and the relations of these boards to the State Superintendent, in the adoption of text-books for use in

Official Labors.

the public schools, are not well understood in some portions of the State. The authority in the matter of change of books, given the State Superintendent in the Revised Statutes, has greatly increased his labors the past year. The neglect or refusal of boards to conform strictly to the law in holding legal meetings when the question of adopting text-books is under discussion by them, and in applying to the State Superintendent for his consent to the change of books previously adopted, has created considerable misunderstanding and ill feeling in some sections. I have strenuously tried to prevent these results by publishing, in various ways, the provisions on text-book adoption and the decisions of my office thereon, and by a considerate treatment of the difficulties which have arisen and come to my notice.

It was the evident purpose of the framers of the law as it now stands, to shield the people of the school-districts from too hasty and sweeping change of text-books in their schools, and from unwise selection of inferior books by district boards. The State Superintendent is required "to recommend the introduction of the most approved text-books, and as far as practicable to secure a uniformity in the use of text-books" in the public schools. It is enjoined upon the district boards to determine, "under the advice of the State Superintendent," what books "shall be used in the several branches taught in the schools." The Revised Statutes forbid these boards not only in the common districts, but in the villages and cities with special systems of school government, from changing text-books, once adopted, "for the term of three years," or "thereafter without the consent of the State Superintendent."

It is the practice of this officer, by recommendation of suitable books, by advice to district boards when they determine what books shall be used in their schools, and by withholding his consent to the change of books formerly adopted and used at least three years in the district, to secure the use of the most approved text-books, and as far as possible a uniformity in the use of the same in the public schools. The most approved text-books are those which are commended by the best informed and unprejudiced teachers, are adopted into the leading schools of the State, and have the sanc-

Official Labors.

tion of the State Superintendent. At least, in each district school a uniformity of books on any branch of study should be secured; and in a town or county such uniformity can be attained only by the co-operation of the several boards in consultation with the State Superintendent. For some time, many of the books now in common use in the State have been approved in a general way by the State Superintendents. It has not been the practice of these officers, for many years, to recommend the adoption of any particular work on any branch taught in our public schools. Owing to the controversies between rival publishing houses, and owing to the fact that there have been, on each branch, several series of text-books of the same or nearly equal merit, each State Superintendent has thus been able to justify this practice.

Any district board or any board of education in our villages and cities, in applying to me for consent to change any text-book, adopted by such board at least three years previous to the time of the proposed change, should furnish me information upon the following points: (1) The date of the previous adoption; (2) The name of each text-book then adopted and proposed to be changed; (3) The time when the board voted to change the books in use; (4) Whether the meeting at which the board thus voted, was legally called; (5) The name of each book voted by the board to be substituted for an old book; (6) Whether the change in any book has taken place prior to the application for my consent to the change, or prior to receiving such consent; (7) The number of the school-district and the names of the town and county in which the district is situated. This information is necessary to enable me to decide whether my consent should be given. It must, in every instance, be furnished by the board, or by some member of the board, who is responsible for the correctness of the information. Whenever it is possible, the clerk of the district board or the secretary of the board of education should conduct the correspondence. Only to each such single board, not to any book agent, nor in a general way, can the State Superintendent grant his consent to a change in a text-book or other article used in giving instruction in a public school of the State.

Official Labors.

It is a matter of importance for district boards to know that the Attorney General of the State has decided that whenever they change the text-books previously adopted, without the consent of the State Superintendent, the latter officer cannot legalize the act by a subsequent assent, nor prevent the forfeiture incurred by ordering, without his consent, a change after the term of three years.

From the returns made "this year by the clerks of school boards, it appears that 2,339 districts in the counties have not yet complied with the law in the adoption of text-books "to be used in the several branches taught in the schools." This is a serious violation of the provisions which make it the imperative duty of every district board to adopt such books. It exposes the schools under their charge to the use of mixed and worthless books, and sometimes to sudden and costly changes of books. It is urged upon the boards which have not chosen books, to consider their duty in this respect, and to obey at once the requirements of the law.

VII. EDUCATIONAL MEETINGS.

Among the documents appended to this Report, are found the full and interesting records of the Semi-Annual and Annual Meetings of the Wisconsin Teachers' Association, the Annual and Semi-Annual Conventions of the County and City Superintendents, the Annual Session of the Principals' Association, and the Annual Meeting of the Institute Conductors. In the performance of the work of my Department, I have attended all the sessions of these bodies. They are composed of the leading, progressive, and earnest teachers and other educators of our State; and their views, expressed with such clearness and force, and relating to the most prominent subjects now under discussion in this country, are entitled to great weight.

VIII. TRAVEL AND LECTURES.

I have spent the larger share of my time out of the office the past year, in visiting the more northern counties of the State; and through their teachers' institutes and in conversation with their school officers and other intelligent citizens, I have become better acquainted with the condition of their public schools. I have been gratified to find that many of the most improved methods of organizing and instructing schools are readily accepted and placed in operation in these more recently settled portions.

Besides delivering lectures before the teachers at the institutes, and before popular audiences, on the present features and the needed improvements of our public schools, I have addressed a number of meetings in different parts of the State, where the people have made efforts to establish free high schools.

OBSERVATIONS ON THE PRESENT CONDITION OF THE PUBLIC SCHOOLS.

I. THE FREE HIGH SCHOOLS.

Ninety-one schools reported this year under the free high school law. One at Oceola Mills, Polk county, has suspended and makes no returns. Four located at Depere, Brown county; Highland, Iowa county; Oregon, Dane county; and Shawano, in the county of the same name, are included in the list for the first time, and have received their portion of the State appropriation of twenty-five thousand dollars. Three others in the villages of Bloomer, Chippewa county; Clinton, Rock county; and Unity, Marathon county, have been established since the first day of September, and will next year be entitled to the State aid.

Twenty of the schools reporting this year have received their share of the appropriation during the first five years after their establishment, — the time limited by the Revised Statutes for granting them assistance. Some of this number will sorely feel the withdrawal of a share of this annual appropriation. It would be good policy to discriminate between the high schools maintained with difficulty in the smaller villages and those situated at the head of vigorous graded schools in our cities; and for the State to continue, some years longer, its help to the former schools.

At least fifteen excellent high schools in operation in the State, have never organized under the free high school statute. They

Observations on the Present Condition of the Public Schools.

have never realized the need of any special pecuniary aid from the State, or they have desired to manage their instruction on a basis independent of the restrictions under the law.

The advantages of our high school system are becoming every year more apparent. In fact, the governing sentiment of the people pronounces the system indispensable. In no other department of public instruction is more rapid progress made toward completing and unifying the organization and the courses of study in all the grades of schools from the primary to the State University. Our high schools are fast supplying the middle and rallying point in our policy of school management, a point hitherto largely neglected, and not yet sufficiently emphasized and enforced. They are alone making it possible for many scores of our youth in different parts of the State, to prepare themselves to receive the culture of our colleges and universities, or to occupy the more responsible positions in business and social life. Other villages and entire towns should be encouraged and guided to open schools similar to those organized the past year. The generous treatment of such efforts by the State should stimulate at least a dozen localities, now without the facilities for giving instruction in the more advanced studies, to establish during next year well-equipped high schools under the law.

There is no serious or organized opposition in the State against furnishing the youth, at public expense, the best opportunities for studying the higher branches of learning. The high schools are such an essential part of the graded school system, that they could not be suspended without serious injury to that system. They are its legitimate and highest product. In most communities where they are located, they express to the people the free privileges vouchsafed by the State in supporting all the departments of instruction, such as the people therein voluntarily establish for the children and youth. The influence of the high schools upon the elementary, connected immediately with them in this State, has always been salutary. They are, in fact, the directing element. We now greatly need to use them as a most valuable agency for inspiring and guiding the rural and separate district schools of many towns, whose pupils can have thus placed before them higher objects to be attained in their study, and in whose methods of teaching can be introduced the newest and most rational suggestions.

II. ATTENDANCE UPON THE PUBLIC SCHOOLS.

In my previous Annual Reports, I have called attention to the comparatively large percentage of the children who each year are not in attendance upon the public schools. It is gratifying to learn from the returns, this year, that there has been some improvement in this direction. The increase in the number of children of school age, enrolled in our public schools, was at least eight thousand; and in the schools of all kinds, nearly ten thousand. In the former, the rate of gain was 2 per cent., and in the latter 2.07 per cent.

Undeniably, this result is chiefly due to the operation of the compulsory education law, which, up to the first day of last September, had been in force one year. It is true that all portions of the State have not, during that time, regarded the law with equal favor; and it cannot be questioned but that many sections have utterly neglected to secure the benefits which the law is intended to provide. But it is very evident that, by the efforts of some county superintendents, teachers, and school boards, the measure had been rendered quite effective in several localities. I select a few items of testimony on this point, from the large number which have been reported to me.

Last winter, D. D. Parsons, superintendent of Richland county, wrote:

"The compulsory law has greatly increased the school attendance in this county, and rendered it also much more regular. It is not uncommon, in my visiting schools, to find pupils from ten to fifteen years of age reading in the Primer or First Reader; and this, in nearly every instance, is the result of the law. The teachers are doing what they can, the officers generally are performing their duty, and the people appear to be in earnest in giving the law a fair trial."

The gain in the attendance of the children under twenty years of age in this county, was 248 the past year. Of the 3,111 chil-

Observations on the Present Condition of the Public Schools.

dren between seven and fifteen years of age, 2,867, or over ninety-two per cent., attended the public schools.

Last summer, D. A. Mahoney, superintendent of Kenosha county, published this statement:

"We believe that the compulsory school law has had the effect of bringing two hundred children into the schools of this county, who were never before at school."

Henry Neill, superintendent of Columbia county, says in his special report this year:

"A comparison with the report of the previous year shows more favorably. While the total number of children reported is 37 less, the number in attendance upon the schools was 243 greater. This difference may arise, in part, from the inaccuracy of returns; but the greater part of the increase I believe to be a fact, and mainly due to the compulsory law. Of their own accord, many parents have taken the hint and sent their children to school; while others have been reminded by the district officers. In the beginning of February, through the columns of the county papers, I called the special attention of the district officers to the provisions of the law, reminding them of their duty, and asking them to enforce the requirements as far as possible. Many gave heed to the summons, and the results have been partially gratifying."

Charles L. Harper, superintendent of Grant county, reports this year as follows:

"One of the encouraging items shown by a comparison of the reports for 1879–80, is the increased attendance. Although the number of persons of school age in the county has decreased 169, there were 191 more enrolled in the schools; and further, the percentage of attendance last year was barely 65 per cent; while this year it is 68⅛ per cent. The compulsory education law, although not so strong nor nearly so perfect as many superintendents and teachers would have it, is undoubtedly bearing good fruit. The provisions and intentions of the law have been discussed at our examinations and teachers' institutes. It is to be earnestly hoped that the discussions of this kind, taken in connection with the timely circular sent to district boards by State Superintendent Whitford, may do much in calling the attention of the people to the law, and paving the way for a new law or amendments to the present law, that will secure to every child in our State the inestimable benefits of a fair common school education. Although no one in this county has been brought before "any court having competent jurisdiction," for neglect of duty or violation of this law, many school officers and patrons have interested themselves in seeing that its provisions were carried out; and the result

III — ST. SUP.

Observations on the Present Condition of the Public Schools.

is that, in some districts, every child, not incapacitated, of the ages required in the law, has been enrolled in the school, and has attended at least the time required."

In this county, eighty-nine per cent. of the children between seven and fifteen years of age, were enrolled the past year in the public schools; and nearly two per cent., in the private schools.

The returns from Vernon County are peculiarly satisfactory. Here an earnest and general attention has been given to the compulsory provisions. The present county superintendent, as well as his immediate predecessor, have labored faithfully to enlist the interest of the teachers, school boards, and other prominent citizens in the different districts, in securing a hearty compliance with the terms of the law. In my opinion, its power to influence parents and guardians in sending their children of the given age to school, has been tested in this county as thoroughly as in any other section of the State. The increase in the attendance of children of school age the past year, was 841, while the increase in the school population was only 100. The percentage of the attendance of these children upon the public schools, was eighty; and of the children between seven and fifteen years of age, it was ninety-one. Nearly four per cent. of the latter were also taught in the private schools. These are excellent results; and if the same could be reached in many other localities, the State would have no reason to complain of the neglect of very many of the citizens to furnish their children, under fifteen years of age, the advantages of an elementary education.

Wm. Haughton, the present superintendent of the county, writes in reference to the facts above stated:

"Doubtless, the compulsory law has much to do with this increase of attendance, and yet I find that Vernon County people are steadily awakening to the necessity of giving their children all the benefits of our common schools."

It is too much to expect that a law of this nature, and one with the operations of which the people were not familiar, should be accepted and enforced within a single year in all portions of the State. To me it is a matter of surprise that it has, during that time, improved the attendance of children as greatly as it seems to have

Observations on the Present Condition of the Public Schools.

done in some counties. Positive opposition to the law has been manifested in only a few localities. Neglect to require an observance of its provisions has been much more general. Yet the expressions of the press, of many teachers, and of prominent business men in favor of the purposes of the law and of its judicious enforcement, have been more universal and more cordial than were expected.

No one claims that the law is complete, and therefore needs no amendment. It is one of the most liberal in its terms of any compulsory attendance measures which have been enacted in this country. It was the most stringent that the Legislature could be induced to adopt at the time of its passage. It was designed to direct the attention of the people to the alarming non-attendance of at least one third of the children upon the schools, to the necessity of using some of the features of a compulsory system in remedying this evil, and to discovering finally the exact provisions of such a system, which could generally be operated and made efficient.

The law should be amended so that at least one-half of the minimum attendance of the children upon school for twelve weeks in each school year, should be consecutive. The provisions of the Revised Statutes in reference to the employment of children in the manufactories, workshops, and other places used for mechanical purposes, should be changed so that no person connected with any such establishment could, without forfeiting one hundred dollars for each offense, set to work therein any child under fourteen years of age, unless it shall have attended during the year some school where the elementary branches are taught, at least twelve weeks next preceding the month in which it shall be so employed. It will be found that the duty imposed upon the director of any school district, or the president of the board of education of any incorporated village or city, "to prosecute offenses under this law," does not meet all the necessities of the case. These officers are inclined, from the nature of their positions, to avoid or neglect such prosecutions. The qualified electors or tax-payers in a district shrink from complaining before these officers of the neglect of their neighbors in requiring the children to attend school the specified time each year. We shall be compelled to follow the example of other com-

Observations on the Present Condition of the Public Schools.

munities which have tested the efficacy and adaptability of such a law, to and provide for the appointment of a police force or special agents in our cities and in districts each composed of several towns or counties, whose duties shall be to look after the dilinquent children, to prosecute parents or guardians for violations of the law, and to prevent children under the specified age from being employed, contrary to the law, in factories, mills, and other mechanical establishments. I urge upon the authorities of the larger cities of the State to provide at once the adequate means for inaugurating such a measure in their own municipalities. They could show its utility to the citizens of the other portions, and thus perform the work which is now being done in some eastern cities of this country.

In opposition to the opinions of many persons, the system for compulsory education has been successful, in a marked degree, in some sections of our country. This is notably the case in Connecticut, where a law of this character has been in force since 1872. In fact, for more than a hundred years some provisions of this law have been in operation in that State. In 1879, its State Board of Education say that the statistics of attendance of the children " furnish evidence that the efforts which have been made, by legislation and otherwise, to secure to all children of the State some opportunities for education, have been attended with a good degree of success, and so give encouragement for the continuance of such efforts." Hon. B. G. Northrop, the Secretary of this Board, states in his annual report the same year, as follows: "The fact that nearly ninety-five per cent. of our children are reported as in schools of all kinds, shows that the law for the prevention of illiteracy has worked beneficently and opened to thousands the door of the school-house, otherwise closed to them forever." In that State, the evidence indicates that calling the attention of parents and the superintendents of factories to the requirements of the law, has generally been sufficient to ensure prompt compliance with its provisions.

III. FINES COLLECTED FOR BREACH OF PENAL LAWS A SOURCE OF THE SCHOOL FUND.

The Constitution of the State defines one of the sources of the School Fund to be " the clear proceeds of all fines collected in the

Observations on the Present Condition of the Public Schools.

several counties for any breach of the penal laws." In the last ten years, only $10,186.72 have been paid into the State Treasury in compliance with this provision. Many times this sum have, in these years, been collected in the counties, as the clear proceeds of all the fines mentioned. In that time, twenty-seven counties, and in the past year, fifty-one counties, have made no returns of these fines to the State. There appears to have been, among the several County Treasurers, no general and authoritative rule which they have followed in reporting and paying, as required, any portion of the fines thus collected. Believing that the School Fund has, in this way, lost large amounts of money justly and legally belonging to it, and realizing the necessity of a decision of our Supreme Court on this question, the Attorney General of the State has petitioned that body to issue a mandamus against one of the County Treasurers, with the view of compelling him to make the desired report and payment to the State of the clear " proceeds of the fines, penalties, and forfeitures collected by him the past year." This will be regarded as a test case in determining the duties of all the County Treasurers in the matter. The schools of the State are under obligations to the Attorney General for the interest which he takes in bringing this subject to an issue and final adjustment.

IV. THE GRADING SYSTEM FOR THE COUNTRY SCHOOLS.

A very encouraging progress has been made this year in introducing this system. Its principal points have been thoroughly explained by the institute conductors to the teachers who have come under their instruction. The plan of the work performed in these institutes embraced, this year, the primary teaching done under this system; and that to be performed the next year will take up the instruction and methods which belong to the intermediate grade of the country schools. Some county superintendents have issued circulars which contain the course of study recommended for this system, but with certain modifications of the course, and with directions for its proper introduction. A few county associations of teachers have forcibly advocated this scheme, as a most important help for securing the immediate improvement of the rural schools.

Observations on the Present Condition of the Public Schools.

Its different features have been investigated by committees appointed by our conventions of teachers and county superintendents, and their views in favor of it have been expressed in well-considered reports.

Last fall I prepared an elaborate circular on this subject, and I have since distributed nearly twelve thousand copies of it among the teachers and district clerks of our country schools. In this work of distribution and of guiding the teachers to use the suggestions presented in the circular, I have been greatly assisted by nearly all the county superintendents. I have been delighted with the particular interest manifested by these officers and by many country teachers, in accepting and testing the proposed plans for the superior management and teaching of the ungraded schools. The progress in organizing the schools on this basis must necessarily be very slow, and will tax for a long time the patience and ingenuity of those most interested in the work. But in this direction is offered the opportunity for promoting the most valuable improvements now required in our public school system.

Many features of the scheme to grade the country schools, can be learned from the following extracts taken from my circular on this subject.

THE FUNDAMENTAL PRINCIPLES.

The object in view is to establish, in the organization of a school with a single department, the principles which are observed in the graded schools. It is not expected that all the methods of operation in the latter schools can be applied as fully, and with the same exactness, in the former. Still there can be designated regular steps in the progress of the elementary instruction. The order of the studies can be arranged on their natural relations to each other, and with reference to their rational adaptation to the development of the faculties of the child. A definite end can be presented for the pupils to attain in pursuing their studies, and a fixed course of action, covering several years, to which they must conform in reaching this end.

The fact that there is only one teacher in the ungraded school presents no insuperable difficulty. The essential point in this system is the adoption of a definite course of study, which embraces the branches required by law to be taught in the school, and is really fitted to the capacities of the pupils, and satisfactorily qualifies them for their future work. The next particular consists in requiring the pupils to observe this course in all its important and *successive details. These* matters can be accomplished as certainly under

Observations on the Present Condition of the Public Schools.

one teacher as under many. The presence of children from the primary to the grammar grade in a single room, furnishes no practical obstacle. By some suitable method for keeping the records of the school, the work of the different grades can be made distinct, as in the schools of our villages and cities. The promotion of the pupil from one study to another, and his completion of the whole course, can be accurately determined as the result of an efficient system of examinations. The truth is, where there is only one teacher, and the children of all grades are gathered in a single room to be instructed by that teacher, there is the most need of a thorough organization.

In the system of grading country schools, the element of time cannot be used in the pursuit of the studies as strictly as in the present graded schools. The attainments of the pupils in the prescribed branches, whether gained in three years or in five, must be the almost sole means of ascertaining their progress. Where the general supervision is not as complete and effective, the teacher must exercise greater care in drilling the classes in their work, and in securing more exact mastery of the subjects or books studied by the pupils. The different grades or sections of the studies composing the course must be as few as possible, and most clearly outlined, otherwise the minds of the children will be confused in the effort to follow the course. In the preparation of the course, and in determining the methods of instruction under it, the proper freedom of the teacher in applying them both should be respected. The fundamental principles and the philosophical methods of teaching the common branches can be faithfully observed; and still sufficient scope can be allowed for each teacher to work "according to the bent of his own individuality."

THE PRINCIPAL OBSTACLES.

The obstacles to be encountered in the establishment of this grading system, should be known and carefully weighed. The principal ones are the following: (1) The irregular attendance of the pupils; (2) The frequent changes of the teachers; (3) The short terms of many schools, and the varying length of the terms; (4) The lack of uniformity of text-books; (5) The unbalanced education of the older pupils; (6) The absence of any reliable record of the work done by former teachers; (7) The unwillingness of many district boards to put into operation such radical changes as this system demands; (8) The indifference of parents to the highest success of the public schools, and to the thorough education of their children in even the common branches; (9) The inability of many teachers to understand the necessity of introducing a definite course of study, and their disinclination to exert themselves properly to establish it in their schools; (10) The want of confidence in the utility or practicability of the system, as shown by some county super-

---

Observations on the Present Condition of the Public Schools.

---

intendents; (11) And the largeness of the field which must be occupied by each supervising officer, preventing very often the necessary concentration of effort in securing the introduction of this scheme.

THE ADVANTAGES CONSIDERED.

The obstacles noticed above can be most effectually and speedily overcome by the adoption of the system for grading the schools in the rural districts. They are also the chief hinderances to the progress of the schools themselves. No greater service can be performed for public education than to effect what is here contemplated. Many of the same difficulties have been experienced in the organization of our graded schools, and they have in a great measure been removed. (1) Evidence shows that wherever similar plans have been adopted for systematizing the instruction and classifying the pupils in the country schools, they have tended, in those places, to improve the attendance of the pupils, making it larger and more regular. (2) In providing a definite system of instruction, it checks the tendency to the constant changes of teachers; and (3) it lengthens the terms in many schools, making them, in the elementary ones, more uniform in this respect. (4) In some districts, it has already aided in correcting the evils arising from too great a diversity of school books. (5) It removes, more than any other expedient, the irregular and unbalanced culture, limited though it be, of many pupils from sixteen to twenty years of age. This system requires that the pupil's mind shall be symmetrically developed, and that he shall be adequately fitted for practical life by the careful study of all the common branches. It serves to prevent the advancement of pupils to higher grades of study, when not entitled to such promotion by their attainments in scholarship. It supplies a most healthful incentive for the pupils to complete the full course of the elementary studies. Too often the case occurs that they are compelled to pursue the same parts of the same subject, term after term, until all ambition is dead and no serious effort is made to advance in knowledge. A definite course of study helps the pupils to do more work in a given time, as it divides their work into successive steps, and thus shows them how much they must accomplish, and how fast they are progressing. (6) It decides for each incoming teacher, by the complete records which are kept, what branches each pupil is prepared to take up at the opening of the term; and it guides the teacher in arranging the programme of the recitations and the hours of study for all the pupils in his school. (7) It educates the people of the school-districts, both parents and school boards, so that they will soon demand that the instruction given the children shall be more systematic and complete. (8) Upon proper trial, many teachers become enthusiastic in the support of this scheme; and, with the changed condition in their schools, they performed more satisfactory work before their classes. (9) It assists each county superintendent in ascertaining the precise instruction given in each school; and it

Observations on the Present Condition of the Public Schools.

enables him, when adopted throughout his county, to direct more judiciously the entire work done in the schools therein. (10) It induces economy in school management, as it reduces, by establishing a thorough classification, the number of daily recitations usually heard in our country schools. (11) It encourages the use of the most approved methods of teaching every step in the several branches pursued in these schools; and, therefore, the employment of the teachers who are best versed in these methods. (12) It prepares a school to be governed more easily, as it supplies the most influential motives to guide the pupils in their work. (13) Children moving from one district to another, experience less difficulty in finding their proper position in the new school, as the instruction in all the districts is quite uniform in consequence of the grading. (14) It paves the way for the formation of high schools in the towns, or adjacent villages, by the graduation of pupils in the studies of the common school course.

WHO MUST ESTABLISH THIS GRADING SYSTEM.

The State directs, through the Revised Statutes, what elementary studies shall be taught in every district school. "Other banches" may be pursued, "such as the district board may determine." There is no general authority for prescribing the arrangement of these studies into a definite course, and the methods to be used in teaching them. The State Superintendent, in the exercise of his powers of "the supervision of public instruction," is required to diffuse, "as widely as possible," "a knowledge of existing defects and of desirable improvements in the instruction of the schools." But he has no power to enforce the adoption of any course of study or any method of teaching. He must supply information on these subjects, and he can advise teachers and school officers what action to take.

The duty clearly belongs to the boards and teachers in charge of the common schools to construct this course and adopt these methods. The law expressly states that the district board shall "advise and consult with the teacher in reference to the methods of instruction, management, and government, and exercise such general supervision as is necessary to carry out the provisions" of the statutes on common schools. This duty does not belong to school boards alone, but to these boards and the teachers conjointly. When the course of study is devised, and when the procedure is selected for introducing this course, then the district board should use all its power in sustaining the teacher in establishing it in the school, and in inducing pupils to observe it in pursuing their studies. The right of the board in this case is strengthened by the provision which gives it the "power to make all needful rules for the government of the schools established in the district." That teacher is not qualified to assume the management of a country school, who does not understand the present need of furnishing a better system of grading the instruction given in such a school; and that teacher is very unfaith-

Observations on the Present Condition of the Public Schools.

ful in the performance of his duty, who does not co-operate with the board in the establishment of such a system. Let me earnestly entreat each board and each teacher in charge of an ungraded school, to recall the in-struction on this subject which has been supplied through our institutes and other sources. Let me urge them to examine carefully the plans set forth in this circular, to put them into vigorous execution, and to adhere to them until they are incorporated into the management of the school.

It is made the duty of the county superintendent " to recommend to school officers and teachers the proper studies and management of schools." It is enjoined upon him "to inquire into all matters relating to the course of study" and "mode of instruction." From these statements it is evident that the framers of our law intended that the county superintendents should exer-cise some degree of power in devising courses of study and methods of teaching for the schools, and in securing their adoption by school boards and teachers. They should note the defects in the course followed in each school, and show its board and teacher how these defects can be corrected. It is clearly within their province to point out to each teacher the imperfect and false methods which are practiced in the work of studying and teaching the elementary branches of his school. They should insist that the teachers under their jurisdiction shall attend the annual institutes, so that they may be instructed upon these important points. They should impress upon their teachers, at the county associations, the value of systematizing and invigor-ating the work done in the schools. On their visits of inspection of the schools, they should ascertain whether the classes are graded according to the course which has been adopted, and should mark the ability of the teach-ers in the management of the schools, in accordance with their success in using this course. On these occasions, they should call the attention of the teachers to articles on this subject which frequently appear in our educa-tional journals, and to the suggestions on the improved methods of giving instruction in the different branches, which are found in our best works on the art of teaching.

Our county superintendents have much greater power in placing in opera-tion courses of study and methods of teaching than they generally exercise. In fact, in their hands is the most effective agency for introducing this grading systems into the country schools. The responsibility of its general adoption and continued use depends very largely upon their energetic and skillful administration. To establish it may greatly increase their labors, but these should be gladly undertaken for the benefits which must accrue to the schools. They should first perceive the imperative need of improving the instruction in the ungraded schools. They should become thoroughly acquainted with all the features of the scheme herein proposed, and so long advocated in the State, for supplying in most part this improvement. They

Observations on the Present Condition of the Public Schools.

should, in each county, send out circulars in which they endorse the suggestions of this scheme; and, if they think best, reduce to the minimum the course of study, or expand them into the fullest details. Knowing clearly the excellencies and the defects of the ungraded schools, they should exactly adapt their modifications of this scheme to the conditions of these schools. To such formidable hinderances as they may meet in the apathy or opposition of district boards and patrons of the school, they should present a warm and intelligent advocacy of the new measures, in their interviews with these persons, and in their public addresses.

After the above introductory discussion in the circular, there follows a full treatment of these points: (1) The course of study; (2) The classification of the pupils under this course; (3) The programme of the daily exercises; (4) The arrangement of the examinations for promotion, with the graduation of the pupils at the close of the course; (5) A simple and yet complete system of keeping the school records.

V. STATE TAX FOR PUBLIC SCHOOLS.

In this country, two methods of direct taxation are used in raising money for the support of public education. They are, first, the levy of taxes on the assessed property in a locality, as a town or a school-district, where the funds thus obtained are expended each year; and second, the levy of taxes on the assessed property of the entire State, and the money thus accruing is distributed each year among the public schools of the State. Under the latter method, our State raised funds, amounting the past year to $237,587.60, to aid in maintaining in part or wholly the free high schools, the State University, and the industrial and charitable schools. Unlike thirty-three of the thirty-eight States in the Union, Wisconsin makes no provision for assisting the common schools by a general tax. Of the $2,697,800.58, the aggregate receipts of public money the past year for the support of these schools, at least ten-elevenths were secured by local taxation in the counties, towns, and school-districts; and the other eleventh was derived from the income of the general school fund of the State, and from the aid to the free high schools. Nearly three-fourths of the entire expenditures for the public schools were met by the taxes voted by the school-districts, and the balance was largely paid from the taxes levied by *the county supervisors* upon the towns and cities.

Observations on the Present Condition of the Public Schools.

LOCAL TAXATION VERY UNEQUAL.

The support of our common schools mainly by local revenue, distributes the burdens of their cost in a most unequal manner. Inthe different municipalities of the State there is no uniformity in the taxes paid for school purposes either on a given amount of property, or for each child of school age. These facts are substantiated by the accompanying tables, in which are given for the localities mentioned,— first, the assessed valuation of the taxable property for 1880; second, the amount of the taxes raised the past year for public schools; third, the percentage of these taxes, expressed in mills and hundredths of a mill, on each dollar of the property; and fourth, the number of children of school age; and fifth, the amount of the taxes paid for each of these children.

The first table gives these items for the regular school-districts in the town of Milton, as follows:

No. of District.	Valuation of property.	Amount of taxes for school purposes	Percentage in mills and hundredths of a mill.	Number of children of school age.	Amount of taxes for each child.
1....................	$77,141	$301 50	3.91	50	$6 03
2....	70,308	200 00	2.85	39	5 12
4....	189,128	600 00	3.12	144	4 16
5....................	172,018	900 00	5.24	151	5 96
6....................	45,778	101 00	2.21	41	2 46
Totals	$554,373	$2,102 50	av. 3.77	425	av. $4 74

The town of Milton is situated in Rock county, about centrally in the southern tier of counties of the State. It has been settled for forty years, contains two small villages, and has quite a variety of soils, which are in an average state of cultivation. The inhabitants support liberally their schools, which are in session about eight months in the year. The districts given in the table are located in the central portion of the town, and are all adjacent to each other. As will be seen, three of them have each from 39 to 50 children, and two of them respectively 144 and 151 children. The taxes on each dollar of property vary, in the five districts, *from* 2.21 mills to 5.24; and the amount of taxes for each child

Observations on the Present Condition of the Public Schools.

from $2.46 to $6 03. In both items, the larger sum is about two and one-third times the smaller.

The cases here cited are by no means extreme but rather average ones. In many other towns of the State, there are unquestionably districts which are required to pay yearly, on each dollar of property, five to eight times the amount of taxes raised in adjoining districts, to maintain the public schools. These districts, like those in Milton, have incurred the past year no extra expenditures for the erection of school-houses, and for the purchase of text-books. Instances can be given where a district paid nine and ten times as much on a dollar of valuation, as other districts in the same neighborhood, for the usual expenses of supporting a public school.

The next table furnishes, for the past year, the same items for several towns in Columbia county, which is situated in the center of the inhabited portions of the State. We have selected the towns which paid, in that time, no expenses for building school-houses. The statistics cover only the ordinary outlay for the support of the public schools. In the list of towns are included the two small cities of Columbus and Portage.

TOWNS AND CITIES.	Valuation of property.	Amount of taxes for school purposes.	Percentage in mills and hundredths of a mill.	Number of children of school age.	Amount of taxes for each child.
Arlington.............	$636,658	$1,425 76	2.24	438	$3 23
Caledonia.............	509,784	1,699 75	3.33	554	3 07
Columbus	716,504	1,248 78	1.74	288	4 34
Columbus City........	789,401	3,757 52	4.76	661	7 50
Fort Winnebago......	185,761	1,269 51	6.82	250	5 07
Fountain Prairie......	434,145	1,650 32	3.80	496	3 32
Hampden.............	615,845	990 67	1.69	345	2 87
Lodi	473.264	2,404 50	5.08	612	3 92
Lewiston	536,698	1,203 96	2.24	438	2 75
Newport	262,616	2,785 87	10.61	598	4 71
Pacific	60,099	287 11	4.77	88	3 26
Portage City..........	1,154,010	6,134 60	5.30	1,561	3 93
Totals	$6,374,785	$24,858 35	av. 4.36	6,329	av. $3 99

Observations on the Present Condition of the Public Schools.

The above table shows that the towns of Columbus, Fountain Prairie, and Hampden, were taxed less than two mills on a dollar for their public schools; that Columbus City, Lodi, Pacific, and Portage City, over four mills and less than six; and that Fort Winnebago and Newport, over six mills — the latter reaching ten and six-tenths mills. In other words, Newport, in which is situated the village of Kilbourn, pays on each dollar of taxable property more than six times as much as the towns of Columbus and Hampden; more than five times as much as Arlington and Lewiston; about three times as much as Caledonia and Fountain Prairie; and at least twice as much as Lodi, Pacific, and the cities of Columbus and Portage. To give a child the privileges of a public school in the city of Portage costs only about half the sum as in the city of Columbus. To furnish the same in the town of Fort Winnebago requires nearly twice as much money as in the towns of Hampden and Lewiston.

The third table gives the items in 1880 for the seven largest cities in the State, as follows:

CITIES.	Valuation of property.	Amount of taxes for school purposes.	Percentage in mills and hundredths of a mill.	No. of children of school age.	Amount of taxes for each child.
Fond du Lac	$3,412,197 00	$20,502 92	6.01	5,482	$3 76
Janesville	8,867,910 00	17,318 75	4.47	3,386	5 13
La Crosse	8,188,133 00	27,457 84	8.52	4,070	6 97
Madison	4,580,499 00	20,445 39	4.47	3,517	5 81
Milwaukee	56,855,966 67	164,570 27	2.87	37,742	4 36
Oshkosh	4,686,310 00	25,000 00	5.12	5,874	4 26
Racine	7,911,330 00	32,025 00	4.05	5,858	5 48
Totals	$84,502,345 67	$307,320 17	av. 5.07	65,929	av. $5 11

It will be noticed from this table that the percentage of the tax on each dollar is the least in Milwaukee, and the greatest in La Crosse, — the latter city raising three times as much as the former. Janesville, Madison, and Racine are taxed at nearly the same rate, which is about one-half of that at La Crosse, and nearly twice as much as that of Milwaukee. For each child of school age, La

Observations on the Present Condition of the Public Schools.

Crosse expends about one-third more per year than Janesville or Racine; over one half more than Milwaukee or Oshkosh; and almost twice as much as Fond du Lac.

As we apply the same tests to the counties of the State, which in this case embrace the school population of the independent cities, we find similar inequalities in the local taxation for the public schools. This fact is shown by the accompanying table, which is prepared from the returns of 1879. A table for the present year would not differ materially from the one given, though the aggregate valuation of property is greater by $19,376,958.00 than what it was last year.

COUNTIES.	Valuation of property.	Amount of taxes for school purposes.	Percentage in mills and hundredths of a mill.	Number of children of school age.	Amount of taxes for each child.
Adams	$936,917 32	$9,193 77	9.81	2,585	$3 58
Ashland.	979,825 00	2,600 00	2.66	377	8 46
Barron..........	844,270 50	9,236 57	10.94	1,977	4 67
Bayfield.........	550,692 23	1,850 00	3.36	271	6 82
Brown...........	6,093,815 65	33,559 16	5.50	13,025	2 57
Buffalo..........	2,877,148 00	23,090 56	8.03	6,209	8 72
Burnett	475,059 80	2,583 48	5.43	677	8 81
Calumet.........	5,992,422 00	17,477 50	2.92	6,360	2 75
Chippewa	5,068,053 00	38,412 11	7.59	4,621	8 31
Clark	2,890,887 00	21,796 47	7.54	3,204	6 80
Columbia	9,928,863 00	51,073 10	5.14	10,996	4 64
Crawford........	2,293,415 00	17,319 86	7.55	6,237	2 77
Dane............	19,577,952 00	76,931 60	3.93	20,150	3 82
Dodge	18,377,220 00	53,035 49	2.88	18,388	3 77
Door............	1,520,904 00	11,479 40	7.55	3,893	2 97
Douglas.........	378,291 00	932 17	2.47	250	3 73
Dunn	3,629,300 00	27,977 07	7.71	5,877	4 76
Eau Claire.......	6,841,966 00	31,656 48	4.62	5,540	5 71
Fond du Lac.....	19,346,102 00	63,450 64	3.27	20,385	3 11
Grant	8,956,949 00	52,351 03	5.84	15,010	3 48
Green	8,414,175 00	34,809 11	4.07	8,356	4 12
Green Lake......	4,598,697 00	19,084 58	4.14	5,410	3 52
Iowa	6,931,521 00	55,446 29	7.99	9,508	5 83
Jackson	2,523,539 00	12,643 84	5.01	4,688	2 69
Jefferson........	11,287,963 00	40,357 12	3.57	13,158	3 07
Juneau	2,343,580 00	19,477 58	8.31	5,800	3 36
Kenosha	6,084,631 00	21,807 18	3.61	5,179	4 21
Kewaunee.......	3,412,721 00	16,658 11	4.88	6,625	2 51
La Crosse........	5,926,504 00	41,180 85	6.94	8,998	4 57

Observations on the Present Condition of the Public Schools.

COUNTIES — con.	Valuation of property.	Amount of taxes for school purposes.	Percentage in mills and hundredths of a mill.	Number of children of school age.	Amount of taxes for each child.
La Fayette.......	$7,227,771 00	$32,048 42	4.43	8,467	$3 78
Lincoln	1,462,015 00	1,912 03	1.31	468	4 11
Manitowoc	10,487,003 00	45,638 12	4.35	16,820	2 79
Marathon	3,699,996 00	20,593 89	5.56	5,160	3 99
Marinette	1,527,490 00	8,781 19	5.75	2,087	4 21
Marquette	1,649,817 00	8,913 61	5.40	3,708	2 40
Milwaukee	47,282,073 00	210,339 92	4.45	45,304	4 64
Monroe	4,078,337 00	31,296 48	7.67	8,172	8 83
Oconto..........	1,511,100 00	12,708 47	8.47	3,098	4 10
Outagamie	7,552,559 00	37,634 79	4.98	10,728	3 51
Ozaukee.........	6,773,488 00	17,940 15	2.65	6,756	2 65
Pepin	1,026,037 00	7,372 46	7.18	2,314	3 19
Pierce...........	4,037,098 00	25,132 29	6.22	6,587	3 81
Polk	1,612,328 00	13,246 92	8.21	3,254	4 07
Portage	2,309,444 00	20,056 99	8.68	5,250	3 21
Price	1,251,536 00	2,500 00	1.99	91	27 47
Racine	15,251,517 00	47,144 14	3.09	11,053	4 26
Richland	2,864,704 00	20,892 63	7.26	7,029	2 97
Rock............	18,735,325 00	75,969 10	4.05	13,308	5 71
St. Croix	5,420,999 00	32,873 53	6.06	6,112	5 32
Sauk.	6,157,928 00	40,479 26	6.57	10,357	3 91
Shawano	2,967,200 00	9,443 86	3.17	3,089	3 05
Sheboygan	13,940,261 00	38,057 56	2.73	14,043	2 72
Taylor	1,111,953 00	5,133 52	4.61	548	9 37
Trempealeau.....	3,405,962 00	21,928 21	6.41	6,471	3 39
Vernon	3,325,384 00	22,705 87	6.83	9,006	2 52
Walworth	13,427,554 00	44,261 82	3.29	9,197	4 82
Washington	10,336,557 00	26,032 63	2.52	9,499	2 74
Waukesha.......	15,308,874 00	38,931 49	2.54	10,609	3 67
Waupaca........	3,783,401 00	24,188 91	6.39	7,872	3 07
Waushara	2,379,787 00	14,427 50	6.06	4,921	2 93
Winnebago......	13,705,174 00	57,722 34	4.21	15,051	8 83
Wood	1,659,759 00	12,189 23	7.34	2,814	4 33
Am't and av'ge.	$406,303,185 00	$1,842,258 86	av. 4.53	483,453	av. $3 81

From the foregoing table, it will be seen that the average percentage on each dollar of assessed property, was 4.53 mills. Of the sixty-two organized counties, thirty-six were taxed at rates higher than this average, and the remainder at lower rates. The highest percentage on each dollar was 10.94 mills, in Barron county, and the lowest was 1.31 mills, in Lincoln county,—the former being over eight times the latter. Six counties paid more than eight mills, and ten less than three. Of the other counties,

Observations on the Present Condition of the Public Schools.

eighteen paid more than six mills and less than eight, and twenty-seven less than six and more than three mills. Not reckoning the taxes paid for each child of school age in Price county, where they seemed to be exceptional, the amount for this object varied in the different counties from $2.40, in Marquette, where it was the lowest, to $9.37, in Taylor, where it was the highest. In fourteen counties, this amount was less than $3.00 per child, and in five, more than $6.00,— over twice the sum. The average in all the counties was $3.81 per child.

A further examination of this table of the counties reveals these other facts:

1. The most recently and sparsely settled counties pay, as a rule, the least amount of tax on the assessed property, and the largest amount for each child.

2. The oldest, most densely populated, and most wealthy counties are generally taxed below the average of 4.53 mills on the dollar, and near $3.81, the average amount paid for each child.

3. The counties between these extremes, such as Adams, Richland, Trempealeau, Vernon, Waupaca, and Waushara, pay, with few exceptions, the highest rates on their property, and below the average amount for each child. This condition arises from the fact that in these counties the property is distributed at a less ratio to the whole population than is the number of children.

LOCAL TAXATION NOT ONLY UNEQUAL, BUT SINGULARLY UNJUST.

After making all due allowances for the variation in the assessment of property really of the same value in different sections, are not the proofs given above conclusive and overwhelming that the burdens of taxation for school purposes are borne by our citizens in a most unequal manner? Shall we not say outrageously and shamefully unequal? But this is not all. These obligations are carried usually by those least able, under all circumstances, to discharge them. It is a general fact that the people in those school-districts, towns, and counties best able to meet their taxes for public schools, pay the least on each dollar; and that the people in those localities with the least property and the largest ratio of children to educate, pay the most. Is not this an injustice which calls earnestly for redress? Does not every fair-minded and public spirited citizen revolt in his thoughts against such inexcusable want of equity? Besides, poverty cannot compete with competence in this work. The miserable hovels in a thousand poor districts can not furnish the complete and attractive facilities for an education, provided in the school palaces of our cities and larger villages. The teachers are inferior, the terms of school are shorter, and the interest in acquiring an education is much weaker. As a result, the children in the less fertile sections must be reared in comparative ignorance, and with all the disadvantage which this ignorance entails. An incalculable injury is inflicted upon the State, as the development of its resources and its progress in the higher conditions of social life are greatly retarded by the want of better intellectual culture among a considerable portion of its inhabitants. Should we longer consent to keep in operation a system which thus discriminates against the indigent class? Shall we not supply those means which are designed to give a more equal start and a fairer race to all our youth?

The only principle on which this inequality and injustice can be defended, is that education is a merely local and personal advantage; and must, therefore, be provided by local income, as in a school district, town, or city, and be gained solely by personal effort, as of the pupil in the school. If we apply this principle to justify the operations of our public school system, we find that it condemns our general School Fund, the State support of the University and the Normal Schools, and all appropriations to the charitable institutions. It destroys all State help for education of any grade But are the benefits of our schools merely local and personal? Such a doctrine is opposed to the best settled convictions of our people. The disadvantages felt by even an insignificant section of the State, affect the well-being of the entire State. The scheme of sustaining a public school entirely or very largely by local revenues, antagonizes the system of State organization for any general purpose. It denies the principle of the common helpfulness of all its citizens. It undermines all plans for the general establishment

Observations on the Present Condition of the Public Schools.

of public schools by the State, as it demolishes the basis of such schools, viz.: that the property of the State must educate the children of the State.

PROMINENT DISADVANTAGES OF UNDUE LOCAL CONTROL.

The slightest examination of our present system of optional taxation in the different localities, will reveal such defects as the following: (1) The school-district is now too independent of State guidance, and is too isolated from outside influence. The income from the State School Fund supplies the pittance of forty cents for each child, and $34.00 on an average for each school-district in the State. Yet this sum serves to bind the schools, in some measure, to the State, and to stimulate them to secure qualified teachers. A larger aid would induce them to manage their instruction with more specific reference to the needs of the whole people. (2) The district system in its present form permits the penurious and the covetous to exert too powerful a control over the management of the schools. They refuse to vote sufficient revenues to provide suitable school-houses and the improved facilities for instruction, to lengthen the terms of the school, and to employ the more experienced and skillful teachers. (3) Now, the citizens who support private schools, and those who are the avowed enemies of public schools, have too favorable opportunities to place restraints upon wholesome movements for general education. The efficiency of the public school being dependent almost exclusively upon the good-will of the people of a district, and upon the money voted annually by them, any active and determined hostility in the district can now be exerted in a most harmful manner in witholding proper support from the school. (4) The districts which most need the invaluable counsel of enlightened and liberally minded managers, are now generally deprived of their assistance both in devising the best methods for the expenditure of the public funds in conducting the schools, and in securing the introduction of better plans in teaching. With the distribution of larger sums of money, the State could direct, more vigorously and with definite ends in view, the the policy which governs each school-district.

Observations on the Present Condition of the Public Schools.

THE EFFECT OF A STATE TAX UPON THE SCHOOLS.

1. It would rapidly increase their efficiency, as this would not be left so greatly to local choice and local enterprise. The two most prominent needs of our public system of education are school-houses with better and more uniform accommodations, and teachers better qualified, receiving larger wages, and more permanent in their positions. A State tax would undoubtedly aid more than the present method in satisfying these needs. The extent of the defi-ciencies of our schools in these respects, as well as in some others, may be judged from the cost of public education in Wisconsin as compared with that of other States. In 1878, this cost per capita of the school children was less with us than any other Northern State, except Maine,— where it was only two cents less. Here it was $4.52; while in the States adjacent to us, it was as follows: Minnesota, $5.50; Michigan, $6.05; Illinois, $7.45; Iowa, $8.22. In Indiana the cost was $7.04; in New York, $6.65; in Ohio, $6 85; in Connecticut, $10.71; in Massachusetts, $15 26. For each child at-tending public school during the same year, Wisconsin paid $7.24; Minnesota, $8.90; Michigan, $10.80; Illinois, $10.63; Iowa, $11.05; Indiana, $9 60; New York, $10.42; Ohio, $9.51; Connecticut, $12.37; and Massachusetts, $14.62. Is it a fact that our State provides in its schools, at a much less expense, instruction superior or even equal to that of most other Northern States?

2. The State has adopted the scheme of endeavoring to increase the attendance, for at least sixty days, upon the public schools, of the children,— especially those between seven and fifteen years of age. The distribution of one-half the State tax among the school-districts on the basis of their attendance, would materially strengthen this effort. It has produced this result in other States. The necessity of such a provision to stimulate attendance at the public schools in our own State, must be acknowledged by every one who considers the facts in the case. While the gain in this attendance the past year was nearly 8,000, yet only 74.2 per cent. of the children between seven and fifteen years of age, and only 61.8 per cent. of the children between four and twenty years, were enrolled during that time in the public schools.

Observations on the Present Condition of the Public Schools.

3. A State tax would tend to discourage the formation of private and sectarian schools in many localities, and to remove therein a serious hinderance to the success of the public schools. While one-half of the tax should be apportioned upon attendance at the public schools, the other half could be paid toward the support of these schools upon the basis of the whole number of children in the school census.

THE AMOUNT RAISED BY SUCH A TAX.

It is not proposed to raise by this method all the revenues accruing from taxation for the support of the public schools. At least one-half could be left to local levy. This would effectually check any tendency to extravagance in the expenditure of money for the schools. It would serve also to cultivate the interest of the people in providing for the education of the children in their own localities. Neither is it expected that this general tax would be additional to the amount now raised for educational purposes. The experience of other States shows that the aggregate taxation for schools is not, at the beginning, materially increased by this method.

This tax should be levied annually upon the taxable property of the State, to the amount of two mills on the dollar. In the other States which raise such a tax, this amount ranges from one to two mills. Six of them have the latter rate, viz.: Illinois, Indiana, Kentucky, Michigan, Nebraska, and Oregon. In New York, it is one and three-tenths mills.

According to the valuation of the taxable property as determined the past year by the State assessors, the aggregate sum raised annually by two mills' tax, would amount to $891,165.44,— less than one-half the expenditures of the State the past year for the public schools. In 1878, the State tax for such schools was at least a million dollars in each of seven States, as follows: California, $1,389,147; Illinois, $1,000,000; Indiana, $1,494,330; Kentucky, $1,084,575; New Jersey, $1,132,502; New York, $2,938,208; and Ohio, $1,531,081.

VI. OTHER PROMINENT DEFECTS IN THE SCHOOL SYSTEM.

1. In various ways, but chiefly through the last Annual Report of the State Board of Health, the attention of the people has, this

year, been called to the sanitary condition of our school-houses and school grounds. As I treated the subject quite at length last year, I need not now discuss it. I understand that this Board will publish, in their forthcoming Report, a timely and well-considered article on "School Hygiene", which I would commend to the notice of teachers and school boards.

2. Many hundreds of the school sites in the country should be fenced and provided with convenient out-buildings; and thousands of them, in villages as well as in rural districts, should be ornamented with trees and shrubs. Will not the school officers throughout the State make it a point, next spring and summer, to perform this simple but important work? Not until this is done, will a majority of them realize how repulsive is the appearance of very many places where the children are trained in the most impressive period of their lives. A large number of the school-houses should be furnished with the improved seats; with blinds or suitable window curtains; with reading and writing charts; with maps of Wisconsin and the United States; with such cheap apparatus as a hand-bell, a clock, a small globe, and mathematical blocks; and with such reference books as a county atlas, a cheap cyclopædia of general knowledge, and a comprehensive history of this country. The State should speedily initiate measures for stimulating and guiding school-districts in the erection of commodious school edifices,— those planned by well-informed and practical architects, and warmed and ventilated on the best approved plans.

3. Our present method of supplying the children with useful information through the few district and town libraries, is a reproach to our school system. Such inadequate means as have been provided for years, are rapidly diminishing. When the township government of the public schools shall be generally adopted, and when the Legislature shall regularly furnish money to aid in the purchase of books, then may we expect that suitable and permanent libraries will be established, not in the school-districts, but in the towns, where they will be better managed.

4. Fewer teachers should be certificated each year, and the more experienced and skillful induced to remain longer in their work.

Observations on the Present Condition of the Public Schools.

To the latter, increased wages should be paid, and the tenure of their positions in the schools should be made more certain by the district boards. Vast amount of labor must yet be done to qualify a sufficient number of teachers with the requisite fitness for our schools. Our condition in this respect is similar to that of Pennsylvania, whose State Superintendent in his Annual Report for this year, says as follows: "No profession or kind of business requires more learning, more skill, more tact, than teaching; and yet four-fifths of all our teachers to-day have made little special preparation for their work. Many of them may succeed in satisfying their patrons, the school boards, and themselves; but if so, it.is because no one concerned in the matter knows what good teaching is. The normal schools, teachers' institutes, and other agencies do much in the way of preparing teachers, but it is to be feared that the day is distant when we shall see a well-qualified teacher, an expert, an artist, in every school room in the State; and, until that day, the system must continue to suffer weakness at a very vital point."

5. Our system of supervision of schools in the counties needs radical revision in some particulars. No officer can properly control, in a single year, more than seventy-five schools, and examine and license their teachers. He should exercise constant and close inspection of every teacher and every class. Yet in this State at least three-fifths of the sixty-five county superintendents have the charge of more than that number. The law which now permits a county having over fifteen thousand inhabitants to be divided into two superintendent districts, should be made compulsory, provided there are more than one hundred and twenty-five schools in that county. Counties which have more than one hundred and seventy-five schools, should be divided into three such districts. In some way the election of incompetent and worthless superintendents, in both the counties and the cities, should be prevented. It might aid to secure so desirable a result, if these officers were required to be graduates of Normal Schools, Colleges, or Universities, or to pass an examination for a State Certificate, or to have had successful experience in supervising public schools for several

Observations on the Present Condition of the Public Schools.

years. If the county superintendents could be assisted, in the examination of teachers, by two persons, qualified for the work, and appointed by some central authority in the county, the business of granting certificates to teachers would not so often be governed by the wish to avoid arousing the ill-will of men who have influence in political caucuses and conventions. More individuals should be encouraged to fit themselves specially for the position of supervising schools. As this is the most responsible office created in our public school system, each incumbent should become thoroughly acquainted with the principles and methods of teaching, and with the particular duties and requirements of the position. Then he should be allowed to fill it with some expectation of permanency.

6. Our school boards should be chosen with a proper idea of their qualifications to do the work which the law assigns to them. At this point the most radical changes will have to be made. It is fast coming to be known that persons with special knowledge and skill in the management of schools, succeed far better as school directors; and the instruction under their care involves far less waste, and develops more accurate and well-balanced culture in the child. The possession of general information on school affairs, and of good business abilities, though valuable, do not qualify one for the complicated duties of selecting teachers, adopting text-books, directing the discipline of the school, devising courses of study, grading the pupils, and examining the classes. Doubtless the first step toward bringing about this improvement, consists in largely reducing the number of school officers by the establishment of the township system.

7. Narrow and false views of economy control too many prominent men who have the management of our public schools, or who resist the enactment of provisions of law for invigorating our school system. They are constantly on the lookout against any increase in the cost of supporting education. In fact, they expect to gain influence in their communities, and to save money themselves, by devising means by which the schools can be maintained at less expense. A measure which promises to improve the schools under their care, or to render more efficient thousands of schools in the

Observations on the Present Condition of the Public Schools.

less prosperous sections of the State, is weighed and decided by them on the insignificant question whether it will increase, by a few dollars, the taxes of the districts or larger municipalities in which they reside. They do not pause to consider that the business of providing for the education of the children is the most important and responsible which the State has assumed to manage; and that by so doing, the training of the children in the elements of knowledge is vastly cheapened, as well as made more general. While they often profess to be the ardent friends of the public school system, they are practically its enemies; for they interpose a most serious obstacle to its further improvement.

VII. PROGRESS IN THE PUBLIC SCHOOLS.

While I describe the imperfect features of our school system, I most readily acknowledge that it has made steady and substantial progress in the past few years. I do not belong to the company who desire to see the school methods of twenty-five and thirty years ago restored. Any one who will examine the facts presented in the statistical summaries at the beginning of this Report, and observe the operations of our public schools of all grades, must see that there has been no retrograde movement. On the contrary, the evidences of advancement in many lines of work are marked, and assure us that our weak points will yet be strengthened. They produce in us the expectation that " the perfect is future." The statistics on the progress of the schools in the past ten years, given in part elsewhere, show that the State has greatly increased, in that time, the number of the school-districts formed, the school-houses built, the graded and high schools organized, the children attending public schools, the students enrolled in the State University and the Normal Schools, the teachers' institutes held and the members taught in them, and the teachers required to instruct the schools. There has been a decided gain in the value of the school property, in the amount of money raised by taxation for the support of schools, in the income of permanent funds for educational purposes, and in the average length of time in which the schools are maintained. The facts are clearly recognized that school

Observations on the Present Condition of the Public Schools.

buildings with better equipment are yearly erected; that a greater number of county superintendents with special qualifications are in office; that teachers who have fitted themselves at our Normal Schools and Colleges, are in better demand; that meetings of teachers' associations are more numerous and better attended; that newspapers in the State are publishing regularly many more items of information in regard to the schools, and excellent articles on practical topics of education; and that improved courses of study and plans for organizing schools are more frequently introduced. In all departments of our public school work, there exist a growing interest and a healthier activity in providing for the children of the State a more thorough training in the elementary and higher studies; and in developing in their character the traits of industrious, upright, and patriotic citizens.

WILLIAM C. WHITFORD,
State Superintendent.

DOCUMENTS

ACCOMPANYING ANNUAL REPORT

OF

STATE SUPERINTENDENT.

REPORTS OF COUNTY SUPERINTENDENTS.

ADAMS COUNTY.

J. M. HIGBEE, SUPERINTENDENT.

I herewith transmit my annual report. Although it is not as complete as I desired to make it, yet it is the best I can do from the records furnished by the different town clerks. The five answers desired under the heading " Questions," were universally returned, "I don't know," except in five towns the last question was answered, four, yes; and one, no, as indicated in the report. These questions have never been discussed by the different towns thoroughly enough to give a correct expression thereto.

We are able to report progress in all lines of school work. Institute instruction is doing more for us than many are willing to admit, yet, as a whole, we are trying to take advantage of this great gift on the part of the State.

I visit the schools twice a year, and in all I endeavor to stay one-half day each visit. Only one new school-house has been built the past year. It is a fine building, seated with the Sherwood furniture.

1 — St. Sup.

ASHLAND COUNTY.

E. C. SMITH, SUPERINTENDENT.

The county of Ashland has adopted the township system of schools, and is divided into two towns, viz.; Ashland and Butternut.

Ashland has three subdistricts, all of which are in the village of Ashland.

Subdistrict No. one was taught last year by Mr. A. Andrew, with good success and general satisfaction. No. two was taught by Miss. Emma Williams, and No. three, by Miss Sara Sherman, — both ladies being held in high esteem by the scholars and parents. Each of these schools was in session ten months. The schoolhouses are in good condition, and are provided with suitable apparatus for such schools.

The town of Butternut has also three subdistricts.

No. one is in the village of Butternut, which is a thriving German settlement, fifty-three miles south of Ashland, on the Wisconsin Central Railroad. The school was taught only five months last year. The teacher, a German, who exhibits much zeal in his work, had good success.

No. two is in the village of La Pointe, on an island in Lake Superior, and was, part of the year, under the charge of Miss Nourse, of Bayfield; and the remainder of the year, of Miss Agnes Thell, a sister of the order of St. Francis. As nearly all the people here are Romanists, she was very much liked.

No. three is at the station on the Wisconsin Central Railroad, forty miles south of Ashland, and is named Chippewa Crossing. There was three months' school here, conducted by Miss Anna Davis, with very few scholars, — never over ten. They have a new school-house and will have five months' school this year.

On the whole, the schools in Ashland county are making as much progress as could be expected under the circumstances, — being so far back in the woods and in sparse settlements.

BUFFALO COUNTY.

J. C. RATHBUN, SUPERINTENDENT.

In addition to my statistical report forwarded a few days ago, I might briefly refer to the educational work in Buffalo county during the past year.

I. THE COURSE OF STUDY FOR UNGRADED SCHOOLS.

This has produced no noticeable improvement in the condition of our schools, owing mostly to the short time elapsed since the initial work. But while our schools show no improvement, I think our teachers are taking an interest in the scheme; and with the proper system of records, they would be instrumental in making it efficient. Irregularity of attendance, in spite of the Compulsory Law, or, perhaps, in accordance with it, is the great drawback to the successful operation of the scheme. But if the mass of the teachers are awake to the need of the gradation of the country schools, and are thoroughly enlisted in the work, our schools cannot fail of being benefited by it.

II. THE ANNUAL INSTITUTE.

Our institute was held during the two weeks following September 13th, and was conducted by Prof. J. B. Thayer, of River Falls. The enrollment showed 48 members,— not as many as there should have been. Deep interest was manifested in the exercises; the attendance was quite regular and the session a very profitable one. It occurs to me that institute work would be more efficient if the same conductor should be sent to this county for three or four successive years. I fail to see the consistency in urging district boards to retain their old teachers, when our institutes, in many cases, are yearly conducted by different persons. I hope, as do our teachers, that we will have Prof. Thayer's services annually for the next few years, at least during the run of the present scheme of institute work.

III. TEACHERS' ASSOCIATIONS.

During the last year, two teachers' associations were formed in the county, with semi-monthly meetings. One continued for a part of the winter and then, for want of interest, was disorganized. The other, in another portion of the county, was kept up during the entire winter. It starts again next winter under very favorable auspices. Its members are quite enthusiastic, and there is no doubt about the meetings being occasions of much profit to those who regularly attend and participate in them.

IV. STATE SCHOOL TAX.

The answers which I have given, in my report, to the questions relating to the Township System, Town High Schools, and State School tax, are the results of my own observations, as nearly all of the town clerks failed to furnish answers. It is very doubtful if the Township System or a Free High School could be secured in any town of the county; while I think, if the matter was thoroughly understood, the people would, almost unnanimously, favor a State Tax for the support of schools.

V. EXAMINATIONS.

The results of my last examinations show that the teachers are bettering their qualifications. More second grade certificates were granted this fall than at any one previous examination. Two years ago, 22.6 per cent. of the certificates granted were of the second grade; one year ago, they numbered 22.4 per cent; while at the last examination, the second grade certificates were 48.4 per cent. of all. The character of the questions and the standard were the same for all of the examinations. The number of first grade certificates remains about the same.

I suppose I am no worse off than other superintendents in being besieged by applicants for private examinations. This class shows a perseverance that should be enlisted in a worthier direction. Just an incident: Last year, a teacher in an adjoining county sent me his certificate from the superintendent of that county, with the statement that he had engaged a school in Buffalo county, which he did not expect to do at the time of my regular examination; and asked that I endorse the certificate he sent. I informed him that such endorsement was not the examination the law required, and appointed a time when I would examine him. He gave up the idea of teaching in this county. Now this fall, the same person sends me a certificate from his county and asks that I duplicate it, stating that he could not leave his work to attend my regular examination.

Such hangers-on are generally frightened away when informed that they are to be treated to what they so much seek to avoid, viz., a thorough examination. I notice that the real honest teacher attends the regular examination.

CHIPPEWA COUNTY.

C. D. TILLINGHAST, SUPERINTENDENT.

I respectfully submit this special report for your consideration.

Chippewa county is about fifty miles in width, and eighty miles in length. Until recent years, the schools of this county have been confined to its southern part. Settlements have been extended to the north, and new schools are being established in remote localities, so that the work of looking after the schools of this county has come to be one of no small proportions. Quite a number of the more remote schools are inaccessible, except in winter.

There are 109 schools in the county, including the several departments of the Chippewa Falls and Bloomer schools. As far as I am informed, every school-district in the county has maintained school during the past year, five or more months.

There are 4,987 children in the county, between the ages of 4 and 20 years. Of these, 3,722 have attended school during the year.

The number of applicants for certificates was 212 Of this number, 170 received certificates. Of these, 1 received first grade, 8 second grade, and 161 third grade. To 111 of the latter were issued six months' certificates. This includes the Fall examination of 1879, held by my predecessor, and of which I have not complete data, showing the number of failures. The questions have been made quite simple, and were designed to test the applicant's knowledge of principles, and their practical application, rather than their ability to solve puzzles. I have found it impossible to raise the average standing required by my predecessor, but I have been obliged to refuse certificates to a number who have heretofore held them. It is my purpose to weed out incompetent teachers, as rapidly as the welfare of the schools and the supply of teachers will permit. I take pleasure in saying, however, that our teachers, as a rule, are earnest, energetic, and reasonably successful. Some teachers labor under serious disadvantages, such as lack of uniformity of text-books, lack of blackboards, and the like; but I believe that these hinderances to success are being removed, and to that end it is my duty and purpose to labor faithfully.

Two institutes were held during the year. Of the Fall institute I cannot speak. The Spring institute, held at Chippewa Falls, and conducted by Prof. Thayer, of River Falls, was attended by 76 teachers, and was a success. The teachers of the county are generally ready to embrace every such opportunity for self improvement. The apparent improvement in the methods of the teachers attending them, is a gratifying evidence of their usefulness and efficiency.

It has been my aim to impress on teachers the necessity and value of a normal training, and I am glad to note that several of our teachers have commenced, the present autumn, a normal course at River Falls.

There are three graded and one high school in the county. Another high school has recently been established at Bloomer. I doubt not that the establishment of these schools will have a beneficial effect on the country schools of the county, by furnishing a better qualified class of teachers than have heretofore taught.

The number of visits made by me during the year is 93. The number of different school-districts visited is 76. A number of the schools were not visited by reason of their inaccessibility. Those visited were found to be in good condition.

Reports of County Superintendents — Chippewa.

In some districts the usefulness of the school is seriously impaired by the neglect of the district boards to secure text-books and other things necessary to the welfare of the schools. There is not generally in such cases a lack of ability, but a want of proper interest in the welfare of the school. The Compulsory Law is rendered largely inoperative by reason of the apathy of the school officers in enforcing its provisions; and also by reason of an inherent defect in that it fails to require that the period of attendance shall be regular and consecutive.

Not very much progress has been made during the year in the matter of the adoption of the course of study for the ungraded schools. It seems that its accomplishment can only be gradual, from the fact that a large number of teachers have as yet no definite or intelligent ideas upon the subject. Many teachers, however, are already interested in the matter, and I confidently expect good results during the coming year.

The extreme tender age at which children are admitted to the public schools, is a serious obstacle in the way of the efficiency of the schools, as well as an injury, in a large number of cases, to the children themselves. Experience has shown, that seven years is a more proper age for the commencement of school life than four years. Children are little more than babies at the age of four years, and are oftener sent to school to get them out of the way than with any expectation that they will accomplish much in the way of learning. Considerations of humanity, as well as of public economy, require a change in the law so that children under six years of age shall be prohibited from attending school.

Before the annual school meetings were held, I distributed through the county, a circular to school boards and others, touching some matters that I deemed of special importance. I herewith enclose, as a part of this report, the following copy of the circular:

The time for the annual school meeting is approaching, and I take occasion to call your attention to some things that are apt to be overlooked at such meetings.

It is an old and generally prevalent custom in the country school-districts, to leave the matter of building fires to the teacher, without any special understanding on the subject. Under such circumstances, the teacher rarely feels under any special obligation to build the fire early enough to have the room comfortable by nine o'clock. As a consequence, that part of the day in which the school room is not comfortably warmed, is wasted. Instead of giving attention to study, the children are engaged in a struggle for a position near the stove, or enduring the cold as best they can. In any event, no study can go on while children are suffering with cold There should be a definite understanding *who* is to build the fires, and *when* they are to be built. Whoever does it should be paid for it, and then require the work to be done at such a time that the school room will be thoroughly warmed when the time comes for opening school. A small sum expended for such work will save time for the regular work of school, which would otherwise be lost. A good supply of dry wood is of great importance. Few school-houses in Chippewa county are so well constructed that they can be kept warm with green wood. There is no excuse for having poor or green wood in a place where wood is so plentiful and cheap.

The matter of keeping the *air* of the school room *pure* as well as *warm,* demands earnest attention. A very simple method of ventilation is described in a pamphlet issued last spring by the State Board of Health, as follows: "A fresh air duct is led into the school room, which terminates under the stove. The stove is surrounded with a sheet-iron jacket, perforated with holes in such a manner to insure the perfect distribution of the air, which is detained in contact with the stove sufficiently long to become warm." The usual means for the admission of air is by opening the doors and windows, and teachers and scholars are obliged to endure the headache and dullness attendant upon breathing the impure air of a close room, or suffer with colds or severe sickness, consequent upon being subjected to alternate heat and drafts of cold air.

A little money judiciously invested in securing good ventilation, would save in some instances a large amount in doctors' bills. Those dreaded scourges of childhood, diphtheria and scarlet fever, are among the diseases generated by impure air.

On the subject of outhouses, I quote the words of the Superintendent of Eau Claire county, in a recent circular: "That any school-house is unprovided with an outhouse, is simply indecent. Two under one roof with doors adjoining, or one used by all, are little better. There should be some portion of every school yard entirely separated for each sex, screened from the view of the other, and from the public road. For the sake of health, modesty, and decency, I hope this matter will receive the attention it deserves."

As a rule, those who make the appropriation for support of schools, are not stingy in the amount voted, but provide sufficient to engage teachers of ability to make the schools profitable to their patrons It is a mistake to offer such low wages that none but the poorer or inexperienced teachers can be obtained. Poor teachers generally estimate their services at near their true value, and consequently offer to teach for wages that good, thorough teachers cannot afford to receive. Let the length of the school be fixed after the teacher is engaged, according to the amount of funds on hand to pay with — but secure a good teacher at all events. Money paid imcompetent teachers, is wasted. Successful teachers should be retained as long as possible. Nothing is more detrimental to a school than constant changing of teachers, provided they do good work.

The seats in a school room have much to do with the success of the school. Children occupying uncomfortable seats, are uneasy, restless, mischievous; and, "fit for treasons, stratagems, and spoils." Such seats are no longer excusable on the plea of economy, when models of ease and comfort can be obtained at a price hardly in excess of the cost of those old-fashioned instruments of torture.

Among other things, a district at a school meeting may authorize the district board to purchase text-books for use in the public school. It is very desirable that text-books be obtained in this way, as it secures uniformity;

and the books may be obtained at a greatly reduced cost, and the expense of furnishing books to those unable to purchase them, will b3 more equally borne by tax-payers.

The district board is required by law to adopt a list of text-books to be used in the several branches taught in the school. This is a matter of great importance, and should be attended to in every district where it has not already been done. It is the duty of every school officer to see that this provision of the law is complied with, and that the books adopted are used in the school. Multiplicity of text-books leads to multiplicity of classes. I have, during the past year, visited schools whose efficiency was seriously impaired by neglect of this requirement of the law. Every school room should be supplied with a large amount of blackboard room. I have noted that this deficiency is generally prevalent throughout the county. A very small expense will set this matter right.

I shall be glad to consult with school officers or friends of the schools, at any time, on matters pertaining to the welfare of the schools.

I have had most gratifying evidences that this circular has accomplished much good, and has largely increased the public interest in the school matters of the county.

Of the school-districts in which the school-houses are not in good condition, or are unsupplied with blackboards or other conveniences, I find the greater proportion to be in the newer and more sparsely settled portions of the county; and that in the older portions of the county, the school-houses are generally comfortable, and provided with the conveniences for teaching.

In a very few instances, the superintendent has been strongly urged to license as teachers, persons of insufficient educational attainments, who, through favoritism of friends or relatives, had obtained schools. This evil, I am glad to know, does not exist to any considerable extent.

There is a growing sentiment in favor of the retention of teachers in the same schools, and against unnecessary changes. Whenever a change is made, it is my intention to have a report left in the hands of the district board, showing the classification and attainments of each pupil, so that a new teacher may be able to obtain needed information on these subjects, without the loss of so much valuable time.

In some localities an erroneous sentiment prevails that pupils must be rapidly advanced in their studies. In such localities this sentiment seriously interferes with the work of thorough, painstaking teachers. It has been my constant endeavor to remove such

views, and to secure careful and thorough work at the hands of instructors.   I have found a very few teachers who had not the moral
courage to withstand this sentiment.

It has been my aim to set before parents, teachers, and pupils
the disastrous results of superficial work.   But the crying evil of
the schools is irregularity of attendance.   I confess that I have not
as yet been able to reach a satisfactory solution of this difficulty.
It is a subject well worthy of earnest thought how best to eradicate
this evil.   Notwithstanding all this, I think the friends of education have reason to be encouraged, and I confidently expect steady
and substantial progress in the work of improvement in educational
methods.

My first year's work has necessarily been devoted largely to ac-
quainting myself with the needs of the schools.   I shall enter
upon the work of the coming year with a lively hope of accomplishing, for the welfare and success of the schools, more than has
been accomplished during the past year.

COLUMBIA COUNTY.

HENRY NEILL, SUPERINTENDENT.

In transmitting this, my first annual report, I cannot draw a
comparison between the present and the past condition of schools
in this county, but I can render a just estimate of the *status quo,*
so far as personal experience will bear me out.

I. STATISTICS.

The "general statistics," returned by the town and district
clerks, have been, on the whole, quite accurate and full.   In the
"special statistics," I have not quite so great confidence.   All the
reports, with two exceptions, were promptly made, and a part of
the summary of these appears as follows:

Whole number of school children in the county.............. 8,513
Whole number of school children attending school 6,613
Pupils under 4 and over 20 years of age attending school..... 77
Pupils from 4 to 7 years of age attending school 1,064
Pupils from 7 to 15 years of age attending school 3,782

Reports of County Superintendents — Columbia.

Twenty-two and one-third per cent., or nearly one-fourth of the entire number of children of school age in the county, have not attended public school during the past year. The number enrolled as attending private schools, that have not been enrolled in the public, is only twenty. Of the number between the ages of seven and fifteen years, about seventeen per cent. did not attend school, while the greatest short-coming in attendance at school, is in that class of children between four and seven years of age, one-third of whom have not received public instruction. The cause of this we infer to be the want of summer and fall terms of school. Few districts in this county have yet adopted the plan of having three terms in their school year, one of which should come in the months of September and October, for the benefit of small children.

A comparison with the annual report of the previous year shows more favorably. While the total number of children reported is 37 less, the number in attendance upon the schools has been 243 greater. This difference may arise, in part, from the inaccuracy of returns; but the greater part of the increase I believe to be a fact, and mainly due to the compulsory law.

II. COMPULSORY LAW.

Of their own accord, many parents have taken the hint, and sent their children to school; while others have been reminded by the district officers. In the beginning of February, through the columns of the county papers, I called the special attention of district officers to the provisions of the law, reminding them of their duty and asking them to enforce the requirements as far as possible. Many gave heed to the summons, and the results have been partially gratifying. There are a good many "loop-holes" in the law, however, and not the least misleading is the plea of "private teaching."

III. EXAMINATIONS.

Since the first of January, or during the Spring examinations, there were 285 applicants for teachers' certificates, of whom one received a second grade, 37 third grade (for one year), and 106 limited certificates. On written petitions, each signed by the three members of the district board, making the request, 15 more were granted licenses or "permits" to teach. The last practice is an evil one, and should be cut off entirely. We mean to follow it only when there is an actual scarcity of properly qualified teachers.

No regular certificates were granted to any one below eighteen years of age, a rule which we intend to follow permanently. Those between seventeen and eighteen years of age were allowed to write and receive their standing.

IV. TEACHERS.

The fact that only fifty per cent. of the applicants received certificates, impressed the successful candidates very strongly with the idea that thorough examinations meant thorough work in the school room, and nothing in the whole range of my experience gives me greater pleasure than testifying to the latter result. With not more than three exceptions, I found the teachers in the summer schools active, hard-working, neat, and orderly. The schools, as a natural consequence, deserve the same commendation.

As another result of the severe examinations, many meagerly qualified, yet otherwise good teachers, have gone back to higher schools of learning, to fit themselves better for the work of the school room. This leaves a stringency in the supply of teachers for the present, with a corresponding rise in the wages, advantage of which can be taken on the return of the better qualified teachers to raise the standard.

V. WAGES.

The villages of Lodi and Kilbourn, each having schools of six departments, have paid their principals respectively $100 and $111.11 per month. Cambria, Randolph, and Poynette, having schools of two or three departments, have paid their principals $65, $50, and $60 respectively per month. Exclusive of these already given, the average per month for male teachers was $31.68; for female teachers, $20.47.

VI. VISITATIONS.

There are 165 school departments in the county, all of which have been visited once; and over two-thirds of them, a second time, making in all 286 visits since the first of January. More were intended, but the open winter and often almost impassable condition of the roads prevented.

In those visits the time was given to observing the work and methods of the teacher, the appearance of the house, and discipline of the children. In nearly all cases suggestions for improvement were made to the teachers privately, by word of mouth or by a written note left in the school register; but the best teacher might not act according to the suggestions made, and that the district might know the condition of its school, a diary of my observations and criticisms was kept and published every week in one of the county papers. Censure was freely given when deserved, and praise as readily bestowed when merited. It was sharp medicine, but always effectual. The better results were every where speedily apparent, and were the cause of frequent remark and discussion. The policy, if policy it might be called, is not a safe one to pursue, if any superintendent is looking solely to his own continuance in office. With the intelligence of Columbia county, it is safe enough; for they are a people who appreciate thoroughness in official conduct, and approve all upright means to promote the interests of their schools.

VII. SCHOOL-HOUSES.

Of the school-houses, 111 are reported as being in good condition, and 93, or a few more than half, as properly ventilated. These figures are substantially correct so far as ventilation is concerned, and also as to the condition, if by " not being in good condition " we mean such school-houses as are not fit, or hardly fit, for children in the winter season. In the weekly diary, I did not fail to call attention to the dilapidated condition of many of the school-houses. The trouble has been amply repaid by the many improvements which are being made this fall, and to which I hope to be able to allude more specifically in my next report. Quite a number of districts are, on their own accord, building school-houses; but three which could not be moved to action by even significant hints, were reminded of the necessity by "condemnation." Two of these districts are now building; but the third, distracted by "internal feuds," can accomplish nothing new.

VIII. APPARATUS.

State and county maps are sadly needed in about two-thirds of the schools, as are, also, globes, charts, and many of those minor contrivances that so greatly aid the teacher in his school work.

IX. TEXT-BOOKS.

Exactly one-half the number of districts in the county have adopted a list of text-books, and few more than half of that number use only the list adopted. In those districts in which a list has been adopted, the uniformity is little better than where it has never been thought of. System or uniformity in books throughout this county, or even a township, under the present system, is worse than a force,— it is a mere delusion. The nearest approach to uniformity is in the case of Robinson's Arithmetic, which is used in 101 schools out of 147 in the county. The next is Sanders' Speller, which is used in 62 schools; then Barnes's History, used in 56 schools; Harpers' Geography, in 53; Swinton's Grammar in 49, and Sanders's Reader in 41. After these, there is scarcely a text-book by any author, on any subject, or in any branch, that is used in 20 schools of the 147. Think of such an obstacle in the way of grading country schools! And yet it is one reason more why they should be graded. Eighteen districts only purchase text-books for pupils, seventeen of which sell them to the pupils and but one adopts the best and cheapest plan of all, viz.; loaning them to the scholars.

X. GRADING SCHOOLS.

Notwithstanding the obstacles in the way of grading our country schools, we mean to give the plan a fair trial the coming year. The "Course of Study for Ungraded Schools" was thoroughly dis-

---

---

cussed in our institute work last spring and this fall; and we mean to do something towards carrying it into our school work this winter. Many are procuring " Lunn's Wisconsin School Register," which will be a great assistance and incentive in the work. To aid the plan in its incipiency in this county and to prepare the way for the Register where not at first introduced, I have prepared a large blank for keeping records, much after the plan of the Register. This will be sent to each district, accompanied by a copy of the " Course of Study," printed on card-board to be tacked up in the school-room; and the more ample exposition of it lately prepared by the State Superintendent.

XI. INSTITUTES.

An institute, of a week in length, was held at Portage last spring, conducted by A. J. Hutton, and was a success in every respect. The character of the work (primary teaching) though not new, was by many comparatively little understood. But as the nature and object of the work unfolded itself during the week, teachers became quite enthusiastic over it, so much so that 75 of the most experienced desired Prof. Hutton to remain on Saturday and give them an extra day, which he did. There were enrolled 130 members with an average attendance of 116. The result of this institute was quite marked in the work of the summer schools, wherever a teacher was found that had attended the institute.

CRAWFORD COUNTY.

J. H. MC DONALD, SUPERINTENDENT.

" Old Crawford " county is slowly but steadily advancing in educational matters. The affairs of the county have been as follows: 1. Tax-payers, whose tax amounts to only one-tenth of that of the average patron, are in the majority, and overrule the minority when appropriations for building are needed. 2. The " hard times," which have discouraged many an ambitious father. 3. The county superintendent not being re-elected. There has not been a case of re-election for the last fifteen years. By the time this officer becomes acquainted with the routes to school-houses, the wants of patrons, and merits of the teachers, a new man is installed, and the old superintendent steps down and out. Many of my co-laborers in the State, who have served two, three, and four terms, will wonder why this is so. That some able, consistent, and impartial men have filled the office, there is no doubt; but as the true cause savors of partisanship, we shall refrain from answering here.

I. VISITATIONS.

One hundred and sixteen visits have been made by myself,— eighty-eight of 91 schools once, and 28 twice. Three either had no schools during the year, or were not in session when I called. One or more districts remarked " that they had not seen a county superintendent for seven or eight years." At these visits I endeavored to spend at least one-half day; and in the time allotted, I heard classes, left written remarks on discipline and methods of teaching, together with reports to the school officers on the meritorious features of the school, and on prominent defects. To reward live and energetic teachers, I published an account of my visits in the educational columns of our local papers. That these reports have awakened teachers to a better sense of duty, and encouraged school officers, I am fully satisfied.

II. EXAMINATIONS.

In all, 160 applicants have been examined the past year, and 130 have received certificates — 15 of the second grade, and the remainder of the third. There are six unexpired first grade certificates, which were either granted or renewed at Supt. Norris's last examination. In a few cases, at the special request of district boards, I have granted licenses. Why school officers employ an inferior teacher when we have a surplus of 39 — all willing to work for equally low wages, I am unable to explain. We are glad, however, to welcome the result of our last annual meetings in " voting male teachers " for the winter term. A few competent male teachers last winter were compelled to take the ax, or enjoy the hospitality of a kind parent, while some schools struggled through with inferior teachers. The standard of attainments for limited certificates has been raised from 40 to 50 per cent.; and I found this requirement fully met with in the papers of the examinations this fall. Many embraced the opportunity of a Normal Training School, conducted by Prof. C. H. Keyes, during vacations; and were much benefited. The plan of grading certificates into three classes, has been adopted, viz.; To those answering 70 per cent., who are successful in teaching, and members of the Teachers' Association, an "A" grade is issued; to only partially successful, and answering 60 per cent., "B" certificates, and to young applicants "C" papers.

III. CRAWFORD COUNTY TEACHERS' LITERARY AND LIBRARY ASSOCIATION.

The county is divided into six association districts, and a meeting of the teachers in each district is held monthly. These meetings do much toward the adoption of new and improved methods of teaching and management. The number attending the meetings has increased from 74 to 115, since January last, and with gratifying results. The usual association work is being done. In the library there are some 66 volumes, which are distributed in nearly every town in the county, and exchanged semi-annually. I hope to be able to increase the number of volumes to 100 before the year closes.

Members of the association are under obligations to Messrs. Merrell, Berryman, and Lacy, editors of the *Courier* and *Union*, for a free column in their respective papers. The interest manifested by teachers and patrons alike, warrants its continuance.

IV. SCHOOL-HOUSES.

The school buildings in many instances are not such as we should have; but are as good as the patrons can afford, owing to reasons elsewhere stated. A few new houses are being built, and old ones repaired and reseated. Soon it will be my unpleasant duty to "condemn" three old structures, the description of which would baffle an architect. Much credit is due to the people of Wauzeka, Belle Center, and Lynxville, for commodious, neat, well.

supplied buildings. The enterprising people of Seneca are also about to adorn the geographical center of the county with a large, frame building.

V. TEXT-BOOKS.

While many districts have adopted a series of text-books, but few have used the list entirely. This brings into use a multiplicity of books, and adds to our slow progress But in districts where they purchase directly from the house, securing an adoption, and loan or sell to pupils, a marked improvement in classification and advancement is noticeable. In my report to the county board, I shall particularly recommend this plan.

VI. INSTITUTE.

The teachers' institute, held at Wauzeka this fall, was a success as regards the amount and quality of work accomplished; but a poor representation of the 151 teachers, licensed during ex-superintendent Norris's administration, there being present but 35. The pleasant and agreeable manner of the conductor, Prof. A. J. Hutton, won the good-will and confidence of all present. The custom of " renewing " certificates sometimes draws a larger number; but teachers who have to be coaxed to an institute, are of but little value anywhere; and I am in favor of a discontinuance of said practice. If the following paragraph were embodied in the certificate, it would awaken some persons to a sense of their duty: The holder of this certificate did not attend the last institute in this county. He takes little or no interest in educational matters, and consequently will make you a poor teacher. This, directed to district boards, would enable them to discriminate between teachers.

VII. CONCLUSION.

In conclusion, I would say that I heartily believe a substantial progress is being made; that school-district officers are in favor of employing a better class of teachers than heretofore, and that our next institute will be largely attended. I am confident that existing difficulties will gradually disappear; and those necessary changes, which now receive but very little attention, will be cheer-

Reports of County Superintendents — Dane.

fully made, and vigorously sustained. Were I to close this report without acknowledging my obligations to the State Superintendent, Hon. Wm. C. Whitford, for his ever kindly advice and assistance, I should be very ungrateful; also, to district boards, and the people at large, for their courtesy and readiness to co-operate in any measure looking to the improvement and welfare of the schools.

DANE COUNTY — FIRST DISTRICT.

C. E. BUELL, SUPERINTENDENT.

The year just closed has, upon the whole, been satisfactory. No radical changes have been inaugurated, but I think more faithful work has been done in our schools than ever before. Each year, our teachers are being better prepared for their work. The number of teachers which our Normal Schools and Colleges have sent forth, has become so great that all can no longer find employment in the village schools, and hence many are engaged in our rural districts. The institutes are also doing much for our country schools. I notice with pleasure that those teachers who attend institutes are doing much better work in our schools than those who do not. I think I speak advisedly, when I say that there is no expenditure of money for educational purposes, on the part of the State, from which so immediate and great returns are secured as from the money expended in conducting institutes. This fall, a two weeks' institute, conducted by Prof. A. J. Hutton, was held at Sun Prairie. This is the first two weeks' institute ever held in Dane county. Judging from the attendance and interest manifested throughout, I think that our institute conductors committed no mistake in making the work this year primary in its nature. It has supplied a want long felt in our country schools.

Just previous to the annual school meeting, a circular was issued from this office to the qualified electors of this district, urging upon them the advisability of dividing the school year into three terms and employing the same teacher throughout the year; of grading our country schools, adopting a course of study, and requiring every teacher at the close of each term to leave a record of the work done by each scholar; of building new school-houses and repairing old ones, giving special attention to heating and ventilation; of procuring more and better school furniture; of building separate and suitable outhouses for each sex; of carrying into effect the compulsory education law; and of hiring more experienced and better qualified teachers, paying them liberal wages.

Since January 1st, I have made 225 visits. In nearly all the schools, I have conducted recitations. I have tried to impress upon teachers and scholars the necessity of system and thoroughness in their work. I have endeavored to secure the co-operation of school boards and patrons in visiting schools, and with some success.

During the year, 249 certificates have been granted to 225 different persons. Of these, 40 were limited. The number of persons required to teach the schools is 136. As but very few gentlemen teach in the summer, we have no excess of teachers. The average wages per month, during the past year, has been $35.02 for gentlemen, and $25.73 for lady teachers. The previous year, it was $32.73 for gentlemen, and $24.50 for lady teachers. With the return of better times, there is a tendency to employ better teachers, and to pay them more liberally, while at the same time many who taught because they could find no other employment, have now engaged in other lines of business. We can well afford to spare such from the profession.

I do not think it will be nearly as difficult a matter to grade our country schools as has been anticipated. All of my teachers at the present time roughly grade their schools. This question was given prominence at the institute this fall, and with the aid which we were able to give my teachers, I think that they will be able to grade their schools much more systematically than before. I anticipate that we shall encounter the chief difficulty in getting the teachers to leave a record, at the close of each term, of the work done during that term. At the present time, a teacher goes into a school with no knowledge of the work done by his predecessor. It takes him nearly a term to determine the proper status of the

Reports of County Superintendents — Dodge.

school, which he might have done at a glance, had a proper record been left by the previous teacher.   At the present time ,we require every teacher to leave a record of the age, attendance, and studies pursued by each scholar, under penalty of forfeiting his wages. Why not require him to leave a record of the progress made by each scholar?

Of the 3,942 children in my district, between the ages of seven and fifteen, 489, or more than twelve per cent., were not in attendance upon our public schools during the year.   As the number of children attending school last year between these ages was not required, we have no means of determining if the compulsory education law has had a beneficial effect.   We also have no data from which to determine how many have attended school the required twelve weeks.   From personal observation I am inclined to think the law is neglected in many localities.

I see no reason why the friends of education should be discouraged.   If we compare our schools with the schools of twenty years ago, we can see that much progress has been made.   Much yet remains to be done.   We should not expect to accomplish great results at once, but should work perseveringly and wait, remembering that the element of time is a very important factor in the accomplishment of anything truly good or great.

DODGE COUNTY.

J. T. FLAVIN, SUPERINTENDENT.

In addition to my annual statistical report, already in your possession, I take occasion to submit a special report, touching a few points bearing on our schools, and the cause of education in general.

I doubt not the experience of all superintendents is very much similar, and endeavoring to bring our district schools to a state of greater efficiency and perfection, experience about the same difficulties, and find their way beset by obstacles that tend, in a great measure, to neutralize the good results that would otherwise attend their efforts.

I. POSSIBILITIES.

The possibilities of our district schools, which it would seem we ought easily to realize under our present system, and which I am striving to reach in this county, are: (1) School-districts, as a rule, of quite uniform size; (2) intelligent, interested school officers; and (3) the retention of the same teacher, — when satisfaction is given,— throughout the school year at least, instead of changing, as is not infrequently the case, two or three times during that period.

II. SIZE OF DISTRICTS.

My unvarying observation has been, that in good-sized districts, embracing necessarily considerable territory, and generally including many families, the burden of supporting the schools thereby falling on the shoulders of the many, that in such districts, schools are maintained a greater number of months during the year, a compensation is paid which is sufficiently liberal to secure the services of good teachers, and far better results are realized, than are possible in our smaller districts, where the expense incident to supporting the school, being borne by the few, is felt more keenly, and the inevitable tendency is in the direction of shorter terms of school, and a compensation so meagre, as to command the services of only the poorer class of teachers.

This is peculiarly the case in this county; and from an interchange of views with other superintendents, I judge it is quite generally true of most other counties in the State.

I recognize the fact that there are seemingly some disadvantages in having large districts, by which children are compelled to journey a long distance to school, but I am firm in my conviction that it would be better to send children two miles to a really good school, than a few rods to a poor one.

In the readjustment of the boundaries of school-districts, and in the change in the location of school-houses, some little effort and expense would be at first occasioned; but I am satisfied that the benefits resulting therefrom would amply repay the outlay thus necessitated.

Reports of County Superintendents — Dodge.

With a less number of school-districts in certain parts of Dodge county, we would, in all probability, have much better schools.

III. SCHOOL BOARDS.

It is to be regretted that the very best men in the different districts are not always selected for school officers. In some instances, perhaps, they could not be chosen, even if willing to serve; but frequently an unwillingness to act in that capacity is manifested by those whose services are sought. With the hearty co-operation of intelligent school officers, a superintendent could render his services far more potent for good. The character of the school very largely depends on the character of the officers. Without the proper kind of officers, we cannot expect to have an intelligent discrimination exercised in employing teachers; merit is liable to go unrecognized and unrewarded; and little distinction is likely to be made between the compensation of teachers of high qualifications and established reputation, and those of limited attainments and little adaptability to the work of the school room.

The duty incumbent upon school officers to visit the schools under their care, is one that is very much neglected; and the urgent invitations uniformly extended them, to be present at the teachers' institutes and examinations, are not as generally responded to as we think reasonable to expect. The relations between school officers and superintendent should be intimate and cordial, and frequent correspondence and consultation should take place between them, in regard to the welfare of our schools.

IV. SCHOOL TERMS AND PERMANENCY.

The number of districts that decide to divide the school year into three terms, increases annually. With the fall, winter, and spring terms of school, and the absolute discontinuance of that practice in vogue in some districts, of maintaining school during the months of July and August, the work of our schools would be of a more vigorous character, and productive of correspondingly better results.

Where a teacher is found to be adapted to a school, and manages the same to the satisfaction of all parties, it is exceedingly unwise to incur the risk that a change involves. A really good teacher, faithful in all respects, should be continued in the same school through many terms, and liberally compensated.

If the district schools, in the length of their terms and the salary of their teachers, were placed on a level with the intermediate departments of our graded schools, there would not be that constant tendency of teachers to quit the charge of the former for positions in the latter. Many of my best teachers sever their connection with the district schools, every year, to engage in the more permanent and lucrative work, than that afforded by positions in the graded schools in this county and elsewhere.

V. Graded Schools.

There are twelve graded schools in this county, and as a rule, they are in charge of a very superior class of teachers. I have taken especial pains to strengthen the corps of teachers in our leading graded schools, inasmuch as those schools are constantly sending out teachers for our district schools, and where the instruction in the former is of a high order, I find it reproduced by those who come forth from them, when they change the role of pupil for that of teacher.

While in the past much care has usually been taken in the selection of principals for those schools, much indifference was often evinced as to the standing of those employed as subordinate teachers, especially for the primary departments. There is now noticeable, however, a growing sentiment in favor of employing only skillful hands to lead and direct the pupils in the lower grades; and there is evidently a real awakening to the vital importance of having children during the first years of their attendance at school, in charge of teachers of special qualification and fitness for doing primary work. Among the recent valuable acquisitions to the corps of principals in this county, are: Mr. L. H. Clarke, a graduate of the Whitewater Normal School, who assumed charge of the high school at Horicon, at the beginning of the past school year; Mr. J. Kelly, a graduate of the Platteville Normal School, who took charge this year of the high school at Fox Lake, and Mr. B. M.

Reports of County Superintendents — Dodge.

Bodle, for several years principal of the schools at Fort Howard, and now principal of the high school in the South Ward of Waupun.

The high school of Beaver Dam, though under city supervision, is one with which our relations have uniformly been of the most friendly character, and in which, from the fact that it furnishes very many teachers for our schools, we shall always feel a special interest, opened this year with Prof. T. B. Pray as its able principal, and I feel confident that it will exercise a salutary influence on the district schools in that locality.

The Fox Lake Seminary, during the past five years, while under the able direction of Prof. A. O. Wright, did a noble work for the cause of education, in that portion of the county in which it is located.

I must here acknowledge the many obligations I am under to Prof. Wright, for the substantial aid he rendered the teachers and superintendent of this county, during his stay with us. Regularly attending and assisting at all of the examinations held at Fox Lake, a worker and lecture at every institute held in this county since his coming here, always ready with wise counsel and helpful suggestions, we owe him a debt of gratitude that deserves something more than this passing notice. His removal from our county is keenly regretted by all.

VI. TEACHERS.

The teacher is the important element in the school. Expensive school-houses, costly apparatus, intelligent supervision, and the cordial support of school boards, will not compensate for a lack on the part of the teachers, of tact, education, or adaptability to the discharge of the practical duties of the school room.

The opportunities for preparation for the intelligent discharge of the duties incident to teaching, are numerous and within the reach of all, and he or she who aspires to the high office of teacher, should first learn how to teach. When schools are in charge of well-qualified teachers, who are zealous and faitnful in the discharge of their duties, the attendance and general condition of the schools are almost invariably satisfactory.

The duty of the parent to visit the school where his children spend five or six hours every day, is one which is sadly neglected. The responsibility which rests upon the parents with respect to the education of his child, cannot be wholly delegated to another; and so long as parents fail to exercise the right and duty of school visitation, our schools will fail of a large part of the good which they might accomplish, if parents would but take a constant and active interest in promoting their usefulness.

VII. EXAMINATIONS.

Eighteen public examinations have been held during the year, which were attended by five hundred and ninety applicants. It has been my endeavor to make my examinations searching and suggestive, with a hope of occasioning subsequent study and investigation, as well as of determining the proficiency of the applicants in the different branches, at the particular time of examination.

Knowing that it is not wise to license a number of teachers largely in excess of the number of schools to be taught, I have, with system and studied effort, tried to elevate the standard of qualification of teachers from time to time; and at present there are scarcely enough teachers available, who hold certificates in this county, to supply all of the schools. We have reached a point where it means something to hold even a third grade certificate.

VIII. INSTITUTES.

At the beginning of the school year, I arranged for and, in connection with Superintendents Collier and Ninman, held a teachers' institute in the city of Watertown. Professors Wright and Viebahn were assigned as conductors, and most faithfully did they discharge their duties. The attendance was very large and regular, and the session proved a marked success. Instructive lectures were delivered by Messrs. Sabin, Wright, Whitford, and Searing.

Following the institute at Watertown, I held one at the village of Juneau, in which Superintendent Delaney co-operated with me. Prof. Beck, of Platteville, labored with us on the occasion, to the entire satisfaction of the large number of teachers in attendance.

Reports of County Superintendents — Dodge.

The two weeks' institute, conducted by Prof. Emery in the city of Beaver Dam, beginning September 20th last, was one of the most pleasant and profitable I have organized since having charge of the schools. I regard Prof. Emery as a most excellent conductor, and one who approaches as near my idea of what an institute conductor should be, as any other I have seen engaged in the work.

If it is the part of a conductor to quibble, be technical, exacting in the extreme, and critically critical with that class of persons who constitute the average institute, thereby destroying the little confidence possessed by some members who are honestly trying to do their best, then Prof. Emery will have to yield the palm. But if on the contrary, a conductor should observe all the common amenities of life, and while thorough in all his work, be courteous, gentlemanly, and considerate; encouraging the timid and inspiring all with his own fidelity, zeal, and enthusiasm, then, in my judgment, Prof. Emery is without a superior in the State.

Disappointment has often been expressed by the institute committee at the failure of so large a number of teachers to take advantage of the opportunity for improvement, which an institute affords; and there is no doubt, in my mind, but that the absence of many is largely due to the dread which teachers have of the undue severity and the studied sharpness of some conductors. Wholesome criticism is desirable; but ridicule and the disparagement of honest effort are to be deprecated, and should he discountenanced.

IX. COUNTY AND SCHOOLS.

In a county so large as this, embracing a territory of nine hundred square miles, we meet many extremes, and observe in journeying through it a great diversity in its resources, physical features, fertility, and productive capacity of the soil.

The condition of the schools is also much diversified, and as a rule, is quite a true index of the condition and circumstances of the people. In certain parts of this county, we find the people as truly alive and progressive in educational matters, and as determined to maintain first class schools in all respects, as are to be found anywhere else in the State, and it is true that the opposite condition of things is not infrequently to be found.

The former is true of localities where the people are prosperous and have accumulated property; the latter, where limited means and poverty prevail. I have very little faith in legislative enactments, or in any remedial agencies other than time, for the bettering of the latter class of schools. The advancement of the schools will not be much, if any, in advance of the improvement of the general circumstances of the people.

X. CONCLUSION.

The entire county came under my supervision on the first of last January, and the work of the office has been very, great. If the days were longer and my strength greater, I could use both to good advantage. There is a sort of inspiration, however, in laboring in a good cause for an appreciative, grateful constituency, and this has cheered me on in my work, never allowing it to become irksome in the least.

So far as the superintendency in this county is concerned, political considerations seem to be entirely ignored, as I have been called for the fourth time to the position; and with the exception of the first time, almost unanimously. The duties of the office have received my undivided attention, and I have spared no effort to advance our schools, without asking to attract any attention from outside of my own field of labor. We have made reasonable progress, I think; scores of teachers having taught successfully in our district schools, are now creditably filling positions in graded schools, in this and other States; implicit confidence seems to be felt by school officers and teachers in the superintendent, so that very many of the former make a general practice of consulting the superintendent in the matter of employing teachers.

Taking an impartial survey of the work that has been done by our schools in this county, I can candidly say that, in most respects, they have met every reasonable expectation; and while the margin for improvement is still great, they will suffer no serious disparagement by comparison with the schools in other counties in the State.

DOUGLAS COUNTY.

I. W. GATES, SUPERINTENDENT.

It gives me pleasure to say in this report that our schools are in better condition than for some years past. An increased interest on the part of parents and citizens is manifested, and a promise for better attendance and more diligent work, is quite encouraging.

Text-books have been furnished free, in part, for some years, and the plan has proved highly satisfactory; and I think the time is near at hand when all the schools of this county will furnish text-books free to all who attend school. One school is now furnishing all necessary stationery to every scholar free; and the plan proves to be not only highly beneficial, but very economical. The advantages of having every scholar "fully equipped" for all work, is very evident to every one. It would seem advisable to shorten the term of school, if necessary, for the purpose of having complete preparation for profitable work during the time of school. More effort should be made to secure good government by self-control on the part of the scholars.

DUNN COUNTY.

MISS FLORENCE TICKNER, SUPERINTENDENT.

In addition to the general statistics contained in my annual report, I submit the following items:

Four new school buildings have been erected during the past year, three frame buildings, and one of brick containing two departments,— all have been furnished with the latest improved furniture, and are neat and commodious.

There is need yet of other school buildings to take the place of those which have become too small to accommodate the number of pupils who ought to attend school.

The law requiring district boards to adopt a series of text-books, has been disregarded by many in this county. Only 64 districts have reported as having adopted text-books; and of these, 45 pur-

Reports of County Superintendents — Dunn.

chase the books, and 28 loan them to pupils, while the remaining 17 sell them to the pupils.

There are some districts in this county, where fully one-half of the benefit which might have been derived from the school, was lost to the pupils, for lack of a proper supply of books.

At the ten public examinations held last year, one hundred and sixty-five applicants presented themselves. Of this number, seven received second grade, seventy-one received third grade, and forty-nine limited certificates.

Quite a number who failed to receive a third grade last spring, attended the fall examinations and passed a good examination, receiving a third grade.

An institute held in Menomonie, beginning August 30th and closing September 10th, was attended by sixty-eight teachers, with an average daily attendance of fifty-five. All seemed very much interested and showed a spirit of earnestness in their work, and undoubtedly will do more efficient teaching than ever before in the school room. The conductors, Profs. A. R. Sprague and G. T. Foster, did good service, and much credit is due them.

Since last January, I have made 114 visits in 85 different schools, in which I found teachers and pupils interested and doing fair work. Many districts cling to the old plan of having two terms, one in the cold weather in winter, the other extending into or through the extreme heat. In each of such schools, I found the attendance small, as the larger boys and girls were needed at home to work, and the smaller children were too tired to attend regularly "in such hot weather."

Money paid for school in July and August, as a general rule, is money wasted. I have urged districts to divide the summer term, closing before July, and, then after the "hot spell" is over, beginning again in September, and having a fall term. Some districts have tried that plan this year, and were well pleased with the results.

Visitation has convinced me that the chief need of our schools to-day is a supply of thoroughly qualified teachers; but just how we are to obtain that supply is not clear. True, the Normal

Reports of County Superintendents — Eau Claire.

Schools are giving us some such teachers, but much can be done by district boards in hiring only those who hold good certificates. Teachers can do much for themselves by studying while they are teaching, — disciplining themselves to think, then they can better teach their pupils how to think for themselves.

I have been urging teachers to try the "Course of Study for Ungraded Schools," as given in the institute circular, knowing that if they succeed in the adoption of it, much will have been gained.

EAU CLAIRE COUNTY.

MISS AGNES HOSFORD, SUPERINTENDENT.

I. SCHOOL-HOUSES.

There are sixty-five districts in the county, and sixty-nine school-houses. Four districts are so large that in each a school is maintained in two places; and in one district, Eau Claire No. 3, in four different buildings; two of these, however, are in the same yard. In two districts, school was kept in rented buildings.

Should any one take the trouble to compare my reports of previous years with the present, the inquiry might arise, "What has happened to the ventilation of the school-houses of Eau Claire county?" Simply this: I have formerly reported according to the returns received from town clerks; this year, I have reported according to my own judgment. Should my right to do so be questioned, the number *sixty-nine* may be substituted in place of *four* under column headed "Number of school-houses properly ventilated." There are three school-houses in Eau Claire, and one in the village of Augusta, in which provision is made for the introduction of warm, pure air, and the egress of foul air. All of the others have been built without reference to ventilation, save that in a few instances a small opening has been left in the ceiling, or in the upper part of the chimney, through which the impure air is supposed to escape.

I believe the people of Eau Claire county are as intelligent, and love their children as much as any in the State. I can account for the lack of ventilation only by supposing that they do not believe pure air is necessary to the preservation of human life and health, or that drafts of cold air from open windows are dangerous. I am sure they desire that their children shall be healthy in body and pure in mind, but they do not provide such means as seem to me necessary to insure such a result. I have not failed to ask the attention of the people to the condition of the school-houses and their surroundings, at least once a year for the last five years. When I learned that new school-houses were to be built, I have written to school officers upon the subject, and sent to them such books as I had, pertaining to the subject. Still, twenty-one school-houses have been built in that time, with no attempt at ventilation; and, in several districts, the outhouses are disgraceful, or the lack of these houses is indecent. Prof. Chittenden's paper upon " Our School-Houses," in the last annual report of the State Board of Health, shows that the people of this county are not sinners above others in disregard of the sanitary conditions of school-houses. The revelations of that paper concerning the condition of the country school-houses of the State, I think, should lead to something more than words. I see no indication that there will be any improvement until some cheap, simple and reasonably effective method of ventilation is devised, and by law required to be used, or some satisfactory equivalent in its stead, in every school-house in the State. The loaning of money by the State for building might be made conditional upon the erection of a comfortable, healthy, convenient house and proper surroundings, the plan for which might be one of several, devised by some competent architect appointed for that purpose.

II. ATTENDANCE.

The school population of the county is 6,002. Of this number, 4,095, or sixty-eight per cent., were enrolled in the schools. The average attendance of those enrolled is reported as sixty-nine per cent., which is probably approximately correct. The number of days in which schools were maintained in each district averages one hundred and twenty-two. Twelve districts maintained school only the length of time required to draw their apportionment from the State school fund. In a few districts, the number of months of school in the year has been increased, and a better arrangement of terms has been secured. The average wages of teachers was less than last year,— the greater decrease being in the wages of gentlemen teachers. The amount spent for apparatus and library was less than in any other year since 1875. The average expenditure per capita of school population was \$6.95; of pupils enrolled, \$10.19.

III. Books.

The plan of district purchase of books has been instrumental in producing a change from the insufficient supply, and vexatious variety of books formerly prevalent. There is now very little ground for complaint from either cause. Forty-four districts have adopted a series of books, and thirty-seven use only the books adopted. Thirty-two districts purchase books, twenty of which loan them to pupils, free, the remaining twelve sell them at cost.

IV. Teachers.

The number of applicants for teachers' certificates during the year, was so small that there were scarcely enough teachers to supply the schools. Ninety-five teachers were needed; one hundred and twenty-nine certificates were issued during the year. The largest number in force at any time was one hundred and twenty-two. Among these, however, were some who held certificates in other counties and found employment there, and some who wished to teach but a part of the year. Twelve certificates were given to persons under eighteen years of age; ten of these were between seventeen and eighteen; two were sixteen. There is evidently a growing desire on the part of teachers for better preparation before commencing the work, — a willingness to receive direction, and faithful efforts to follow it. Educational books and periodicals are more read than formerly. Notwithstanding the improvement in intellectual attainments and the use of such aids in teaching as are attainable, I am more than ever convinced that the great need of the district school is teachers who have received special training for that work.

GRANT COUNTY.

CHAS. L. HARPER, SUPERINTENDENT.

With the close of the school year, a retrospect of the work done, a comparison of the statistics required in the annual reports for 1879–80, and other items showing something of the progress and present educational condition of the county, are presented, trusting that they may be of some interest, if not of value:

I. SUMMARY OF STATISTICS.	1879.	1880.
Number of children between four and twenty years of age	15,016	14,847
Number of such children who have attended public school	10,862	11,053
Number of such children who have attended private school only	330	288
Number of persons under four and over twenty who have attended school	126	60
Whole number of persons who have attended school.	11,318	11,401
Whole number of days school has been taught by qualified teachers	33,912	33,165
Average number of days school has been maintained in each district	160	158
Number of public examinations held during the year	23	26
Number of applicants for certificates	796	732
Number of certificates granted	346	396
Number of persons required to teach the schools.	247	250
Whole number of different persons now holding county certificates	....	320
Average wages of male teachers per month	$32 78	$36 47
Average wages of female teachers per month	22 27	21 87
Number of graded schools	16	17
Number of high schools	5	5
Number of districts reported	212	210
Number of districts that have adopted a list of text-books	82	95
Number of districts using only those adopted	54	75
Number of districts that have adopted a course of study	....	26
Number of private schools reported	10	12
Number of days of institute work in the county	20	20
Number of persons enrolled in the institutes	155	155
Cash value of school-houses	$155,216 00	$169,263 00
Cash value of sites	9.874 00	9,989 00
Cash value of apparatus	4,980 00	5,790 00
Total amount of money received during the year	74,325 18	75,879 30
Total amount of money paid out during the year	60,767 51	60,552 29
Money on hand August 31st	13,557 61	15,327 01
Number of official visits made by county superintendent	177	188

Reports of County Superintendents — Grant.

The statistics given above are substantially correct. Many of the town clerks have held the office for a number of years, well understand what is required of them, and are generally interested in seeing that the reports of the district clerks are correct. A very few of the districts have not furnished this year some of the special statistics required, because the school register did not show them, and they were unable to obtain them from the teachers. District clerks and county superintendents will hail with pleasure the universal adoption and use of Lunn's School Register in the schools of the State. Until its introduction, it will be almost useless to expect absolutely correct statistics from some of our school-districts; and statistics, in order to be of any true value, must be correct.

II. ATTENDANCE.

One of the encouraging items shown by a comparison of the reports for 1879–80, is the increased attendance. Although the number of persons of school age in the county has decreased 169, there were 191 more enrolled in the schools; and further, the percentage of attendance last year was barely 65 per cent., while this year it is $68\frac{1}{8}$ per cent. The compulsory education law, although not so strong and nearly perfect as many superintendents and teachers would have it, is undoubtedly bearing good fruit. The provisions and intentions of the law have been discussed at our examinations and teachers' institutes. It is to be earnestly hoped that discussions of this kind, taken in connection with the timely circular sent to district boards by State Superintendent Whitford, may do much in calling the attention of the people to the law, and paving the way for a new law or amendments to the present law, that will secure to every child in our State the inestimable benefits of a fair common school education. Although no one in this county has been brought before "any court having competent jurisdiction," for neglect of duty or violation of this law, many school officers and patrons have interested themselves in seeing that its provisions were carried out; and the result is that, in some districts, every child, not incapacitated, of the ages required in the law, has been enrolled in the school, and has attended at least the time required.

III. SCHOOL TERMS.

Several of the more sparsely settled districts maintain school only five months during the year, generally commencing about the middle of November. The attendance during the winter term is usually excellent. Many other districts have divided the school year into two terms, one of five months, beginning about the first of November, and the other of two or three months, beginning about the middle of April. A majority of the districts that maintain school eight months, have a fall term of two months, a winter term of four months, and a spring term of two months. By this arrangement all children in the district of whatever age, can attend and receive due attention, the older ones in the winter, and the younger ones in the fall and spring. The " keeping " (for but very few can do much *real* teaching) of school during the months of July and August, has been discouraged; and, as a consequence, very few schools will be found in session at that time. In some of the villages and more thickly settled districts, ladies have opened private schools during the heated term; and in several instances, they have been well sustained and productive of much good.

IV. CHANGING TEACHERS.

The evils and losses arising from an unnecessary and too frequent change of teachers, are too many and various to admit of discussion in this connection. This is certainly one of the greatest drawbacks to progress in our country schools, and can hardly be too earnestly deprecated. Too many of our school boards contract with as many different persons, during the school year, as they have terms of school in the district. While in some instances this action may be unavoidable, yes, even desirable, its effects are only too apparent in the dead, non-progressive condition of things, that can not only be seen, but *felt* at once, on entering the school-room in a district where " change " is the rule. Generally speaking, the wide-awake, go-ahead schools are found in the districts where it is the custom to employ the teachers for the year, — a custom that I am pleased to say is becoming more common, and promises, in time, to do much toward making the teacher's tenure of posi-

Reports of County Superintendents — Grant.

tion depend more on the quality of the work done in the school room, than on the mere whim of some irate parent or fault-finding member of the school board.

V. TEXT-BOOKS.

We have not escaped the importunities of irrepressible representatives of several school book publishing houses. However, they came none too soon; and, although they were successful to a considerable degree in their efforts, we have no reason to regret their coming. There was at one time, many years ago, something like a uniform series of text-books in most of our schools; but very soon new and revised editions were issued and purchased, with now and then some new book recommended by a teacher, until the condition of things was something astonishing as well as appalling to the teacher who was daring enough to attempt to classify his school. It was no uncommon thing to find thirty or more different classes in a school of not more than forty pupils.

By judicious introduction of books, the number of classes has been reduced to eighteen or twenty (depending somewhat on the advancement of the pupils), thus enabling the teacher to do something like good work, which was almost impossible under the previous state of affairs. By judicious use of the power now placed in the hands of school officers, much may be done toward advancing the best interests of our schools, and the much agitated text-book question can be satisfactorily settled, without any further action on the part of our State Legislature.

VI. SCHOOL-HOUSES.

We have, in common with many other counties, I presume, school houses existing under all conditions of fitness and unfitness known to school officers and teachers. One is valued at $20,800, two at $12,000 each, and quite a good number from two to seven thousand dollars each. These buildings, in common with a large number of others, less pretentious, are well furnished and conveniently arranged.

There are still a few log structures in the more remote districts,

that were " put up " when the districts in which they are, were first
established, and were, at that time, designed as mere make-shifts.
The condition of things under which they were erected, has long
since passed away, and the dilapidated log structure is their only
monument. I have, however, very good reasons to believe that
another year will close the existence of most of them, and we may
then look for substantial and commodious structures that will be
sources of pride and satisfaction to the districts in which they
stand.

VII. VENTILATION.

Under the head of " school-houses properly ventilated," I have
returned one hundred and eighty-one. From my acquaintance
with the condition of the school-houses in this county, I judge that
the district clerks have read the heading *well*, instead of *properly*.
There are, without doubt, some that are *well* ventilated. On this
subject, I agree exactly with the town clerk who, in his report,
says: " Five are so reported to me, but I don't believe there is one
in the *county, properly ventilated.*"

This subject should receive much more attention from teachers
and school officers than it now does. There are good reasons for
believing that the ill-health of many of our teachers and pupils
during the year, was chiefly owing to the fact that they were, for
the greater part of the winter, confined to school rooms so ill ventilated that the process of breathing was little less than a process
of slow poisoning, from which it may take years to recover. The
circular, " Our Public Schools and School-Houses," has done much
good in calling the attention of the people to this subject, as well
as to many other serious evils arising from neglect and ignorance.

VIII. EXAMINATIONS.

Twenty-six examinations have been held during the year, each
occupying two full days; and I think I am within bounds when I
estimate the written work handed in for marking, at 18,000 pages.
It has been my aim to make the questions used, plain, practical,
and comprehensive; of such a nature as to require thought on the
part of the applicant, and to bring into full play his knowledge of

---

Reports of County Superintendents — Grant.

---

the different branches. Whether or not my aim has been realized, those examined are left to decide. The standing required for the different grades of county certificates, was raised in the spring of 1879. There was, as a consequence, quite a falling off from the usual number of teachers in the county, but just so soon as applicants learned that the percentage required was rigidly adhered to and was the dividing line between failure and success, the more ambitious, energetic ones placed themselves well up in the list of qualified teachers, while the non-progressive ones, barnacles on the educational ship, dropped off, and but little has been heard from them since. The effect has, on the whole, been highly beneficial, and our schools are in the hands of the more wide-awake, progressive teachers; and, if we are not making the progress we should, the fault is not altogether theirs by any means.

IX. PERMITS AND CERTIFICATES OF INCOMPETENCY.

These are almost wholly unknown in this county. When granted, it is only to persons who have passed a tolerable examination, and who then present a "request for license," signed by all the members of the school board of the district in which they expect to teach. Two different grades of certificates may not be enough for the State, but three different grades are certainly enough for the county. The custom of granting anything below the full third grade certificate, should be persistently cried down by every true teacher, and carefully guarded against by every earnest superintendent. It is customary in some counties to grant certificates "good for six months," to numbers of young persons at spring examinations, in order that they may teach summer schools. It is true that most of the pupils enrolled during the summer term are young, and the work to be done is of a primary nature; but our experience with the syllabus used in our institutes the past year, shows plainly that it requires judgment and skill, which are not always found in young beginners, to do primary work intelligently. It is also an act of injustice to teachers who have passed satisfactory examinations, to grant this class of certificates. The older and more successful teachers are quite often crowded out of positions by these semi-qualified beginners, who can afford to teach for low wages, and who can certainly do no better work than those who are fully qualified. The refusal to grant " fourth grade " certificates has produced a healthy educational sentiment among the people of this county, that is highly encouraging.

X. INSTITUTES.

Two teachers' institutes were held during August. The number of members enrolled was, at Platteville, 77; at Fennimore, 78. Very nearly all of those enrolled at Platteville have, at some time, availed themselves of the advantages offered by the Normal School, and, I think, there need be no hestitation in saying that better or more thorough work has not been done at any institute organized in the State. The institute at Fennimore was the first ever held in that village, and the interest and hearty co-operation of the citizens contributed largely to our success. The work done by the teachers was highly commendable, and a more earnest class would be difficult to find. The average age of the members was 21.3 years; the average experience in teaching, 23.75 months; and the percentage of attendance, 96.56.

Prof. A. J. Hutton conducted the work at Platteville; and Prof. Geo. Beck, at Fennimore. These gentlemen have merited and won the highest esteem and confidence of the citizens of this county, and will always receive a hearty welcome at their hands. My thanks are due Miss Emma Watkins and Mr. C. Showalter, of Lancaster, for valuable assistance at Fennimore, and to J. L. Krueger, one of the best penmen in this part of the State, who took charge of the work in penmanship, at Platteville.

We were fortunate in having with us at Fennimore, for one entire day, State Superintendent Whitford, who gave us many valuable suggestions and much excellent advice on points relating to school management. He lectured before the citizens and teachers in the evening, on the subject of " High Schools." The remarks were excellent, to the point, and well received; and I will, without doubt, in my next annual report, have the pleasure of returning one more high school organized in this county, at Fennimore.

Reports of County Superintendents — Grant.

One great benefit that we are deriving from our institutes, is uniformity in methods of teaching. When uniformity of methods is secured in our schools, we will not feel, to such an extent as we now do, the evils arising from frequent change of teachers. Every citizen having the welfare of our educational system at heart, should do all in his power to increase the interest manifested in institute work, and use his influence in encouraging attendance, by giving a decided preference to those teachers who are willing to sacrifice time and money, that they may be able to attend and better prepare themselves to take up intelligently their work in the school room.

XI. VISITING SCHOOLS.

My time for this, the most enjoyable part of my work, is necessarily limited by the unusual amount of other work that demands attention. During the past year, one hundred and eighty-eight official visits have been made. My endeavor has been to remain one-half day in each school, visits of a shorter period being. generally, unsatisfactory. Programmes and methods have been examined, and such changes made and suggestions given as were deemed prudent. Especial attention has been given to the discipline of the school room, and it is with pleasure that I can say that we are making rapid improvement in this direction. The people are generally awake to the fact that but little or no benefit can be derived from our schools, unless at least a fair degree of order is maintained; and with few exceptions, they cheerfully give their hearty support to the teacher who strives to make his school what it should be in this particular.

A county superintendent can certainly do a great deal toward promoting the efficiency of the schools under his supervision, by frequently visiting them, encouraging what is good, discouraging what is bad, counseling with parents and teachers, and using his influence at every opportunity to promote a harmony of feeling and purpose, and a wholesome educational sentiment. However, there is one thing that is absolutely essential in order that the greatest good may be derived from the work of a county superintendent, and that is this: The number of departments under his supervision must be something less than one-quarter of a thousand.

XII. Educational Advantages.

It is with pride we enumerate the educational facilities offered by this county. Of the two hundred and ten schools reported, seventeen are graded. These are under the management of instructors who are thoroughly interested in the work, and who are worthy of the confidence placed in them. The Normal School at Platteville is constantly sending out numbers of trained teachers, who exert an influence that is one great cause of our educational vigor. Twelve private schools, not incorporated, and mostly denominational, are reported. One incorporated institution, St. Clara Academy, beautifully located on Sinsinawa Mound, and under the management of Sisters of the Order of Saint Dominic, is in a flourishing condition. Besides giving instruction in branches usually taught in our higher schools, much and excellent instruction is here given in painting, crayon drawing, and music.

Five weekly newspapers freely offer space and kindly invite communications on educational topics. One, the Platteville Witness, has placed, wholly at the disposal of our teachers, an entire column under the management of Prof. Geo. Beck, who earnestly invites communications relating to the work from all interested. I regret to say that this column has not yet received from us the support it deserves.

XIII. Conclusion.

Pleasant and encouraging as this retrospect has been, the prospect is doubly so. With the usual good feeling attendant on periods of general thrift and prosperity, the subjects of new school buildings, new furniture, additional and necessary apparatus, fences and trees for our school grounds, and better wages for our teachers, were brought up and favorable discussed at very many of our annual meetings. We not only hope, but rest assured that much will be done in the near future to add to the appearance and comfort of our school-houses and their surroundings. The earnestness and devotion of our teachers, united with better preparation, the general and hearty co-operation of parents, officers, and teachers, the growing determination on the part of the older pupils to fit themselves for the duties and responsibilities of life, all point with unmistakable emphasis toward gratifying success.

GREEN COUNTY.

D. H. MORGAN, SUPERINTENDENT.

There is general complaint that the district reports are incomplete. The truth is that many of the district clerks do not know how to fill the blanks, and some think that it is of no consequence, except the number of children, and are indifferent. Could there be a day set by law for the district and town clerks to meet, and then a day for the town clerks and county superintendent to meet, I think we might be able to obtain reliable reports.

Another thing we need, and that is a uniform school register; the same throughout the State. As it is now arranged, district clerks buy the first one that comes in their way, scarcely any dealers keeping a uniformity. If you, or the publishers of the kind which you recommend, will send me a copy, I will do all I can to have it introduced into general use in our schools.

I am satisfied that the district clerks have underrated the number between the ages of seven and fifteen years who have attended school. From personal observation and inquiry, I am very sure that very few between these ages do not attend school, at least a portion of the year.

It may be owing to the imperfect manner of keeping the school registers, that the clerks are not able to make better reports.

I shall call the teachers together early in November, and give them instruction in keeping the register; and at that time, I should be glad to exhibit the one you approve, and may get our booksellers to lend a helping hand.

I believe the people of Green county will be glad to have a law that will levy a State tax to aid in supporting the public schools.

I wish, too, that the State would establish the township system of school government. We might then get one much more systematic. It would then be easy to have and maintain a uniform course of study throughout a county.

JACKSON COUNTY.

T. P. MARSH, SUPERINTENDENT.

It affords me much pleasure to be able to report some progress in the schools of Jackson county, during the past year.

I. TEACHERS.

The class of persons applying for certificates was much better acquainted with the duties pertaining to teaching, than heretofore. There has been manifested an earnest desire, on the part of many of the best teachers of the county, to reach a higher standard of qualifications; and as a sure result, much better work has been done in the school room. I have endeavored to raise gradually the required standard, and put into the schools only such as were capable of doing good work. The supply is not equal to the demand. The best teachers, with those patrons of the schools who take a live interest in educational advancement, gave their cordial support to all measures inaugurated for improvement. Necessity sometimes compels me to license some for the work, who show a lack of those qualifications which are necessary in order to render one eminently successful in school work. In other branches of business, there are persons who are qualified for their duties, and they faithfully and effectively perform them; while others are making repeated failures, because they are attempting to do something they are totally unqualified to do. There must be an aptitude for one's business, in order to insure entire success. Just so it is in teaching. I am satisfied there are many teachers who could do better work, if they only had the proper means to do with, such as good school rooms, properly arranged and furnished with the needed apparatus, as outline maps, globes, charts, and plenty of blackboard.

II. TEXT-BOOKS.

The text-book muddle prevents many from doing as thorough and efficient work as they could, were there a nearer approach to uniformity in this particular. I am glad to be able to say that there has been a decided improvement in this direction during the past year.

III. SCHOOL BUILDINGS.

There have been two new buildings erected during the year, and there are other districts contemplating building houses, during the coming year. Some of the old buildings have been repaired, yet truth compels me to say that some of the school-houses furnish an unfavorable commentary upon the educational indifference that allows the school work to be retarded for the want of better build-ings. There are many buildings though, which conclusively show that the spirit of progress is animating the patrons of the country schools of Jackson county.

IV. HIGH SCHOOL.

The high school at Black River Falls has never been more effi-ciently managed, nor accomplished more thorough work, than during the year ending June 18th, 1880. The school now contains a very efficient corps of teachers; and, I think, will compare with the best of high schools in this part of the State.

V. NORMAL INSTITUTE.

An institute was held at Black River Falls, from August 30th to September 9th, under the able supervision of Prof. J. B. Thayer, assisted by myself. Fifty-one members were enrolled; the average daily attendance being forty. Hard and earnest work was a char-acteristic feature of the session. I am satisfied that much good will result to teachers in their school work, from the many hints relative to teaching, given by Prof. Thayer.

VI. CERTIFICATES.

The total number of certificates issued during the year ending August 31st, is one hundred and forty; three first grade, twelve second grade, and one hundred and twenty-five third grade. To forty-four applicants I refused to grant certificates, because they lacked sufficient learning. Examinations were held at three different places in the county. A few applied for private examination. I try to discourage such examinations as much as possible, as I think it better to do so.

VII. School Visitations.

All but twelve of the schools were visited by me during the winter, and all but one during the summer. I have endeavored to visit the schools twice during the year, but in some instances I could not do so, on account of the shortness of the terms and the irregularity of commencing. I have given words of advice where needed, and tried to stimulate all to do better work in the future.

In conclusion, I would state that it shall be, as it always has been, my earnest endeavor, while connected with the schools, to labor for their success, as therein lies our hopes of future safety and prosperity. I hope to receive the aid and hearty co-operation of school boards and all patrons of the common schools. Very much good can be accomplished by the people becoming thoroughly in earnest, and taking an active part in making the schools better. School boards sometimes need to be reminded of their duties. I hope the time will soon come when the questions asked by them of teachers will be, " what are your qualifications; " and not, " how cheap will you teach our school."

JUNEAU COUNTY.

W. G. SPENCE, SUPERINTENDENT.

I. Teachers and Graded Schools.

Juneau county, according to the report just furnished, contains ninety-five school-districts. Each of five of these districts contains a school of more than three departments, and is under the immediate supervision of experienced and successful teachers.

The village of Necedah has the largest enrollment of any in the

Reports of County Superintendents — Juneau.

county. The seven teachers employed there have nearly all received a normal course of instruction. Prof. O. N. Wagley and Miss Ada Dann, teachers of the high school, are graduates of the Whitewater Normal.

The village of New Libson, in its early settlement, was fortunate in securing citizens deeply interested in educational matters. The public school is the pride of the village, and money expended for teachers' wages or school supplies, is considered well invested. Prof. George T. Foster, of Beloit College, and Miss Dedie S. Beebe, of the State University, have charge of the high school.

The village of Mauston is about to erect a new school building, which will compare favorably with the other buildings of the town. Messrs. Edbrooke and Burnham, architects, of Chicago, have prepared the sketches. The Ruttan Company, Chicago, furnish the system of warming and ventilation; and, when completed, the building and school will have few equals in this part of the State. Prof. John A. Anderson, of the State University, class of '78, is principal of the high school. Necedah, Mauston, and New Lisbon enroll each about three hundred and thirty-seven pupils, or over one thousand in all.

The village of Wonewoc has at present the best school building in the county. This school, which has three departments and four teachers, is in charge of Prof. I. A. Sabin, a teacher of thirty years' experience, and is in excellent condition.

The village of Elroy has been signally favored, during the past six years, with a Seminary supported by the United Brethren denomination, and under the immediate charge of Prof. F. M. Washburn. The village, heretofore, has recognized the usefulness of the Seminary, and patronized it to such an extent that it has been allowed to usurp the place of a high school. Prof. Washburn having left for another field of labor, the people in favor of a public school have seized the opportunity and organized a graded school with four departments. Prof. Johnson, a graduate of the Platteville Normal, has the school in charge.

II. STATISTICS.

Of the 116 teachers employed in the public schools of this county, 26 hold positions in the graded schools, and are largely graduates of the higher institutions of the State. · Most of them are teachers of experience and ability, and one must go far to find better methods or more thorough instruction than is imparted in these schools.

We wish as much could be said of the mixed schools. Some of them, indeed, are doing good work, and have pleasant, home-like rooms, well-lighted and ventilated. Some have patent furniture, a good supply of blackboard surface, globes, maps, charts, etc. On the other hand, many of the districts in the more sparsely settled sections are less fortunate.

III. EXAMINATIONS.

We have raised the standard of qualifications sufficiently to reduce the number of teachers to 125 — nine more than the number of different departments in the county.

We have aimed to select 125 of the best teachers in the county, and notice that these are not forced to go to Minnesota or into other counties of our own State, to find employment.

We have endeavored to make candidates realize that examinations mean something, that a certificate is a record of proven attainment. A large number of students of our high schools are taking their examinations in second and first grade branches, just as regularly as they do their finals; and we have reason to hope that, during the coming year, we shall have a larger number of teachers, holding well-earned first grade certificates, than ever before in the history of our county.

IV. SCHOOL-HOUSES.

During the past year, I sent a written report of each school visit to the clerk of the district, giving condition of the school, so far as any good could be accomplished by so doing, and calling attention to the condition of the school property. Where repairs were needed, where curtains, apparatus, blackboard, etc., were wanting, I urged,

---

Reports of County Superintendents — La Crosse.

---

often in strong terms, that these be supplied; and I was more than pleased with the results in this direction.

Many hideous. gloomy rooms were cleaned and repaired, curtains were hung at the windows, pictures were brought in by teacher and pupils, and rooms made home-like, cleanly, comfortable.

During the past year, three new houses were built, additions were made to several, and a large number have made substantial repairs.

We have yet a number of houses entirely unfit for school purposes. Local district quarrels, disputes regarding the site of the new house, and petty jealousies, are the most common hinderances.

V. THE OUTLOOK.

On the whole, the educational outlook in Juneau county is quite encouraging. Wages is still low, but the return of good times, better qualification on the part of teachers, and better schools have caused the market price of such service to look up.

We have a county teachers' association with four divisions, which will each hold meetings regularly during the winter months.

The "Course of Study for Country Schools" we hope to see adopted in all of those schools this winter; and, altogether, we see in the past and the immediate future no uncertain signs of progress.

LA CROSSE COUNTY.

C. S. STOCKWELL, SUPERINTENDENT.

I have the honor to transmit herewith my third annual report.

The whole number of children of school age in the county (La Crosse city not included), is 4,601. Whole number enrolled, 3,042. Whole amount expended for teachers' salaries, $15,232.90, or $3.31 per capita of school population. The whole expenditure for school purposes, including building and repairing, furniture, fuel, and incidentals, is $20,636.72, or $4.48 per capita.

I. SCHOOL VISITS.

I have made, during the year, one hundred and seventy-one school visits, devoting usually a full half day to each visit. By

reason of the sickness of the teacher, or the prevalence of diphtheria, closing the school unexpectedly, two or three districts have
been visited but once. All others have been visited at least once
in each term, and many of them much more frequently. In those
districts where I knew the teacher, and felt satisfied that he was
doing good work, I have made my visits when it has been most
convenient; but where schools were in charge of new and inexperienced teachers, I have made it a point to satisfy myself as
early in the term as practicable as to the kind and character of
their work.

Monthly reports have been required from all the schools, the
teachers being supplied with printed blanks on postal cards. I
find that the adoption of the postal card report insures more regularity in the reception, as out of the whole number of teachers in
the county only two failed to report regularly.

II. EXAMINATIONS.

Ten public examinations were held, at which two hundred and
one applicants were present; one hundred and thirty-four of these
received certificates, viz.; four first grade, seventeen second grade,
and one hundred and thirteen third grade. As the schools of the
county employ but seventy-four teachers, there has been no scarcity,
and yet the supply is not so far in excess of the demand as the
figures appear to indicate. About one-half of our schools are still
managed on the " time honored " plan of a male teacher for the
winter term and a female for the summer. This system is gradually
growing unpopular, although there are quite a number of districts
that do not seem to realize that a change of teachers involves a
loss of time; and for the sake of saving a few dollars in the way of
salary, will change teachers every three months. My observation
leads me to believe that each of those changes costs the district, on
the average, at least one-half a month's salary, as it takes a new
teacher about that time to get matters straightened around so that
he can do effective work. The adoption of a uniform course of
study, with careful grading and an intelligible system of records,
might, to a certain extent, obviate the waste of time; but a more

simple, and, on the whole, a better remedy is within the reach of every school board,— that is, do not change. If a teacher is succeeding in awakening an interest in study, if he is a successful teacher, it is poor economy to exchange his services for those of a stranger, even if a dollar or two be saved thereby.

III. SCHOOL-HOUSES AND GROUNDS.

There are yet a few poor school-houses in the county. It is gratifying to be able to report that they are rapidly disappearing. Three new buildings have been erected this year, and at least five new ones will be erected the coming year.

District No. 3, of the town of Washington, has built a very fine stone building this year, 30 by 42 feet in size, well supplied with blackboard surface, and is a credit to the enterprise and intelligence of the district. Quite a respectable number of our districts have large, roomy playgrounds, attached to their school buildings; but, in a very few instances, has anything been done in the way of ornamentation or improvement. The school yard devoid of shade, the school room without blinds or curtains to keep out the intolerable heat of the sun, no well or other supply of water without going one-fourth of a mile to a neighboring farm-house, where, perhaps, the school-house water pail has long since ceased to be a welcome visitor, is it surprising that the child looks forward to the close of school with about the same feeling that the prisoner does to the time when he shall regain his liberty?

Indications are, however, that there is a growing interest in this matter, and I confidently expect that the close of the present school year will see a much less number of barren, unattractive school yards.

IV. SCHOOL-DISTRICT RECORDS.

I am convinced that a somewhat faulty system of book-keeping prevails among a large number of those who have charge of school-district records. My convictions in this direction come from this: The balance on hand for August 31, 1879, as shown by the report of that year, was in the aggregate $4,275.66.

The first item called for in the report for this year, is balance on hand August 31, 1879; and in this year's report, the same balance that was reported last year as above, is reported as $5,455.27. I confess that I cannot understand it; and referring to the several town reports, I find decrepancies amounting to several hundred dollars in some cases, and in nearly every case the amount is reported larger this year than last. Going " behind the returns," and making a comparison between the district reports, I find thirty-two of them return an amount on hand at the beginning of this year differing from the amount on hand at the end of last year.

That this comes from errors or carelessness is quite evident, as in nearly every case the balance is increased. In some instances it varies by only a few cents; in others, by one or two hundred dollars. Can not some system of book-keeping be devised, that will help this matter?

V. BLACKBOARDS AND APPARATUS.

Nearly every school room in the county is supplied with something in the way of a blackboard; yet in very many of them the blackboard surface is very small,— indeed, not more than one-third can be said to be well supplied. About one-half are supplied with globes and outline maps. Webster's Dictionary is, of course, found in every school room.

VI. SUPPLY OF TEACHERS.

As before stated, I have examined 201 applicants for teachers' certificates; sixty-seven failed to reach the required standard (seventy per cent.), and were refused certificates. It has been my aim to keep the standard as high as possible, and supply the schools. Until the present, there has been an oversupply of teachers for our winter schools; but this fall, so far, the supply is not equal to the demand. The short supply is due to other causes than rigid examinations. There has been a considerable " exodus " of teachers, in the direction of Colorado and Dakota, since last winter, and their places have not been filled. The result has been a slight increase in teachers' wages, and a lively demand for teachers.

VII. TEACHERS' INSTITUTE.

Two institutes have been held; one at Bangor, in March, attended by fifty-nine teachers; and one of the regular series, appointed by the State, at West Salem, in September, at which the enrollment reached fifty-two. At each of these, the interest in the school work and methods manifested by those in attendance was very gratifying to those in charge of the work. These institutes, notwithstanding the fact that the attendance was not as large as usual in September, are growing in favor with our teachers, a majority of whom realize that they are worth more to them than any other means of instruction within their reach.

VIII. TEACHERS' ASSOCIATION.

The La Crosse County Teachers' Association still lives, and, during the past winter, held regular meetings. The interest in these meetings is confined to about twenty; but these realizing the good work it is doing, are not faint-hearted, and are determined that the Association shall live; that its influence for good on our public schools shall not be permitted to wane. The Association has accumulated a library of about fifty volumes of professional works, and if it shall accomplish nothing but this— the establishment and maintenance of a Teachers' Library in the county — its efforts will not have been in vain.

IX. EDUCATIONAL JOURNALS.

Ninety per cent. of our teachers are readers of educational journals. The practical aids in the preparation for the arduous duties of the school room, are fully appreciated.

X. CONCLUSION.

Though there has been no marvelous improvement in our public schools, yet, on the whole, the schools of La Crosse county have made creditable and substantial progress during the past year. The majority of our people are earnest and liberal in their support, and, with a healthy public sentiment to back them, their future is full of promise.

LA FAYETTE COUNTY.

C. G. THOMAS, SUPERINTENDENT.

Two well-arranged school-houses have been built during the year, and several old ones reseated with patent desks. A general improvement is observed in most of the buildings and grounds. The high school at Darlington has been provided with a new fur-nace.

The demand for teachers holding the higher grade of certificates, has been greater this year than ever before. I have been raising the standard of certificates every year that I have been in office, and I find that the teachers are doing better work. Whenever I find that the teachers as a class are deficient in any one branch, at the next two examinations, I furnish a thorough test in that branch. When I first came into office, I found that, as a general thing, teachers were not posted in orthoepy, and in this study they have improved much. As a general thing, most of the teachers are trying to improve in school work. The institute was fairly attended, but not as well as it should have been; but I think by next year that the attendance will be a third larger.

In marking teachers in theory and art, I take into consideration the work performed in the school room during my visits, as I then always mark teachers on order and manner of conducting classes.

I am gaining the confidence of the school boards, as this year quite a number of them have come to me to ask advice in hiring teachers, as regards their qualifications. I find that the people of the county like to have the superintendent visit their schools, if they themselves do not ever visit them; and I have urged it upon school boards, that it was their duty to visit the schools, to see for themselves the work performed there, and not to depend upon the children for their information.

My report is as near correct as I could make it from the town clerks' reports, and from my own knowledge of the schools.

In closing, I would say that it gives me great pleasure to be able *to report* a very perceptible progress in the condition of the schools,

---

Reports of County Superintendents — Marathon — Marquette.

---

and in the qualifications of the teachers. In many districts, the work is not such as ought to be demanded; yet I can see considerable improvement, and an increasing demand for better teachers.

MARATHON COUNTY.

THOS. GREENE, SUPERINTENDENT.

Hon. W. C. WHITFORD, *State Superintendent:*

DEAR SIR — A few days since I forwarded to you my annual report.

In addition, I have the pleasure in saying that a very general interest is felt at present in our schools. There is a great demand for competent teachers, who are willing to work for their wages. I am glad to be able to report that the teachers of this county are trying to improve themselves; and that they realize the demands which the school laws have upon them, and are determined, as far as possible, to obey them. Proof of their sincerity was given me at the examinations. Nearly all have been successful in raising their standing.

Our institute held in Wausau, the first week in September, was not well attended. Out of 102 teachers licensed during the year, 9 males and 40 females only attended the institute.

In reference to holding institutes, the law ought to be amended so as to compel teachers to attend.

MARQUETTE COUNTY.

R. G. O'CONNOR, SUPERINTENDENT.

Each recurring school year develops some progress in the cause of education. When we compare the present with the former time, we have reason to rejoice that we live in a land of schools, as well as in a land of bibles. The school system of our State rests upon a firm basis. It takes hold of the mind and the heart of the people, and sways an influence beneficent in its results, that grows broader and deeper each passing year. The condition of schools in this

county, taken as a whole, is encouraging. In many localities there
is a marked improvement, while in others there is yet a want of
that interest necessary to improvement, and which should charac-
terize an intelligent people.

Notwithstanding all the advancement made in the great cause of
educating our children, physically, morally, and intellectually, for
which our hearts rejoice, there is yet indifference and ignorance
rearing their repulsive forms here and there, in our midsts, for
which we mourn; but not without hope, for the growing sentiment
of the people in favor of all right objects is gradually overcoming
every obstacle in its onward march. But thanks to a progressive
age, light steadily comes in; virtue and intelligence ultimately will
be the common inheritance of all people. The want of a liberal
patronage in behalf of some schools in this county, is seen in dilapidated school-houses, the use of roads for playgrounds, the hiring
of cheap teachers, the grumbling at every tax, finding fault with
teachers at imaginary wrongs, and irregular attendance or non-
attendance of pupils, which, in spite of our compulsory law, we
find several hundreds of the required school age in the county, who
have not attended school.

The number of school-districts under my supervision, the school-
houses of which are in this county, is fifty-nine. All these districts have maintained school five or more months, employing
seventy-four different teachers. The whole number of children of
school age in the county, is three thousand three hundred and
fifty-four, of which number one thousand eight hundred and seven
are males, and one thousand five hundred and forty-seven are
females. The whole number reported as attending school, during
the year, is 2,379. The average wages per month for male teachers was $27.50; for female, $17.37.

In the town of Newton, two new school-houses have been built this
year, and one new district organized. Several other districts are
preparing to build the coming summer, while in other districts
there would have been appropriations made for building this fall,
were it not for being voted down by men whose children had grown
up, and by others who care nothing for the education of the rising

generation; and these would not pay one dollar for school purposes, were they not obliged to by law.

Five candidates from this county have been recommended for admission to the Normal Schools. We trust that right material has been selected, and that they will return to us the fruits of their labor, such as will prove the efficiency of the schools they have attended.

It is pleasant to be able to say that the teachers, with few exceptions, have labored hard and faithfully, and have done their work well.

As a rule, the teachers of this county are putting forth every effort to excel, not only in literary acquirements, but also in the best methods of giving instruction. Many yet fail in securing good order, though in this respect there is much improvement. We have a few teachers who are too old to teach, but a very large share are much too young. It is strange that so many people have an idea that a young boy or girl, some sixteen or eighteen years old, can take charge of a school of large scholars and control them without the co-operation of the board. We find in many districts that even old, experienced teachers cannot even do this when the people of the districts are indifferent toward the teacher.

An institute was held at Montello, commencing September 6, and lasting ten days. Eighty-nine members were enrolled; the average daily attendance was 77. Hard work was a characteristic feature of the session. There was no hedging on the part of the conductors in charge, Profs. C. A. Burlew and J. H. Gould; and no teacher was allowed to shirk his duty. The discipline maintained was nearly perfect. The conductors required, and, by the character of their work, commanded, the closest attention. The teachers who deprecate communication in school, were thus afforded an opportunity to illustrate by example the advantage of their theory. The papers written at the examination which took place after the institute, by those who attended, were far better than the ones written by those who did not attend the institute. State Superintendent Whitford was present during the last week, and lectured to a large and appreciative audience. We earnestly hope to have the pleasure of having him with us again at our next institute.

I have issued, during the year, 101 certificates of all grades, viz.: Three of the first grade, seven of the second grade, and 91 of the third grade; of which 12 were to males, and 89 to females. A number of six months' certificates were issued at the spring examination, mostly to those who had never taught. The most common defects noticed in teaching are hearing a recitation instead of conducting the same; failing to commend when commendation is due; exhibiting unnecessary authority, thereby provoking children to wrath; asking questions in such a manner that no thought is required in the answer; and, perhaps, if the answer does not come up to the standard required by the teacher, a "blockhead" is the first word that comes from the teacher, or perhaps something worse; preparing a recitation to be recited when visitors are present; a neglect to impress upon the children the fact that, in a few years, they will cease to be children; that they will want to use the lessons which they are now reciting; that the responsibilities of life must be met, and that mental discipline is indispensable to complete success in any pursuit.

Thankful for the prosperity of the past year, and hoping we may, by our efforts, merit a still greater degree of the same in the year before us, is the wish of the teachers of Marquette county.

MILWAUKEE COUNTY — FIRST DISTRICT.

JAS. A. RUAN, SUPERINTENDENT.

I am sorry to be obliged, in this report, to say that the public in this portion of Milwaukee county do not take an active interest in educational matters; only a few of the school officers manifest any anxiety to secure active and competent teachers. They refuse to pay sufficient wages to secure teachers of the required ability, and thus our best teachers seek employment elsewhere. Yet there is some hope that the people may be aroused from their present lethargy, for the average attendance of the children is 68 per cent.

The number of applicants for certificates, during the past year, has been sixty-five. Of these, fifty-two received certificates, eleven of the second, and forty-one of the third grade. I have refused to grant any limited certificates, for I consider that, no matter how well a person may be able to communicate his knowledge, he cannot be a successful teacher unless he has the required learning.

One school-house has been built of frame, veneered with brick, in the town of Oak Creek, and it will comfortably accommodate fifty scholars.

An institute of one week's duration was held at Hale's Corners, beginning October 4th. It was very ably and interestingly conducted by Prof. Albert Salisbury. The attendance was large in comparison to that of former years, there being a daily attendance of twenty-two.

The number of school-houses in the district is 35. The number of teachers required to teach is 44.

During the past year, I made two visits to each school, and found to my joy that the teachers showed great zeal for the advancement of their pupils. But the best efforts were only in the districts which are supported by the parents of the children or by the district officers, who visit the schools.

MONROE COUNTY.

A. F. BRANDT, SUPERINTENDENT.

I. GENERAL STATISTICS.

The census of August 31, 1880, shows 8,243 children of school age, which is 71 more than was reported last year.

The total number who have attended school, during the year, is 5,756, which is 98 less than last year.

The number of days school has been taught is 20,463.

The number of schools in the county is 127; of this number, two are high schools and five are graded schools.

The number of teachers required to teach the schools is 144.

The number of different teachers employed is 223.

Highest wages paid to teacher of high school, per month, is $120.

Highest wages paid to teacher of common school, per month, is $50.

Lowest wages paid to teacher of common school, per month, is $15.

The average wages, per month, of male teachers is $34.96, 90 cents more than last year.

The average wages per month of female teachers is $20.73, $1.38 less than last year.

The number of districts which have adopted a list of text books is 68.

II. INSTITUTE.

An institute of two weeks' duration was held at Sparta, commencing March 29th. Prof. A. J. Hutton conducted the institute. The teachers, 120 in number, were highly pleased with the work done by Prof. Hutton. On the evening of the last day of the institute, Superintendent Whitford delivered us an able and interesting address.

III. EXAMINATIONS.

During the year, 343 applicants were examined, and 258 licensed. Of this number, three received first grade, 24 second grade, and 231 third grade certificates. Of those receiving third grade certificates, 63 received certificates at both the Fall and Spring examinations.

IV. VISITATIONS.

Since January 1st, I have made 170 visits. During these visits, I closely examined the work done by the teacher and the pupil, and I am pleased to report that I found the schools, with few exceptions, in good working order.

OUTAGAMIE COUNTY.

J. A. LEITH, SUPERINTENDENT.

I have not yet been one year in office, and consequently cannot give that information which I hope I may be able to give next year; and, as my time is limited, my special report this year must be brief.

Reports of County Superintendents — Outagamie.

I. VISITATIONS.

Last winter, I was unable to visit all the schools. At my first visit it required more time to ascertain the condition of the schools; and as the longest session of these was but four months, a few were closed before I could make the circuit. But I began in the summer where I left off in the winter, and have visited about all the schools twice. In my visits throughout the county, I have been hospitably received and find a great many warm supporters of education. The growing sentiment of the people seems to be, "Give us good teachers. Let us have better schools."

II. INSTITUTE.

A pleasant and profitable institute was held in the city of Appleton, the first week of September, 1880, conducted by Supt. B. R. Grogan, assisted by Prof. R. H. Schmidt, with an enrollment of seventy-one active members. Hard work was the characteristic feature of the session, both on the part of the conductors and the members. The instruction, although primary, was no less thorough and practical, such as can be applied to the every-day work in the school room. Supt. B. R. Grogan and Prof. R. H. Schmidt are able conductors, and have the well wishes of the teachers who have attended their institute.

III. VISITATION BY PATRONS.

Schools are not visited as they should be. They ought to be visited by the parents at least twice a term, to ascertain the improvement made by the pupils. This would encourage both scholar and teacher, and would otherwise have a beneficial effect on the school.

IV. EXAMINATIONS.

Since I have filled this position, 265 have been examined. Of these, 2 have received first, 2 second, 55 third grade certificates, and about 60 limited. Of those holding limited certificates, a portion, I am afraid, will make poor teachers on account of their lack of education. I have given but four permits, and these were granted on the petition of the entire district. Under no other circumstance are they given. It requires 113 teachers to fill all the schools. There were not enough certificates granted at the last regular examination to fill all the schools, even with those given last spring. Consequently, I was obliged to call a supplementary examination, and supply the demand. We have two good schools in the city of Appleton for preparing parties to teach, namely, Lawrence University and the High School. I am in hopes that those holding limited certificates will take advantage of circumstances and become better equipped for the business in which they desire to be engaged. The time is not far distant when a limited certificate in Outagamie county will play but a small part in the instruction of our schools, no matter who is superintendent; and the sooner this can be brought about, the better it will be for the schools.

V. SCHOOL TERMS.

I notice that the school terms in many districts of the county are so arranged as to have their vacation occur through the sultry weather of July and August. This is quite commendable, and I hope the time is not far distant when every district in the county will economise the expenditure of the public school fund, and so arrange the school terms that school will be taught only at such times as will best accommodate the inhabitants of the district; and so avoid the most unfavorable part of all the year, July and August.

VI. CONCLUSION.

In conclusion, I will say that a great amount of good can be accomplished for our schools by the co-operation of the school officers, teachers, and superintendent. Without this co-operation, progress will be slow and uphill work. Just as long as school officers will insist upon employing inferior teachers, because they can be obtained for a dollar or two a month less, or because they have friends or relatives in the district, and just as long as teachers will insist upon imposing themselves upon the people before they are qualified, and superintendents will license them for fear of losing their patronage, just so long will our schools suffer in consequence. Can

---

Reports of County Superintendents — Ozaukee.

---

we expect honesty and justice from our representatives of honor and trust, if we, for the sake of gain, will perpetrate fraud and injustice even upon our own children? This county, with its healthy climate, productive soil, its manufactures, and inexhaustible water powers, will soon be second to none in the State. But I fear it will require some time before we can say as much of our schools; and to advance our schools with equal pace, it will require a vast amount of labor, hard, earnest, honest labor on the part of teachers, officers, superintendents, and all others concerned.

OZAUKEE COUNTY.

WM. F. SCOTT, SUPERINTENDENT.

Hon. W. C. WHITFORD, *State Superintendent:*

DEAR SIR — In addition to the statistical report which I sent you a few days since, I now have the pleasure of transmitting to you the following special report of the present condition of the schools of this county, and of the work done since January 1st, when I entered upon the duties of this office.

I. STATISTICS.

Cash value of all school-houses	$38,825 00
Cash value of all school sites	4,608 00
Total amount paid out during the year	22,406 71
Average wages of male teachers per month	41 00
Average wages of female teachers per month	21 59
Highest wages paid per month	122 28

Number of children between the ages of 4 and 20 years	6,565
Number of children who have attended the public schools	3,298
Number of school-houses in the county	60
Number of teachers required to teach the schools	70
Number of districts which have adopted a list of text-books	36
Number of visits made by superintendent	114

In these statistics, I observe with much surprise and regret that more than forty-nine per cent., about one-half, of the children of school age in this county, were not in attendance upon the public schools, during the past year. The number of children who attended private schools is comparatively very small. At present, I have no accurate means of determining their number. I believe that this number is considerably less than ten per cent. of the total number of children between the ages of four and twenty years. It is then, from these facts, very evident that about two-fifths of our youths are approaching maturity in ignorance, in idleness, without that training which prepares them for the intelligent discharge of the many incumbent duties of later life. I know no valid reason for continuing this sad condition of our educational affairs. When we consider the great sum of money which is annually expended for purposes of education, in connection with the fact that only three-fifths of the children of the State are directly benefitted thereby, it would seem that prompt, decisive, and effectual remedies were imperatively called for. We have, it is true, a compulsory school law; but that law, in consequence of its numberless provisions, is almost necessarily nominal in this county. I believe it is the same in other counties. I have yet to learn of the first case of prosecution under the law. School officers seem unwilling to enfore it, principally because the law provides for the defendant so many avenues of escape. To me that law seems utterly inadequate, and will be productive of very little good, unless it be to pave the way for something better.

II. INSTITUTE.

Our institute this year was in every respect a decided success. It was conducted by Supt. Edward McLoughlin, of Fond du Lac county, who is thoroughly acquainted with the present requirements of our district schools. His clear, courteous, and persuasive manner of conducting the exercises, soon obtained for him the entire confidence and esteem of the teachers. A spirit of earnest work prevailed throughout, and the best of results were obtained. The teachers went away with broader and higher conceptions of their work, and deeper and clearer insight into the various methods of instruction and school management.

The number of teachers enrolled was fifty-five, of whom forty-nine had experince in teaching. Eighty per cent. of those who attended are now engaged in teaching in the schools of this county.

Reports of County Superintendents — Ozaukee.

III. EXAMINATIONS.

Since January 1st, I have examined 73 teachers. Of this number, three received certificates of the first grade, six of the second grade, and 42 of the third grade. To others, 18 in number, whose standing, as determined by the examination, was below that required for a third grade, I issued limited certificates or permits. In the greater part of the work of examining applicants, I have followed the written method. I used carefully prepared questions, in which I endeavored to embody principles rather than facts or puzzles; and written answers were required. The written method, I believe, more accurately and thoroughly determines the attainments of the applicant in the several branches.

Following the examination, I addressed a circular to the school officers, informing them of the names of the well-qualified teachers, and urging them to secure the services of such teachers for work in their schools, during the coming year. Our experience thus far in the work of the examinations, has not been altogether pleasant. Nearly all of those who received " permits " this fall, held, heretofore, third grade certificates; and a few of those who barely passed the standard required for a third grade, formerly held second grade. There is, therefore, since the last examination, considerable disaffection among a number of teachers and their immediate friends. In this we clearly see the utility and wisdom of the measure proposed by you a short time since, providing each county superintendent with two assistant examiners. The results of each examination, as then ascertained and published, would be immediately acquiesced in by the relatives and friends of those who are refused certificates, and would, moreover, be accepted with a much greater degree of confidence by the public in general. The measure is a wise one. If it is enacted into a law, as we hope it will be at the next session of the Legislature, it will result in much good to the cause of the public schools.

iV. VISITATIONS.

Since entering upon the duties of this office, I have visited all the schools in the county once, the majority of them twice, and a

5 — ST. SUP.

few of them three times. It was my intention to visit each school
twice at least, but through the early closure of some of them, I
failed to do so. Much the larger number of districts in this county
have no summer term. They have but one term a year, consisting
usually of seven or eight months, which commences early in the
fall and closes in the spring.

The greater part of the work of school visitation must, therefore,
be done in the winter or not at all; and when the winter is open,
as was last winter, with extremely muddy roads, this work becomes
very laborious.

I do not lightly estimate the work of school visitation. I consider it, rather, the greatest factor for promoting the progress of
our public schools; and these visits should be made, not for the
mere purpose of spending an hour or two in the school, but to
criticise all pertaining to the workings of the school, to examine
the pupils, and note their progress, to give credit and encouragement where it is due, not omitting censure when deserved. It
also affords an excellent opportunity for the superintendent to
make the acquaintance of the earnest, faithful, and efficient teachers, whom he may select for more difficult and more lucrative situations.

V. TEACHERS' ASSOCIATION.

Our teachers' association was organized in September, 1877, and
since that time, has held its regular sessions upon the last Saturday
of each month, with the exceptions of the months of July and August, when vacations have been taken. The sessions of the association have been, in general, pretty well attended by teachers and
patrons. During the first year, the exercises of each session consisted mainly of music, essays, declamations, select readings, and
debates. At the first session of the second year, a new feature,
class exercises, was introduced. These class exercises have since
been continued with excellent results. They have been very suggestive of methods of study and of the presentation of thought,
and have aided many of the teachers in their efforts to improve
their knowledge of several branches.

The association owns a library of 120 volumes, in which there

Reports of County Superintendents — Ozaukee.

are many excellent works for teachers — such as those written by Page, Northend, Holbrook, Phelps, Wickersham, and others, and many well-selected works on biography, poetry, and history. Our library has accomplished much good for the cause of education in this county. It has, we believe, materially increased the membership of the association and the attendance of each session.

VI. TEACHERS — SCHOOLS.

The large majority of the teachers in this county are deeply interested in the cause of education. They are earnest, faithful, and efficient workers, who realize the importance of their positions and their responsibility, and I am pleased to report that their labors are fully appreciated by the people of the districts in which they labor.

Quite a number of our teachers were prepared for the work in the academies and normal schools of Europe, and have in the fullest sense of the term, made teaching their " life work." Several of them have taught more than twenty-five years, and the greater part of that time in the public schools of this county. On visiting the schools taught by these teachers, it was a great pleasure to observe how quietly, thoughtfully, and effectually they pursued their labors, although their manner of presenting thought and developing ideas partook of a foreign cast.

In our teaching force here, as elsewhere, there are some who seem to be mere creatures of salary, without love or respect for the work, without an interest in the future well-being of their pupils. They are, as a class, possessed of little or no intellectual qualification for the work of teaching. We consider it our duty to eliminate them from the schools as soon as possible. By informing the school officers, who were well-qualified teachers and who were not, and urging them to employ only well-qualified teachers, I have freed the schools of several of this class. They have spent neither time nor money in preparing for the work, and can, consequently, offer their services (dear at any price) for much lower wages than good teachers can who have spent both time and money in preparing for the work. Through erroneous ideas of economy, they are too often employed. The schools suffer in consequence. When refused certificates, they usually plead poverty as the reason why they should be given something upon which to teach. In their view, the money raised for the support of the public schools is a charity fund for their special benefit, or a premium upon their indolence and incompetency.

· Your predecessor once spoke of the schools in this county as "rather backward." He spoke truly. My predecessor, in his last report to you, said our schools were not up to the "standard." Very true. But why is this the case? Not because good teaching is here unappreciated and poorly paid. The average salary of our male teachers is higher by $3.25 per month, than the average wages of male teachers in the rural districts of the State. The real and sole cause of the backward condition of our schools, is the custom, so long prevalent in this county, of granting certificates of high standing to the class of teachers above referred to; these certificates were palmed off upon the district boards, by whom they were received in good faith, as evidence of scholarship and ability to teach, when the holder in fact possessed neither.

Our schools, nevertheless, have been in a progressive state since the fall of 1877. The sessions of our teachers' association and the annual institutes have done much to improve the condition of our schools. The benefits of the same are limited, however, inasmuch as there are many teachers who attend neither. In the demands now so frequently made by school officers for better teachers, we see a hopeful future for our schools. The demand for better teachers far exceeds the local supply. As a result, we were obliged to send to one of the Normal Schools for teachers. Improvement in our educational affairs is thus seen, and it is the earnest hope of many that it will continue until our schools have reached, at least, the average standard of efficiency. In conclusion, I tender my thanks to the State Superintendent for his advice and assistance; to the school boards for their cheerful and prompt co-operation in all matters looking to the improvement and welfare of the schools; to the people in various parts of the county, for the kindness, courtesy, and hospitality shown me when visiting schools.

PEPIN COUNTY.

WM. E. BARKER, SUPERINTENDENT.

Having occupied my present position as superintendent of schools but little more than a month (commissioned Oct. 20th), my knowledge of the condition of the educational work of this county is, as you may suppose, somewhat limited. The late Superintendent, J. H. Rounds, died October 13th, after a brief illness.

He was serving in this capacity for the fifth year, having been elected three times. As an officer, he was earnest and faithful; as a citizen and a christian, he ever maintained a character without reproach. As a tribute of respect to his memory, I beg leave to insert the following resolutions, adopted by the Teachers' Association, at Durand, November 6th:

" WHEREAS, Death has taken from our ranks our esteemed friend and co-worker, Superintendent J. H. Rounds; therefore,

" *Resolved*, That while we bow in submission to the Divine will, we extend to the bereaved family our heartfelt sympathy.

" *Resolved*, That in the death of Mr. Rounds, this Association has lost a valued member, and the cause of Education an earnest worker.

" *Resolved*, That while we greatly deplore the death of our honored friend, we will ever cherish his memory, and emulate his many virtues."

I have already spent some time in visiting schools, but my acquaintance with the teachers has been formed mainly in institute and associational work, in which I have ever felt a deep interest.

As a class, I feel sure that our teachers are in earnest, and endeavoring to improve. They are mostly young, however, and of little experience in the work.

Of the whole number licensed during the year for which the statistical report is made, I notice that about three-eighths are yet in their "teens," while six-sevenths are less than twenty-five years of age. It is almost a curiosity to find a teacher who has been long in the work. I am aware that our county is not alone in this respect. It seems to be generally true with regard to the profession,— can it be called such? — throughout the country. What other recognized occupation can be named, which is universally carried on by persons so young in years and experience? And does the work of training our youth for the duties and responsibilities which await them, really demand so much less of tact and skill than any other? We want more teachers who will give their *lives* to the work.

It is to be feared, however, that the number of these will not be greatly increased, until a more liberal provision shall be made for their support. The average wages of female teachers has been a little less than $25 per month; of males, about $31. Most of our districts have but six or seven months of school during the year. The average yearly salary is, therefore, from $150 to $200.

In regard to attendance of children at school, I do not know that any effort has been made to enforce the compulsory law. About one-fourth of the number of persons of school age have not been enrolled in the schools, and a considerable portion of the remaining three-fourths, have been in attendance only a very small part of the year.

As stated by Superintendent Rounds, in his last annual report, "Our Free High Schools are an important factor in the educational work of the county." I have no means of knowing exactly, but I think it safe to say that fully one-third of the number now teaching in the county have been students in these schools, during some part of the past school year. The school at Durand has been rather unfortunate in not securing a permanent teacher. Since the close of the winter term of 1879, three changes have been made in the principalship, and the present incumbent does not expect to remain after the close of the fall term. The school at Pepin retains its principal another year.

A live institute, conducted by Professors B. M. Reynolds and J. H. Gould, was held at Pepin during the last two weeks of August. At its close, nearly every teacher seemed to feel more like work, and better fitted for it than before. The *Wisconsin Journal of Education* received prominent attention, and I believe the greater part of our teachers are now among its subscribers.

Reports of County Superintendents — Pierce.

On account of the peculiar shape of our county, it was thought best to form two branch teachers' associations. These have been organized, and are now in successful operation, holding regular monthly meetings. They are known as the Durand and Lake Pepin Associations. Arrangements are in progress for a general session of two days' length, to be held at Durand, early in January, at which time we hope to secure the attendance of nearly every teacher in the county.

PIERCE COUNTY.

JAS. T. MC CLEARY, SUPERINTENDENT.

On entering upon my duties last January, I appreciated the truth of the statement so often made by superintendents, that January is not the best time for the official term to commence. After much consideration, and bearing in mind that it would be impossible for me to visit all of the schools before the close of the winter terms, I concluded to do my best to reach and help all by means of a series of meetings described below.

I. TEACHERS' MEETINGS.

Dividing my county into four districts, I outlined work for a series of eight meetings — two in each district. The scheme of work, given below, was neatly printed, and furnished to teachers and to many other friends of education in the county.

RIVER FALLS, Wis., January 9, 1880.

Fellow Teachers: Opposite is the scheme of work for our winter meetings. The scheme has been prepared with the view of presenting work of practical value. It is hoped that each teacher will use the means at his disposal to prepare for each meeting in his district, and then come to the meetings to work. Bring note-books and pencils. Some of the best teachers of the county will conduct exercises.

The advanced pupils of the schools and all friends of education are cordially invited to attend.

First Meeting in Each District.

READING. Kinds — (a) Silent; (b) Oral; Objects of each; how to attain them.

SPELLING. What should be taught and how. Word analysis.

ARITHMETIC. Notations and reductions.

GRAMMAR. Sentences: Classification — (a) by use; (b) by structure. Capitals; terminal marks; analysis.

HISTORY. Great events of the XVth century. Discovery and settlement of America.

CONSTITUTION. Comparison of Articles of Confederation with the present Constitution. Origin of the Constitution.

GEOGRAPHY. Earth as a planet: Its position in the solar system; its form; its motions. Location of lines upon the globe.

PENMANSHIP. Methods of teaching.

THEORY OF TEACHING. School organization.

Second Meeting in Each District.

READING. Emphasis, inflections: definitions, kinds, uses. Illustrations.

SPELLING. Rules: final e silent; doubling final consonant.

ARITHMETIC. Fundamental principles and operations

GRAMMAR. Sentences: Analysis continued; uses of comma, semicolon, and colon.

HISTORY. Chief events of colonial history. Brief accounts of leading men.

CONSTITUTION. Legislative department — especially organization of Congress, mode of making laws, and the powers of Congress.

GEOGRAPHY. Causes of — (a) variety of seasons; (b) varying length of day and night.

PENMANSHIP. Analysis of short letters.

THEORY OF TEACHING. School discipline.

The meetings were productive of much good. The institute at the close of the series was very successful, thanks to the enterprise and spirit of the teachers attending, and the hospitality and interest shown by the citizens of Ellsworth. Forty working members were enrolled, and the room was filled with visitors nearly every day. During the institute, two very entertaining and instructive lectures were delivered: the first, by Dr. D. W. Woodworth, of Ellsworth,— subject, "The Blood;" the second, by Prof. F. H. King, of the River Falls Normal School,— subject, "How to Construct Simple and Inexpensive Apparatus to Illustrate Instruction in Science."

II. EDITORIALS.

Some time before my official term began, at the invitation of the enterprising proprietors of the River Falls *Press*, I began to edit, in their paper, a column devoted to Education. This work I have continued. While aiming to give special prominence to methods of teaching, and valuable but not easily obtained information, a portion of the column is devoted to educational news and personal mention of specially worthy workers. I have the promise of much valuable aid for the coming year, so that I hope to accomplish much good by this means. The paper is now read by a majority of the teachers, and its circulation amongst them and the patrons of the schools, is constantly increasing.

III. VISITATION.

During the winter and summer terms, I made over 100 visits to schools, staying from one hour to a half day, principally the latter. In addition to private criticism of the teacher's work, either written or personal at recess, I usually tried to leave something for the pupils to think about until my next visit. For instance, in the old experiment of nearly filling a cup with water, covering it with thick writing paper, and then inverting it, the fact that the water does not run out, though seemingly unsupported, is a great wonder to the pupils of most of the schools. Having performed some such experiment, which takes only a moment, I ask them to think about it until I come again. I ask them not to question any one about it until they have formed an opinion in regard to it, then to compare opinions, ask questions, and read. My object is to "wake up mind," as Page puts it.

In my conversation with teachers at their schools, in teachers' meetings and institutes, and through the columns of the papers, I endeavor to impress upon them the necessity of having a good private library of professional and reference books. But very few of such books were reported in the spring, now quite a number are reported. Last spring, not one in a certain teachers' meeting could name half a dozen great teachers. I hope to be able to say in my next report that my teachers can name a dozen great educators, and tell wherein their greatness consists, and what they have done for education.

IV. EXAMINATIONS.

Last spring, 151 candidates were examined, involving the careful reading of some 3,000 pages of manuscript. Seventy certificates were granted. It was no gratification to me to refuse so many; it was a very unpleasant duty. But, as I look at it, it is the special duty of the Superintendent to protect two classes: (1) The public, and especially the children, from the worse than useless work of unqualified teachers; and, (2) those persons who expend time, money, and energy in preparing themselves for the proper discharge of their duties, from the competition of those who make no such effort. I am a great believer in the efficacy of a fair examination with honest marking — an examination in which the questions are wisely framed and are a test of one's qualifications, and a marking that shall show what one earns, no more, no less. I am no believer in fancy markings. They are at first deluding to both teachers and school officers, and finally lose the respect of both. A superintendent in conducting an examination is acting in a judicial capacity, and should know no friends, no foes; no rich, no poor; but should let each candidate succeed or fail purely on his or her merits.

V. Progress.

1. During the year, six new school-houses were built, — nearly all good buildings. The most expensive, that at River Falls, costs $15,000. This village claims to have one of the handsomest and best planned buildings in the State. An effort is being made, all along the line, this fall, to put the buildings into good condition for the winter.

2. Few districts, comparatively, have voted to have less than seven months of school for the coming year; many are to have eight months, and a few nine months.

3. There is a great call made upon me for good teachers, at fair wages. In fact, as I wish my recommendation to be and remain at par, I am a little embarrassed by the number of calls. Good buildings and appliances, long terms, and good teachers should result in good schools. Another hopeful sign is an evident disposition to engage teachers by the year. Through the efforts of an agent of one of the leading publishing houses in Chicago, aided by my predecessor, uniformity of text-books exists in most of the districts. I shall try to secure the adoption of text-books in the remaining districts.

Reports of County Superintendents — Pierce.

VI. CIRCULARS TO SCHOOL-DISTRICTS.

Some time before the annual meetings, I sent to each district in the county the following circular, from which I select a few points: —

LENGTH OF TERM.— Among the most important of the duties of the annual meeting is the determination of the amount of school to be held. The amount is generally too small. Not fewer than seven months should be voted; in most cases eight would be better. In dividing the school year, the practice in the best schools is to have three terms. If you have seven months, you might have a fall term of two months, commencing about September 20th; a winter term of three months, commencing about December 1st; and a spring term commencing about April 1st. If you have eight months, it might be best to let the fall term run three months, and open for the winter term after New Years. In any case, try to avoid having school during July and August.

HIRING TEACHERS.— This is the most important of the duties of the Board, and I ask your careful consideration of these points:

1. Seek your teacher. Do not wait for some one to "apply" for the school. The best teachers do not have to wait. They are engaged early. You probably know teachers whose skill is unquestioned. Seek one, and offer him or her fair wages. (I can always send a good teacher, if notified in time.)

2. Get a good teacher. Do not say, "Oh! any one can teach our school." If you do, the chances are that the school will always remain so that " any one can teach it." " Do not ask me to issue " licenses," as they are called, to persons who are unqualified. It is an injustice to those who spend time and money in fitting themselves for the proper discharge of their duties, to have to endure the competition of those who do not try to prepare themselves. Of course, a person may have a good education and not be successful as a teacher. So, also, a man might own a good set of engraver's tools and not be able to make a picture. But as the best engraver in America could not make the picture without the tools, so I hold no one can be a very good teacher without a good education. Hence, I ask you in making a choice to examine the certificates carefully. Generally, the teacher having the highest standing will do the best work. Do not expect to find many tens. There are few who attain perfection in anything. Nine is a very good standing, and anything above seven is good. A fair knowledge is indicated by six. I try to put reliable markings upon the certificates. Notice the " attendance on institutes and teachers' meetings." As a general thing, the best teachers give most time to these meetings. Good teachers, also, are in the habit of taking educational papers, and of buying professional and reference books. Note all the items in the middle column of the certificate.

3. Engage for the year. This is the practice in all the best schools, and is one cause of their being " best." Many advantages are gained. Work can be planned to better advantage; pupils proceed at the beginning of a new term from the point where the work was dropped at the close of the preceding one; the time otherwise spent in " getting acquainted " is saved, etc.

COMPULSORY LAW. A law passed during the legislative session of 1879, makes it the duty of the director to see that all children between 7 and 15 years of age, be given the advantage of school for at least 12 weeks of each year. The purpose of the law is good I ask you to give it a fair trial. A few may grumble at first. But if you do your duty calmly, kindly, and firmly, you cannot fail to secure the respect of all right minded persons.

Reports of County Superintendents — Pierce.

VII. COURSE OF STUDY.

In the latter part of August, I issued a circular on a course of study for the country schools, from which the following programme of the studies is taken:

BRANCHES.	"D" GRADE, AGE 5 TO 7.	"C" GRADE, AGE 7 TO 9.	"B" GRADE, AGE 9 TO 12.	"A" GRADE, AGE 12 TO 15.
Reading including spelling.	Words and sentences from board, cards, and books.	Second reader. Special attention given to calling words readily.	3d and ½ of 4th. Special attention to use of dictionary and synonyms.	4th, 5th, and selections. Special attention given to analysis of thought.
Numbers.	Counting and grouping. Writing to 1,000. Denominate tables.	Elementary processes and simple problems. Introduce simple fractions.	Fractions, common and decimal, and compound numbers. Require analy's.	Finish. Special attention to mensuration and percentage.
Handicraft.	Printing. Splint-work. Copying forms.	Writing words. Drawing simple forms.	Writing sentences. Drawing — elements of perspective.	Correspondence. Business forms and single entry book-keeping.
Object lessons and Geography.	Forms. Colors. Common objects.	Animals. Plants. Minerals.	Geog. { Town. County. State. U.S. — Political.	World. U.S. — Commercial. Outline of Physical Geog.
Language.	In object lessons see that accurate observation is followed by correct expression. Teacher to set an example in the use of pure English.		Composition and simple analysis. Punctuation and capitalization.	Analysis and grammar with text-book. Special attention to syntax.
History.	General for first three grades. Interesting historical stories.			Formal with text-book. From facts develop the philosophy.
General.	Physiology and Vocal Music.			

Reports of County Superintendents — Polk.

Already one class is reported as working for graduation.

It is my purpose to issue an explanatory and suggestive circular on organizing and teaching in accordance with the above course. This is to be backed by a series of sixteen teachers' meetings — four in each district — and, probably an institute. With the hearty co-operation of teachers and friends of education, I look for an unusually prosperous year.

POLK COUNTY.

HENRY B. DIKE, SUPERINTENDENT.

During the past year, there has been an appreciable improvement in the efficiency of our schools. School officers and patrons are waking up to the fact that the great demand of the schools is for live, earnest, conscientious and well-qualified teachers; teachers who realize the grave responsibility connected with their labor in the school room. As a consequence, the major portion of the districts, at their annual meetings, took action in the matter of more school, better teachers, and better pay for their services.

Three new school-houses have been built during the year; while the buildings are neat, and the exterior appearance is good, no attention whatever has been paid to the important item of ventilation.

The Superintendent's office has been provided with a full set of record books, in which are kept the various statistical items furnished by the teachers in their monthly reports, the financial condition of each district, and the general notes by the superintendent, based upon his visitations to the schools of the county. These records, if properly "kept up," will furnish, for the present and in the years to come, full historical information of the progress of each school in this jurisdiction. In the early part of the school year, the town of Clear Lake reorganized under the township system of school government, and the result has been, a marked improvement in the character of the schools, longer terms, better teachers, better supervision, less expense, and a general increasing interest on the part of patrons. While the town of Clear Lake is among the newer towns, its schools are the peers of any in this county, and they are on the road to higher and still better results. In this connection, it may not be out of place to state that to Dr. P. Gates, the present efficient secretary of the school board, credit is largely due for the excellent condition of the schools of this town.

During the month of August, Pres. W. D. Parker and Miss Mary A. Kelley, of the River Falls Normal School, conducted a teachers' institute at Osceola Mills; and despite the fact that, at that time, our farmers were busy taking care of their crops, the institute was the largest one which we have ever held in this county; and I attribute much of the increased interest of our teachers to the instruction given and the enthusiasm awakened during its session.

An effort is being made to introduce into our schools the " Course of Study for the Ungraded Schools; " and I hope, in my next report, to be able to note its general introduction. I have presented and urged this matter upon the attention of teachers at all my examinations, and whenever an opportunity presented itself; I see in it a potent power for elevating, systematizing, and rendering more efficient our country schools.

In conclusion, the outlook is all encouraging, and we are earnestly working for better schools, better teachers, and an increased interest on the part of our citizens in this important work of training and developing the moral, intellectual, and physical natures of our boys and girls.

PORTAGE COUNTY.

ANDREW P. EEN, SUPERINTENDENT.

There are 85 school-houses in the county. A few of these are in poor condition; yet on the contrary there are many fine, comfortable school-houses. The new ones have been built during the year.

At the institute held at Plover, last spring, 100 members were enrolled. Prof. Albert Salisbury, the conductor, had not fully recovered from a severe attack of illness which he had undergone shortly before our institute commenced; yet he did good work. The institute instruction this year being mainly of a primary nature, was perhaps not so interesting to teachers generally as the work of former years; yet it was undoubtedly of more practical benefit to them. The number of teachers required to supply the schools of the county, is 88. In our examinations we have endeavored to give the schools the benefit of the best teaching force possible, by fixing a high standard to be reached in order to gain a certificate. A superintendent can, perhaps, do more good for the schools of his county, by being careful in granting certificates than he can in any other work that he has to do in connection with them.

In visiting schools we have tried to become acquainted with their condition and needs, and by short addresses to the pupils have endeavored to encourage and stimulate them in their work.

Our schools and educational interests, I think, have been advanced during the past year. Last winter teachers' associations were held in different parts of the county. These meetings are a source of great benefit to teachers, especially to the younger members of the profession.

RACINE COUNTY.

C. A. MORSE, SUPERINTENDENT.

My report to you of October 10th, shows that, out of the 5,514 children of school age in Racine county, only 2,273 have attended school during the past year; showing a total of 2,792 who have not availed themselves of the privileges offered by our public school system. Of this number, 530 are between the ages of 4 and 7, 642 between 7 and 15, and 619 between 15 and 20. This much-to-be-regretted fact is one that deserves the earnest consideration of all thoughtful citizens. Whether each one of these 642 children furnished some " good excuse," thereby satisfying the requirements of the law, or not, I cannot say. We need not fear for the future of the State when most of the children are being educated; but when such is not the case, there is danger.

VISITATION.

I have been in the office during the last eight months of the school year just closed. In that time, 94 visits have been made, and 73 out of the 76 schools under my charge have been visited. My object in this work has been to encourage both teachers and pupils to more earnest, systematic, independent thought. I have criticised where I thought criticism would lead to improvement, and commended where commendation was merited.

The teachers of Racine county are a class of earnest workers. There are a few exceptions, but there are few other vocations in life that can show a more lively interest on the part of the worker.

Two examinations have been held, spring and fall, in each of the three inspection districts. There were 176 applicants, and 97 certificates granted, of which 15 were second grade, and 82 third. There was no application for a first grade. The examinations have not been so easy as to admit the poorest in scholarship, nor has the possession of a certificate in time past insured success in all cases. In my opinion, present qualifications should be made the test, and teachers who will not advance, must be left behind. Scholarship is not the only essential requisite, but it is one of the things every teacher must have.

ASSOCIATIONS.

Associations were held during the winter, and were regularly attended by a few of the best teachers, who, by their earnest efforts, made them a success, and were mutually benefited thereby. The teachers of Raymond, owing to bad roads, organized an association of their own, showing by their zeal that their heart was in the work. If therein every town had followed their example, better school work would undoubtedly be the result.

INSTITUTE.

An institute of two weeks was held at Rochester, commencing August 9th, under Profs. A. Salisbury and E. R. Smith. The work done was practical, and just what was needed. More attention was paid to theory and practice than to the accumulation of facts preparatory to examination. The true province of the institute was kept in view, and the universal testimony of the teachers seems to be that they were well paid for attending. At this time, 76 were enrolled; average daily attendance was 66. Thanks are due to the conductors for their effective work.

There seems to be a growing tendency on the part of school boards to exercise more care in employing teachers. The idea that anybody can teach school is giving place to the inquiry, "Who is the best teacher." This is a healthy indication, and it is hoped that poor teachers will soon be out of demand.

There is but one high school in the district, that at Burlington. Its principal, Edwin R. Smith, and his able corps of teachers are doing an excellent work. The influence which the school exerts for good cannot be estimated.

ROCK COUNTY — FIRST DISTRICT.

JOHN W. WEST, SUPERINTENDENT.

I. PROGRESS.

I am pleased to state that there is an increasing demand for a better class of teachers; and the cheap, unqualified, and would-be-aspirant is held, as he should be, at a low estimate, while the honest and faithful finds ready employment with a fair compensation.

II. ATTENDANCE.

Irregular attendance is more prevalent than non-attendance, yet only 78 per cent. of the children of school age have been in attendance the past year. Tobacco culture has become one of the leading interests to the farmers of Rock county; and children of all ages, especially those of school age, both girls and boys, are kept out of school to aid in its culture. This has its discouraging effects on teachers and schools. The compulsory law, though highly commended, has not, to my knowledge, yet been enforced. The three term system is quite common, and wherever adopted is generally approved; and by this arrangement, teachers are employed by the year, and the older pupils have the benefit of more school than by the old system. A less frequent change of teachers than we have had in the past, is desirable.

III. CERTIFICATES.

The whole number of applicants for examination since January first, has been 235. Of this number, 47 failed, 7 hold first grade certificates, 25 second grade, and 156 third grades. No "permits" were granted. By request of the superintendent of the Janesville city schools, we have examined, each spring, the graduating class, and granted third grade certificates to such members as passed the examination,— thus increasing our numbers from 12 to 15 that are not included in our teaching force.

IV. VISITATIONS.

I have visited all the schools once, and nearly all twice, during the year,— the number of different visits amounting to 190. That these visits have been productive of much good to teachers, and in many cases to school boards and patrons, I am satisfied. Space will not permit me to enlarge upon the amount of good that may be done by this means.

V. SCHOOL-HOUSES.

Generally, the school buildings are properly and pleasantly located, necessary repairs have been made, quite a number have been re-seated with modern, patent seats, and one new building has been erected. School grounds are not properly adorned by shade trees, except in the villages, and a few of the wealthiest country districts.

VI. TEXT-BOOKS.

There has been a lull in the agitation of the text-book question. District officers are generally posted on their duties respecting the formal adoption of school books, and have, in most districts, complied with the law. The plan of free distribution to pupils is not extensively favored.

VII. LIBRARIES.

Two years ago, an attempt was made to awaken an interest on the subject of school libraries, but without any satisfactory results. There are two town libraries, several Sunday-school libraries, and libraries belonging to special organizations in different parts of this superintendent district, to which children have access; so that people seem to think that this is an uncalled for enterprise, and manifest but little interest in it.

VIII. EXHIBITION OF SCHOOL WORK.

With us, this matter is yet in its infancy, but we expect to see a healthy growth the coming year. Our best teachers are satisfied that the benefits and pleasure derived from an exhibition of their school work, will amply repay them for their extra time and labor in preparation. I shall have their co-operation, and think we shall be able to furnish specimens from this winter's work.

IX. COURSE OF STUDY.

I am glad to state that the "Course of Study for Ungraded Schools" is hailed with joy by our leading, thoughtful teachers, and many school officers and patrons. It seems to be the one thing needful to facilitate the teacher's work, to economize time in the school room, and to properly and systematically educate the children of our State. The purposes and objects of the Course have been clearly explained at our teachers' institutes, and now we shall endeavor to put into practice these well-grounded theories and suggestions; as to how well we succeed, you shall hear in future. Those of our teachers who have used the Course, speak in the highest terms of its superior merits. Twelve school-districts have already adopted the course.

X. TEACHERS' INSTITUTE.

Our annual teachers' institute, held at Evansville, last spring, under the direction of Prof. Albert Salisbury, was one of unusual interest. We had an enrollment of eighty-four members. The lecture by our State Superintendent was filled with excellent thought, and listened to by an attentive and appreciative audience. Teachers who attend the institutes are more zealous, have broader views, and are generally more successful than those who do not.

SAUK COUNTY.

JAS. T. LUNN, SUPERINTENDENT.

I. STATISTICAL.

Children of school age...	10,330
Children from 4 to 7 years of age....	2,436
Of whom there did not attend public school....	1,228
Children from 7 to 15 years of age....	5,085
Of whom there did not attend school....	675
Number of situations for teachers	190
Visits made by county superintendent....	248
Total school expenditures	$49,464

II. THE COMPULSORY LAW.

This law has made scarcely a ripple of excitement in the county, and the attendance is rather against its efficiency, as there is an actual decrease of 59 from last year's enrollment. Failure to comply with the law must have occurred, as for instance in one district which failed to maintain any school; but officers and others do not care to embroil themselves in vexatious lawsuits, about schooling the children of negligent and sometimes vicious parents; hence, the law seems a dead letter, so far as this county is concerned, this year. Again, the onus and odium of starting a lawsuit against delinquents, have to be borne by officers who receive no compensation for their official services, which are sufficiently complex and burdensome in times of legal peace to deter them from increasing their burden by a legal war, in which not a director could engage without pecuniary loss to himself.

Another item is that the lawsuit is too cumbersome, and the burden of proof is in the wrong direction. A plan, which seems to me preferable, is that each teacher should keep a sworn register, from which each town clerk charge on his tax roll against each de-

linquent patron or guardian, ten cents per day for each day's failure
to comply with the law by any of his children or wards; and that
the treasurer collect such levy, unless such patron prove an error
before some officer duly authorized to determine such cases, and to
confirm or to discharge the levy. This would put the running,
worry, and proof on the transgressors; and so far as the register is
concerned, none will now be taken in evidence without attestation,
which a teacher, after months of absence, would be loth to make
strong enough to withstand an attorney. As the law now stands,
it seems capitally drawn to scare the timid, and to wink at the bold.

III. Course of Study for Country Schools.

This course has been so pertinaciously pushed as to lead most
teachers to think it worth their while to make its intimate acquaintance. Before examination, each applicant has to promise that, in
case he teach a country school, he will guide his work by this
course, a copy of which, with explanations, is posted in every such
school. It has been advocated and explained at institutes and associations; examination questions in theory and practice have been
taken from it; and teachers have been plainly told that, if there is
any good in the course, we wanted to get it out for the advancement of Sauk county schools; and that those who were unwilling
to lend a hand in such consummation, were not wanted as teachers.
A project is maturing for a uniform examination throughout the
county, of the several grades of pupils, by means of questions sent
in sealed envelopes, to be opened on specified days only, and the
answers thereto canvassed by more than one teacher before being
credited to the authors.

So far, few teachers have been very zealous in its cause, and
many regard it as an unwelcome innovation on the time-honored
"go-as-you-please" style of teaching, which is much in vogue with
the conceited, the erratic, the transient, and the "don't-care"
teachers, who form no small part of the fraternity. Regarding the
course as tentative merely, I cannot but ask that the view of many
of its friends in favor of its definitive expansion, be not disregarded; for by such feature alone can the course reach the class

most needing aid, and without it the course will soon be laid on the shelf, as one of the hobbies which intermittently fever the educational crowd.

IV. FREE HIGH SCHOOLS.

Baraboo, Reedsburg, Sauk City, and Spring Green each maintain a school of this grade, at which the united enrollment for 1880 is 285 pupils, of whom 121 studied algebra and geomotry; 67 physiology and physical geography; 81 modern languages; and 16 ancient languages. At these four schools a large share of our teachers perfect their education for examination, and many others prepare for the University or for college; in some of these schools the tendency is too much toward such preparatory collegiate course, regardless of pupils' intentions or opportunities to pursue it, and hastening over and leaving pupils poorly grounded in the more commonly used branches.

V. TEACHERS.

To fill the 190 situations in this county, 349 applicants were examined, of whom 273 or nearly 80 per cent. were passed to teach; and of 144 applicants this fall, all but 13 were passed, not because much more than one-half are thought to be qualified to teach, but because nothing better seems procurable. Even with this leniency, a scarcity of teachers yet exists, though, of course, all schools will eventually be supplied with some material or other.

It is deplorable that in this old settled county of Sauk, with 30,000 population and 11 graded and four high schools, that there are not fairly educated persons who will conduct its schools and deliver pupils from the incoherent work of our boy and girl teachers; and that a county superintendent in keeping up the standard and trying to secure thorough teachers, is subject to the virulence and malice of many tax-payers, whom he is trying to shield from such educational shams or weaklings as ask good wages without being able to render an equivalent.

In a few districts such an anti-improvement spirit exists that teachers therein report that they are commanded by the boards not to use any "new fangled notions," but to keep an old style school, which means to let pupils do about as they please.

Reports of County Superintendents — Sauk.

It is a gratification that many of our teachers are attending Normal Schools for their professional improvement, and that several graduates and past attendants are teaching in the county. I have not observed an instance in which attendance at our State Normal Schools is not followed by improved teaching, and it is hoped that more of our teachers will accept their benefits.

For country teachers, the average wages per month for males is $31, and for females, $23; which, with the average of six months' schooling per country district annually, gives a yearly income of $186, and $138, respectively, an amount not calculated to inflate aspiring youth with the prospect of sudden or great riches; but rather to become economically inclined, while considering the number of things which this sum cannot buy.

VI. INSTITUTE AND ASSOCIATION.

Our institute at Prairie du Sac was the most gratifying of any with which I have been connected as conductor. The attendants were more mature and advanced than is wont, and they devoted themselves with the best of good will to the mysteries of primary methods, which were most aptly developed by Prof. C. H. Nye, of whom it is noted by the attendants that " he never smiled again " during the institute, even while often getting off something which provoked an audible smile from all present; and he left behind him the impression of a most genial, cultured gentleman, who came to treat teachers as friends, without any of the browbeating and hectoring by which some conductors seek to add to their stature. Kindergartening was united with, or rather led drawing. Several dollars' worth of genuine kindergarten material was procured from Springfield, Mass., and from Chicago; and was placed in attendants' hands for manipulation. Such material was selected as can be most noiselessly used in the usual school, and the varied designs, bright colors, and unforseen developments interested the brains and busied the fingers of scores of attendants, from whose minds the foreign mists which enshroud this name, were swept away, and they were led to see that it is *an art of pleasing children.*

Divested of the abstractions and exaggerations of its foreign worshipers, and remodeled to suit American conditions, and mainly as an art of pleasantly busying children while resting from close study, I think that kindergartening is yet to play an important part in improving our schooling.

VII. TEACHERS' ASSOCIATION.

Our county association has held its semi-annual sessions, with interesting programmes and full houses. We propose to take an onward step in the line of society library, exhibit, etc. Inquiry has developed a willingness to contribute to a library fund, and to draw books when within reach. Several local associations and teachers' meetings have been held. Some think they do but little good; and one person asked me but a day or two ago whether I thought they were of any benefit, to which I replied that those were benefited who go wishing, yea, yearning, to be aided; and those who go for curiosity, or company, or to keep right with the powers that be, went away as poor as they came.

SHAWANO COUNTY.

WM. SOMMERS, SUPERINTENDENT.

With pleasure I report from Shawano county the condition of schools, their progress and aim. Three years ago, when I held my first teachers' examination, more boys and girls presented themselves to be examined than real teachers; and as I was determined to hold an examination for teachers only, I discharged them by telling them then and there, that this examination was only intended for teachers, and that I would give the boys and girls an examination at some future time, if I should find it necessary, and would give notice of the same, through the paper; but I never found it necessary to do so. There are always enough qualified teachers to be had, who, if not discouraged by the intruders or would-be teachers, cutting down the wages, are willing to abide by the profession, as long as they can get living rates; and I find, that those district boards, who are impartial as to uncles, cousins, or aunts for teachers, are making the best progress; while, on the other hand, those districts, favoring a medium pet, who cannot work out an examination nor get a certificate, and requesting the superintendent to grant them a license or permit, to those "Dear favorites" for the term, are but little better off than if they had had no school at all. Strong as the assertion may seem, it is nevertheless true, and to object to it would be objecting to the truth, though I am happy to say that such districts are but few, and, in general, the schools are progressing. Some school boards now are not satisfied by seeing the badge that entitles the holder to teach, but prefer those teachers with the highest standing attained at the examination in the various branches. This fact has induced those "who try to improve themselves," to study up, so that now, seven hold second grade, and three first grade certificates. I must say that, in general, the teachers of Shawano county are working hard; and it is only once in a while that one is found, who has missed his calling, and ought to be employed at something else besides teaching. Out of the 101 applicants who were examined last year, 18 failed, 11 received limited, and 62 full third grade certificates.

Our usual fall institute, conducted by Prof. A. F. North, proved a most happy success, and all the teachers expressed their hearty thanks to the Professor; and others that have abandoned teaching, and were not enrolled as working members, acknowledged the benefit which they received, and the ability of the Professor to conduct institutes. It will afford great pleasure to the teachers of this county to resume institute work under the leadership of one whose competency and kindly interest in teachers are so manifest.

School-houses are improving. In the last year, six new ones were built; three belong to newly created districts, and three large, commodious frame structures take the place of the old, low, log buildings, which had been, heretofore, used for the purpose. One of them, the best in the county, with a belfry, " but no bell as yet," is taking the place of what has been the poorest in the county. One more would have been built, in the most flourishing village of the county, if disagreements had not arisen in regard to the road that should lead to it, which caused the delay in erecting the same; but I shall be able to add it to the list of new ones next year.

During the year, I made 154 visits. The acquaintance which naturally is formed between the superintendent and the scholars, makes each recurring visit a pleasure; as the scholars seem to feel the need of the encouragement' which they always expect to find in the visit. Knowing 'that I have done all that was in my power in that direction, I am happy to say that I enjoy the confidence of the teachers and scholars in this county.

ST. CROIX COUNTY.

MISS BETSEY M. CLAPP, SUPERINTENDENT.

The work in St. Croix county is advancing but slowly. The old story of poor houses, no ventilation, discomforts, and even abuse to the children, is still true in a large class of districts, and that too where the wealth and ability of the people are equal to better things. Three new houses have been built the past year; two on a division of district, and one to replace a very good house destroyed by fire.

Slowly the districts are throwing aside old books and adopting new ones, but too many are still compelling their pupils to waste time and lose heart in companionship with old uninteresting excuses for books.

The plan of organization and course of study presented last year, has not been rapidly or generally introduced. Teachers were not prepared to take hold of it; and, consequently, very little that can be seen has been done. What has been done, has been with the teachers in the way of appreciating the advantages and the possibilities of the course. Still we are hopeful of a long step in advance the coming year.

We have now 100 districts in the county, and 105 rooms; and 141 persons are now holding unexpired certificates. Eight of these are teaching in other sections, and several are yet students who do not wish to teach the coming term.

Reports of County Superintendents — Waukesha.

There is a growing demand for the best class of teachers, and a growing inclination in school boards to seek teachers, instead of expecting teachers to seek schools; all of which is looking in the right direction.

We held an institute in the spring, two weeks in length, conducted by Prof. J. B. Thayer, and thirty teachers were in attendance. The institute work was calculated to meet our greatest need, primary work; and the best attention and interest were manifested during the whole session. Altogether, the school work in St. Croix county has some hopes for the future.

WAUKESHA COUNTY.

JOHN HOWITT, SUPERINTENDENT.

In addition to my fifth annual report to your department, I herewith submit this special report, which may throw some light on the educational interest and work of Waukesha county. The spirit of real improvement in this county does not look backward, but forward to a brighter and more glorious future. Many obstacles to the cause of education have been removed, and much has been accomplished in different directions in past years; still there are opportunities for improvement. Great credit is due to the citizens of this county, for the great interest they have taken in the cause of education, and the supporting and upbuilding of their common schools. Much of the success of our schools is due to the educated, energetic, and thorough superintendents who preceded me, and it is justly due them that a place should be given to their names in this report, — Profs. E. Enos, A. D. Hendrickson, I. N. Stewart, W. Green, and A. F. North.

In relation to the school-districts of this county, I would report: Number of regular school-districts or those whose territory is situated in their respective town, 76; number of such districts reported, 76; number of joint districts, 42; number reported, 42; total number of school-districts, 118; number of parts of school-districts, 106; number reported, 106. From the above, you will notice all the reports required have been received from the regular districts, joint districts, and parts of districts in the county; and from these reports, as well as from information gathered during the past year, a statement will be made, as brief as possible, of the condition of the schools in this county.

The total number of male children over four and under twenty years of age, 4,165; female, 4,907; total number over four and under twenty, 10,072; number attending public school, 6,757; total number attending public school in the county, 6,810. Total number last year, 6,710. Then the total number of male and female over four and under twenty, was 10,610; this year, there is a decrease of 538, yet the number in attendance is greater than the previous year, which is partly attributed to the compulsory law of 1879. To this law the attention of district boards, parents, guardians, and other persons, has been respectfully called in our reports. The percentage of attendance has increased in certain districts, since the passage of said law, and it is expected of all persons having charge of children to comply cheerfully with the provisions of the compulsory law, without coersion during the coming year. In my opinion, it is a law which has long been needed, and the people of this county seem well satisfied with it, as only a few have to be coersed to comply with its provisions.

In relation to the statistics of private schools, we found it impossible for the town clerks to get a correct report from all; as in some no records are kept. I feel quite confident if a blank was supplied to the private schools at the commencement of the year, containing such items as would be required, a correct report could be given; but as it is they do not know what is expected of them to report. The following is the report of six private schools: Number of male teachers, 4; female, 6; number of days school has been taught, 576; number of pupils registered that have not attended public school, 194; average number in daily attendance, 298. Six private schools are not reported, still the daily attendance is 91 greater than last year.

There are 118 school buildings in the county, which will accommodate 8,258 pupils. This includes the graded schools buildings,

Reports of County Superintendents — Waukesha.

viz.: Waukesha Union, consisting of nine departments; Oconomowoc City, six; Pewaukee, No. 1, three; Pewaukee, No. 3, two; Menomonie Falls, two; Merton, two; Delafield, two; Hartland, two; Genesee, two; Sussex, two; Mukwonago, two; Eagle, two. Total number of graded schools, 12; number of departments, 36, which added to the district (or ungraded) schools, would make 132 rooms, which is equal to the number of teachers employed when the schools are in session. As there are 10,072 children of school age, if all attended, it would give to each teacher 71 pupils, but of those attending it gives an average of about 50 pupils to each teacher. From this, conclusions are drawn that some of the schools are very much crowded, and so they are; and it has been recommended, for the common good of teachers, pupils, parents, and all concerned, that additional departments be established in the overcrowded schools. From forty to fifty is a sufficient number for a teacher to do good thorough work; but in some schools I find from sixty to seventy-five and even more enrolled. Total number of children in the county between 4 and 7 years of age, 2,158; number attending public school, 1,388; number between 7 and 15 years of age, 4,778; number attending public school, 4,002, which would leave 776 between the ages of 7 and 15 who do not attend public school; but as we have 12 private schools in this county, and taking in consideration those attending private school and receiving home instruction, the percentage of those who come under the compulsory law, not receiving an elementary education, would be quite small. It is expected a better report will be made in relation to this matter the coming year.

The total valuation of the school-houses is $104,433; cash value of sites, $11,983; cash value of apparatus, $3,894.95. Total valuation of school-houses, apparatus, sites, etc., $130,315.95. Number of school-houses of stone or brick, 48; number in good condition, 98; number properly ventilated, 98. Twenty school-houses are reported as not being in good condition, and twenty as not being properly ventilated. I have no doubt if an expert were to examine the school buildings, this number would be increased. The attention of school directors, parents, teachers, and all others con-

cerned, has been called to the dangers which may easily arise from
ill-ventilated, poor school-houses and impure water, also from im-
proper lighting.   I would report that a large majority of the school
houses are in excellent condition, and well furnished.   The old log
school-houses have disappeared, and fine-structures replace them.
A great interest has been taken, throughout the county, during the
past years, in rebuilding, repairing, etc.   A person who visited the
schools a few years ago, and visits them again to-day, would be
surprised at the change in buildings, seating, furniture, etc.   Yet
a great change is still needed in a number of districts.

I find that $5,640.60 were paid, the past year, for building and
repairing, and $1,218.18 for school furniture.

Three new school buildings have been erected, during the past
summer, at Delafield, with two departments, in the town of Merton, and in New Berlin.   All are fine structures, well furnished,
and an ornament to their respective districts.   Hartland has made
arrangements to erect a fine building of two departments, the coming year.   All the schools are reported as having blackboards.
Number each having a map of Wisconsin, 63; map of the United
States, 70; Webster's Unabridged Dictionary, 108.   Number of
districts adopting a list of text-books, 80; number which use only
text-books adopted, 74; number which purchase text-books, 62;
number which loan to pupils, 4; number which sell to pupils, 59.
I would here state, in my opinion, in our existing text-book laws is
to be found all that is needed for uniformity of text-books, changes,
etc.; but I am sorry to report that I do not think the best books
have been adopted in certain districts.

The teachers of the county, as a class, are ambitious, awake, and
earnest, and seem to put forth every effort toward improvement in
the school work, as well as to secure a higher grade of certificates.
The following gives, by sexes, the synopsis of certificates issued
during the past years.   Number granted to male teachers, first
grade, 3; second grade, 5; third grade, 32, — total, 40.   Number
of certificates granted to female teachers, first grade, 2; second
grade, 5; third grade, 162, — total, 169.   Total number granted
during the year, first grade, 5; second grade, 10; third grade, 194, —

Reports of County Superintendents — Waukesha.

total, 209. Number of male applicants refused certificates, first grade, 3; second grade, 8; third grade, 22, — total, 33. Number of female applicants refused certificates, first grade, 3; second grade, 6; third grade, 83, — total, 92. Number of different persons employed during the past year is 212. The deficiency of teachers was supplied by those holding State certificates and first grade certificates. I endeavor to make the examinations thorough, practical, and impartial. I still think it would be well to have the questions for examination prepared by a State committee, as some of the older States do; thereby, the county superintendent would have more time for other important duties.

Our institute, as usual, was a success. It was interesting and profitable to the teachers of the county. It was held at the Union school building in Waukesha, commencing August 30th, and continuing one week. Conductors were Profs. Beck and Rait, who showed great skill and tact in conducting the institute. Lectures were delivered by Hon. W. C. Whitford, State Superintendent, and Prof. James MacAlister, Superintendent of the Milwaukee schools.

One essential element to our educational system has closed; that is Carroll College, which has furnished us with excellent teachers from year to year. We hope that it may soon be re-established in its former glory. Pewaukee high school continues in a prosperous condition; number enrolled, 64.

During the year, I have visited each school in the county twice. I have endeavored to make my visits informal and unexpected, and to acquaint myself with regard to the attainments of the scholars, the progress they are making in their studies, deportment, classification, etc., as well as to the ability of the teacher in relation to government, tact, and ability to teach. I have found the schools doing well and making commendable progress. Teachers have shown an intelligent zeal in their duties, and have made marked improvement in both the science and art of teaching; and I would still report that the efficiency and usefulness of our schools are steadily increasing.

WAUSHARA COUNTY.

J. H. TOBIN, SUPERINTENDENT.

I herewith respectfully submit my report for the year 1880, giving a general statement of the condition of the schools under my charge.

During the year, $21,839.28 were received, and $17,402.06 were paid out for educational purposes, — an increase of $748.81 in the amount received, and a decrease of $733.77 in the amount paid out for 1879.

Of the amount expended, $12,859.31 were for teachers' wages, which is $334 less than last year. Average wages of male teachers, $26; of female teachers, $17.64 per month.

Every district has maintained school for at least five months. Number of children enrolled is 3,502. Number over four and under twenty years of age is 5,008. Number of regular school-districts, 46; of joint districts with school-houses in the county, 48. Total number of school-houses, 94. Number of teachers required, 99. Number of different teachers employed, 165. Several of these teachers are counted twice. Of the 152 certificates issued, 16 were of the second, and 105 of the third grade for one year, and 31 were granted for six months. Of the last, 11 were from private examinations where the standing would entitle the holder to a certificate for a year, if it were not limited by law. Whole number of applicants throughout the year was 268. At the present time, there are 125 holding certificates in this county, 3 of the first, 16 of the second, and 106 of the third grade. Number holding certificates in the county, granted for at least one year, 104.

Two county institutes, of five weeks each, were held, one at Pine River, and the other at Hancock, with S. Barker as assistant. Prof. R. Graham had charge of the first for two weeks, conducting it in his usual masterly manner. Number enrolled at this institute was 84. All who attended were deeply interested in the work, while the people of Pine River vied with each other in their efforts to make the term pleasant and profitable to all concerned. The

Reports of County Superintendents — Waushara.

second, at Hancock, had an enrollment of 60.   This small attendance was due to the fact that two terms of institute work are held
in this county during the year, and nearly all of the teachers attend at least one of these.   Many could not afford to attend, owing
to the low wages received for teaching.   The citizens of Hancock
were also liberal, and did everything for the comfort and convenience of the teachers.   It was the opinion of the best teachers
present that the time was well spent, while the records show that,
though the daily attendance was not large, the average per cent.
in recitations ranks higher than ever before.   In my circular for
this institute, the condition of the schools was discussed and suggestions offered to remedy their most prominent defects.   All but
five of the ninety-nine schools are reported as having blackboards,
though many have them only in name, since they have been in use
several terms without being repaired, and are nearly worthless.
Twenty-seven have each a map of Wisconsin; fifty, a map of the
United States; and eighty-two, a copy of Webster's Unabridged
Dictionary.   The value of each of these is apparant to all, and it is
hoped that these almost indispensable aids to the progress of the
schools will soon be supplied in all.   Monthly reports, showing the
condition of the schools, were received from nearly all the teachers.
These reports also showed the names of pupils neither absent nor
tardy; those who were ninety per cent. in examination, and those
with good deportment.   In nearly every instance the reports
showed the true status of the school.   I am proud of these lists, for
they indicate the future character of those enrolled, and it is my
intention to publish all lists received during the winter.

The course of study for ungraded schools has generally been a
failure.   The better way would be to have the State Department
prepare a course that is sustained by law, and require teachers
to be familiar with it after a certain date, and then to be compelled
to teach by it.

Every school in this county has been visited at least once.during
each term, and the number of different visits was 200.   The winter
schools were well attended; but during the heated term, the schools
were quite small.   It is certainly a grave mistake to continue

7 — ST. SUP.

school through July and August. In regard to the law compelling the attendance of pupils, I have not heard of one instance where it was legally enforced, though threats of enforcing it have stimulated the attendance of many.

In conclusion, it gives me pleasure to state that in looking over the year's work, I feel very much encouraged. True, there have been some disappointments, yet, taken as a rule, our schools have been prosperous, and I look for better results during the present year. I am happy to state that the careless teachers are becoming less in this county, and that there is a demand for a higher stand-ard of education, and that there is a general disposition to retain competent teachers.

TREMPEALEAU COUNTY.

STEPHEN RICHMOND, SUPERINTENDENT.

Since I came into the office of county superintendent of schools, on the fifth day of January, I have spent much of the time in school matters. I have made 122 visits, examining into the methods of instruction and discipline, the condition of school rooms, yards, and out buildings; and, in a general way, have tried to get at the real situation of our schools.

I. School-Houses.

There are 86 school-houses in the county,— 16 of these are poorly fitted for the purposes for which they are employed, and 9 of the 16 are in no sense to be considered as proper places in which to educate children. It is barbarous to compel their attendance in them at some seasons; and at no time can it be considered pleasant to these children, or to their teachers, when such teachers are per-sons qualified in education, morals, methods, and spirit for their work. Several of these 9 school-houses are not worth to exceed $10 each. The remaining 70 are fair, comfortable rooms, in ordin-ary condition, and include the six graded school buildings in the county.

II. SOME STATISTICS.

We employed 96 teachers last winter, 83 of whom I visited during that time. Of these, many were doing and did good work; some did ordinarily well, while others failed absolutely to do anything worthy of commendation.   True, they were not always wholly to blame, " for their machinery and tools were very poor. Manufacturers find it for their interest to have the best machinery and tools, and always obtain them as soon as possible for their employes." Why should not teachers have the best helps that can be obtained for them, as well as mechanics? And why should not school officers look for and obtain the best tools, such as good, comfortable rooms, well-seated, lighted, and maps, globes, etc., as well as manufacturers? The number of children of school age in the county, on September 1st, as reported, was 6,409, of which 4,082 attended school some portion of the year. The sum expended for school purposes, as nearly as I can approximate, for the town clerks' reports are very imperfect and many of them are quite incomplete, was $25,221.13. Of this sum, male teachers, with average wages of $34.71 per month, received, $8,951.70; and females, with average wages of $25.64 per month, received, $11,362.12.

III. CERTIFICATES, ETC.

One nomination to normal schools was made. Three permits were granted last winter, and the time of five certificates has been extended. The number of different persons licensed to teach, between September 1st, 1879, and August 31st, 1880, was, males 56, and females 82,— total 148.

IV. EXAMINATIONS.

Since January 5th, 1880, two regular examinations, and one supplementary examination, have been held, as follows: In the spring, at five points in the county, and for a period of three days at each point; in all, 15 days. At this time, 119 applicants wrote, 74 receiving certificates as follows: 5, first grade; 4, second grade; 28, third grade for one year; and 37, third grade for one-half year.

In the fall, the regular examinations were held at three points, and for a period of four days at each point; in all 12 days. At this time, 104 applicants wrote, 93 receiving certificates, as follows: 7 first grade; 6 for the full time, and I for one year; 8 second grade; 47 third grade for one year; and 31 third grade for one-half year.

The supplementary examination was held at Arcadia, October 15th and 16th. Six applicants were present, five of whom were licensed till the time of next regular examination of teachers. To each certificate granted this year, the experience, as a teacher, of the holder, has been added, as an element of information to district boards.

V. NORMAL INSTITUTE.

A teachers' normal institute of two weeks, was held in the village of Blair, commencing August 16th, and conducted by Prof. J. B. Thayer, assisted by myself and by Mrs. Louise Parker, principal of the primary department in the River Falls Normal School. She was present during the first week only. The institute was, in every respect, successful. Prof. Thayer has conducted our institutes successfully for six years, but never before so fully displayed his complete mastery of didactics, and of every detail of school teaching. His spirit and effort were seconded by all present, and the result was highly satisfactory. No man in the State has greater claims upon the people in this county, than Prof. Thayer. He has, by example and precept, done a great deal for our teachers, and hence for our schools.. Mrs. Parker gave us a fine exhibition of primary teaching. Her methods and work, I consider the best it has been my pleasure to witness. We shall be pleased to see her again in our institute work.

VI. OUR UNIVERSITY.

The Galesville University has supplemented a " normal training course," in which methods, discipline, and school organization will be taught as systematically and thoroughly as such work is done in any regular normal school. A thorough normal teacher has been employed, and good class has been in attendance during the fall. It is expected and desired that a still larger number will avail themselves of the opportunity thus offered them so conveniently, and I might say, so generously by the University Board. We hope that a strong demand for teachers who have had some prcfessional training, will grow up in our country districts. Our effort will be in. this direction. It is hoped that it will no longer be necessary to grant " six month " certificates, in order to get teachers to supply our schools. That only those, able to take a full certificate will be licensed, should be the rule. All others should be neglected, till fully qualified to reach that standard.

VII. ASSOCIATION.

A teachers' county association for the purpose of improving our teachers, elevating the school work of the county, purchasing school furniture and text-books at the lowest rates, and gathering a teachers' county library, was organized at the close of the institute. The first regular meeting to perfect the organization was held in the University building at Galesville, October 1st and 2d. A full attendance was had. A strong, active, educational interest is manifested by all our teachers. Much good will grow out of this organization, if our teachers will only make it a means to an end, or rather to the many ends which they are seeking to reach.

VIII. COMPULSORY EDUCATION.

A circular containing the compulsory school law, with comments upon it, and some suggestions to school officers, was issued early in August. A copy was sent to each district clerk, and many were distributed through the county, hoping to make all familiar with its provisions, and to create a strong public sentiment iu favor of its enforcement. A larger number of children were enrolled in our schools last year than heretofore, and yet, fully 1,000 failed to comply with the law.

VERNON COUNTY.

WM. HAUGHTON, SUPERINTENDENT.

In addition to my annual statistical report for Vernon county, I now furnish some special memoranda in connection with our public schools.

Reports of County Superintendents — Vernon.

My late efficient and indefatigable predecessor in the Superintendent's office had done such good work in this county, during the past six years, that little more remained for me than to adopt his methods, and carry out his plans of labor. I have made upwards of one hundred school visits, during the past nine months, and I have sought, by every available means, to encourage teachers and pupils in their labors, assisting and counseling when assistance or counsel was necessary. The great object was to secure, as far as possible, uniformity in programme, classification, and method of instruction.

This I considered essential, in view of the fact that few of our teachers are normal trained, and that constant changes are made in the selection of teachers, and for single terms. I have advocated earnestly the necessity of less change in this direction; of keeping the old teachers in the old place, engaging them if possible by the year, and of encouraging them by liberal salaries and frequent visits to the school. I am happy to be able to add that both teachers and school patrons have held up my hands, and co-operated with me in this. Our people of Vernon county take an honest pride in their schools and in the advancement of education, and encourage me in seeking to secure a staff of well-qualified and efficient teachers. I have given lectures on educational matters where and whenever I could find opportunity, and have spent a great part of my time amongst the schools and their patrons, carrying from one district to another any method in teaching or discipline I found successful. Indeed, I have been much gratified by the experience and good judgment manifested by many of our teachers, and the readiness with which others avail themselves of all such aid.

Our staff of teachers has been large — too large for the number of our schools; hence, bargaining at low salaries, and in some cases underbidding, has been the result. The supply has been greater than the demand, and the only remedy in this case is to thin the ranks of the less capable, and, for a time at least, keep out young aspirants for the teacher's office. This I have sought to do as wisely and as judiciously as possible. A higher standard of qualification must be set, and greater efficiency exacted. This will, I think, in time regulate the matter.

Reports of County Superintendents — Vernon.

Sixteen public examinations have been held at the most available points in the county of easy access to the candidates. Notwithstanding this, many seek private examination. It is to be regretted that either feigned or real causes hinder any from attending the largely advertised public examinations. The work has been both oral and written, and the papers placed on file for future reference. Those grading seven and upwards on a scale of ten, other things being equal, have received a year's certificate. Those grading less have received their standing on a license for six months, on the express condition that no further certificate would be given without a marked improvement at the next examination.

These examinations have been largely elementary, for it is not so much scholarship we need in our teachers as ability to train others, and impart instruction. Special attention has been called to the proper ventilation of the school room, the hygiene of pupils and gentlemanly or lady-like deportment toward each other. The teacher in this, as in other things, instructs by example as well as precept.

A normal institute of two weeks' duration, under the able management of Prof. Hutton, closed about the middle of September. An enrollment of one hundred and twenty-two represented every town in our large county. These institutes are of incalculable benefit to our teachers, one of many good results is that we are having a more uniform course of study in our schools, and as a consequence one teacher will be less likely to spend part of his time in pulling down what another has built up.

The following items from our statistical reports for the years ending August 31st, 1879 and 1880, offer a favorable showing of some increase in school attendance, and the amount paid for school purposes:

	1879.	1880.
Number of children of school age.	9,006	9,106
Number of children who have attended school......	6,482	7,323
Number of days scoool has been taught.............	21,603	24,976
Number of one year third grade certificates	163	150
Whole amount paid for school purposes............	$29,023 00	$29,141 00
Average wages paid teachers, both sexes.............	22 50	22 50

Doubtless the compulsory law has much to do with this increase of attendance, and yet I find that Vernon county people are steadily awakening to the necessity of giving their children all the benefits of our common schools.

We have a high school at Viroqua, under the management of Prof. O. E. Larkin, and one at Hillsborough, under that of Prof. I. F. Mack, both graduates of Milton College and gentlemen of ability and culture. These schools offer large facilities to young people preparing for the more advanced studies, and are largely attended by non-resident pupils.

We have also an excellent graded school in Ontario, and another at De Soto. The former is under the care of Mr. Mahoney, and the latter under that of Mr. Chapman; both are doing good work.

In conclusion, I am happy to be able to add that a few very comfortable and commodious school-houses have been built during the past year, and some others neatly furnished. Many district boards have adopted and purchased a series of text-books, and are favorable to some uniform course of study. Our progress, if slow, is steady and assured. We hope the time will soon come when no way-side hovel, in the shape of a school-house unfenced and neglected, will be an eye-sore to the traveler and a slur upon our people; but that one and all will feel that money cannot be more wisely or more nobly expended than in aiding education and beautifying the school-houses of Vernon county.

WINNEBAGO COUNTY.

W. W. KIMBALL, SUPERINTENDENT.

I. STATISTICS.

Number of children between the ages of 4 and 20 years	7,010
Number of the same who have attended school	4,969
Number of school houses in the county	101
Number of teachers required to teach the schools.............	113
Number of visits made by the superintendent during the year..	164
Amount paid male teachers during the year...................	$6,708 00
Amount paid female teachers during the year.................	13,444 00
Average wages of males per month	32 32
Average wages of female teachers per month..................	21 84
Total amount paid out, during the year......................	27,205 00

II. SCHOOL-HOUSES.

With scarcely an exception, the school-houses are in good condition throughout the county. A number of districts have purchased patent desks, while many others are thinking of doing the same. The plea for better blackboards is being recognized, and, in the new houses, good boards are the result. Many improvements are observed in the other and older ones. The map of Wisconsin is found in 73 schools, and that of the United States in 59.

III. TEACHERS.

There have been 218 applicants for certificates, and of the 158 licenses granted during the year, 8 were first grade, 4 second, and 146 third. Of these but a small percentage are males, whose members seem to be rapidly decreasing in this county, owing to the reduction of salaries, which is being brought about by the present condition of the schools, as regards the age and number of the pupils. The marked difference between a term in the summer and one in the winter, seems in this county a feature of the past.

Female teachers are preferred, as a rule, for the winter, where they have given good satisfaction during the summer. This idea is gaining ground, is being recognized by the teachers, and a feeling of competition is the result. Many of the older teachers of the county, being, this year, in attendance at the Normal School, are determined to compete with the younger teachers who have had the advantage of a more extended course at school.

I am doing what I can to have the school-districts secure permanent teachers, believing that until this is done, we can do but little toward establishing a course of study throughout the county.

IV. INSTITUTES.

Two institutes have been held, each of one week's duration. At Omro 52 teachers were present; at Neenah, 44. There was a marked co-operation between the teachers and Prof. Graham, at each place. We believe that much needed good was accomplished, and that to-day, the teachers throughout the county more deeply feel the need of institute drill, and are more anxious to avail them-

selves of every opportunity for self-improvement, and that they realize that Prof. Graham is a true friend to every district school-
teacher.

V. TEACHERS' MEETINGS.

Owing to the bad weather and poor roads, but three county associations were held last winter. We hope to do much better the
coming year. The county being naturally divided into two districts,
we purpose holding monthly meetings at the most convenient
points in each, and continue systematically the work begun at the
institutes; and then at the close of the year, meet in joint session
for a two weeks' institute.

REPORTS OF CITY SUPERINTENDENTS.

HUDSON.

R. B. DUDGEON, ACTING SUPERINTENDENT.

Owing to the size of our little city, and our limited means, the schools under the city arrangement have not been all that we could wish. The salary of the superintendent has been so small that no man would be justified in neglecting his private business for school work. Under the circumstances, very much credit is due our city superintendent. Upon the reorganization of the school board last April, it was determined to make the position of superintendent merely nominal, and to place the management of the schools in the hands of the principal. That the principal might be relieved of a part of his class room work, the services of an additional teacher were secured for the high school.

Since the opening of the present year, we have given special attention to the work of the different grades. In some cases the course has been slightly changed. When scholars were found, who seemed capable of doing more work than the average scholar in their grade, we have given special examinations and passed them into higher grades. Our schools are now thoroughly graded, and all seem to be working advantageously. The work of our higher grades is especially worthy of mention. The amount of good, honest work now done will compare favorably with that done by any school of corresponding grade.

In bringing up our schools to the proper standard, we find that our teachers' meetings, which we hold once in two weeks, are of inestimable value. They are full of interest and eagerly attended by all teachers. We have a regular programme for each meeting, which includes select readings, discussions on special school topics, regular class drill, and general work which is of value to the teachers in their daily duties.

Our course includes the English branches and the Natural Sciences. No place has been given to the Classics, which fact we regret. It is our aim to prepare young men and women for the active duties of life, and to send them out well prepared, at least in the rudiments of an education.

We regret to say that some of our school rooms are dark, gloomy, and very uninviting. We feel that our citizens are not thoroughly impressed with the importance of furnishing the children with pleasant school accommodations. They do not seem to realize how much the young and growing mind is influenced by its surroundings. We believe that beautiful school buildings, with well-lighted, clean, inviting rooms, surrounded with tastily arranged grounds, have an influence in cultivating the tastes of the young, which cannot be overestimated. They furnish a part of the child's education, which cannot be obtained in any other way. No community can afford to neglect these influences. Even the tax-payer should bear in mind that money spent in making schools attractive, will save expenses and taxes for poor-houses, prisons, and police forces. We trust that our people are waking up on this matter, and that they will realize more fully that the intelligence of a community can be rightly judged by the school facilities which it offers.

JANESVILLE.

R. W. BURTON, SUPERINTENDENT.

As compared with 1879, the school census of 1880, in our city, shows a decrease in its school population of 172 children, between the ages of four and twenty.

Of the 3,386 returned by the enumerator, 1,728, or about 51 per cent., have been enrolled in the public schools. On number enrolled, the records show an attendance of 76.3 per cent.; while on number of members, our regular attendance rises to 94 per cent.

In punctuality our schools have maintained their usually high standard. Cases of tardiness number 344; or in other words, for the thirty-seven weeks of school, our per cent. of punctuality was

Reports of City Superintendents — Janesville.

99.8.   For the week ending June 11th, there was not a single case of tardiness.

For the year ending June 25th, the high school enrollment was 161, and average membership, 117.   This is not quite up to last year's report, but much in advance of those of its predecessors.   April the 16th, a class consisting of four boys and ten girls was graduated, four of the girls entering immediately upon the work of teaching.

Five years ago our lowest grades were crowded to excess, while our grammar departments were few, and only partially filled.   As a rule, the reverse is now true.   The necessity for more room in the grammar grades became so pressing in May last, that a second grammar department, representing the seventh year of the course, was organized in the First Ward.   As the cause of this change in conditions, we must recognize the systematic division of the work, and the enthusiasm which pervades the department.   The resultant of these forces is a thorough preparation on the part of a large majority of pupils in each room, upon the limits assigned, enabling them to pass the annual test successfully.   Those reaching the required standard move forward, while the new levies have hitherto been insufficient to keep the number good in the lower departments.

Our experience in a practical test of the Grube method throughout our primary grades, has proven very satisfactory.   As compared with the old method, it is the *living truth.*   By an application of its principles, both in spirit and in letter, a higher life in class can be maintained, a clearer understanding of numbers and their relations secured, and a greater facility in their combination acquired.

The advantages arising from the purchase of school books with public funds, and loaning them to the pupils, should commend the plan to every district in the State, and especially to the populous cities like our own.   As a matter of economy, without doubt, it is the best thing to do.   The plan tends to lessen the necessity of compulsory laws by removing obstacles in the form of school book expenses, deterring many children from entering school, and, in not a few cases, driving them from school into idleness or a premature self-support. In addition to the advantages often cited, the purchase of school books by the district or city, gives pupils the benefit of a supplementary series of books — just now claiming public attention,— so essential to thoroughness in certain directions. For instance, all learn to read by reading; and a fresh book, unfamiliarized by weeks of thumbing, will impart new zest to the exercise in class. Where books are the property of the district or city, supplementary series of readers can be provided with slight expense, and placed at the service of teachers in sufficient numbers to furnish a grade or class for an important exercise, calculated to test the ability of pupils to make a practical use of the power acquired, while it stimulates to better effort. Save the charges made to pupils, the workings of the free text-books principle are fairly illustrated by the library system in our Normal Schools.

During the year, our manufacturing interests have been extended by the establishment of a knitting factory, promising employment to fifty young women. Besides this, the facilities of other manufactories of longer standing, have been increased. The effect of all this is to reduce the attendance upon the daily sessions of our schools, and to voice emphatically the claim of those youthful employes to the benefits of a free night school, whose establishment was advocated in our report for 1879. A longer delay in this matter would seem to do violence to the general well-being of this community, while the individual interests, present and future, of a worthy element in its society, are being ignored.

Our usual teachers' meetings have continued throughout the year with unabated interest. These meetings occur semi-monthly, and are of three hours' duration. The greater part of the session is devoted to class exercises in subjects that have a direct bearing upon the daily work of the departments. A space of forty-five minutes, or an hour, is spent upon what is termed an " outside subject," or one that is general in its bearing upon the ordinary work of the schools. Last year the outside subject was Universal History; this year it is American Literature. In all cases the work is laid out two weeks in advance. In literature, papers embodying the biography of the author, the history and criticisms of his works,

---

Reports of City Superintendents — La Crosse.

---

are carefully prepared and read by members of the class. These papers are subject to discussion, time permitting. One or more parties are always appointed to present literary specimens, illustrative of the style of the author under consideration. The force of these outside studies is potent in strengthening the teacher's habit of investigation, and stimulating a greater love for reading. To meet the demand of these exercises, a certain amount of literary study cannot be avoided. Thereby a broader intelligence of the teacher results, giving high promise for the future progress of our schools.

Gradually we are approaching that satisfactory condition when it may be said, "Our schools are supplied with all necessary apparatus." The condition of the treasury being favorable, but little argument is needed with our Board of Education to secure the essentials in this particular. As the fruit of this year, a liberal supply of globes and historical charts adorn our school rooms.

LA CROSSE.

J. J. FRUIT, SUPERINTENDENT.

During the seven or eight years last past, the public schools of La Crosse have been gradually improving in thorough and efficient work.

The present condition of our schools can be attributed to no one cause. A liberal appropriation, made by our judicious councilmen from time to time, deserves commendation. With this appropriation, the enterprising men who have composed our Board of Education have provided and furnished school buildings, and have placed in charge of the various departments an efficient corps of teachers, who have worked faithfully with the Board and Superintendent in accomplishing what we have.

ATTENDANCE AND PUNCTUALITY.

While circumstances beyond our control (such as good weather, and the absence of contagious disease), have been very favorable to good attendance and punctuality during the past year, the hearty co-operation of parents, children, and teachers, has added largely to the result attained.

From an enrollment of nearly 1,950 pupils, there were only 237 cases of tardiness during the year; the per cent. of attendance on the number belonging during the year, is a fraction above 97.

VOCAL MUSIC.

During the spring term of 1880, Vocal Music was introduced in the grammar and intermediate departments, by way of experiment, as a regular branch of study. From a trial of three months it was deemed advisable by our board to employ a teacher of music regularly, during the year (1880–81),—which has been done. Both pupils and teachers are pleased with it; and so far as I am able to ascertain, this exercise has the approval of the patrons.

I hope and trust that this branch, which gives such culture to the better emotions, may soon be adopted as a part of our course of study.

The people of our city have begun to feel greatly interested in maintaining the credit of their present school system; and we look forward to such work and results, if not already attained, as shall be second to none in the State.

NEENAH.

JOHN B. RUSSELL, SUPERINTENDENT.

The general condition of our public schools during the past year, has been very satisfactory.

The attendance has not materially increased over other years. The several departments have been well filled. The teachers have been attentive and faithful in the discharge of their duties. The conduct of the pupils has been good. There have been no cases calling for interference on the part of our school board, and no case of expulsion, and but one of suspension; and the latter only for a limited period, till the pupil should conform to certain rules.

Our high school, under the management of Prof. H. A. Hobart, has been a decided success in all its departments. At no time

Reports of City Superintendents — Neenah.

since its establishment, has it rendered more effective service or made more satisfactory progress, than in the year just closed. It affords me great pleasure to be able to state that there has been a thoroughness in teaching the most useful branches of the English course.

The teachers in charge of the high school appreciate the importance of thorough work in those studies which are of practical advantage, and have the most commercial value in the great struggle of life, and are available on the farm, in the workshop, or in the marts of commerce.

The exercises of the high school graduating class for 1880, were conducted by Prof. Hobart. They were of an interesting character, creditable both to the teachers and pupils. Twenty-seven pupils graduated in what is known as the short term or nine years' course, and nearly all of the graduates have returned to school, to finish by graduating in the long term or eleven years' course.

We completed our new high school building last April, at a cost of $25,000. In architectural style and everything that pertains to the health and comfort of scholars, it is unsurpassed by any other school building in the State. The main part is 100 feet square, and contains eight departments, five on the first floor and three on the second. Except in the high school room, which is 15 feet high, the rooms have a uniform heighth of 13 feet. Each department has a main entrance from corridors, and two cloak rooms corresponding in size with the seating capacity of the rooms. These cloak rooms open into both the class room and the corridor, to facilitate the exit of children, especially in case of fire. All the doors open outward, thus preventing a panic.

The heating of the building is the most perfect system known, except, perhaps that by steam. It is known as the Ruttan System. The heat is supplied by three large furnaces in the basement. The air warmed is pure, for it is admitted to the furnaces from outdoors; and contrary to the old idea of ventilating at the top of the room, the foul air is carried off through registers near the floor to the great ventilating shaft, where it is carried into the open air. The shaft is heated by the smoke flues, thus creating a current or draft.

8—ST. SUP.

The school building has a seating capacity of 800 pupils. The floor space is 8,214 feet on each floor, the cubic contents being 120,422 feet.

We moved into it on the first of May last, much to the delight of the teachers and pupils; and on occupying it, we found, for comfort and convenience, and adaptability to uses intended, our schoolhouse is all that is claimed for it, — the model building of the State.

We have added largely to our school apparatus in the purchase of globes, maps, charts, etc., which aid the teachers materially in describing, illustrating, and demonstrating.

At the commencement of the school year, we changed our system of purchasing school books. We now buy the books directly from the publishers, and place them in the superintendent's office in the high school building; and put them in charge of the janitor, who sells them to the scholars at actual cost. Those who are too poor to buy, are furnished free, — the city paying the cost of freight and express. Thus the books are placed in the hands of the pupils at three-fourths the former price; and we find the plan working very satisfactorily to all concerned.

PRAIRIE DU CHIEN.

A. C. WALLIN, SUPERINTENDENT.

Special reports are intended to give further statistical details, to summarize or generalize, to draw comparisons or correct errors; if these, or any of these purposes are not accomplished, then a special report, as such, fails of its object.

The school census of this district for this year shows an increase of twenty-nine over last year's report. The increase is the result of an enlargement of this district. The portion annexed has a school population of twenty-two.

By reference to my annual report, I find that of the four hundred and ninety-four children between the ages of " 7 and 15," five hundred and ten have been returned as in attendance at the public and private schools! A pretty good showing! No intentional error has been made. Private schools reported to me the number of pupils between "7 and 15," attending such schools, without ascertaining whether any of those pupils had been registered in the public schools or not. Allowing that a number of those attending private schools had, for some portion of the year, attended the public schools, and we have nearly all pupils between the ages specified in attendance upon some school, during the greater part of the school year.

Although in this district, those in charge of private schools have been very obliging in giving me information in relation to those statistics which were asked for in the annual report, there is nothing in the law which compels them to give those statistics. These reports are compulsory on the part of public school officials; I think they should be made compulsory on the official in-charge of a private school. There is no other way by which accurate statistics in relation to attendance, such as would be required in order to carry out the provisions of the amendment to the school law, entitled, "An act to secure to children the benefit of an elementary education," can be obtained. A canvass of the district would not show a result as accurate as that obtained from the registers of the schools. To illustrate: This year I took the school census of this district, expecting to get accurate results. Parents reported to me two hundred and seventy-five pupils between the ages of 7 and 15, who had attended the public schools during some part of the school year. I find recorded in the teachers' registers the names of two hundred and ninety-five different pupils between the ages specified. No deception could have been intended by the parents. During some part of the year, a child had been in attendance at the public school, but for the greater part of the year had attended a private school. The parent, at the time when the census taker calls, forgets the fact of attendance at the public school, and so an error occurs in his report. To make that provision of the law effective, managers of private schools should be required to report to the clerks of districts in which such schools are located, the names of all children attending such schools, with the aggregate number of days' attendance for each child, said reports to be due at the clerk's

office on the first day of February, and the first day of September
of each year. I believe it to be a wise provision of the law, and
hope the act may be made enforceable.

STEVENS POINT.

FRANK L. GREEN, SUPERINTENDENT.

In submitting the Annual Report of our schools, some advances
are to be noted, and some characteristics presented, which may be
of interest to others by way of comparison or for forming an estimate of the school work, and the success here.

The schools of our little city possess some features peculiar to
themselves, and without which it would be difficult for one to form
a correct judgment of the progress made.

The year has been one of growth and financial prosperity.

The census of June last gives the city a population of 4,445. On
August 31st, there were 1,408 children of school age. Of these,
877, or 62 per cent., were enrolled in our schools during the year,
with an average daily attendance of 505. In comparison with the
preceding year, this shows a decrease of one in the number of school
age, an increase of 57 in the enrollment, and of 85 in the daily
attendance for the year. The percentage of attendance on membership was a little over 86, — more than two per cent. higher than
ever attained before. The wide disparity between the number of
school age and the enrollment, as well as between the enrollment
and daily attendance, arises mainly from three causes; first, the
compulsory law is not enforced: secondly, during the season for
manufacturing lumber, a large number of boys are engaged in the
mills; and thirdly, one ward is made up largely of foreign population, in which the Polish predominate. These take very little interest in educational matters, and are very irregular in attendance.
The enrollment is exclusive of one parochial and two private
schools, whose numbers reach above 250.

Situated on the border of the pineries and at the base of the line
opening to the north, our population is more fluctuating and less

Reports of City Superintendents — Stevens Point.

permanent than in the Southern cities of the State. This fact renders it more difficult for school officers to provide the necessary facilities, and for teachers to secure regularity and satisfactory advancement. Few schools require so severe work from their teachers. The primary and intermediate departments cover three years each, under one teacher; and for each teacher below the high school, there was a total enrollment of 87, and a daily attendance of 51. In the year just entered upon, the increase in some schools is so great as to necessitate an addition to the teaching force, and indicates a farther enlargement soon. Hitherto, too little attention has been given to the grammar school. There are especial reasons why it should receive every encouragement, and have the best of teachers and the best of support. It is the main feeder to the high school, whose success depends largely upon it. It gives to a certain class all the education they ever get in the schools; and for that reason alone, it ought to be most thorough and practical.

The greatest benefit which the people could confer upon the schools, would be an active expression of interest in them. Very few ever visit them, and too often parents are apathetic and think the teacher's efforts to secure punctuality a bore. The school board, however, seem desirous of good teachers, good schools, and the best possible returns.

A systematic code of rules and regulations for the government of the schools, and an excellent course of study, have been adopted, — the latter covering eight years of study for entrance to the high school. These are printed in a neat circular, in connection with the catalogue of the high school; and supply a long-felt need. The objects sought are greater unity and certainty of action on the part of teachers, greater zeal and a higher ambition on the part of pupils, and more permanency and solidity in the character of our schools.

The financial management of the schools has been very economical, leaving a handsome balance in the treasury. The cost per capita of the pupils for teachers' salaries, exclusive of the high school, computed on the year's enrollment, was $4.52; on the average daily attendance, $5 82. The cost for each pupil, including the high school, was $7.84 — a sum small indeed, compared with the cost in many other cities.

There are some needs which we hope to see supplied during the coming year. The primary teachers have not sufficient helps, and generous additions should be made to the high school library and apparatus.

Teachers' meetings are held one evening each week, for the purpose of reports, consultation, study, and general intelligence and criticism. In connection with the necessary business of the meeting, we are now carrying on a course of study in history and government. This interchange of views gives rise to a feeling of fellowship and mutual helpfulness, and to the study, we believe, of a wider mental scope, and better work.

An effort has been made to give to our high school the system and the influence which are the strength and the fruit of every well-conducted high school. Two carefully arranged courses of study have been adopted in place of the old "go as-you-please" style, and have been issued in the catalogue already referred to, for general circulation. The English Course covers three years' study, and is intended more particularly for those who are preparing to teach in the public schools. The Latin Course extends over four years, and gives an ample fit for the University.

The reorganization of the school upon the new basis was no easy task, but it has been successfully accomplished, and the present senior class of nine, now pursuing plane trigonometry, natural philosophy, and Virgil, will be the first to graduate from the school.

The enrollment for the year in the high school was 95; the average membership, 60. This difference arises in part from the fact that many pursue their studies a portion of the year and teach the remainder.

Some old teachers are returning to the school, for the purpose of securing a certificate of higher grade. Thus the high school comes to have a stimulating and elevating influence upon the schools of a considerable territory. Pupils are constantly coming in from the towns of this and adjoining counties.

The study room contains an excellent reference library, and there

Reports of City Superintendents — Stevens Point.

is no feature of the school more gratifying than the constant and intelligent use of these books of reference.

Centrally located as we are, with no Normal School near us, and the country rapidly developing to the north of us, there seems to be no reason why our high school may not, with proper care and support, become a strong educational force in this part of the State.

University of Wisconsin.

UNIVERSITY OF WISCONSIN.

BOARD OF REGENTS.

STATE SUPERINTENDENT OF PUBLIC INSTRUCTION,
Ex-Officio Regent.

Life Member... .... C. C. WASHBURN.................... Madison.

Term Expires First Monday in February, 1881.

7th Congressional District.......... CHARLES D. PARKER .... Pleasant Valley.
5th......do...........do ... ... HIRAM SMITH....................... Sheboygan Falls.
2d ......do...... ....do .... J. C. GREGORY...................... Madison.
4th......do...........do .... GEO. KOEPPEN ....'.... Milwaukee.

Term Expires First Monday in February, 1882.

State at Large...................... GEORGE H. PAUL.................. Milwaukee.
8th Congressional District .... J. M. BINGHAM .... Chippewa Falls.

Term Expires First Monday in February, 1883.

State at Large...................... E. W. KEYES....................... Madison.
1st Congressional District .... J. B. CASSODAY [1] .... Janesville.
3d ......do...........do .... W. E. CARTER...................... Platteville.
6th......do...........do .... L. B. SALE .... Green Bay.

OFFICERS OF THE BOARD.

GEORGE H. PAUL,
PRESIDENT.

W. E. CARTER,
VICE PRESIDENT.

JOHN S. DEAN,
SECRETARY.

STATE TREASURER,
EX-OFFICIO TREASURER.

EXECUTIVE COMMITTEE.

E. W. KEYES,   J. C. GREGORY,   W. E. CARTER.

FARM COMMITTEE.

HIRAM SMITH,   C. C. WASHBURN,   CHAS. D. PARKER.

COMMITTEE ON LIBRARY, COURSE OF STUDY, AND TEXT-BOOKS.

W. C. WHITFORD,   L B. SALE,   GEORGE KOEPPEN.

COMMITTEE ON LAW DEPARTMENT.

J. C. GREGORY,   J. B. CASSODAY,   J. M. BINGHAM.

[1] Since resigned, and Hon John G. McMynn, of Racine, appointed to fill the vacancy.

University of Wisconsin.

ANNUAL REPORT OF THE BOARD OF REGENTS.

To His Excellency, WM. E. SMITH, *Governor:*

The generally satisfactory condition of the University of Wisconsin, in both its financial and educational departments of government, is exhibited in the accompanying reports and statistics for the year ending September 30, 1880. The attendance upon the collegiate courses has continued to increase, the standard of instruction has been elevated, and, through the intelligent munificence of its founder, the Washburn Observatory has been considerably enlarged, and with the further additions contemplated and progressing, promises to become a permanent and unexpectedly affluent source of valuable accessions to astronomical science.

Progress and enlargement, however, develop the needs and deficiencies invariably incident to new conditions of growth and usefulness. A higher grade of capacity and experience in the instructional department, a greater quantity and better quality of illustrative apparatus, a more complete and comprehensive cabinet and library, and more commodious recitation rooms, are conspicuous among the present necessities pressing upon the consideration of the Board. These necessities are the evidence and outgrowth of increased prosperity and strength, and therefore not to be deprecated. And inasmuch as they refer to a more effective application of existing capacities and resources, prompt concession to them is a positive economy.

Recently it has been the policy of the Board to give greater prominence to those departments of instruction which more particularly relate to the practical industries of our State. Reference is made especially to the departments of agriculture and practical mechanics. These are branches of study which must ultimately and inevitably exercise a large and wholesome influence upon the development of the material interests of Wisconsin, and should tend to command for the University the sympathy and support of large classes of our population less immediately concerned in abstract and professional instruction. A wider diffusion of practical and scientific knowledge, through the departments named, without

University of Wisconsin.

detriment to the highest practicable standard in the classical and purely scientific courses, is an educational policy commended by the best examples and the spirit of the times, and which largely tends to equalize the public benefits conferred by the University.

The details of expenditure included in this report exhibit the manner in which the annual income of the University is applied. This income is not sufficiently large to enable the Board to meet all the demands to which reference has been made. It is possibly large enough, but certainly not too large, to cover an economical current expenditure, exclusive of the cost of additional buildings or permanent improvements required.

In this connection, your attention is respectfully invited to the fact of a considerable diminution in the University fund income, arising from the failure of the State to invest the whole of the principal fund. As stated in the communication of the Secretary of the Board, included in this report, the amount remaining uninvested at the close of the financial year just terminated, was $41,896 72, and the diminution of income for the year, from this cause, as compared with the year ending September 30, 1878, is $3,185.23. The tendency to reduction in rates of interest renders further deficiencies in the product of the permanent fund probable, as compared with past years, and enforces the propriety of such additional legislation as may be necessary to secure a more uniform and complete investment of the principal.

Under all the circumstances, and with special reference to the exigencies of the future, the Board feels impelled to recur to the original relations of the State to the University, and to the just conditions of the trust imposed upon the State by the federal government. To divert the annual and appropriate income of the University from the necessary purposes of current support, does not accord with those relations, and the obligations imposed upon State by the terms of the national endowment. The act of Congress granting lands to Wisconsin for the benefit of agriculture and the mechanic arts, from which grant the present income of the University is derived in part, is especially emphatic upon this point, in declaring that no portion of the fund derived from the grant or

University of Wisconsin.

the interest thereon, "shall be applied directly or indirectly, under any pretense whatever, to the purchase, erection, preservation, or repair of any building or buildings." The language of this act, as well as the provisions of previous enactments, construed with reference to existing circumstances, seems to remove all doubt as to the appropriate policy of the State and the Board of Regents in respect to permanent improvements and additions to real property in future.

Under the laws of the State, the University is now free to both sexes, and its courses of instruction such as to extend the facilities of a higher education to nearly all classes of citizens. Graduates of the institution inhabit nearly every county, and frequent nearly every profession and path of industry. Its growing strength is imparted to our entire system of public education, and in numberless unseen ways it contributes to the intelligence and permanent happiness of our people. Certainly, there is no source of enlightened progress or of material prosperity more justly entitled to liberal and reliable public support. Fortunately no additional number of buildings is imperatively required at the present time. The immediate modification and better equipment of University Hall, however, for the accommodation of class recitations, is a pressing necessity which relates as well to the health as to the convenience and progress of students, and which may be supplied at a comparatively trifling cost. For further particulars concerning this proposed improvement, we respectfully refer you to the facts presented by the President of the University in his communication to the Board, accompanying this report.

During the past two years, the University has experienced great and exceptional misfortunes in the death of some of the ablest and most valuable members of its instructional force. These losses are now sadly supplemented by the decease, since the introductory clauses of this report were written, of Professor James C. Watson, Director of the Washburn Observatory, as he was crossing the threshold of a new career of public usefulness, with the promise of brilliant achievements in the near future, for himself and for the University, to which he had but recently transferred the wealth of his learning and reputation. The severity of this affliction, in its relations to the University and the public, can be justly appreciated only by those upon whom is imposed the duty of endeavoring to supply his place.

Respectfully submitted,

GEO. H. PAUL,
President of the Board of Regents.

MILWAUKEE, November 25, 1880.

UNIVERSITY COLLEGES.

REPORT OF THE PRESIDENT OF THE UNIVERSITY TO THE BOARD OF REGENTS.

To the President of the Board of Regents of the University of Wisconsin:

The past year, closing with September, has been one of growth. The Assembly Room and Library have been completed. The advantages to be derived from these two accessions will steadily disclose themselves, from year to year. Only one urgent demand remains in the farther improvement of our buildings, and that is the renovation of University Hall.

University Hall was never a fortunate building, and the University has long since outgrown the accommodations this hall offers. Its recitation rooms, which are in constant use, and with which the comfort of the great majority of our students is closely involved, are very small, are ill-furnished and ill-ventilated. They also open into halls much too narrow for our increasing number of students. The renovation of this building has long been recognized as something of great moment to the immediate comfort and good order of our students. The improvement has been deferred from year to year, on account of other undertakings, and these have now so absorbed our funds as to make this most needed change impossible without a small sum from the State. The urgency of the case is

University of Wisconsin.

so obvious that it will be at once perceived by those who give the subject any attention. These rooms are not only unworthy of a University; they are inconsistent with the most ordinary conditions of health.

There has been rapid progress, during the year, in the preparation for astronomical work. Prof. Watson has erected a fine Solar Observatory; also a working Astronomical Observatory for students. This latter building will greatly increase the facilities for instruction. Ex-Gov. Washburn is also enlarging the Astronomical Observatory, with the expectation of still further enlargement in the spring. The best astronomical instruments are in the process of construction, and we shall soon have one of the most complete observatories, in its appointments, to be found on the continent.

The most marked fact in the internal history of the University during the past year, has been that it has brought to a close our preparatory work with the exception of the Greek Class. This is a step which has been taken not without some solicitude, and one which was urged upon us by the High Schools. The ultimate results, we believe, will be favorable, but some immediate results are to be deprecated. The High Schools of the State are not yet in a condition to do all the work required of them. In many portions of the State, no convenient transition is open from the common school to the University. The number of High Schools is still insufficient, and these schools tend to be very local in the provision they make for instruction. This limit arises from two facts. The High Schools are organized and sustained in the interests of a narrow territory just about them. Those persons outside of the established limits are not recognized as having any claims upon them. As a liberal spirit, however, usually prevails in this respect, the narrowness of their work is not so marked in this particular as it is in another respect. High Schools are ordered in their courses and in their rapidity of progress to meet the wants of comparatively young scholars who live at home. They do not, therefore, meet well the necessities of a young man, who, lacking early instruction and somewhat advanced in years, resolves to secure an education. He cannot, without some loss of self-respect and much loss of time,

University of Wisconsin.

reduce his pace to that of the young pupils about him. It remains, therefore, painfully true, that a good many young men and women whom the University would especially wish to help, find great difficulty in making their way into it.

A partial remedy for this evil, which cannot be wholly removed, might be found in the encouragement of the few academies scattered through the State. They are fitted to do the work of preparation for the University more freely and rapidly than are the High Schools. They have no special constituency. They gather their students from far and near, and students well advanced in years. It lies, therefore, quite in their line of work to bridge as quickly as may be the space which separates the preparatory student from the University. We do not think our system of public instruction would be unfavorably affected by an occasional vigorous academy.

Yet in this State, as in other States, the High Schools are fast reducing the academies. The result, as a whole, we rejoice in, but would invite the attention of the academies that still remain to the fact that the field most open to them is this of general preparatory work.

The multiplication and improvement of High Schools must be our great resource. There are few of the educational provisions in the State likely to work more strongly and favorably on our school system than the High School law. It is only to be regretted that the sum distributed is so small, and the period for which it is granted so short. Five years do not give the feeble schools time enough to strike root. The period suffices fairly well for the large villages, but not for the more rural districts. Under this law, which has been in operation five years, there are now organized ninety-five High Schools. The smallest sum received by any school last year was forty-six dollars and five cents; and the largest sum, three hundred and twenty-eight dollars and ninety-three cents. The law decidedly favors the formation of schools in the smaller villages, and in country districts, by giving to these schools a sum relatively larger than that which the older schools receive. The law, the longer it remains in force, will be increasingly efficacious in

University of Wisconsin.

bringing into existence High Schools at secondary centers. Indeed, the whole constructive force of it is now felt at these points. The cities and larger villages put more into the fund by taxation than they take from it by appropriation, and in some instances decline the returns that would fall to them. There are fifteen of the stronger schools of the State not organized under the law. The law distinctly recognizes the principle that education in the State can not be left simply to districts, towns, and cities, but that the State must be responsible for the State. Not only may we hope that High Schools will slowly increase in number, but that the one hundred and ten now in existence will steadily improve in quality. The system is already, by the encouragement of the law, working its way into thinly populated regions, while corresponding improvement in the quality of instruction is made in the schools already established.

There are two sentiments which work against the entire success of the law in its relation to the University. The first is the disposition to make each district and town exclusively responsible for its own educational work, and the reluctance of the larger cities to contribute to education outside their own limits. The country must always suffer severe limitation in the matter of education as compared with the city. The High School law was designed to reduce and is fitted to reduce somewhat this inequality. The ultimate wisdom of the policy can hardly be doubted, though its first results are in conflict with the limited principles which are usually carried into business. The prosperity of our cities and villages must finally be determined by the wealth and intelligence of the surrounding population, and these centers and heads in our social system cannot afford to divorce themselves from the dependent members. The prosperity of the State is one, and must be treated collectively; and that prosperity is identified with its educational institutions. This should be with us a first principle of statesmanship.

A second narrow sentiment that the High Schools have to contend with is that they are diverted from their primary and more local work by any shaping of their instruction to fit students for

University of Wisconsin.

the University. This sentiment, like the previous one, springs up so naturally and is so favored by first appearances as to require some deliberation and breadth of view for its correction. If it be true that the work done for the University diverts attention from the much more important work to be done for scholars who go no farther than the High School, we should accept the objection as a fatal one to any effort to unite the higher and lower grades of instruction by means of the High Schools. On the other hand, we are fully persuaded that the High Schools of the State will never attain to their true development in their strictly home relations without fully accepting the upward relation, and fully meeting its duties.

In the first place, the spirit of a High School which makes itself a door, both in science and language, to the great stores of knowledge beyond its own instruction, will be very different from that of the school which seems to say to its students, " We are the end-all of attainment so far as you are concerned."

Spirit is a very impalpable thing, but a very potent one. The spirit of the teachers and the place is that which makes the great difference between one instructor and another; between one school and another. Without a large spirit, and an enthusiastic one, no extended and stimulating work can be done. Both the spirit of the place and the instruction will be very different in which these two things are combined, awakening the mind to continuous activity and fitting it for its immediate work, from that which is sure to prevail where the exclusive consideration is the practical bearing, so called, of instruction. Though education must do cheerfully and thoroughly its hourly work, it must also be allowed the enthusiasm of a larger outlook and more generous devotion to knowledge. It is by no means those alone who advance, who feel the inspiration of the march, but all who witness it and catch the feelings that prompt it. Spirit is the supreme thing.

A second gain to the High School from a liberal course of instruction, is the much stronger inducement it thereby offers to advanced students, both those advanced in age and those advanced in work. The evil already spoken of — a course adapted exclusively to young

University of Wisconsin.

scholars who have plenty of time, — is greatly increased when the High School is not a recognized avenue to anything beyond it. In that case, it is drawn downward by the work below it, while there is nothing above it to pull it upward. The moulding influences lie all in one direction. The High School, as the end of the school system, is left, with no vital connection with the liberal education above it, to bear alone all the backward pull. The result is not difficult to predict. The High School will easily lose educational ground, and will gain it with great difficulty.

Another very efficient force works in the same direction. There are a few in every community thoroughly interested in the education of their own children. They do not propose to stop short of a collegiate course. It is from this class that schools have the most to expect. But if the common schools and High Schools announce themselves as not in the line of a liberal education, these persons must withdraw their children and seek instruction elsewhere. If this is done, they feel little interest in the High School. They owe nothing to it, and they may easily come even to begrudge the money spent upon it with no personal return. When the High School has thus separated itself from the most intelligent sentiment in the community to which it belongs, what can it reasonably expect? Those take the shaping of it, who are not over confident of the value of education, and who wish to make it at least minister in the cheapest and most direct way to business interests. Educational institutions have never grown up under such an inspiration, and will never greatly prosper by it. It is a spirit that takes only a narrow view of immediate results. It substitutes economy for enterprise, shrewdness for wisdom, and the present for the future. Nothing great can grow out of such a root of parsimony, or thrive when grafted on it. Among the things that the University of Wisconsin is striving to do and helping to do, there will be none of more permanent value than its share in the effort to bring into existence and into line a strong body of High Schools scattered throughout the state. In furtherance of this purpose, it has striven to keep its terms of admission within reach of these preparatory schools, and yet, from time to time, to so far advance these terms

University of Wisconsin.

as both to make way for improved work on their part and to call it out. As a movement in the same direction, it has now laid aside almost all its preparatory work, retaining Greek instruction simply because the general educational sentiment of the State is not yet strong enough to take it up.

The growth of the University in the past five years is chiefly indicated in its advance in scholarship, and in the steady increase of students in higher work. We add a statement of the last five years. Special students with us grade as collegiate students. We require for them essentially the same terms of admission; they work with the collegiate classes, and are constantly passing into those classes:

Year.	Ancient Classical.	Modern Classical.	Scientific.	Special Students.	Young Women.	Out of the State.	Whole Number.	Preparatory.
1875–6	39	26	135	49	71	17	249	71
1876–7	41	28	99	57	65	15	225	72
1877–8	57	54	77	57	66	14	245	109
1878–9	62	78	72	78	75	13	280	120
1879–80	66	83	82	91	94	19	324	105

There are some obvious facts contained in this presentation. The two classical courses have rapidly gained ground, and to that degree that the classical, literary, and the scientific tendencies at present show an almost equal strength with us. The number of special students has increased relatively to regular students. This arises from two reasons: the increase of elective work, and the use of the position of a special student as a transitional one to membership in a regular class. We have designedly enlarged this vestibule of the University, as a means of reducing the friction of entrance examinations. An advanced student is now freely admitted as a special student in a probationary way, and when he has declared by actual work with us his true status, we are able to assign it to him with maximum correctness and minimum labor. The young women have, notwithstanding our advanced scholar-

University of Wisconsin.

ship, maintained their relative numbers. Students from out of the State have not increased in number. We have advertised the University less and less year by year, and our reputation has been correspondingly local. I think we should do well to compete more strongly for foreign support. A University, like a High School, is benefited by competition and a large constituency. It can very easily become too local for its own profit. We see from the above presentation that there has been a gratifying increase of numbers in collegiate studies. The advance of the terms of admission served for two years to reduce the numbers; they then began to increase, and have gained in four years, forty-four per cent. At the erection of Science Hall, it appeared to some quite disproportionately large for its work, and yet there is already an overflow in its most important room — the qualitative chemical laboratory.

It will also be observed that during this period of growth, the preparatory work has been increased, in consequence partly of more extended requisitions for admission to the University classes. The preparatory work has not been laid aside by us because it was disappearing of its own accord, but simply from a desire on our part to offer no obstruction to High School work.

We rejoice in the yearly increasing interest of the State in its University, and renewedly and hopefully commend it to the most patient and wise provision of its Regents.

JOHN BASCOM.

ANNUAL EXAMINATIONS.

REPORT OF THE BOARD OF VISITORS TO THE BOARD OF REGENTS.

To the Honorable Board of Regents of the University of Wisconsin:

The small fraction of the Board of Visitors appointed by you for the present year, who have met at this time, feel that they have but little to report except the failure of the Board to perform the duties expected of it. Former Boards have visited the University

University of Wisconsin.

in a body and formed their impressions of its work from examinations made for them at the close of the year. These examinations have been discontinued, the design being to have the Board visit the institution during the year. Owing to the lack of any organization of the visitors as a Board, any division of labor among them, or any understanding as to what was expected of them, no visitations have been made during the year by a large majority of the Board, and but four members are present at this time. Each one of those four has visited the institution one or more days during the year, but under such circumstances as to learn but little.

We would suggest that some plan should be devised for organizing the Board of Visitors early in the year, and dividing their work, that each member may know what is expected of him. This might be accomplished by some person being designated by the Regents as chairman of the Board of Visitors, upon whom would rest the duty of perfecting the organization and laying out the work of the Board. Being appointed from the four quarters of the State, and no meeting being contemplated until the close of the year, it seems impracticable to effect anything like an organization, or create a feeling of responsibility in any other way.

So far as our observations have gone, we have, as a general thing, been favorably impressed with the workings of the institution. The professors and teachers in all departments seem to be able, earnest, and thoroughly alive to their work; and with a single exception, remarked by one of our number, the students, during recitations observed, seemed attentive, interested, and well-prepared with their lessons.

We were especially impressed with the excellent facilities afforded by the University for instruction and education in all scientific and mechanical branches. While too much cannot be said in praise of this, it has seemed to some of our members that there was a tendency to advance the interests of this to the neglect of the classical department.

While our examination has been so cursory and disconnected that we do not feel justified in criticising, lest by so doing we should but show our ignorance, those of our members who were on

University of Wisconsin.

the grounds during morning prayers were impressed with what appeared to them a prevailing sentiment of disregard, if not disrespect, to those exercises. Out of an attendance upon the institution of between four and five hundred, less than thirty attended these exercises. During their progress, the great majority of students whose recitations immediately followed, were lounging upon the grass around the building, or engaged in conversation or sports in the halls, attended with such noise as to disturb those in the chapel. It would seem that since the completion of the Assembly Hall, which affords accommodation for all the students, some improvement might be made in the matter of attendance upon the chapel exercises. If not, and the instance observed is a fair sample, it seems questionable whether it would not be advisable to discontinue the exercise.

Finding no students in, and learning of no graduates from, the agricultural department, we have sought for an answer to the oft-repeated question, What, if any, benefit the State is deriving from that department? We have been gratified to learn that much valuable work is being done, but from which but little benefit has flowed, owing to the ignorance of the people regarding it. This work consists largely in experiments with fertilizers and different varieties of grains, the result of which, if known to the farming community, would be of great value. No systematic means have been heretofore employed for disseminating this knowledge among the people. It has seemed to us that steps should be taken to have this knowledge brought prominently before all agricultural societies at their annual fairs, by thoroughly competent persons. This would tend not only to benefit vastly those now engaged in agricultural pursuits, but to familiarize the people with the advantages to be derived from a pursuit of the studies of that course. We are gratified to learn that the defect that we have noticed has been at your present session a subject for action, and that steps have been taken to secure a competent person, one of whose principal duties will be to bring the agricultural interests of the State into closer relations with this department and its benefits. The only recommendation that we can offer is that this work be done thoroughly.

University of Wisconsin.

One matter observed during our visit has so engrossed us that we could not refrain from mentioning it here, although perhaps outside the province of this report; that is, the very valuable work being done by the lady who fills the position of library attendant. The library, though not as large as it should be, is yet something of a wilderness to the student who consults it for light on most any subject. The attendant, we are informed, spends her time in digesting the contents of the books, arranging the matter in permanent form for reference, so that the student can be referred to any and everything in the library upon any topic that he may be investigating. Such a work, if properly prosecuted to completion, would be invaluable, and should, as it undoubtedly does, receive proper recognition and encouragement at your hands.

As our visits have been made by us severally, and not jointly, and there has been no meeting until this time for any interchange of views, it naturally transpires that many things have been observed by one member, not seen or noticed by others. In regard to such matters, as no opportunity remains for further investigation, it is impracticable to present our views as a Board. Trusting that the difficulties under which we have labored may be avoided by our successors, we will not attempt further comment, but join with our predecessors in congratulating your honorable body and the people of the State upon the flourishing condition of the University, and the excellent facilities afforded by it to our youth for obtaining a thorough education.

SAM'L D. HASTINGS,
ROBERT GRAHAM,
S. S. ALLEN,
JOHN BRINDLEY.

MADISON, June 23, 1880.

The Normal Schools.

THE NORMAL SCHOOLS.

BOARD OF REGENTS.

GOVERNOR WILLIAM E. SMITH,

STATE SUPERINTENDENT WILLIAM C. WHITFORD,

Ex OFFICIO REGENTS.

Term expires first Monday in February, 1881.

J. H. EVANS,	PLATTEVILLE.
C. DOERFLINGER,	MILWAUKEE.
A. O. WRIGHT,	MADISON.

Term expires first Monday in February, 1882.

S. M. HAY,	OSHKOSH.
JAMES MacALISTER,	MILWAUKEE.
J. PHILLIPS,	STEVENS POINT.

Term expires first Monday in February, 1883.

W. H. CHANDLER,	SUN PRAIRIE.
A. D. ANDREWS,	RIVER FALLS.
T. D. WEEKS,	WHITEWATER.

The Normal Schools.

OFFICERS OF THE BOARD.

PRESIDENT,
J. H. EVANS.

VICE PRESIDENT,
JAMES MacALISTER.

SECRETARY,
W. H. CHANDLER.

TREASURER, EX OFFICIO,
RICHARD GUENTHER.

COMMITTEES OF THE BOARD.

EXECUTIVE,

| J. H. EVANS, | W. H. CHANDLER, | T. D. WEEKS. |

FINANCE,

| S. M. HAY, | J. PHILLIPS, | C. DOERFLINGER. |

EMPLOYMENT OF TEACHERS,

| W. H. CHANDLER, | W. C. WHITFORD, | J. MacALISTER. |

INSTITUTES,

| W. C. WHITFORD, | W. H. CHANDLER, | W. E. SMITH. |

SUPPLIES,

| T. D. WEEKS, | A. D. ANDREWS, | S. M. HAY, | J. H. EVANS. |

EXAMINATION OF GRADUATING CLASSES,

| J. MacALISTER, | W. H. CHANDLER, | W. C. WHITFORD. |

COURSE OF STUDY AND TEXT-BOOKS,

| A. O. WRIGHT, | C. DOERFLINGER, | W. E. SMITH. |

INSPECTION OF SCHOOLS AND BUILDINGS,

| A. D. ANDREWS, | S. M. HAY, | A. O. WRIGHT, | J. H. EVANS. |

The Normal Schools.

EXTRACTS FROM THE REPORT

OF THE

PRESIDENT OF THE BOARD.

To His Excellency, WM. E. SMITH,
Governor of Wisconsin:

SIR — In compliance with the requirements of law, I have the honor to submit the annual report of the Board of Regents of Normal Schools for the year ending August 31, 1880, including statements and exhibits of the Productive Fund, the Income Fund, receipts and expenditures at each of the four Normal Schools, expenditures for teachers' institutes, reports of the presidents of the schools, and such other information concerning the condition and work of the schools under the charge of the Board, as may be deemed of public interest.

THE BOARD.

There were no changes in the *personnel* of the Board during the year. Special sessions were held at Madison, in the office of the State Superintendent of Public Instruction, on September 23–24, 1879, February 24–26, June 29 to July 1, the annual session July 14–15, 1880. At these meetings the ordinary routine work of the Board was transacted, abstracts of which have been published.

THE SCHOOLS.

The Normal School problem involves, in each country and to some extent in each locality, peculiar conditions which must not be ignored in its solution. In the old world with its established system of apprenticeship to the work of teaching, the conditions of the Normal problem are very different from those found in this

The Normal Schools.

country. In the eastern portion of our own land, too, with its excellent and well-supported academies and colleges, Normal Schools
can do a kind of work for which there is only a very limited demand in this newer West of ours. That the Normal Schools of
Wisconsin have thus far done work for which there has been demand, and have fulfilled the expectations of their projectors in the
matter of attendance, is evident from the fact that two of the
buildings have been very considerably enlarged to accommodate
increasing numbers, and the growing demand for professional
work; and that a third is about to be enlarged for similar reasons.
Again, the demand for a product may safely be taken as an index
of the estimate put upon it. From this stand-point, there are
grounds for believing that these schools adapt their management
and instruction to the wants of the people. Their students are in
demand throughout the West, and are meeting with commendable
success.

The management of the schools is, in its character, progressive.
Gradually the professional element is assuming more prominence,
and the academic element given a place in which it can be used in
the interests of the professional. Each year a perceptible advance
is made in the amount of time given to the study of Methods of
Teaching and the Philosophy of Education, and in the interest
manifested in these studies. It is the settled policy of the Board
to make as rapid progress in this direction as may be justified by
circumstances. They consider it a pleasure and a duty to give
every encouragement and official aid in perfecting appliances for
the furtherance of professional training.

Any school or system of schools may be aided by a skillful use of
what may be called its traditions. Each class strives to excel its
predecessors in that feature which is characteristic of the school,
and through this striving comes progress. The traditions of our
Normal School system are not yet numerous, nor are they of sufficient age to command veneration; yet each school is even now
beginning to feel the stimulus which comes to it from the acknowledged success of those who attribute their attainments to its
influence. Such traditions differ only in age from those that are,

The Normal Schools.

at the same time, the best advertisements and the most valued possessions of old and celebrated institutions of learning.

TRAINING DEPARTMENT.

Practice teaching is considered an important feature of our schools, and is believed to be in a very satisfactory condition. The management of this part of training is substantially the same in all the schools. The Director of the Training School has special charge of this work. He directs the preparation, supervises the teaching, and criticises the work. The plan of the lesson must meet his approval before the teacher goes before his class. Every possible precaution is taken to avoid mistakes in facts or failures in methods. The teacher is held responsible for the management and instruction of the class, and is helped in his efforts to strengthen himself in points in which he shows weakness. Persons unacquainted with this work, naturally entertain the idea that practice teaching in our Normal Schools, must be crude, inaccurate, and largely experimental; that it must be much inferior to the work of paid and mature teachers. A statement of the conditions under which the teaching is done, ought to be sufficient to dispel this notion. Besides, it must be remembered that many of these pupil teachers have taught school before entering upon the normal course; that all are required to study school economy before being assigned to do practice work; that they had been members of the school for at least one year; and that, when they entered the school, they had sufficient scholarship to entitle them to a third grade certificate from a county superintendent. These pupils are in demand as teachers; they take charge of our district schools, where they do acceptable work without supervision. In the Normal School, with its aids in special preparation and its close supervision, the work done by practice teachers is of a very creditable character. The Board commends the efforts of our schools toward perfecting this important feature of a Normal education; and they have reason to believe that the advantages afforded will be so highly appreciated, and so well improved, that hereafter " to

The Normal Schools.

present a candidate for graduation is to vouch for his professional skill."

The future promises an improvement on the past. With increased accommodations and appliances; with a growing confidence in the ability of the Normal Schools to give such training as can be utilized in our common schools; with a settled policy on the part of the Regents to make them more and more professional in character; and with a continuance of the cordial co-operation always manifested by the teachers in charge of the Normal Schools in carrying out this policy, there is reason to expect that the work of the coming year will be instrumental in increasing the interest in these schools, and in still further strengthening their hold upon the hearts of the people.

ENROLLMENT.

The following table shows the total enrollment of pupils attending the four schools during the past year:

	Normal.	Preparatory.	Grammar.	Intermediate.	Primary.	Kindergarten.	Total.
Platteville	219	......	137	42	48	......	446
Whitewater	279	......	96	48	26	......	449
Oshkosh........	332	71	109	39	38	25	614
River Falls	128	55	71	57	60	......	371
Totals	958	126	413	186	172	25	1,880

Being an increase of 77 over the preceding year. Every county in the State, excepting seven, viz.: Adams, Ashland, Bayfield, Burnett, Langlade, Price, and Vernon, was represented in the Normal Departments of our schools during the year.

Students resident in the State, sixteen years of age, and complying with the regulations for admission, receive instruction free.

The Normal Schools.

Those who cannot fulfill these requirements are classified in the preparatory or model schools, and are charged tuition as follows:

Preparatory and Grammar Grades .... 40 cts. per week
Intermediate Grade .... 25 cts. per week
Primary Grade... 20 cts. per week

The amount of tuition collected at the several schools during the year was:

Plattevi'le.. $2,273 20
Whitewater 1,781 50
Oshkosh 2,722 90
River Falls... 2,111 60

    Total......... .... $8,880 20

The aggregate salaries paid the instructional force of the Preparatory and Model grades of the schools for the year, were as follows:

Platteville.. $2,850 00
Whitewater* 2,800 00
Oshkosh† 3,050 00
River Falls... 2,050 00

    Total. $10,750 00

By this statement it will be seen that the cost of instruction in the Preparatory and Model schools, exceeds the sum received for tuition by $1,868.80.

GRADUATES.

The number of students completing the prescribed courses of study at the several schools during the year, is as follows:

ELEMENTARY COURSE.

Platteville 9
Whitewater.. 23
Oshkosh 29
River Falls........ 5

    Number certificated.................................. 65

* Deducting half salary of principal of Academic department for work done in Normal department.
† Not including Kindergarten.

The Normal Schools.

ADVANCED COURSE.

Platteville...........	1
Whitewater	5
Oshkosh.......	5
River Falls............................	2
Number graduated...........	13

TEACHERS' INSTITUTES.

At the last annual meeting of the Board, the Committee on Institutes reported in full the work performed the past year, under their special supervision. It appears that during the four months beginning with August, 1879, fifty-one institutes were held in forty-nine counties and superintendent districts. This is a larger number than is usually organized at that season of the year, and was necessitated mainly by the few institutes held the previous spring. Three-fourths of the fifty-one were appointed, at the request of county superintendents, for August and the first week in September; this fact compelled the employment of an unusually large number of assistant conductors,— forty-two in all. These were selected from the leading teachers of the State, who had acquired skill in the charge of institutes. Besides aiding the four regular conductors in a portion of their institutes, they gave the entire instruction in thirty others. This arrangement required the expenditure of more funds than is usual in the series of summer and fall institutes. Last spring, the committee provided for only eleven institutes in the same number of counties. These were instructed by the regular institute conductors.

The sixty-two institutes of the past year were in session one hundred and four weeks,— one for four weeks, thirty-nine each for two weeks, and twenty-two each for one week, being four more than were held the preceding year, with eight weeks more time. There was a slight decrease in the number conducted each one week, and an increase in those conducted each two weeks.

The attendance in all the institutes was:

Males...	1,335
Females...	3,630
Total....... .... ,................. ...	4,965

The Normal Schools.

This is a gain of 542 over the enrollment of the preceding year. In the counties where the institutes were held, 5,718 teachers are required to teach the public schools — in number only 753 more than the enrollment of the institutes, a conclusive proof that a very large percentage of the teachers of the State avail themselves of the privileges afforded by this branch of Normal instruction.

The annual report of the State Superintendent presents the statistics in many items which are omitted in this statement. It furnishes the names of places where institutes were held in the different counties; the time of the opening and duration of each institute; and the names of the regular or assistant conductors in charge of each institute. It shows the number of the attendants who hold the different grades of certificates granted by the county superintendents; the average experience in months of teaching of those who have taught; the number of persons not having taught, but intending to teach; the number having previously attended institutes; and the number having attended schools of different grades.

The following statement shows the condition of the fund set apart for the support of teachers' institutes, including an exhibit of the expenditures for the present year:

RECEIPTS.

Appropriation by the State.....................	$2,000 00
Appropriation by the Board of Regents.....................	5,000 00
	$7,000 00

EXPENDITURES.

Salaries of conductors.................	$4,260 50
Expenses of conductors.......	2,242 31
Incidental expenses and for lectures	707 23
	$7,210 04

Of this amount, $9.00 were paid for a bill incurred during the preceding year. The appropriation for the ensuing year was anticipated to the amount of $201.04, in printing for the next series of institutes, making the net amount expended for the past year just the sum appropriated, viz., $7,000.

The Normal Schools.

The outline of studies taught during the summer and fall of 1879, embraced the third and final part of a course of instruction which extended over a period of three years. This outline was published in pamphlet form, and was furnished to the conductors and county superintendents in sufficient number to supply the members of all the institutes.

At a joint meeting of the Institute Committee and the regular conductors, held in January last, a general programme of instruction for the next three years was adopted. The work for this year, embracing the institutes of the spring and fall, was confined very largely to primary teaching in our public schools. This scheme, as far as it has been tested, is very satisfactory. It is based on the idea that this grade of teaching in the State is greatly in need of radical improvement. The outline of the studies for this year was printed last spring and distributed among the institutes then held.

The Institute Committee and Institute Conductors held a meeting in Madison in July last, during the yearly session of the State Teachers' Association. This meeting was attended not only by members of the committee and by the conductors, but by many other leading teachers of the State. The exercises consisted of the careful discussion of the subjects to be taught this year in our institutes. Much interest was added to the occasion by the exercises in primary work, presented by a class of pupils from the Model department of the Platteville Normal School. The instruction here given was enjoyed by all in attendance; and, without doubt, materially aided those who conducted the series of institutes held immediately subsequent to this meeting.

The institute work is steadily growing in favor throughout the State. Its usefulness is more apparent with each succeeding year. Its effect upon the teaching in our common schools was never more visible than during the past year. To focus the instruction, for one year, of at least twenty-five trained conductors, and the minds of thousands of teachers in our public schools, upon the most elementary subjects taught to our pupils, is an achievement which must speedily result in great good to these schools.

The Normal Schools.

KINDERGARTEN.

After much deliberation and discussion of the principles, objects, and practices of the kindergarten, the Board of Regents, at their meeting held in February last, determined to establish a kindergarten in one of the Normal Schools, as a model for observation and practice; and thereby make the philosophy of the kindergarten system a more prominent feature of instruction in the Normal departments of our schools.

The arguments presented against the practicability of making use of the kindergarten in public school work, were carefully considered; and the fact that the subject was discussed for several years, shows that the conclusion of the Board was not a hasty one, when, in May last, they opened at the Oshkosh school the first kindergarten officially and directly connected with any State Normal School in the United States.

The Board realize that it was a " new departure," but one that they confidently hope will be received with warm approval by the people of the State; as it has been by prominent and active educators forming the " State Teachers' Association," and by many members of the press throughout Wisconsin.

It may not be out of place to sketch the main features of the Froebel Kindergarten, and the reason for its introduction into our Normal School System.

Kindergarten culture is designed to correct many of the faults of our common schools, where knowledge is generally imparted in a concentrated form by teachers and text-books; where the child is crammed with the greatest possible amount of what might be termed positive knowledge in the least possible time, in many instances to the detriment of his healthy development. Kindergarten work will develop healthfully and harmoniously all the faculties of the child; it treats the child as an organism that needs but to have its surroundings brought into harmony with its nature, to grow into beauty and usefulness. It does not *drive*, but *leads*. The restless disposition of a child, so trying to the parent and teacher, and so often forcibly repressed, is made useful, and a source of happiness

10 — ST. SUP.

The Normal Schools.

and pleasure to the true kindergartener.   The methods and discipline ordinarily pursued in our common schools have a tendency to dwarf the physical development of a child; the kindergarten cultivates the same by frequent changes, and a wise combination of exercises of body and mind.   While the school often overtaxes memory, and imposes upon the young child intellectual work that does not properly belong to it, the kindergarten seeks to create the most favorable conditions for the natural development of his perceptive, reasoning, inventive, and formative faculties, using all opportunities and taking time to instil into the child's mind pure moral sentiments and good social qualities, too often overlooked in schools where the race for individual standing is the one absorbing idea.   An important feature is the loving, motherly supervision which the child receives in the kindergarten, and which forms the natural connecting link between home and school.   The mental and practical possibilities of the child, when his powers are cultivated and developed by the seeming play of the kindergarten without over-exertion of mind or body, are wonderful.   Prominent educators, speaking from experience and observation, inform us that children having the advantages of kindergarten culture learn more rapidly in their advanced school work; these children are keen observers, their powers of analysis and synthesis have been trained naturally and systematically in early childhood; they desire useful employment, because this employment has been to them a source of pleasure.

Kindergartening in the common schools of our State may not be an accomplished fact for many years to come, but the Board of Regents have thought it wise to give our Normal pupils a theoretical and practical knowledge of its principles, aims, methods, and apparatus, in order that they may be able to apply those methods and principles in their future school work, as far as circumstances will permit.   If our students are to be missionaries for higher views of the objects of education, they should certainly be made acquainted with all the educational systems and methods deserving consideration.   Among these systems none has received more earnest attention at the hands of prominent educators than Froebel's system of kindergartening.

The Normal Schools.

LIBRARIES.

All text-books used in Normal Schools· are purchased by the Board from the publishers at wholesale rates, and furnished pupils at a rental not exceeding three dollars per year, or sold to them at actual cost, if preferred. By this plan, the pupil is furnished the necessary books for pursuing a course covering a wide range of studies at much less expense than if compelled to purchase at ordinary retail rates. The income derived from rentals and sales of text-books, is sufficient to keep the text-book libraries replenished, pay the salaries of the librarians, and make substantial additions to the reference libraries, books from which are used by pupils without charge. Below will be found a statement of receipts from rents and sales of text-books, and of expenditures for the purchase of text and reference books, and salaries of librarians, for the year 1879–80:

RECEIPTS.

Platteville, book rents and sales.......	$996 00	
Whitewater, " " " "	968 34	
Oshkosh, " " " "	1,038 52	
River Falls, " " " "	624 20	
		$3,627 06

DISBURSEMENTS.

	Text.	Reference.	Librarian salaries.	
Platteville	$396 29	$165 47	....	
Whitewater..............	644 58	74 60	$100 00	
Oshkosh.................	277 37	39 07	100 00	
River Falls.........	515 85	74 65	100 00	
	$1,834 09	$353 79	$300 00	$2,687 88
Balance to income fund.................................				$939 18

BUILDINGS AND GROUNDS.

During the year, the Executive and Visiting Committees have made careful inspection of the grounds, buildings, and other property belonging to the schools, and report the same in good condition, with few exceptions.

Substantial improvements were made at Whitewater, by laying

The Normal Schools.

a new hard wood floor in the assembly room, and re-furnishing the same with single desks; also, making some changes of partitions, needed to facilitate the work of the Normal department.

Plans were submitted by the Executive Committee, and adopted by the Board, for the erection of an addition to the Platteville building, with a proviso that the addition, including heating apparatus, should not cost to exceed ten thousand dollars. The contract for the erection of the building was let to Messrs. Nye, Traber & Co., for $9,297.84. This addition will make the Platteville building about the same in size as those at Whitewater and Oshkosh. It will be 45 by 65 feet, with basement and two stories, and will include an entrance hall and stairway, one school room, six recitation rooms, and the necessary cloak rooms; thus affording ample and much needed accommodations for the growing wants of this school.

An appropriation of one thousand dollars was ordered for the purpose of improving the grounds surrounding the school buildings; said sum to be expended under the direction of the Executive Committee, who were authorized to employ a competent landscape gardener to furnish a plan for each school.

TABULATED STATEMENT — RECEIPTS AND EXPENDITURES.

The following tables show the amount disbursed and received at each Normal School, during the school year 1879–80, and the purpose of each disbursement and the source of receipts:

EXPENDITURES.

	Salaries.	Text-Books	Reference Books.	Stationery.
Oshkosh	$15,840 25	$277 37	$39 07	$130 38
Whitewater	15,788 75	644 58	74 60	126 85
Platteville	14,600 00	396 29	165 47	159 19
River Falls	11,640 00	515 85	74 65	123 87
Total	$57,869 00	$1,834 09	$353 79	$540 29

The Normal Schools.

EXPENDITURES — continued.

	Fuel and light.	Furniture.	Repairs.	Building.
Oshkosh......................	$755 75	$371 67	$869 72	$171 75
Whitewater..................	995 32	44 77	612 56	20 00
Platteville	498 69	245 10	623 88	....
River Falls	658 80	51 85	8,975 72	3 00
	$2,908 56	$713 39	$6,081 88	$194 75

EXPENDITURES — continued.

	Printing.	Cabinet and apparatus.	Miscellaneous.	Totals.
Oshkosh.	$179 45	$144 41	$698 27	$19,478 09
Whitewater...............	157 40	374 56	101 60	18,940 99
Platteville	172 35	110 39	103 87	17,075 23
River Falls	282 15	208 80	986 33	18,521 02
	$761 35	$838 16	$1,890 07	$74,015 33

RECEIPTS.

	Tuition.	Book rents.	Book sales.	Other sources.	Totals.
Oshkosh.......	$2,722 90	$755 45	$283 07	....	$3,761 42
Whitewater....	1,781 50	851 40	117 34	$152 14	2,902 38
Platteville	2,273 20	746 20	149 80	3 80	3,173 00
River Falls	2,111 60	486 35	137 85	....	2,735 80
Totals.....	$8,889 20	$2,839 40	$687 06	$155 94	$12,572 60

The Normal Schools.

SUMMARY.

The summary shows the aggregate expenses by the Board the past year at the several schools, the expenses for Institutes, Regents' expenses, salary of Secretary, printing, and incidentals:

Disbursements at the schools $74,015 33
Disbursements for institutes 7,210 79
Regents' expenses attending meetings of the board 563 42
Services and expenses of committees........................... 1,652 44
Salary of secretary........................ .... 300 00
Printing and incidental expenses 192 55

    Total $83,935 53

Your attention is respectfully called to the accompanying reports of Presidents McGregor, Stearns, Albee, and Parker, for further and special information relating to the condition and work of their respective schools.

Respectfully submitted,

J. H. EVANS,

President of the Board of Regents of Normal Schools.

THE REPORTS

OF THE

PRESIDENTS OF THE NORMAL SCHOOLS.

PLATTEVILLE NORMAL SCHOOL.

PLATTEVILLE, WIS., August 31, 1880.

Hon. J. H. EVANS,
    President Board of Regents of Normal Schools:

SIR — I have the honor to present to you my report upon the condition and progress of the State Normal School, Platteville, for the school year 1879–80.

Since the date of the last annual report, no change has taken place in membership of the Faculty of the school.

STATISTICS.

APPLICANTS.

	District School.	Graded Schools.	Normal Schools.
In what schools prepared	32	62	41
Number having previously taught	24	4	....

Whole number of applicants for admission to Normal Department, 135.

The Normal Schools — Platteville.

EXAMINATIONS.

	FALL TERM.		WINTER TERM.		SPRING TERM.	
	Gents.	Ladi's	Gents.	Ladi's	Gents.	Ladi's
Number examined	26	60	24	21	25	31
Number admitted to first year	11	29	6	3	3	1
Number admitted to preparatory class	3	12	3	3	......	......

TOTAL ENROLLMENT BY CLASSES.

	Months of membership.	Average age.	Number of pupils.
Normal Department, fourth year	24.	6.25	1
third year	26.3	7.7	18
second year...................	20.	7.75	31
first year	19.	7.1	144
Model Department, Grammar grade................	17.3	5.55	160
Intermediate grade	11.42	7.	43
Primary grade.................	7.5	7.02	47

Entire enrollment in Normal Department:
  Fall term —
    Gents 62
    Ladies 100
  Winter term —
    Gents 66
    Ladies 101
  Spring term —
    Gents 49
    Ladies 88

Number of different students enrolled in Normal Department:
  Gents 89
  Ladies 130

    Total.. 219

Enrolled in Training Department:
  Boys 129
  Girls 122

    Total... 251

The Normal Schools — Platteville.

Number enrolled since organization of Normal Department:
Gents 574
Ladies 684

Total.. 1,258

Number in Training Department since organization of school:
Gents 1,036
Ladies 959

Total.. 1,995

Total number of graduates, by sexes:
In elementary course —
  Gents 35
  Ladies 45

  Total.. 80

In advanced course —
  Gents 62
  Ladies 58

  Total.. 120

Twice counted fourteen ladies and fourteen gentlemen who completed both courses, giving 172 as the number of different persons who have graduated. Of this number there were, during the past year, connected with schools as teachers, superintendents, and students, 123; ladies, married and not teaching, 19; deceased, 21; not in active employment, 5.

It is impossible to ascertain the exact number who have taught after leaving school, but it is known to be over ninety per cent. of the enrollment. In addition to this, many of those who were classified in the Grammar grade taught after leaving school.

Whole number of students who have practiced during the year, 67. Number of weeks of practice teaching, 678, or an average of ten weeks and nearly one day for each student.

Two students, James Adams, of Argyle, La Fayette county, and J. Frank Smith, of Werley, Grant county, completed the full course of study, but chose to have their graduation deferred until 1881. The Elementary course was completed by nine students — seven ladies and two gentlemen,— to each of whom the proper certificate was issued.

The Normal Schools — Platteville.

RELATION TO THE COMMON SCHOOLS.

It is unquestionably the chief, if not the exclusive, object of our Normal Schools, to elevate the character of our Common Schools. The State has a right to expect, that through the agency of this branch of its school system, the schools of the people shall be improved in every particular to which the influence of Normal Schools may be made to reach. Wisconsin tenders an education to its youth through the medium of its common schools, and, in a measure, compels the acceptance of it whatever may be its character. The conditions existing in many school-districts are such that teaching, satisfactory either to teacher or taught, is impossible. In many cases the remedy is not within the power of any body of teachers, however zealous and well-trained they may be. Still the course of study pursued by Normal pupils makes them acquainted with the subject of School Economy; and, to some extent, qualifies them to suggest and to make such improvements in school appliances as may increase the possibilities of effective work. As teachers increase in professional qualifications, the demand for more comfortable school-houses, more pleasant surroundings, and more suitable appliances, increases. The powerful, though silent, influence upon pupils, of school grounds, furniture, and apparatus, becomes a subject of consideration. Communities are slowly learning that expenditures incurred in improving the condition of their schools is the wisest economy. They naturally look to teachers who profess to have special training for their work, for aid in removing the hinderances to effective teaching that inevitably multiply under the direction of those who are ignorant of the conditions necessary to success. Thus, the Normal School becomes an educational center, from which is disseminated information bearing upon the conditions that make a good school possible.

In addition to exerting their influence in improving the school accommodations, it is also an important object of Normal Schools to give more stability to the professsion of teaching. No school can be in a prosperous condition in which change of teachers is the rule. There is serious waste in connection with a change in any calling, in none is it more serious than in teaching. At every

The Normal Schools — Platteville.

change there is a waste equal to the amount of time needed by the newly installed teacher to learn the condition of the school in general, and the advancement, disposition, and ability of each of the pupils. Most of this knowledge is of a kind that cannot be communicated by others, but must come by actual intercourse with the school. Therefore, the loss is distributed through a less or greater time, according to the experience of the teacher and his familiarity with human nature as manifested in youth. It follows that the school that has been for a term of years in charge of a teacher of even moderate ability, is in better condition than it would have been, had several equally good teachers been, in time, employed. Of course, it is admitted that changes are frequently profitably made, but where change rather than permanence is the rule, the district suffers in its most vital interests; hence the prosperity of a school demands that a change of teachers shall be made only when it is imperative, or when it promises a very positive advantage. The reasons for making changes are various, the general effects of change are constant and injurious.

We have no means of showing conclusively that teachers who have attended Normal schools are less likely to change than others are, or that communities are less willing to have them change, yet a comparison of graduates' registers of this school for any two consecutive years, shows that changes seldom exceed ten per cent. of the number teaching. In the case of undergraduates, the rate is doubtless much greater. But if Normal schools cannot, to any considerable extent, diminish the number of changes, they can very materially diminish the waste now incurred by the change. As our communities are constituted, probably there will be instability in the teacher's calling hereafter as heretofore. Circumstances, such as short terms of school, with long intervals between, inadequate pay, small districts, etc., are directly opposed to stability or permanence. We must therefore accept the conditions, and devise means for making the loss as light as possible. Granting the changes will be frequent, there is only one way left by which the injurious results incident to these may, to a reasonable extent, be neutralized; and that is by taking the work of teaching out of the

The Normal Schools — Platteville.

realm of imitation or mere chance, and putting it upon a basis of correct principles.   Normal school training is based upon very similar principles wherever found, and in a system of schools under the same mananagement there can be but little variety.   These institutions give a uniformity to method, which cannot be reached by any class of schools not giving special attention to that department of professional training.

When a change is made, the teacher trained in methods of teaching as his predecessor was, can take up the work with little loss of time.   In this way, there is a great diminution of the waste incident to the employment of teachers untrained in the principles of teaching.   At present the great majority of teachers in our district schools have no special training for their work, except what they receive in attendance upon teachers' institutes for a few days each year.   They teach largely, as a matter of course, by imitating the manner of some other teacher, and know next to nothing of method or the principles upon which it is based.   Imitating and experimenting may lead to success, but to a success purchased too frequently at the expense of the school.   It is not at all strange that there is an enormous waste in schools taught by untrained teachers. It is clearly the work of Normal Schools to effect a change in this particular.   Let these schools reach by their influence the schools of the people, so as to systematize the work done in them, so as to give a degree of uniformity to the teaching; and they will, by this one thing alone, establish their right to be considered indispensable to the success of our common schools.   In all the professional training of this school, the condition, the wants, and the possibilities of our common schools are kept in view, and the instruction shaped to meet their requirements.

During the year, practice teaching has been made as prominent a feature of the school as was possible with existing accommodations.   Students are not only willing, but anxious to engage in this work.   The amount of practice teaching has reached what seems to be the maximum, without impairing the quality of the work done.   The very limited number of recitation rooms connected with the training departments, renders it impossible to reduce the

The Normal Schools — Platteville.

membership of classes to what seems just either to the teacher or pupil. However, improvements in the building, recently ordered by the Board of Regents, and already in progress, encourage the hope that hereafter it may be possible to subdivide classes, so as to give to Normal students that amount of practice teaching to which they are entitled, and yet leave a large part of the teaching to be done by the employed instructors. This most important feature of Normal School training should be encouraged by every means possible; and the facilities for carrying it on, increased and improved.

Each member of the Normal Department has been encouraged to observe the work done in the training school, and required to make a full report of the same in writing. Two classes have been formed each term for the purpose of observing, each class numbering from twenty to forty members, and continuing through a term of six weeks. It is believed that this phase of professional training compares favorably in value with other exercises considered indispensable to the success of Normal Schools.

The training department is always open for observation to teachers who are not members of the school. Such persons are cordially welcomed, and every opportunity afforded for observing in such departments of the school as they may prefer. Many have availed themselves of this privilege, spending considerable time in observing the lines of work in which they had special interest.

Since the date of my last annual report, three additional recitation rooms have been provided for the use of the Normal Department, thus enabling each teacher to have exclusive use of a room. The heating and ventilating apparatus in a considerable portion of the building, has been renewed and re-arranged, and is now in a tolerably satisfactory condition. With the changes now in progress, and the improvements to be completed before the close of the ensuing school year, the accommodations of the school will be greatly increased, and some of the hinderances to the most efficient work removed.   Respectfully submitted,

D. McGREGOR.

WHITEWATER NORMAL SCHOOL.

Hon. J. H. EVANS,

   President of Board of Regents of Normal Schools:

SIR — I have the honor to submit to you the annual report of the State Normal School, at Whitewater, for the year 1879–80.

ENROLLMENT.

The enrollment for the year in the several departments is as follows:

NORMAL DEPARTMENT.

Ladies	191	
Gentlemen	89	
		280

BY CLASSES.

Senior year	5
Junior year	26
Second year	79
First year	144
Preparatory	26

MODEL DEPARTMENT.

Grammar grade	96	
Intermediate	48	
Primary	26	
		170
Total		450

In this statement one person is counted twice, leaving the total of different persons 449.

Examined for admission to Normal Department	117	
Withdrew to teach during the year	59	
Number who graduated during the year		5
Number who certificated in January		13
Number who certificated in June		23
Total from both courses		89

PRACTICE WORK.

There has been a gratifying increase in the attendance upon the intermediate and grammar grades of the Model School, which are

The Normal Schools — Whitewater.

now as large as the rooms permit or the wants of the school require. The extent to which these schools serve as instruments for the training of teachers, is shown by the following statements of the practice work during the year:

Practice teaching in preparatory classes......................... 92 weeks.
Practice teaching in grammar grade .... 131 weeks.
Practice teaching in intermediate grade .... 185 weeks.
Practice teaching in primary grade .... 76 weeks.

    Total... 484 weeks.

Number of persons who have taught 52
Average time of each, in weeks, 484 divided by 52....... .... $9\frac{4}{13}$

To complete the estimate of their practical worth as instruments for the training of teachers, it will be necessary to take into account, also, the fact that they serve as models for the observation of those who have not yet obtained the grade in the school which entitles them to commence teaching. The value of the observation and practice work to Normal students can only be fully appreciated by those who have had opportunity to watch their effects. Teaching is an art, and therefore it cannot be acquired by the study of principles alone. Skill in discerning what is needed in each case, and tact in the application of principles to the varying conditions of school work, can be acquired only by direct contact with classes, and can be acquired most rapidly and successfully under the guidance and criticism of one who has had experience, and is skillful in pointing out errors and suggesting improvements. In this most important particular, and in the careful preparation of the student for his work before he is allowed to take it up, the practice work of the Normal School differs most widely from the "experience" which young people get by keeping school. The latter may confirm them in wrong ways only, while the former carefully fashions them to right ones. In its practice work the Normal School recognizes fully that "the material is too noble" for crude and undirected experimentation.

The chief defect of practice work, it has been often said, is that it does not afford, and from the nature of the case cannot often afford, practice in school management. This is, I am convinced, more an apparent than a real defect. He who learns to conduct a class, not mechanically and by inspiring fear, but by calling out, guiding, and controlling the activities of the children to happy, orderly, and profitable exercise, has discovered the secrets of good management, and needs to learn only the general principles of school organization, and to have been a member of a properly managed school, to be as well prepared to enter upon his profession as can be reasonably demanded.

THE NORMAL SCHOOL AND THE PROFESSION.

To elevate teaching into the rank of a profession, into which persons enter with a view to making it a life work, was one of the aims of those who were most instrumental in the establishment of Normal Schools. That substantial progress has been made in this work, is evident. There are causes, some temporary and others permanent in their operation, which tend to bring about more changes in this profession than in others. The very large number of schools which employ a teacher for only a few months in a year, makes it necessary that there should be a large body of persons temporarily or practically attached to the profession, who teach school only as a make-shift until something better offers, or to eke out other inadequate means of support. To diminish the number and provide for the better management of these schools, in which occurs the greatest waste at present existing in our educational system, is one of the most important problems now demanding attention. But, besides this, it is unfortunately true that, even in schools whose terms are of longer duration, the teachers' tenure is needlessly uncertain, so that a large number regularly spend the summer vacation in school hunting. They are made to feel that their place is held only from year to year; and, being anxious to obtain a permanent settlement, many seek it by taking up some other pursuit. Moreover, the notion that any one who can read, write, and cipher can keep school, though steadily losing ground, has by no means disappeared; and while it lasts, there must be a large body of persons who teach without being teachers, hangers-on to the skirts of the profession, until something better offers. Among the per-

The Normal Schools — Whitewater.

manent causes of change, may be mentioned the larger number of women employed in this profession than in all others together, to whom marriage means an end of professional labors.

It has been expected that Normal Schools would do something to counteract all these tendencies; that they would not only elevate the popular ideal of school-teaching, but, attracting to themselves the more earnest and ambitious persons who wish to teach, would prepare them properly for their work, and bind them to it as a profession, to be followed for life. Statistics show that the school has done this. Last winter I addressed a circular to the graduates, licentiates, and many former pupils, asking particulars with regard to their work since leaving the school. Of the sixty-two persons who replied to the circular, but nine are not teaching, and forty have taught ever since graduating. I find from the returns that three have taught upwards of one hundred months; five others, upwards of ninety months; seven more, upwards of eighty; and fourteen of the remainder, between fifty and eighty. The following table shows, as far as they are known, the occupations of all the graduates of the school during the past year:

Teaching	68
Lawyer	1
Minister	1
Physician	1
Students (college)	4
Editor	1
Unknown	3
Deceased	1
Married (ladies)	14
Total	94

It will be seen that the number who have entered other professions is very small. Among the licentiates a similar statement of occupations for the year past shows results equally satisfactory:

Teaching	66
Students	16
Farmers	2
Lawyer	1
Clerk	1
Married ladies	6
Unknown	7
Total	99

The Normal Schools — Whitewater.

Of the sixty-four who answered the circular, all but seven are teaching, and twelve have taught forty months and upwards.

The same circular was sent to those who had been at the school between the years 1877 and 1879, but had not graduated nor taken the certificate. Of these, one hundred and seven answered; all but nine have taught since attending the Normal School, and eighty-six are teachers or expect to teach during the present year. As stated in former reports, it is through these students, and those who teach while pursuing their studies, that the Normal School most directly influences the ungraded schools. Every year's experience serves to strengthen my conviction of the necessity of doing the utmost possible for the professional instruction of these students who remain so short a time in the school.

RELATION TO THE SCHOOLS.

From these statements, it will be seen that the Normal School is represented in the schools of the State by students in all stages of progress, from those who have spent only a few weeks in the school, to those who have completed the full course. Doubtless, some misunderstandings and some misrepresentations result from this state of things; but it is a necessary consequence of the present stage of educational progress, in which the public is being educated to recognize the need of a professional standard, and the way prepared for the establishment of one. Meantime, it is evident that the worth or influence of the Normal School cannot be estimated by counting up the number of its pupils, or reckoning the length of their time of service. It ought to be a center from which new ideas are disseminated among the schools of the State. It ought to reach and influence far more teachers than ever enter its classes, because right methods of procedure recommend themselves to right-minded persons, and need only to be seen and understood in order to influence their ideals and endeavors. The thought of the time has dealt as fruitfully and transformingly with education as it has with science and philosophy. It has not only labored to build up a body of educational doctrine, but has striven to bring practice into accord with it. One who wishes to realize how great the progress

The Normal Schools — Whitewater.

is, has only to compare a well-conducted primary school of one of our large cities with work of the same grade in the less progressive district schools. In the one, he will see skillful and constantly varying adaptations to the needs of the children, so that not only is the management of the school suited to their physical condition, but the methods and matter of instruction keep the child happily and eagerly active; in the other, he will see routine, mechanical methods, dullness, and indifference or aversion. It has become established to the satisfaction of all who are capable of judging in the matter that, at least in the primary school, teaching is an *art*, which requires, in addition to natural aptitudes, some knowledge of the mind to be worked upon, and of the best means of working upon it. If it is impossible for a school to make good teachers of all who come to its halls, it is at least equally impossible for those who have the most tact and good sense to divine all, or even the greater part of the best modes of procedure, which have been wrought out by the experience and thought of many. A comparison of the hard, dry, and barren teaching of English grammar, still generally prevalent in the schools, with the progressive, interesting, and practical language lessons which are beginning to precede, and in some degree supersede, the grammar, will be equally instructive.

THE ADVANCED COURSE.

It has been well said, "All teaching need not be deep, but all teaching should be founded upon depth." Other things being equal, the wider a teacher's culture, the more valuable will his services be to those who come under his instruction. The narrowness of the teacher, whose acquirements do not reach beyond what he teaches, leaves his pupils unstimulated and their acquisitions consequently barren. He should be able to give a wide significance to what they learn, to make each step in advance bring with it a new horizon inviting them on, so that their minds will be always eager for more knowledge and higher skill. "How," exclaims Carlyle, "How can an inanimate, mechanical verb-grinder foster the growth of *anything*, much more of mind, which grows, not like a

The Normal Schools — Whitewater.

vegetable, by having its roots littered by etymological compost, but, like a spirit, by mysterious contact with spirit-thought kindling itself at the fire of living thought. How shall he give kindling in whose inner man there is no live coal, but is burned out to a dead grammatical cinder? How, indeed, shall he give kindling whose inner fire is not kept alive by a constant supply of fuel?" Those who wish to teach come to the Normal School to learn what is necessary for the successful pursuit of their profession. Unless this school is prepared to admit only those who have such attainments as every common school teacher ought to possess, except professional training, I do not see how it can properly neglect the duty of giving instruction up to the grade required. Although comparatively few, at present, take the full course, the tone and character of the school is largely affected by it, and would be materially lowered by any shortening of it.. While I realize fully the desirability of emphasizing the importance of the full course, so as to bring larger numbers into it, I doubt the expediency of dropping the certification at the end of two years. Students are drawn to the school by various motives, some to coach for the county examinations, others to get a certificate, who, if these motives were withdrawn, would not come at all; but brought under the influence of the school, their views and purposes expand, and they are carried beyond their original intentions. It seems to me that the difference between graduates and licentiates should be made clearer in the school and out of it, and that the attendance upon the advanced course will increase as this is done.

Respectfully submitted,

J. W. STEARNS.

WHITEWATER, October 5, 1880.

The Normal Schools — Oshkosh.

OSHKOSH NORMAL SCHOOL..

Hon. J. H. EVANS,

President of the Board of Regents of Normal Schools:

DEAR SIR — The report of the work and aims of the Oshkosh Normal School is herewith submitted for consideration:

	FALL TERM.		WINTER TERM.		SPRING TERM.		Total.
	Men.	Wom.	Men.	Wom.	Men.	Wom.	
No. examined for admission..	46	82	40	60	48	54	330
No. admitted to Norm'l course	20	31	19	23	13	13	119
No. admitted to Prep. Class.	17	37	17	23	21	32	147

No. of different applicants during the year................... 247
No. admitted to Normal Course........... 119

WHERE PREPARED.

Of the 119 admitted to the Normal Course,

7 were graduates of High Schools.
27 were prepared in graded schools.
28 were prepared in ungraded schools.
50 were prepared in both graded and ungraded schools.
7 were prepared in other schools.
55 had previously taught.
Average experience in teaching, three terms.

ENROLLMENT BY TERMS.

NORMAL DEPARTMENT.	Men.	Women.	Total.
Number registered..........................	155	248	403
Average membership	99.6	155.7	255.3
Average daily attendance	95.2	151.5	246.7
MODEL DEPARTMENT.			
Grammar Grade.......	48	61	109
Intermediate Grade.....	15	24	39
Primary Grade...........	20	18	38
Kindergarten.............................	14	11	25
Total enrollment......................			614

The Normal Schools — Oshkosh.

CLASS STATISTICS.

NORMAL DEPARTMENT.	Average age.	Terms exp. in teaching.	ENROLLMENT.			Taught during year.
			Men.	Women.	Total.	
Post graduates................	....	....	......	2	....	2
Seniors	25.8	9.4	4	3	7	2
Juniors....................	23	5.3	5	8	13	8
Second year	21.1	2.2	43	72	115	42
First year..	18.6	2.1	86	109	195	102
Preparatory................	....	....	29	49	78	16

Of those enrolled during the year,

     213 had taught an average of 4.2 terms.
     172 taught a term during the year.
     174 will teach during the ensuing term.
     109 are members of the school.
      5 students graduated in the Advance Course.
     29 students received certificates of Elementary Course.

OCCUPATION OF GRADUATES.

     24 students have completed the advanced course.
     87 other students have completed the elementary course.
     18 graduates of the advanced course are teaching.
      2 graduates are superintendents of schools.
      1 graduate is student in college.
      1 lady has never taught.
      2 are in other business.
     65 of the elementary course are teaching.
      1 is superintendent of school.
      7 are in advanced course.
      1 is in State University.
      5 ladies are married.
      4 gentlemen have left the profession.
      2 gentlemen have died.
      2 ladies have ceased teaching on account of failing health.
      1 of the last class is not teaching.

With three exceptions, all students of both courses have taught since graduation, and 90 have taught continually since completing course.

The Normal Schools — Oshkosh.

AMOUNT OF STUDENT TEACHING.

GRADES.	FALL TERM.		WINTER TERM.		SPRING TERM.		TOTAL FOR YEAR.	
	Teachers.	Weeks.	Teachers.	Weeks.	Teachers.	Weeks.	Teachers.	Weeks.
Grammar	24	237	13	110	12	106	49	453
Intermediate	7	52	5	45	5	47	17	144
Primary..............	13	104	10	73	6	43	29	220
Total..........	44	393	28	228	23	196	95	817

SCHOOL ORGANIZATION.

The steady increase of applicants from year to year has been attended with a commensurate improvement in the grade admitted, while the subdivision of the larger classes into *sections* has enabled instruction to become more closely adapted to individual needs. Still there are certain conditions affecting the work unfavorably.

The ideas of those entering the Normal School contain few elements favorable to immediate growth in the essential preparation for good teaching. It is not merely the *lack* of thought incident to early youth, for an inspection of the foregoing table shows a high average age for efficient thought. The student usually has a surplus of distorted ideas, and these constitute the chief obstacles to progress in the early and most important period of his course.

Briefly stated the leading errors are these:

First, that he needs only to increase his technical attainments to become fit to engage in teaching; second, that scholarship consists in a specific knowledge of facts, regardless of their related influence or of the possessor's power to apply them to further acquisition; third, that the teacher needs neither technical nor general knowledge of branches beyond those to be directly taught by him.

The Normal Schools — Oshkosh.

CAUSES.

These views are impressed upon him from several sources.

The perfunctory tasks of his previous school life, limited to few topics, and these usually bounded by the phrases of the ever present and all important (?) text-books, have been graven in his mind as the beginning and end of school work. That the phrasing and retention of terms and facts is the immediate end for which schools are organized and children compelled to attend, he vaguely but unhesitatingly believes.

Second, the minimum legal requirement for teaching embracing so limited a knowledge of a narrow range of topics, is largely responsible for his shrunken ideas; and this misleading test is the embodiment of a wide-spread view that some knowledge of the *instrument* is not merely an essential, but a *sufficient* qualification for this most delicate and complex of all arts.

Thirdly, making due allowance for the foregoing causes, it is a matter of experience that the courses of study in Normal schools, crowded with food inciting to more acquisition, must also bear a share of responsibility for this one-sided and inadequate conception of the equipment essential to good teaching. While there is a real and quite definitely conceived purpose to use the topics in every exercise as a means to the making of each student skillful and intelligent in his dealing with mind, most applicants are so deficient in knowledge, both of the facts and logical relation of topics in the most elementary branches, that more attention is necessarily devoted to securing clear conceptions of the subject-matter, than to an examination of the mode by which the mind most readily grasps and investigates.

Thus at the best, the *child*, in his nature and manifold traits, is a contingency so vaguely future to many students, while the laws of language and mathematics grow so formidably present that the relation of matter and thought in the teacher's problem is but dimly apprehended by many.

Under these conditions must the Normal Schools of the State aid teachers to attain a higher excellence in the most intricate task of the century. Some of the difficulties inhere, and must remain

The Normal Schools — Oshkosh.

inevitable, though not insuperable, obstacles; others can be removed by the slowly eliminating processes of interaction between
teachers, officers, and communities. Yet others are being overcome
in a commendable degree by the unremitting efforts of a few class
teachers who comprehend how far short merely scholarly discipline
comes in the preparation of students for the business of exciting
and directing thought.

REMEDIES.

All the forces at present operating must necessarily occupy gen-
erations in achieving satisfactory results, if unaided by improved
organization of the State system.

What tests shall determine " fitness to teach " have been fixed
by statute, and by law may be modified to meet whatever conditions the best interests of this all-important function of society
may require.

Is it not time that this commonwealth takes another step forward
by prescribing that some definite instruction in school management,
and at least one term's apprenticeship under the best teachers of
respective communities, or in the normal school, shall be had by
the candidate before being licensed for an independent position as
teacher? We have but to examine the requirements in most other
civilized nations to perceive that in this respect we are much behind those whom we aspire to lead.

Secondly, Normal Schools need to emphasize far more than heretofore, the practical, face to face work of student with classes in
the School of Practice. Notwithstanding a decided advance has
been made in this respect during the last five years, both in the
greater amount of supervision given to student teaching and in
the placing of many lower class students in the work instead of
reserving it for members of the senior class; yet even now a comparatively small part of the normal student life is devoted to gaining a systematic acquaintance with this part of his business.

The numerous proofs and unvarying testimony of students as to
the value of this phase of normal work so far as it has been conferred, indicate that its benefits should be reaped by all students
who are sufficiently proficient in elementary branches to undertake

the work; and that a considerably larger part of his course should be devoted to the observation of participation in school management.

It may fairly be questioned whether some class teaching may not profitably and logically precede the more formal work in the "theory" of teaching, thus securing a concrete basis for a better reflection upon the abstract principles of pedagogy.

The partial relief in text-work afforded by the lengthening of time to be devoted to the Elementary Course, will enable us to carry this training for practical skill to more satisfactory results.

If the committee on Senior Classes were to so modify their examination as to include manifest ability in class work with the scholarly tests heretofore employed, it would constitute still another progressive step in behalf of true ideals of the teacher's office.

KINDERGARTEN.

The organization of the Kindergarten grade in the Model Department of this school, during the last term of the year, was the result of much examination and reflection on the part of Normal Regents and leading teachers in the State.

·The strong tendency of teachers, especially those inexperienced and fresh from student work in advanced grade, to rely too exclusively upon the assignment of tasks for solitary study, has been a marked defect in most primary school work. This isolation of the child is particularly marked in the rural, ungraded school, where a multiplicity of exercises affords occasion for great neglect in dealing with the few small children mingled with the numerous classes of older and more clamorous youth.

Usually, the few precious minutes per day given to the "primer class" are nearly wasted, because the teacher has gone through a long course, calculated to lead him to forget his early craving to handle, hear, or look at everything presented for his consideration. He has been used to taking his later gleanings from the broader field at second-hand, and fails to realize the intensely concrete nature of the child's thought-world. It is this wide difference between the needs of the child, and the necessities and habits of the man, that makes much sad waste in school and family.

The Normal Schools — Oshkosh.

The "object-teaching" reaction in vogue during the last generation, has often proved only a re-action, and has not, as it ought, become the universal door-way leading from the play-ground to the independent reflection and investigation of later youth; because it has fallen into the hands of teachers knowing more of the *object* than of the child.

As possessing a strong tendency to correct this vital error, by illustrating *positively* the right attitude of the teacher as a guide and stimulant in the child's development, we value highly this addition of the Kindergarten to our facilities for training teachers. Here, in the hands of a thoughtful and well-trained teacher, all students see the processes of mental and moral training, unobserved by memorized phrasing. No child is encouraged to think he knows more than he has tested, of things knowable. A clear distinction between his knowledge and his beliefs is a marked characteristic of every exercise in the Kindergarten.

But this methodical, eager, clear-headed dealing with facts would be but one step better than the unquestioning attainment and acceptance of statements, so rife in advanced grades, were it not intimately associated with a constant intelligent exercise of the *imagination*.

By idealizing the material, its manifold relations, readily suggested by things known when the train of fact and fancy is fired by a hint from the thoughtful guide, become logically arranged in the child's mind; and an otherwise bald, unfruitful fact is made to teem with possibilities.

These methods of wise development of power to do, to think, and discover are, unfortunately, in this grade, designated by a foreign, yet fairly significant term; and the ordinary mind views it as an *excrescence* instead of the *germ* of all primary method. It cannot be reasonably doubted that the principles upon which Kindergarten processes are founded, are the basis of all skillful mental discipline looking to ultimate symmetrical growth.

Its special excellence as a school of observation lies, first, in the free expression of the child's thoughts and impulses, and the worthy direction given these by the teacher.

This expression guided, instead of represssion under dictated formulas, is to the observer what the analytical outline is to the student or the specimen to the naturalist, the source and center of all just inference. Here the *child* is all, and the means clearly subordinated to the unfolding of his powers.

Secondly, the class of occupations here employed so readily enlist the interest of children that, even when the immediate influence of the teacher is removed, their work does not flag; and the observer gathers many a suggestion by which to meet the ever recurring question of the overworked teacher, "what shall we do with the little ones?"

For these increased facilities, and the thoughtful care that has left no plainly essential appliance unprovided, it shall be our endeavor to make return by a closer study of school processes so far as they furnish and discipline the man.

Respectfully yours,
G. S. ALBEE.

OSHKOSH, WIS., December 6, 1880.

RIVER FALLS NORMAL SCHOOL.

RIVER FALLS, WIS., August 31, 1880.

J. H. EVANS, Esq.,
   President of Board of Regents of Normal Schools:

DEAR SIR — Agreeable to law, I report as follows for the year ending at date:

The work of the school has been prosecuted with sustained interest during the year, and comparatively few discouragements have come to those students whose purpose to study could be assured.

The withdrawal of two teachers, May 1st, on account of sickness, imposed additional service upon the remaining members of the faculty, and teachers worked through the year cheerfully and effectively, though certain departments of the school suffered in interest.

The influence of more than a thousand students of all ages, the observation of the current work itself by hundreds of intelligent

The Normal Schools — River Falls.

visitors, and the teaching done by its students, have marked the career of the school during the first five years of its history, with reasonable results in the transformation of neutral attitudes and adverse criticism, to loyal support of its regime, and have assured the desire for study that shall be self-sustaining after formal instruction has ceased.

At the annual commencement last June, one class was graduated from each of the courses of study, — having passed the usual examinations instituted by the Board and the faculty. These classes were likewise inspected by the committee appointed by the State Superintendent.

During the year, the Normal faculty taught 128 different Normal students, and 55 preparatory students, whose study ranged through a five years' course.

The Model School, having dual functions, has grown in importance, and it bears the fruition that the zealous friends of the Normal expect, and the intelligent citizens applaud. As a graded school, creating and maintaining the habits that imply good citizenship, the model grades seem to be a good type.

The freedom of classification of individuals, the unity of growth of the literary, rhythmical, and moral practices, the adhesion of parental faith to children's real delight,— all these features are apparent, and it is believed that they fully justify the continuance of the present state of the Model School. Following is the enrollment in the Model grades, for the year:

Primary	60
Intermediate	57
Grammar	71
Total	188

Making 371 different students enrolled in the Normal school during the year.

The text-book and reference book library has been enlarged by the purchase of publications that facilitate the work. The chemical and philosophical apparatus has been maintained at its former efficient stage, and additions have been made to the cabinet, and a catalogue of cabinet specimens is in a good stage of progress.

The Normal Schools — River Falls.

The anticipations incident to the introduction of adequate apparatus for warming and ventilating the house, have been fully realized in the experience of the year, and it is believed that the building exemplifies a perfect system in the two important particulars.

Thanking the Board of Regents and the committees for the courtesies of the year, I am,

Respectfully,

W. D. PARKER.

REPORTS OF VISITING COMMITEES.

TO THE PLATTEVILLE NORMAL SCHOOL.

Hon. W. C. WHITFORD, *State Superintendent:*

The committee appointed to visit the State Normal School at Platteville, respectfully present the following report:

A mere visit cannot suffice for more than a glance at the externals of an educational institution, and perhaps to note the regularity and order of its administration. The real internal work of a school depends as much, perhaps more, upon the class of students in attendance, as upon the teachers placed over them. With students of a lower grade of intelligence, much energy is necessarily expended in securing outward conformity to the requirements and discipline of the institution, with which the teacher is not always credited in the judgment formed of his or her work. Outward conformity on the part of the pupil is for the teacher, in many cases, an expensive achievement, which still leaves scholar and teacher only in a position of advantage for real work. The teacher only can know the cost in time and energy of this outward conformity, this lifting students into a position of advantage for effective work. Teachers are too frequently contented when that is physically accomplished, while it is more important to acquire a position of advantage mentally. Less mechanical accuracy might be consistent with, an even production of, free mental work.

A visiting committee, therefore, can form only a general and often an imperfect impression of the material upon which teachers are at work; and hence the student factor is, to a certain extent, an unknown quantity in the judgment passed upon the work of an educational institution.

The pupils of the Normal School at Platteville are, to all appearances, in a position of advantage for good work, and there is a substantial ground for thinking that good work is being done. So much precision in the Model department would be painful, if these were signs of suppression; but when brought about by unfelt guidance and direction, it can result only in the greatest economy of energy and the highest achievement possible. The instruction and methods of instruction deserve to be taken as models, and more than exemplify the precepts received by the student of the Normal department. Many teachers from the surrounding counties avail themselves of the privilege, cordially extended to them, of visiting the Model and Practice departments of the school. Instances have come under the notice of members of your committee where the most gratifying changes in methods of instruction were brought about by a visit of only a few days to these departments.

Abundant opportunity could be had for further experience and practice, if room could be had for practice classes. The more advanced students would thus be able to take full advantage of the instruction, observation, and experience, which the institution would afford. The friends of the school will be glad to know, however, that additional room is being provided, when observation and practice will enter more largely into the work of the Normal students. But observation and practice alone cannot prepare pupils for the work of teaching. A thorough knowledge of the various branches to be taught, is the prime requisite; and the time is far distant when Normal Schools can take the knowledge for granted, and devote their time and attention to instruction and training in the methods of teaching. Without doubt, the branch best taught in our common schools is that of Mathematics, which is largely, if not entirely, owing to the fact that instruction in Mathematics is more thorough and precise in the Normal Schools, than instruction in the other branches. A thorough knowledge of Geography and Grammar is more important to the teacher than a thorough knowledge of the best methods of teaching Geography and Grammar. More thorough and advanced instruction in Language, History, and Geography, would result in a marked improvement in the instruction given in those branches in the common schools of the country.

We do not advocate lowering the standard of mathematical instruc-tion, but believe in elevating the standard of instruction in Lan-guage, Geography, and History. This can be accomplished only by narrowing the field of work assigned to each teacher by increas-ing the number of instructors, or diminishing the subjects of in-struction. Better results, we believe, would be obtained by resorting to either of the above methods, than by the present sys-tem of jaded instructors and attenuated instruction.

The faculty must be credited with producing results which chal-lenge adverse criticism, when the conditions under which they labor are fully comprehended. The teacher should be given time not merely to prepare for the next day's work, but to be himself a student. When the progress of a teacher in knowledge is arrested by the weight of the work of tuition, instruction from that source must lose its freshness and force. The additional room which will soon be available, will materially add to the efficiency of the school in removing disadvantages and facilitating the further application of the observational and experimental features of the course of instruction.

E. D. HUNTLEY,
R. B. ANDERSON,
W. A. JONES,
Committee.

TO THE WHITEWATER NORMAL SCHOOL.

Hon. W. C. WHITFORD, *State Superintendent:*

The committee appointed by you for the inspection of the Nor-mal School at Whitewater, respectfully submit the following obser-vations:

PHYSICAL ENVIRONMENT.

The physical circumstances of the school were found, in no very essential respect, different from those prevailing in the immediately preceding years. Located on a gentle, swelling eminence, the building is at all times bathed in the purest available atmosphere, and exposed to its free and elevated currents, which, though they sometimes sweep with something of rudeness, yet, in the main, are eminently salubrious and invigorating. The declivities of the surface on all sides, and the gravel substratum furnish prompt and efficient drainage, and that degree of earth aëration so essential to the entire wholesomeness of site. In short, the native sanitary conditions of the immediate surroundings are exceptionally excellent; and there are no remote sources of noxious exhalations, either natural or artificial, that give occasion for serious apprehension.

Within the building, the appointments are comparatively excellent, but not entirely above criticism or beyond improvement. The original architect was unfortunate in not utilizing to greater advantage the unlimited solar exposure of the building. Too large a proportion of the best sunlit compartments are devoted to halls and anterooms, thus forcing a corresponding portion of the more constantly occupied apartments into inferior situations. It is true that there is no study room, and but two recitation rooms, we believe, that do not receive, at some time of the session, a limited portion of sunshine obliquely; but the utilization of this important sanitary agency is scant where, in our judgment, it should be ample. The architects, earlier and later, have sacrificed a certain measure of wholesomeness, economy, and attractiveness to conventionalism in architecture, without being eminently successful in the latter respect. Not that the error is a very grave one, but, since school architecture demands a much more careful and intelligent consideration than it commonly receives, the subject deserves passing consideration. The facilities for ventilation in many parts of the building are excellent, in others only fair, and, in a few, somewhat inadequate, requiring special attention and care to secure an entirely innocuous atmosphere.

The relation of the recitation rooms to the main assembly hall was originally far from being fortunate. Too much time was consumed in the movement of classes; and, in individual states of health, too much climbing of stairs necessitated. The later addition to the building alleviated this to some extent, but the difficulty, in a measure, remained at the time of our visit. Remedial plans

Reports of Visiting Committees — Whitewater.

were being matured, which, we are informed, have since been executed, but it is evident that a perfect remedy is incompatible with the complete utilization of the building in its present form, and that a similar fault is presented by a large number of the High School buildings of the State. We know of no perfect remedy, but a radical change in the prevalent form of school buildings, which shall give greater lateral extent and less hight. In the furnishing of the building, we observed minor changes that looked toward greater comfort and convenience; and, among the apparatus and collections, some accretions that add to the already excellent facilities for illustrative instruction and experimental study.

In the material subject-matter of esthetic culture, while something has been attained, there is yet large room for development. Costly works of art are doubtless unattainable, and, if they were within reach, would not best subserve the end desired, since they would constitute an example entirely beyond the possibility of imitation in the public schools. But the cheaper, and yet excellent, copies of masterpieces, the various resources of an ingenious modern, or, perhaps, more strictly, modernized decorative art, and the infinite possibilities of nature, tastefully handled, furnish unlimited material, everywhere available, for esthetic culture and its consequent benign influence, a fertile field, which might, we judge, profitably receive a somewhat additional measure of consideration.

The combined effect of the physical circumstances and appointments of the school — so largely propitious, so slightly prejudicial, as to make our trivial criticism seem almost cynical — appeared to us to find appropriate expression in the large measure of respect shown by pupils of all ages for the school property. We observed only a minimum tendency, even among the young children of the training schools, to that misuse and defacement of exposed property which is the especial disgrace of American youth. Amid the prevalent vandalism, it is both gratifying and encouraging to witness comparatively unsullied buildings and furniture, and unmarred lawns of flower beds. Undoubtedly, the remedy for the common evil lies in rendering the buildings and grounds attractive, and in cultivating a pride, instead of contempt of school premises.

The general health of the students seemed excellent. Here and there were forms and faces that indicated weakened or vitiated vitality. A few of these seemed constitutional for which we would not recommend either school training or school-teaching as a remedy. We question the propriety of fitting such for the exacting and exhaustive duties of the teacher. Beyond question, such should not be employed to teach. A few seemed due to individual violations of hygienic laws in no way occasioned or necessitated by their duties. A few others seemed worn and nervous from the stress of duties, probably not from actual overstudy, which, in our observation, is a rare occurrence, but from the anxiety and nervous strain attendant upon competitive and stimulative comparisons in class work, comparisons which inhere in the very nature of vigorous class exercises. The remedy, in our judgment, is to be sought not so much in a lessening of mental antagonism and mutual measuring of intellectual strength in the class room as in the inculcation of better mental habits, the conversion of nervous anxiety into mental concentration. We would recommend an increased attention to both mental and physiological hygiene,— not that these seem to be neglected subjects, as custom goes, but from the conviction that in our schools and communities generally there are at once extensive waste and vitiation of both physical and mental energy from its injudicious and diffusive application, as well as from positive violation of sanitary laws, and that it is the appropriate and imperative function of our educational agencies to remedy this.

We were agreeably disappointed in regard to the average age and individual maturity of the body of students. In our higher educational institutions there is generally observed a decline in the average of student age, correlated, apparently, with the progressive development of our material as well as educational institutions. At Whitewater there seemed to be a greater age at a given stage of study than in average institutions within our observation. This, we judge, does not so much indicate tardiness of development as frequent alternations of study and teaching and a persistent seeking for higher fitness, a favorable index.

Reports of Visiting Committees — Whitewater.

INTELLECTUAL CONDITIONS.

Turning from these, perhaps too prolonged, observations on the physical and physiological aspects of the school, we observe that the intellectual attitude was healthful and vigorous. In the limited time available to us for observation, it is quite possible that, in the details of instruction and administration, we might fall upon exceptional states and stages, as indeed, in part, we did. We therefore sought to discern the permanently moral and intellectual expression of the school, believing that there is a definitely fixed mental accretion, both of substance and habit, that is the truest index of the work done; because it underlies and outlasts all. Viewed in this regard, our judgment was favorable. There were prevalent both an acquisitive and a receptive state, a readiness to receive and a promptness to seek. Correspondent to these, there were manifest acquisitions and as manifest intellectual thirst for more. There was likewise at once a deferential and an independent attitude, a due respect for intellectual authority, with a due questioning of the grounds of belief, a forecast of teachers that will be neither the slaves of text-books and popular methods nor, on the other hand, flippantly contemptuous of past experience. We remarked a frankness and honesty of spirit toward truth that seemed to seek unbiased knowledge, forgetful of personal attitude to it. The mortification of being found in error seemed to be more nearly recompensed by learning the truth than is common to self-mindful human nature. The exercises indicated a habit of searching for knowledge beyond the fixed and often straightened lines of thought of the text-book, and showed that something of skill in such search had been acquired, — an important acquisition, since it is the type of practical education in the business of life, to which text-books are, in the main, inapplicable. We noticed some innovations in methods, wherein more original investigation and individual ingenuity were demanded, and were gratified at their evident success. The methods of instruction generally were natural and wholesome, but few appearing artificial and constrained. The recitations, in the main, were not trammeled by needless formalities; much less were they fettered by dogmatism on the part of instructors. Freedom of inquiry, of argumentation, and of dissent, were prevailing characteristics. Freedom of criticism, explicitly expressed without attempt at softening or circumlocution, was generously indulged in, and as generously received. Responsiveness to the suggestions of teachers was a conspicuous trait. But slight tendency to wandering thought in recitation was observed. Active mindedness characterized most recitations.

To the training school we cannot give a space that adequately represents our estimate of its value, indeed of its necessity as an element in professional training. The attention given to this very practical constituent of the preparation of Normal students for their chosen profession, indicates that this is not considered in this institution a matter of trivial importance. To the committee the work seemed to be conscientiously and carefully performed. The double and difficult duty of being faithful, at the same time, to student teachers, that they may be led into correct methods, and to pupils, that they may not suffer from inexperienced instruction, seemed to receive due, and, in a measure, successful attention. The instruction even by student teachers appeared excellent so far as observed by the committee. The watchful presence of the supervising teacher, suggestive of criticisms to be rendered, seemed to rouse the pupil teachers to their best efforts both in preparation and execution.

The committee was favorably impressed by the fact that there seemed to be but one practice critic. The supervising teacher had the whole management of the training classes, responsible to the president, it is true, but fortunately to an officer who made his suggestions to the critic in charge, rather than directly to the student teacher. There is thus, presumably, secured a more methodical criticism and more considerateness in its application, the student teacher being spared the confusion of discordant suggestions, and the danger of being overwhelmed by criticisms of the principal, superadded unknowingly to those of the regular supervising teacher, at times when these may, perchance, be all the young teachers in training can for the time endure. The general conduct of the training department impressed us favorably.

Reports of Visiting Committees — Whitewater.

In the primary departments, we observed some features that were evidently adopted from the kindergarten system. They appeared to be excellent and to well illustrate the beneficent influence of that system on American primary education. There is every reason to believe that the principles and methods of the kindergarten may be very extensively adapted to our common schools, even when the full system is wholly impracticable; and to this end, among other reasons, we recommend the establishment of a kindergarten in connection with the school.

While a disposition to be thorough was largely manifested, the examination by a committee of the Regents, in progress during one of our visits, showed that the classes were strangers to many questions asked, either because the topics were unfamiliar, or were presented in an unaccustomed phase. We do not offer this as an adverse criticism upon the instruction of the teachers, or the application of the students. However, thorough going and devoted these may be, the time allotted to the coure is inadequate to exhaustive study of the several branches. This presents a difficulty felt by the administration, felt by observant teachers everywhere. The question is not, Ought the studies attempted, to be pursued to exhaustion? The amptitude of knowledge in all branches is now so great that exhaustive study in school is impossible, and to attempt it is absurd. Nor is it mainly a question of thoroughness of method. So much as is attempted may be thoroughly done, though it be but a small part of the entire subject. Though we may not encompass the entire circle of a subject, we may traverse with exactness and precision one of its innumerable diameters. If but a single day could be given to chemistry, and it were confined to a searching definition of its sphere and functions, it might be a very thorough-going and profitable lesson. Exhaustiveness of a branch of knowledge being impossible, a thoroughness of method in the treatment of selected topics being, in a measure, possible in any case, the question is one of judgment as to the most profitable distribution of effort; whether it shall be comprehensive or concentrated. The practical questions with the Whitewater school are: (1) Shall some branches be thrown out, and more time given to others; (2) Shall

fewer topics under each branch be attempted, and these more fully
mastered; (3) Shall the time for the course be lengthened; or
(4) Shall the requirements for admission be raised. Without
transcending our limits by discussing so broad a subject, we would
suggest an answer to the first question by an affirmative reply to
the last. While it would be impracticable to dismiss entirely any
of the fundamental branches from the course, the burden of elementary instruction might be relegated much more largely to the
public schools and the preparatory department, and thus give additional time for professional work and advanced study. We also
urge the affirmative of the second question; and, by advocating
advanced terms of admission, we practically favor an extension of
the course. Custom in the higher institutions of learning has fixed
upon a four years' curriculum, and it may not be wise to force that
fashion; but a more prolonged course of study is eminently to be
desired, and may be secured, as it has been in those institutions, by
persistently advancing the terms of admission till the requisite
grade is obtained. Of the nearly seven thousand teachers needed
to supply the schools of the State, the Normal Schools can directly
furnish but a small proportion. The remainder must come from our
other schools. They certainly should not come from any grade
lower than our High Schools,— whatever may be the present fact,
and through these schools only can come a large percentage of the
qualified supply of teachers. But, at present, Normal graduates
are inadequately fitted for taking charge of the better class of High
Schools, and are thus practically shut out from this most effective
avenue of influence upon the district schools. As it now is, the
majority of the better class of Normal graduates neither go directly
into the district schools, nor do they have charge of the higher
schools, that are the main factories of qualified district school-
teachers. They largely do an intermediate class of work that does
not directly affect the country schools, either by person or product.
The shortest road to the district schools, in their totality, is through
the higher schools that furnish them with teachers We do not
say that the work now done by the Normal Schools is not good; on
the contrary, in its degree, it is effective; but a higher, more effectual, and more economical work is, in our judgment, possible.

Reports of Visiting Committees — Whitewater.

The effort of the president to foster a public discrimination between those who have received certificates of the shorter course and diplomas of graduation, and thus prevent misapprehension and misjudgment of the institution, from its cheaper products, is laudable; but we cannot comfort him with the conviction that it will be, in any great measure, effectual. We confess to a prejudgment against such a course, at least against granting any formal graduation or certificate; but if it shall, as claimed, lead ultimately to the completion of the longer course by a larger number, the public misapprehension may be ignored as a comparatively trivial matter.

SOCIAL AND MORAL ASPECTS.

Passing to the social and moral aspects of the school, we remarked great apparent harmony and cordial co-operation among the members of the faculty. In like manner, the relations of instructors and students seemed of the kindliest character. With great freedom and friendliness of intercourse, there seemed to come no disrespect, but rather a more sincere regard. Here, at least, reserve and dignity do not seem to be essential to impressive influence or commanding authority. The administrative discipline appeared to be gentle and considerate, but effectual. Were the institution simply for itself and its own, the government would near the ideal; but as the prototype of discipline to be exercised under less favorable conditions, by young teachers of less commanding personality, a somewhat more pronounced and impressive regimen might, we judge, be profitably exercised, that, without involving objectionable constraint, might develop greater power to control self and command others. The danger, we apprehend, is that the students, not having felt it themselves, will go out unimpressed with the gravity of administrative discipline and unprepared to meet its responsibilities.

The moral expression of the school was excellent. The most noteworthy innovation of the year is a change in the opening exercises, by which the reading of the scriptures and prayer have been omitted, and brief conversational lectures or equivalent exercises, having a more or less moral bearing, substituted. This, we are assured, was done, not as a concession to opposition, nor from a want of appreciation of the good influences springing from religious exercises, but from a conviction that greater good might be accomplished by the method adopted. Whatever may be thought of the ultimate results of the permanent adoption of this plan, it will, at least, be conducted by eminently considered and conscientious hands, and characterized by an effort for the real moral education of the students. The subject is one of transcedent importance. The greatest good and the greatest evil to the Commonwealth, are alike dependent upon the moral education of its youth; and perhaps the strongest justification of universal taxation in support of public education, is the dependance of national security and permanence upon intelligence and morality, — upon morality at least equally with intelligence. It will be extremely unfortunate and ultimately dangerous to the public school system, if religious narrowness on the one hand, and atheistic bigotry are the other, shall interfere with, or in any way trammel, the full exercises of all those influences which the highest reason and the experience of the ages have proved efficacious in moral education. Avoiding sectarianism on the one hand, and negativism on the other, it is to be hoped that our Normal Schools will be pronounced advocates of a positive sterling morality, both in personal and civic relations.

T. C. CHAMBERLIN,
M. T. PARK,
CHAS. W. ROBY,
Committee.

TO THE OSHKOSH NORMAL SCHOOL.

HON. W. C. WHITFORD, *State Superintendent:*

Your committee, appointed to visit the State Normal School at Oshkosh, respectfully report for the school year ending August 31, 1880, as follows:

Arrangements were made for a visit by the committee together in February, but by reason of sickness and other unavoidable causes, only one member was able to make the visit at the time agreed upon. Each of the other members of the committee spent

Reports of Visiting Committees — Oshkosh.

at different times about a week in the school during the month of April, and one made a second visit in June, during commencement week.

The president and the other members of the faculty placed every facility at the disposal of the committee to assist them in their duties, and extended such courtesies as made their visits exceedingly enjoyable.

The time spent in visiting enabled the committee to be present at recitations in all the branches of study pursued, and to witness the work of each member of the faculty. The school was found to be full, particularly the Normal department, which was taxed to its utmost capacity. The industry of the students, as manifested in the preparation of lessons, their attention and promptness at recitation, and their general bearing and deportment, were all calculated to impress the committee with the fact that the spirit and tone of the school is all that can be desired. The influence of a directing and controlling mind is everywhere apparent, producing unity and harmony in the workings of the school to a marked degree. It was an agreeable surprise to the committee to find so large a proportion of the Normal students of mature years, and the fact that so many of this class are found in the Normal Schools of the State, argues hopefully for the cause of education within her borders.

Your committee refer to this matter with pleasure, and wish to aid, so far as any words of theirs may have weight, in removing the impression entertained by many that the Normal Schools are filled with boys and girls of immature years. Nothing could be farther from the truth, so far as the school at Oshkosh is concerned.

The best, and indeed the only fair ground of testing the character and the value of the work done in a Normal School, is found in the results produced, — in a comparison of the crude, and, in many cases, limited attainments of the students at entering, with the professional skill and general culture of the same after completing there the prescribed course of study and training.

The ideal Normal School, where the work performed is strictly professional as distinguished from academic, exists in the newly settled States of our country, if at all, in the distant future.

Reports of Visiting Committees — Oshkosh.

The discussion of the desirability of such schools is at present. useless; for, as has so often been shown, the material for the strictly professional and training school does not exist, and the severely practical question of the hour is, how the scores of young men and young women who are constantly knocking for admission at the doors of our Normal Schools, and whose advantages and opportunities for academic culture and training have been limited, can be best fitted for the work which they are to undertake in the public schools of the State.

In the opinion of your committee, a solution to this question is happily reached at Oshkosh. In connection with thorough academic work in the Normal department, where good examples of teaching are constantly presented to the students, there are arrangements for a comprehensive course of practice by the students in the Model school. This work is under the general supervision of an able director, who has time to make his supervision a fact, rather than a pretension, as is the case too often; and it is usually performed in the presence of an experienced critic teacher. A noticeable feature of this practice work is the evident method and care with which it is conducted, and it certainly forms a distinguishing characteristic of this school. Viewed in its relation to the Normal student, it seems that no doubt can be entertained of the benefits resulting from it; as it furnishes him with a generous amount of work, as similar as the circumstances can admit of, to that which will await him when he enters upon his actual school room duties. The committee were, in the main, well pleased with the character and quality of the work performed by the practice teachers. Much of it seemed worthy of special mention, and the average was not below that seen in the primary and grammar school departments of the graded schools of the State. And while it is true that some students who succeed in practice work, may meet with failure when thrown entirely upon their own resources, in actual school experience, so it is true that some teachers who are regarded as successful in one field of labor, will fail in another under different circumstances, and with different surroundings.

This practice work, carefully laid out and supervised, and daily

Reports of Visiting Committees — Oshkosh.

subjected to the friendly criticism of experienced teachers, would seem to be well calculated for fitting and training those who engage in it for the active duties of the school room. It certainly possesses many of the factors requisite for such a result. There is the incentive arising from others being engaged in the same work, the thought constantly before them that they are on trial, the stimulating influence resulting from the suggestions and criticisms of those of long and well-proven experience, and the confidence that any trouble and difficulties which may arise, will be shared by those who are able to bear the burden. Of course, the question may arise whether some of the factors spoken of above may not prove at times, for certain students, elements of weakness rather than of strength. With what minuteness the work of a subordinate ought to be laid out, arranged, and limited; to what extent it may be criticised, and yet leave the individuality of the worker impressed upon it; and whether the handling of a class in the presence of the director or critic teacher furnishes the opportunity of sufficiently proving the powers in school management, are questions which cannot be decided by speculation, but by the severe test of experience.

The committee found the discipline of the school excellent. While there was no effort at display in handling the school, and while apparently there was the utmost freedom of action on the part of every student, yet all movements were executed with commendable promptness, and nothing, on the part of the students, had the appearance of being done in an indifferent or perfunctory manner. The intercourse between the teachers and students at all times, and between the students at recess, was free and unrestrained; and neither word nor act was noticed, not in accordance with the strictest requirements of propriety and good-breeding.

The kindergarten, which was opened the latter part of April, was seen by only one member of the committee. The importance of schools of observation, where the Normal student may witness true kindergarten work successfully performed, catch something of its spirit, and carry its methods, so far as practicable, into the schools of the State, can be questioned by no one conversant with the possibilities of genuine kindergarten training.

Reports of Visiting Committees — Oshkosh.

The committee have been pleased to learn that the Board of Normal Regents have decided to continue the kindergarten department at Oshkosh, and believe that the experiment there will prove so successful that, at no distant day, kindergartens will be established in connection with the other Normal Schools of the State.

The various rooms in the building seemed to be well ventilated, and the health of the pupils, so far as could be learned, was generally good; and although there were indications of weariness at the end of the week, an evidence that work had been done, still it was noticed that the students came to each day's duty with cheerfulness and energy. On the part of the teachers there were indications of overwork. Whether this was owing to the demands made upon them in the performance of their daily school duties, or to an excessive professional enthusiasm, was not apparent to the committee.

At this point, the committee would venture upon a word of criticism. It is thought that too much sharpness and severity, both in manner and in language, was at times manifested by some of the teachers towards students who made mistakes in recitations, or who failed in presenting statements in a satisfactory manner, but who apparently were doing as well as they could do. This criticism is made reluctantly, as the committee are well aware of the fact that circumstances may exist, which, if known to visitor, would call for a suspension of judgment, if not a complete change in opinion.

The lectures given by the president in the theory and practice of teaching, are very suggestive and stimulating. From this lecture room the students must go to the preparation of their daily tasks, to their practice work, and finally to the other school rooms of the State, deeply impressed with the responsibility of the teacher's calling.

In this report it has been no part of the plan of the committee to speak in detail of the work performed by the different teachers, but to present their views upon the general management and character of the school, and to discuss briefly such points as appeared to them of special importance.

In conclusion, the committee express the opinion that the Oshkosh Normal School is organized and administered in a masterly manner; that the instruction in the several departments is thorough and accurate; that practice work is skillfully directed; and that in all respects the school is performing the duties for which it was organized, and that it is worthy of the continued patronage of the people of the State.

Respectfully submitted,

H. C. HOWLAND,
GEO. M. GUERNSEY,
J. T. FLAVIN,
Committee.

August 31, 1880.

TO THE RIVER FALLS NORMAL SCHOOL.

To Hon. W. C. WHITFORD, *State Superintendent:*

Considering the act of the legislature providing for the thorough inspection of the educational institutions of the State from different stand-points eminently judicious, your committee gladly accepted your appointment to visit the State Normal School at River Falls. Believing that a mere perfunctory and formal execution of this trust is worse than useless, each member of the committee visited the school twice and spent from three to nine full days examining its condition; listening to recitations under every member of the faculty in all the departments; looking over the papers of the pupils preparatory to admission to the classes, and also those required for graduation; witnessing the work of the students conducting classes in the Model departments, and the criticisms and suggestions of the Director of Practice work thereon; observing the discipline of the school, the spirit and temper of the students; and endeavoring to estimate justly the influence, which, from their training in this institution, they may be expected to exert as teachers upon the schools of the State.

In performing this work, we did not forget that the River Falls School is the youngest Normal School in the State, and is so situated that it must draw the great body of its students from a region where their educational advantages, aside from the common district schools, have been very limited. We had no expectation, therefore, that its chief work would be technically Normal.

We have, however, words of commendation only, for the educational enterprise of the people in that more recently settled portion of the State, which has caused them to organize and sustain so well the district schools, where the desire for something higher has been called forth. It augurs well for the future that such earnest, self-reliant, and persevering pupils from these schools, are availing themselves of the advantages afforded by the State for a thorough preparation for the teacher's work.

It was gratifying to us to find the scholars in the Model departments so delightfully interested in their studies, — a fact due, doubtless, to the admirable manner in which their exercises were conducted, and equally gratifying were the energy and devotion of the Normal students in their special work; and we were pleased to find that, in the main, the recitations were so conducted as to draw the attention of the students to methods of presenting the various branches of learning so as to develop thought and intelligence. By this course, coupled with the opportunity of seeing exemplified in the Model departments the best methods of instruction and government, while at the same time being themselves governed by a method and spirit nearly faultless, the essence of Normal training is amply afforded; and students availing themselves of these opportunities, are prepared to make their work in the schools, to which they may be called, fruitful in the great work for which our common schools are instituted.

We noted favorably the republican simplicity and fitness of the building for the purposes for which it was designed, except that the recitation rooms and some of those of the other departments were too long for their breadth, placing those in the back part of the room too far from the teacher, and the scholars at the extreme ends out of good hearing distance of each other. Particularly well pleased were we, with the scrupulous neatness and manifest care throughout the building and its appendages, and with the means of heating and ventilating, which seemed to be meeting, in a satisfac-

Reports of Visiting Committees — River Falls.

tory manner, the modern demands of sanitary science in these particulars.

We approved of the morning exercises, a most admirable means of having the Bible exert its due influence upon the school without giving them the character of a sectarian exercise, — thus allowing no foundation for complaint that these schools are being made proselyting institutions.

We admired the grave, mild, and efficient administration of Pres. Parker; the quiet but incisive work of Prof. Thayer; the practice of Prof. King, in having his scholars *see, and handle, and observe the facts* of physical science, and the modest manner in which he does it; the happy influence of Miss Foot's rare good taste and judgment in English literature, well exemplified in the closing exercises of her class; the fruitful promise in the work of Miss Hatch; the thoughtful training of Mrs. Jenness; the genial and successful work of Miss Jones; the thorough and energetic work of Miss Kelley; and the kind, motherly, yet authoritative, and most effective work of Mrs. Parker, giving what the little ones need — the largest amount of liberty, without the least taint of undue license.

Through conversations with leading citizens, by individual members of the committee, and by visits to some of the schools in the country tributary to River Falls, it was found that the influence of the school for good is already manifest.

But notwithstanding the great amount of really excellent work that has been done in the River Falls School, it is the opinion of the committee that there is room for a great advance in the scholarly attainments of those who may hereafter be graduated; and that the time has arrived when the school requires, in its faculty, somewhat of an addition to the strong intellectual force which goes so far to mould the character of scholars, a thing especially needed in an institution whose function is to send out those who are fitted to give a favorable bent to many others.

J. Q. EMERY,
A. F. NORTH,
J. S. DORE,
Committee.

STATE TEACHERS' ASSOCIATION.

SEMI-ANNUAL MEETING.

MONDAY EVENING, Dec. 29, 1879.

The Association met in joint session with the Academy of Science, Arts, and Letters. Dr. A. L. Chapin, of Beloit College, delivered an address on " The Nature and Methods of Science." The following resolution, submitted by Prof. W. S. Johnson, was adopted:

" *Whereas*, On the present evening the State Teachers' Associations of six adjoining States — Illinois, Indiana, Iowa, Michigan, Minnesota, and Wisconsin, are in session;

Therefore, be it resolved, That congratulatory dispatches be sent to each of the other Associations, and that the following gentlemen be chosen to draft such dispatches: W. H. Beach, S. S. Rockwood, G. S. Albee, L. D. Harvey, and E. Barton Wood; and that the Treasurer be authorized to pay for such dispatches from any unappropriated moneys now in his hands. In accordance with this resolution, the following messages were prepared and sent to the presidents of these bodies:

To Prof. O. Whitman, St. Paul, Minn.:

The Wisconsin Teachers' Association, assembled in semi-annual session, send a cordial greeting to the Minnesota teachers, now in session.

To W. J. Shoup, Independence, Iowa: — *The Badger State Teachers, Greeting:* May the Hawkeyes be far-seeing in council, temperate in feasting, and prosperous in all things.

To E. A. Strong, Lansing, Mich.:

The Badgers greet and emulate our brothers of the Wolverine State. May our " Forward " never need to countermarch in search of our elder brethren.

State Teachers' Association.

To Prof. Alf. Harvey, Bloomington, Ill.:

The Badger State pedagogues, in holiday session assembled, send greeting to the pedagogical Suckers. May you safely swim down the streams of knowledge, till they debouch in the ocean of wisdom that floats the intellectual and moral argosies of the world.

To J. T. Merrill, Indianapolis, Indiana:

From the school-masters of Badgerdom to their Hoosier brethren, greeting. Shake!

TUESDAY MORNING, December 30.

The Association was called to order at 9:30, in the Assembly Chamber, by Pres. W. H. Beach, of Beloit. Prayer was offered by Rev. J. B. Pradt, of Madison.

The first paper presented was that of State Superintendent W. C. Whitford, upon "The Present Condition of the Schools of the State," giving a comprehensive survey of the educational field of labor from the University down to the common ungraded school.

Next followed a paper on "The Possible Reading Class," by Miss M. E. Hazard, of Beloit. Pres. Bascom, of the State University, extended an invitation to the teachers to visit the Washburn astronomical observatory.

Supt. Dore, of the Committee on Compulsory Education, asked for more time for the further preparation of a report. Leave was granted.

Prof. I. N. Stewart, of Berlin, submitted the report of the Committee on Relations of High Schools and Colleges, which, after considerable discussion, was, on motion, received and placed on file.

A letter from the President of the Women's Christian Temperance Association, concerning school text-books on temperance, was read by the Secretary.

Pres. Bascom moved that the Association invite the attention of the educational boards of the State to the Temperance Lesson Book, by Dr. Richardson, of England, as fitted in intermediate schools to enforce the most important moral lesson by physiological facts. After some discussion, the letter and resolution were received and placed on file.

Pres. Parker moved that the Committee on Exhibitory Department be discharged, and the whole matter placed in the hands of a new committee. Lost.

The following resolutions, moved by W. H. Chandler, were adopted.

Resolved, That the Association gratefully acknowledges the valuable services of the public press in promoting that better training of teachers and that general improvement of the public schools so observable in the history of this country during the past thirty years.

Resolved, That in the great improvements still to be accomplished, we believe that the powerful agency of the press must be employed to a still greater degree, and .we therefore urge superintendents and teachers to use their influence to induce editors to give more attention to educational subjects, and wherever it is possible to secure the establishment of educational departments in the local and general newspapers.

Resolved, That our special acknowledgments are hereby made to those newspapers that have taken the lead in according to educational matters stated columns in charge of special editors, who make the operations and wants of the public schools a subject of continual investigation and report.

Adjourned.

TUESDAY EVENING.

The Association met in joint session with the Academy of Science, Arts, and Letters. Rev. S. S. Peet, of Clinton, Wis., read a valuable paper on " The Emblematic Mounds of Wisconsin," which was followed by a very instructive and entertaining lecture on " The Arts of Etching and Engraving," by Prof. Jas. MacAlister, of Milwaukee.

WEDNESDAY MORNING, Dec. 31.

Association called to order at 9:30.

Moved and carried that the sum of twelve dollars be appropriated from the funds of the Association to reimburse Prof. MacAlister for telegraph and express expenses in securing materials for his lecture last evening.

State Teachers' Association.

Telegrams in response to those previously sent were received as follows:

BLOOMINGTON, Ill., Dec. 30.

W. H. Beach, President Wisconsin Teachers' Association:

Four hundred Suckers return the greeting of the Badgers. May they never have to swim or take to their holes.

A. HARVEY,
President.

INDEPENDENCE, IOWA, Dec. 30.

The Hawkeye State to the Badger, greeting: May your feasts be as delicious and councils as enthusiastic as ours, and may the ocean of your zeal and success break upon no *beach.*

A. J. SHOUP,
President.

LANSING, MICH., Dec. 30.

The Michigan Association of Teachers accept the greeting of their Wisconsin brethren, and thanks. We bid you Godspeed in the glorious work of education.

E. A. STRONG,
President.

ST. PAUL, MINN., Dec. 30.

Two hundred teachers of the Minnesota Educational Association, assembled in convention, respond most heartily to your greeting.

O. WHITMAN,
President.

INDIANAPOLIS, IND., Dec. 30.

Five hundred Hoosier school-masters to the Badger brethren "shake," by order of the Association   J. T. MERRILL,
President.

The following telegram was also received:

DENVER, COL., Dec. 30.

Colorado to Wisconsin, greeting: Though far away we are with you.   J. A. SEAWALL,
President.

State Teachers' Association.

To which the following response was sent:

Wisconsin Teachers' Association to President J. A. Seawall—

Wisconsin to Colorado Teachers: Greeting acknowledged and returned. May your work be as productive and enduring as your everlasting hills.

W. H. BEACH.

Prof. J. Burnham, of La Crosse, read a carefully prepared paper on "The Limits of the Teacher's Authority." An extended discussion followed in regard to recent supreme court dicisions on educational questions, and their effect upon the school interests of the State.

On motion, Prof. Burnham was requested to furnish a copy of his paper for publication in pamphlet form for distribution.

President Parker followed with a paper on "Mathematics: Its Scope and Place."

Prof. Richardson, of the Committee on Kindergarten Teaching, presented a satisfactory report, which, on motion, was adopted as the sentiment of the Association.

Pres. Parker, gave an account of his recent visit to the kindergartens of St. Louis, speaking in high terms of their efficiency.

Prof. A. F. North, of Pewaukee, from the Committee on the Agitation on Popular Education, presented a report, which was adopted.

State Supt. Whitford, from the Committee on Course of Study for Ungraded Schools, presented a report, urging continued effort in the perfection of the course already sent out to the schools of the State.

Prof. R. W. Burton, of Janesville, from the Committee on Relations of Ungraded Schools to High Schools, presented a brief report, which was adopted.

Supt. Dore, from the Committee on Compulsory Education, presented a report, which was adopted.

Pres. Parker, from the Committee on Exhibitory Department, reported in favor of a new committee consisting of W. H. Chandler, Mrs. Sarah F. O. Little, J. Burnham, Mattie E. Hazard, and

State Teachers' Association.

Agnes Hosford, to arrange and report a plan for further work in the direction of Educational Exhibits. Adopted.

WEDNESDAY MORNING, Dec. 31.

Prof. De La Matyr offered the following resolutions, which were adopted:

Resolved, That this Association is under obligations to Dr. De Motte and the Misses Eddy and Ritscher, for this wonderful exhibition of the capabilities of mutes, and the great care, patience, and skill of their instructors.

Resolved, That these mutes have our heartfelt thanks for this interesting entertainment, and that they and their companions at Delavan receive our sympathy in their struggles to obtain an education.

Prof. North offered the following resolution, which was adopted:

Resolved, That this Teachers' Association recognize and highly appreciate the courtesy of the *Wisconsin State Journal*, *Madison Democrat*, and the *Milwaukee Sentinel*, in giving daily and continuous reports of the doings of this body, during its present session.

Association adjourned, *sine die*.

FRED. W. ISHAM,   W. H. BEACH,
        Secretary.   *President*.

ANNUAL MEETING.

The twenty-eighth annual session of the Wisconsin Teachers' Association was held in the Senate Chamber of the State Capitol, at Madison, commencing July 6, 1880.

TUESDAY EVENING, July 6.

The meeting was called to order by Pres. W. H. Beach, after which a chorus was rendered, by a choir led by Prof. Brand, followed by prayer by Rev. J. D. Butler.

Pres. Beach announced the resignation of Secretary F. W. Isham, and A. R. Sprague, of Black River Falls, was chosen to fill the vacancy.

State Teachers' Association.

W. D. Parker, Railway Clerk, spoke of the arrangements for the entertainment of teachers, and moved the appointment of Prof. Shaw, of Madison, to direct such arrangements; and announced the receipt of correspondence in reference to the proposed excursion to the Dalles, giving rates to teachers.

Prof. Joseph Emerson, of Beloit College, delivered a lecture on " Some National Experiments in Education."

Adjourned.

WEDNESDAY MORNING, July 7.

The session was opened at 9 o'clock, by prayer offered by Prof. Emerson. Following this, congregational singing was led by Prof. Brand.

Pres. Parker stated the desire of the railroads as to commutation rates on return tickets. Prof. Salisbury was called to the chair, and the President delivered the annual address.

On motion, it was referred to Messrs. Kerr, Graham, and Howland, for the assignment of its several topics.

Supt. Viebahn presented a paper on " The Developing Method."

Pres. Stearns presented a paper on " Some Incalculable Elements of School Work."

Recess of ten minutes.

The Association was called to order and listened to a song by a trio of male voices, consisting of Prof. Brand, and Messrs. Bross and Rowland.

After some explanations and instructions by W. D. Parker, Railroad Clerk, the committee to whom was referred the President's address, reported the following disposition of topics:

State University — Samuel Shaw, J. Q. Emery, and E. B. Wood.

Colleges — T. C. Chamberlin, Albert Salisbury, and J. H. Terry.

Normal Schools — W. C. Whitford, W. G. Clough, and J. T. Lunn.

Institutes — W. H. Chandler, Agnes Hosford, and W. H. Cummings.

Primary Education and Kindergarten Work — James Mac-Alister, Mary Brayman, and Jesse B. Thayer.

State Teachers' Association.

School Supervision — Duncan McGregor, John Howitt, and C. F. Viebahn.

The Practical in Education — George S. Albee, A. J. Hutton, and A. R. Sprague.

Miss Brayman, of the Platteville Normal School, with her class, presented an illustrative exercise in primary object teaching. After the exercise, questions were asked by the audience, and answered by the class and teacher. The class was then excused, and after some discussion upon the subject, the session adjourned.

WEDNESDAY EVENING.

After music by the choir, the President named the following committees:

On Resolutions — S. S. Rockwood, M. S. Frawley, and C. E. Buell.

On Honorary Members — I. N. Stewart, A. F. North, and Miss Hattie Bacon.

On Nominations — J. T. Lunn, E. B. Wood, and Miss Ella Aspinwall.

On Finance — H. C. Howland, J. Q. Emery, and Miss Emily Webster.

It was moved and carried that Pres. Stearns be requested to furnish, for early publication, a copy of his address delivered this morning.

Pres. Parker moved that the Committee on Employment of Teachers, formerly existing, be revived, and that Pres. Albee, Prof. Emery, and Miss Agnes Hosford be appointed such committee. Carried.

After music by Prof. Brand's quartette, the President introduced Rev. Mr. Rose, of Milwaukee, who delivered an address upon the "Inabilities and Disabilities of the Teacher's Profession."

At the close of the lecture, Mrs. Brand sang a solo, after which the session adjourned.

THURSDAY MORNING, July 8.

After the usual exercises, the minutes of the previous sessions were read and approved. Mr. Viebahn then offered the following resolution:

State Teachers' Association.

Resolved, That this association considers the law passed by the legislature during its last session, providing for the granting of State certificates to the graduates of colleges and other institutions, whose courses of study may be deemed equivalent to the course of study of our State University, to be unjust, impolitic, and contrary to the best interests of our public school system.

On motion, the resolution was made a special order for the first day of the winter session.

Supt. Somers and Prof. Sawyer being absent, the association passed to the next exercise on the programme, a paper on "The Province and Function of a Normal School," by Pres. G. S. Albee.

Recess of ten minutes.

The next order was an essay, "The Kindergarten," by Rev. J. B. Pradt.

Supt. MacAlister opened the discussion on the above paper, urging the value and efficiency of proper kindergarten training; that the education of the child begins at the very earliest moment; and that the kindergarten comes in to shape and rightly form the nature of the child, and is an essential part of any system of education.

Supt. Whitford made an announcement from Prof. Watson, as to the hours of reception at the Observatory.

A. O. Wright followed in the discussion on the paper read, endorsing Supt. MacAlister's views, and urging that the methods of the kindergarten should be adopted and used in our graded schools.

Pres. Albee followed, heartily endorsing the true philosophy and methods of the kindergarten.

Mr. Clough, of Portage, thought that the German system should not be copied, but that we should work out improvement of methods in our primary schools.

Pres. Shepherd, of the Winona State Normal School, Minnesota, did not wish, at so late an hour, to discuss the question, but only to say that he had received an immense amount of inspiration from this work in Wisconsin.

Mr. Andrews, of Chicago, urged the necessity of completeness *in the* kindergarten work.

State Teachers' Association.

Miss Beebe, of the Racine Private Kindergarten, was called for, and urged the introduction into our primary schools, at the earliest moment, of such methods from the kindergarten as are practicable, and thought that very many *are* practicable.

Another speaker thought that one needed reform should be at once begun; that our primary departments should be made smaller than they are in very many schools, and not more than forty scholars should be placed in charge of one teacher. Teachers to be trained in this work should be carefully selected. The experience of St. Louis shows this.

THURSDAY AFTERNOON.

The President appointed the following named persons as a committee to report on the resolution pertaining to State certificates on the first day of the winter session: C. F. Viebahn, T. C. Chamberlin, and T. F. Frawley.

The following committees asked leave to report at the winter meeting, viz.: Committees on University, Colleges, and Normal Schools.

Prof. Samuel Calvin read a paper upon " Natural Science in our Schools."

The Association, by vote, requested a copy of the paper for publication.

The report of the Treasurer having been approved by the Finance Committee, was adopted by the Association, as follows:

The Treasurer of the Wisconsin Teachers' Association respectfully submits the following report of receipts, disbursements, and present condition of the finances of this Association, for the year ending July 8, 1880:

RECEIPTS.

July 11,	1879	To amount received of T. F. Frawley, ex-Treas'r.	$110 92
July 11,	1879	To annual dues of one member	1 00
Dec. 30-31,	1879	To annual dues of thirty-five members..........	35 00
July 7-8,	1880	To annual dues of one hundred members.......	100 00
		Total receipts.........................	$246 92

Superintendents' Convention.

EXPENDITURES.

Dec. 31, 1879	By expense of Art lecture..................	$12 00
Dec. 31, 1879	By expense of exhibit	4 50
Dec. 31, 1879	By bill of Railway Clerk...................	9 50
Dec. 31, 1879	By printing, postage, telegrams, and express-age....	25 73
Mar. 4, 1880	By printing Mrs Little's lecture............	15 00
July 7, 1880	By expen-es of lectures....................	43 25
July 7, 1880	By expenses of primary class...............	16 20
July 7, 1880	By expenses of music.........	13 00
July 7, 1880	By bill of Railway Clerk	17 43
July 7, 1880	By printing, p stage, telegrams, and express-age...........................	31 41
	Total expenditures..............	$188 02

Cash on hand.................................. $58 90

H. A. HOBART, *Treasurer.*

The committee on Honorary Members reported the following names for such membership: Rev. H. T. Rose, Milwaukee; Prof. Joseph Emerson, Beloit; Prof. Samuel Calvin, Iowa; Pres. Irwin Shepard, and Prof. E. Gilbert, Winona, Minn.; and Prof. Davis, Rochester Minn.

The officers of the Association were then elected, as follows:

President — I. N. Stewart.

Vice-Presidents — Alex. Kerr, E. A. Charlton, and Miss Agnes Hosford.

Secretary — J. H. Gould.

Treasurer — Alfred Thomas.

Executive Committee — W. H. Beach, A. R. Sprague, H. A. Hobart, C. F. Viebahn, and J. B. Thayer.

The Association then adjourned *sine die.*

W. H. BEACH, *President.*

A. R. SPRAGUE, *Secretary.*

CONVENTION OF SUPERINTENDENTS.

ANNUAL SESSION.

The annual meeting of the county and city superintendents was held in the Assembly Chamber of the State Capitol, at Madison, in the afternoon of December 31, 1879.

Superintendents' Convention.

The convention met at 2:10 P. M., and was called to order by State Supt. Whitford.

State Supt. Whitford was elected President, and Supt. Lunn Secretary of the convention.

The following county superintendents were present: J. C. Rathbun, Buffalo; J. S. Dore, Clark; K. Scott, Columbia; H. Neill (elect), Columbia; C. E. Buell (elect), 1st district Dane; M. S. Frawley, 2d district Dane; Agnes Hosford, Eau Claire; E. McLoughlin, Fond du Lac; W. G. Spence (elect), Juneau; A. Heidkamp, Ozaukee; W. F. Scott (elect), Ozaukee; D. D. Parsons, Richland; J. W. West, 1st district Rock; Betsey M. Clapp, St. Croix; J. T. Lunn, Sauk; F. W. Isham, Walworth; W. R. Taylor (elect), Walworth; J. Howitt, Waukesha; J. H. Tobin, Waushara; T. E. Nash (elect), Wood.

Also the following city superintendents: G. M. Bowen, Columbus; R. W. Burton, Janesville; J. J. Somers, Milwaukee; A. C. Wallin, Prairie du Chien; C. F. Ninman, Watertown.

State: W. C. Whitford; J. B. Pradt, Assistant.

Supt. Whitford addressed the convention in advocacy of the following stated features:

1. Superintendents should incite or personally edit more educational columns in county papers. Those columns containing most local items of school doings and management, teachers' queries, explanations of interest to officers, and in general school news, excite more popular attention than those containing more extended and elaborate productions.

2. County superintendents might prepare, in durable pamphlet form, for general circulation, a compilation of county educational statistics, information, advice, rules or regulations, course of study, advocacy of reforms and advancement, etc.

3. Special effort should be made to secure the fullest possible attendance, at our public schools. Some county superintendents report most gratifying results in this direction. The compulsory law should be thoroughly advertised.

4. During the past year, too many third grade certificates and licenses were issued in many counties to indicate any intention by

their superintendents to revise the standard of education of teachers.

5. The reports of the State Board of Health are eminently worthy of superintendents' sanction and aid in circulating. Much good may result from the interest manifested by this Board in the matter of school edifices, management, and hygiene.

6. Educational attainments by superintendents may yet become a necessity to deliver us from incompetent ones, who, knowing but little, exact less from their teachers, and perpetuate poor schooling.

7. The course of study printed in the institute syllabus is recommended for thorough trial.

8. For insertion in the Annual Report of the State Superintendent, special reports from superintendents are solicited, as it is noticed that such special reports constitute a very interesting feature. It is recommended that superintendents select some one or more items for thorough observation and cultivation, and embody results in their special reports. In this way, a mass of reliable information could be gathered for the main report.

9. Acknowledged the courtesy with which the State Superintendent had been received throughout the State, and the general educational interests maintained.

Supt. West read a paper on "Supply of more Efficient Teachers," which treated carefully the following points: 1. Teachers' lack of thorough information in the common branches. 2. Similar lack of general information, the teacher's education being usually very narrow in text-books alone. 3. Effort to procure more information in the above particulars, may be stimulated by searching examinations. 4. Many teachers content themselves with an education barely sufficient to obtain the lowest grade of certificate or license. If such persist in this condition, they need weeding out, leaving their places vacant for more promising material. 5. Some teachers have education enough, but are very poor in discipline. These may be improved by judicious criticism during visitation. 6. Normal training should be within the reach of more teachers, and institutes should be more generally attended.

A discussion followed.

Superintendents' Convention.

Supt. McLoughlin: Before we can have much more efficient teachers, we must have officers who demand them, and are willing to pay them, which is seldom the case. Only a minority of our teachers are interested attendants of our institutes and associations. Meetings of school officers may do good by discussing the qualities of good schools and good teachers, and endeavoring to demonstrate their economy, until a demand for them is created.

Supt. Ninman: Demand creates a supply, and if the demand be for low qualifications, teachers possessing such will be supplied. It will be hard for us to reverse the law of demand and supply. What can be done toward such reversal?

Supt. Rathbun: The number of certificates issued should be but slightly larger than the number of situations for teachers, in any county. By this, the better qualified would be authorized to teach, and would secure the situations.

Supt. Parsons: Enough full grade certificates are not issued in Richland county to fill all its schools. For the remainder of the situations, limited licenses are issued to the most worthy of those failing to obtain full certificates, bearing in mind personal qualifications, as energy, tact, etc., and educational opportunities and interest.

Assistant State Supt. Pradt read a paper on Securing Better School-Houses.

Prof. North thought the convention of superintendents a proper body to institute action in the matter treated in this paper.

Prof. Wright spoke of schools kept in veritable hovels, through which the wind swept unchecked, dark, deskless, and floorless; one in particular, in which the seating was a simple ridge of earth. Such houses are a needless disgrace, which no poverty can palliate, and the sooner they are swept away, the better for our advancement.

As Executive Committee for the ensuing year, the chair, on motion, appointed Supts. Lunn, Ninman, and Rathbun.

Carried that the Executive Committee provide for a summer session, in connection with the State Association.

J. T. LUNN,   W. C. WHITFORD,
    Secretary.   *President.*

Superintendents' Convention.

The semi-annual meeting of the superintendents was held in the Senate Chamber of the State Capitol, at Madison, in the afternoon of July 7, 1880.

Meeting called to order at 2 o'clock P. M., by Supt. J. T. Lunn.

On motion, State Supt. Wm. C. Whitford was elected President, and Supt. Ed. McLoughlin Secretary.

The following superintendents responded to roll call: J. C. Rathbun, Wm. B. Minaghan, Henry Neill, James McDonald, C. E. Buell, M. S. Frawley, J. T. Flavin, Miss Florence Tickner, Miss Agnes Hosford, Ed. McLoughlin, C. L. Harper, C. L. Hubbs, D. A. Mahoney, C. G. Thomas, C. F. Viebahn, C. A. Morse, J. W. West, Wm. Jones, Miss Betsey M. Clapp, J. T. Lunn, John Howitt, W. W. Kimball, Samuel Shaw.

By request, Supt. M. S. Frawley was called to the chair, during the reading of the address by State Supt. Wm. C. Whitford.

Among the many good points of this address, the following were noticed:

1. It was a fortunate day for education when the county superintendency was adopted.

2. County superintendents should be graduates of a normal school, college or university, or should pass examination for a State certificate.

3. Counties of more than 175 districts should be divided into at least two superintendent districts; and, in counties of 15,000 or more inhabitants, the law dividing them into two districts should be made compulsory.

4. No superintendent can properly care for more than 75 schools. Such supervision would allow time to visit each school from two to five times a term.

5. Each superintendent should be assisted by two competent assistants, to be appointed by the county board of supervisors for two years, and paid by the day for actual work.

6. Higher qualifications for teachers. Certificate only a few more teachers than enough to fill the schools.

Superintendents' Convention.

The address was followed by an animated discussion, in which the following superintendents participated: Lunn, Mahoney, Viebahn, Buell, and Shaw.

Supt. M. S. Frawley, of Dane county, read a paper on the "Proper Tests in Teachers' Examination, and How Exercised." This paper was filled with excellent suggestions. The following were noticed: (1) Oral examinations are good, and remedy defects in written examinations. (2) Too much trouble is taken with courses and grades. (3) Teachers should be able to solve practical problems and answer practical questions. (4) A legislative enactment relating to the qualifications of superintendents would prevent many wrongs in examinations.

The discussion on this paper was opened by Supt. Buell, followed by Supts. Neill, Mahoney, McLoughlin, Lunn, and Viebahn.

Supt. Parsons being absent, his paper on "Teachers' Libraries" was read by Supt. Rathbun. This paper related the origin, progress, and present condition of the teachers' library in Richland county.

Discussion on the subject was opened by Supt. McLoughlin, who was followed by Supts. Lunn, Harper, and Viebahn.

"Superintendents' Duty and Action toward the Course of Study for Ungraded Schools," a paper read by Supt. Agnes Hosford, summed up the many present questions that form *the* issue in the higher and better condition of these schools.

Discussion on this topic was opened by Supt. Howitt, who was followed by Supts. Viebahn, Rathbun, Mahoney, Neill, Flavin, and others.

Moved and carried that this paper be requested, for publication in the *Journal of Education.*

Moved and carried that we adjourn.

ED. McLOUGHLIN,   W. C. WHITFORD,
     Secretary.   *President.*

14 — ST. SUP.

PRINCIPALS' ASSOCIATION.

PROCEEDINGS OF THE ANNUAL SESSION.

TUESDAY AFTERNOON, December 30, 1879.

In the absence of all the other officers of the Association, it was called to order by the Secretary, and Mr. Wood, of Oshkosh, was made President *pro tem.*

Owing to the absence of Mr. Burton, the topic next on the programme, "The Marking System," was brought forward by Mr. Beach, who thought that the best results could be obtained by averaging the marks of the daily recitations, with those of written examinations, and with a judgment mark which should express the teacher's estimate of the scholar's work.

Prof. Chamberlin, of Beloit College, thought some record of scholarship desirable, and knew of no better way to get this than to use some modified form of the marking system. Pupils must acquire *mental power;* and whatever hinders this must be put aside. If the marking system should so intrude, it should not be used.

Principals Clough and Bowen strongly favored the practice of daily marking, making the record either during the recitation or immediately after it.

It was urged by another principal that the necessity of marking the definite result of each recitation is too mechanical, the teacher being tempted to put the questions in such shape that the answers may easily be marked. He also alluded to the utter worthlessness of marks when used to estimate the comparative standing of different departments of a school.

Mr. Webb, of Milwaukee, was strongly opposed to the use of the ystem as emphasizing a wrong motive.

Mr. Willis, of Baraboo, did not indorse it.

Mr. Pray, of Tomah, thought that in this way the best work of the scholar would rarely be recorded.

Prof. Kerr, of Madison, thought it not altogether good but necessary. He quoted Mr. Porter in defining what a teacher

Principals' Association.

should be, viz : " An investigator, a communicator of knowledge, an examiner."

Mr. Stewart, of Berlin, thought that the practice utterly bad, — worse than worthless.

The sentiment of the Association seemed to be that the practice of daily markings should only be used where some stimulant is necessary, and when no other device seems effective.

Mr. Wood, of Oshkosh, next presented his paper, — " Some needed Reforms in Graded Schools." He spoke of the need of more tact and sympathy in primary teaching, and said that salaries should be graded by success. As perception and memory are most active in the younger scholars, the grade work should be arranged with reference to this fact. Accuracy and rapidity of work should be obtained in lower grades. Individuals and classes should be promoted at any time when they are ready for it. He thought most High School courses too long. He would advise that a certificate be given to each scholar upon his completing each study of the course, after a thorough examination, and that he be graduated only after he has obtained the requisite number of certificates. He regarded the supervision of most graded schools, as very defective. Each room needs *every day* the presence of a Principal.

Mr. Stewart then read the report of the committee appointed to report on State certificates, the report having been written by Mr. Frawley, of Eau Claire, who was absent.

After reading, it was moved to lay over the report until to-morrow. The Association then adjourned until two o'clock in the afternoon of the next day.

WEDNESDAY AFTERNOON, Dec. 31.

The Association was called to order by Vice-President Emery, of Fort Atkinson. After roll-call, Mr. Burton, of Janesville, read a paper on the topic, " Should the High School be organized as supplementary to the Common School, or as preparatory to the University or College," giving the opinion that the former should be the work of the smaller High Schools, and that the larger schools should be organized so that they may accomplish both objects.

Annual Meeting of Institute Conductors.

The report of the Committee on State certificates was then taken up and discussed at some length.

Mr. Wood thought the present system undesirable.

Mr. Richardson, of Milwaukee, thought the examination too technical, and the experience required too limited.

Mr. Albee called attention to the real purpose of the State certificate, and urged that we press for severer and surer tests of success, as a prerequisite for a State certificate.

After the discussion, the report, which strongly condemned the present system, was adopted by the Association.

On motion, a committee was then appointed by the chair to nominate officers for the ensuing year. The committee, composed of Messrs. Wood, Burton, and Sprague, reported the following names: For President, J. Q. Emery; for Vice-President, S. A. Hooper; for Secretary, I. N. Stewart.

The report of the committee was adopted, and the persons named therein were declared elected.

The Association then adjourned *sine die.*

A. R. SPRAGUE,   J. Q. EMERY,
          Secretary.   *President.*

ANNUAL MEETING OF INSTITUTE CONDUCTORS.

MADISON, WIS., July 5, 1880.

The Annual Meeting of the Conductors of Teachers' Institutes convened at the High School building at 9 A. M.

The meeting was opened with prayer by Rev. J. B. Pradt, after which the organization was effected by the election of State Supt. W. C. Whitford as Chairman, and A. A. Miller as Secretary.

The first subject on the programme, " Teaching the First Reader," was presented by Prof. Robert Graham. Preliminary to the exercise, he remarked that this occasion reminded him of the first meeting of the kind, held at Sparta seven years ago. The presentation of this programme of work to the teachers of the State, is evidence of progress since then. Last spring, great solicitude was felt con-

Annual Meeting of Institute Conductors.

cerning its success. The results of the spring institutes give great reason to hope for its ultimate usefulness.

The subject was presented as a class exercise. The chief points elicited were: Reading is finding the thought expressed in printed matter. It is of two kinds — oral and silent.

Two objects are sought in primary reading, viz.: (1) To give the child the power to recognize words at sight from the printed signs. (2) To give him the power to find the thought expressed by the words. Most teachers have no object at all before them in their work.

The spoken sign should be associated with the written character. The letter method is unreasonable. No unnecessary burdens should be imposed upon the child, as is done unavoidably by this method. Prof. Graham thinks by whatever method we start, we shall soon meet on a common plane. There are some advantages even in the letter method.

The pictures in reading books are of use: (1) As a test of knowledge; (2) as a means to transfer the idea of the object to the picture, and thence to the word; (3) as giving opportunities for language lessons.

The sounds of letters may be taught by slowly pronouncing the word, and repeating more and more slowly until each sound stands out distinctly and separately.

Following this, came the subject of Primary Arithmetic, by Prof. A. J. Hutton.

Formerly arithmetic consisted in ciphering; now everything is analyzed and methodized until the pupil is lost in a tangle of words. The formation of the elementary combinations swiftly and accurately, is the first requisite. The use of language is but of secondary importance. The art of arithmetic logically precedes its science, which should be deferred until pupils have passed their twelfth year. Numbers are best arranged in columns for addition. Even fractions follow the same law. All this work pertains to the first or primary form in the course of instruction for graded schools. Incidentally to this, some knowledge of powers, roots, prime and composite numbers, factoring, etc., may be acquired.

Annual Meeting of Institute Conductors.

To do this work well, requires the teacher to know *all* of arithmetic. In the solution of problems, all operations should be indicated by signs before any work is done.

This exercise closed with a desultory discussion on the correct interpretation of the signs of addition, subtraction, multiplication, and division.

The subject of "Penmanship as taught to Primary Pupils," was treated by Prof. J. B. Thayer.

Penmanship is the most neglected of primary studies, especially in the first or primary form. Here pupils should be able to write answers to questions legibly. Legibility is the point to be emphasized. To this end the powers of perception must be cultivated; also the ability to execute.

The desirable material for pupils in the primary form is, (1) slate and pencil, (2) crayon and blackboard, (3) paper and pencil, and (4) rulers for slate and blackboard.

The steps in the work are: 1. Drawing on slate and blackboard lines in different positions, from copy. 2. Drawing simple forms from copy. 3. Printing words learned from reading. 4. Change from the print form. 5. Capitals from copy. 6. Copying written language lessons.

MONDAY AFTERNOON, 2 o'clock.

The first subject in the afternoon was "United States History and Government," presented by Prof. Albert Salisbury.

This exercise is intended to give teachers a method of studying history. Some commence this study at the beginning of the period, others at the end. A combination of the two modes is preferable. Let us trace the national characteristics from the present to their origin in the early history of the people. For example, How came this to be an English speaking nation? What else could it have been? Take up the claims of the different nations. Determine the territory claimed by each, and the basis of the claim. How were the various claims of all these nations extinguished?

Another example: How came this government to be a federal republic? The nations sought to impose forms more despotic than

Annual Meeting of Institute Conductors.

they had at home. The growth of the notion of a centralized government from one of complete localization, was very gradual. The first union was the New England Confederation, formed in 1643. It originated through fear. To the time of Franklin's plan, in 1754, the desire for union was forced upon the colonies by external pressure. Afterwards, it was urged on by forces operating from within.

To stimulate the imagination is an essential element in teaching history. The constant use of the map is very necessary to teach or study history successfully. To secure this use will require perseverance on the part of the teacher.

The subject of Primary Geography had been assigned to Miss Rose C. Swart. Supt. Whitford stated that she had been prevented by illness from attending the meeting, and that the subject would be discussed by the regular conductors.

Prof. Thayer began by explaining the scheme as laid down in the syllabus. The work in geography should exemplify in the institutes the work proper to be taught the first and second reader pupils. He sometimes asks members of institutes to think as pupils of this grade naturally would do. The work should not be so exacting as to restrain the thought of pupils concerning objects surrounding them. An effort should be made to cultivate the correct use of language.

Prof. Salisbury thought two courses exist in geography, — preparatory and scientific. This scheme contemplates the former. It should consist in a series of object lessons. In the institute, he takes a specimen animal and treats it exhaustively. He disposes of the second division of the syllabus by a lecture.

Prof. Hutton thought the form of the earth and its proofs too difficult for primary pupils. The simpler portions should be taught, and proofs taken on trust. So, also, should the motions of the earth be treated.

Prof. Graham thought the scheme admirable. He gave an exercise showing what may be done in the way of teaching primary geography, by requiring pupils to describe the objects which they had seen in a single morning on coming to school.

Annual Meeting of Institute Conductors.

The work of the afternoon was closed by a paper on "Spelling taught Primary Classes," by Prof. J. Q. Emery. The ability to write words correctly is the object of learning to spell. Spelling is more difficult to acquire than any other branch. This is due to the fact that one letter may represent several sounds, and *vice versa*. Spelling should follow reading. Its teaching should conform to the law that all instruction should follow an understanding of its meaning. The written method should be employed chiefly. Whatever cultivates accuracy and quickness of perception, is an aid to spelling. The pupil needs to learn words he will use. A spelling-book has no place until the third reader is reached. All words in first and second readers should be first spelled correctly. Daily attention should be given to new and unfamiliar words. In oral spelling the syllables should be pronounced. The word should be spelled once and only once. It is the conductor's duty to recommend only methods that are old and well tried.

A lively discussion here arose upon the utility of pronouncing syllables, resulting in the prevalence of the opinion that it is no help to spelling, but may be to pronunciation.

MONDAY EVENING, 8 o'clock.

The meeting was held in the Senate Chamber of the State Capitol. Prof. Graham presented a paper on the "Introduction of the System of Grading Country Schools."

Some superintendents have spoken favorably of the scheme; some have condemned it; most have treated it with indifference. The future of the attempt seems unpromising. No results are obtained by our present system. In Massachusetts, whose system is the best in America, the results of an examination, in the county of Norfolk, in arithmetic, reading, and writing, were discouraging. Two grades were examined,—one reading in the third reader, and the other in the fourth. Many of the averages fall below fifty per cent., none reach seventy per cent., while the average is but fifty-seven per cent. If such is the result in Massachusetts, there would certainly be little in a Wisconsin examination to flatter our vanity.

More depends on the supervision of the schools than upon any-

Annual Meeting of Institute Conductors.

thing else. We can improve by the earnest co-operation of all the teachers and by the organization of efficient supervision.

Supt. Whitford thought that some progress has been made in introducing the system. Conductors have generally presented it at the institutes. Some superintendents have made earnest efforts to introduce it, and a fair number of teachers have, during the past year, tested its practicability. That no greater progress has been made, is not at all surprising to him. There will be cause for rejoicing, if the system is established in a majority of the schools in a dozen or fifteen years. One obstacle is the non-agreement of authorities, as to how the work should be done. He hopes to prepare a comprehensive circular on the subject, at an early date.

County Supt. J. T. Lunn said his teachers complain that the scheme is too indefinite — wanting in particulars. Those who have tried it, say it is good as far as it goes. He has made many explanations to teachers. It will be a long time before it is uniformly introduced into any county. He has faith in a course of study for such schools, but it must be more explicit.

Regent Chandler said the work must be slow for a time. Much will be done towards organization that will be unobserved. There has been a decided gain already. We have begun in the wrong place, without proper preparation. Patrons and boards have been neglected, and teachers alone have been enlisted in the work.

Supt. J. T. Lunn presented a paper on " Programme and Records for Grading Country Schools." He said that all successful business men and manufacturing establishments have an extensive system of book-keeping. Should a business man neglect his books, his business would soon be ruined. Teachers alone assume to conduct an important enterprise with inadequate records, or with none at all. The forms prescribed by the State authorities are of no great value.

Mr. Lunn was requested by the convention to place on a blackboard a specimen page of a register which he had devised to meet the existing want. He said he would do so to-morrow.

Annual Meeting of Institute Conductors.

TUESDAY MORNING, July 6, 9 o'clock.

The session opened in the High School room, with prayer by Rev. M. Benson, Pastor of the Methodist Episcopal Church of Madison.

Miss Mary Brayman, of the Platteville Normal School, presented the subject of "Teaching Numbers to Primary Pupils." She had a class of seven boys and girls, her pupils. The exercise was remarkable in many respects; notably as showing the great interest taken by the pupils in the work, their accuracy in recitation, the precision with which they worked, the readiness with which they wrote numbers previously unfamiliar, and the beauty of the figures when written. Miss Brayman uses objects in illustration as far as 1,000. Before reaching this point, she finds her pupils pushing ahead in forming abstract ideas of numbers.

Drawing was next considered, a paper being read on the subject by Prof. A. J. Hutton.

Drawing is worthy a place in every school as an adjunct to writing. It should not be permitted to usurp the place of any other branch. Too much is now attempted in the institute, and drawing may well take a back seat. If introduced at all, let it come two days and writing three days each week. Conductors should show that it need not be an expensive study. Pupils should be set at work.

Just here the convention switched off into a discussion on teaching penmanship.

Prof. Salisbury would have drawing this year to the exclusion of penmanship. It is impossible to do both.

Supt. Lunn said the use of drawing was to keep the little children busy and to interest them.

Miss Brayman here gave a class exercise with primary pupils on beginning the subject of numbers.

By means of objects, pupils are taught to select numbers from one to nine. Then take up addition, then subtraction. Multiplication is begun by marks on the board, and continued by means of objects. Division is taught in this connection. All this work takes one year.

Annual Meeting of Institute Conductors.

In teaching language to primary pupils, Prof. Thayer strives —

(1) To bring out what the child has learned before entering school in the acquisition of his tongue. What method has the child used? Answer. Imitation. In what order has he acquired it? Answer. (*a*) Name words, (*b*) quality words, (*c*) action words, (*d*) simple statement.

(2) To show the ways in which the child should be taught language in the early stages. Use the child's habit, viz.: (*a*) By objects, questions and answers; discourage analysis. (*b*) Teacher furnishs correct questions leading to correct answers; criticism in a kindly spirit. This refers to oral work. When it comes to written work, strive to exercise the memory, as reading a story and asking the pupil to re-write as well as he can.

(3) A book should not be put in pupil's hand, making it a separate study, until the intermediate or the grammar form is reached. Technical grammar has no place in the common school, save in exceptional cases.

Prof. Salisbury thinks we always acquire language just as the child does, by imitation and practice. Teacher's criticism of errors must be persevering. He should refuse to accept ungrammatical expressions from pupils. Every reading and spelling lesson should be a language lesson.

TUESDAY AFTERNOON, 2 o'clock.

Prof. Emery presented a paper on "School Organization." The best classification of the objects is that given by Gill (to which the reader is referred). Loosely, they are study and recitation. The authority for the organization rests immediately in the teacher and the board, but ultimately in the State constitution. Teachers must carefully avoid transcending their power. All innovations should come jointly from teacher and school board. The enrollment should take place near the close of the first day. The basis of classification should not be size nor age, but ability and attainments. No set rules can be given,— teachers must exercise their tact and judgment. It may not be determined in a day, but should be at first an experimental one.

Annual Meeting of Institute Conductors.

The teacher should secure enough information before school begins to enable him to form the programme for the first day. Pupils may select their own seats, subject to change for cause. Reading and arithmetic are the best basis for classification.

Mr. Lunn explained a new form for school records, a specimen page of which he had placed on the blackboard. It embraces the usual register of attendance, with room for summaries, as well as of punctuality, deportment, recitation, examination, classification of school, programme of study and recitation, progress of pupils, time engaged in study, and advice where each pupil should begin the next term.

A " General Exercise in Teaching History to Primary Classes," was presented by Prof. Salisbury.

Begin by reading or telling a story to the pupils each day, questioning daily on what was read previously. Prof. Salisbury considered the convention as a district school for the time being, and showed how he would conduct such an exercise. He considers that there is great value in pictures as a means of stimulating the imagination.

Finally, the discussion on the subject of spelling was resumed for a short time. This resulted in the determinatian of nothing in addition to yesterday's debate.

Adjourned *sine die.*

A. A. MILLER,　　　　　　　　　W. C. WHITFORD,
　　　Secretary.　　　　　　　　　　　　*Chairman.*

Wisconsin Industrial School for Boys, at Waukesha.

REPORTS OF

REFORMATORY AND CHARITABLE INSTITUTIONS.

WISCONSIN INDUSTRIAL SCHOOL FOR BOYS, AT WAUKESHA.

(From the Managers' Report.)

The undersigned, managers of the Wisconsin Industrial School for Boys, in accordance with the law, respectfully present herewith the twenty-first annual report " of the performance of their duty " in the management of the institution under their charge, for the fiscal year ending September 30, 1880:

Number of boys on roll October 1, 1879	431
Received by commitment	108
Returned from " out on ticket "	10
	549

Released, " home on ticket "	97
Released, out to place	7
Dismissed	2
Died	5
Escaped	8
On roll October 1, 1880	430
	549

Average number of boys during year	427 $\frac{23}{100}$
Highest number of boys at any one time	438
Lowest number of boys at any one time	418
Total number enrolled since July, 1860	1,801
Total number dismissed, escaped, and died	1,371
Leaving on record as above	430

The report last year said that after completing the buildings then in progress, there would be left of the appropriation for that purpose an estimated amount of $5,201.74. The actual amount was $6,765.95. That report also said a hospital was needed, and gave the reasons therefor, and that they proposed to take the money left to erect such a building. They said, " We also propose to build an ice house with refrigerators sufficiently large to hold all the beef and other articles required to be put therein, and to make such other permanent improvements as are needed, and there are such." They complete the paragraph as follows: " The labor of our boys on and about the new buildings, in preparing the stone, etc., has saved us all of the sum now on hand, and therefore we feel warranted in using the money as we propose."

The ice house with refrigerator was first built at a cost of $1,181.23. It is a success and of great value.

After due deliberation and consultation, we decided to have new water tanks made in place of those on hand, that were no longer safe, and to expend the money for what we felt were our most pressing needs. We put up stone walls, and raised the laundry building one story, purchased a steam engine and boiler of sufficient capacity to run all the machinery of the laundry, boot and shoe shop, and carpenter shop, should one be erected. The cost of building tanks, laundry extension and washing machine, large brick chimney outside the building, engine, boiler, shafting and belting, was $4,770.94, leaving balance of building fund in the treasury of $813.78.

The need of a hospital was set forth at length in our last annual report, to which we respectfully refer. We ask for an appropriation to build a two story building according to plan furnished by Dr. Reeve of the State Board of Health, of ($6,000) six thousand dollars.

The building now used as a bakery, boys' kitchen and wash room, and for family of 30 boys, is of wood, two stories, with stone basement. It adjoins the shop building, and should it get on fire would endanger them all. It is an old building, unfit for the purposes used, and any longer delay in replacing the wooden with a stone structure, would be little short of criminal. We ask an appropriation of eight thousand ($8,000) dollars for that purpose.

The rooms that have heretofore been used for carpenter and paint shops, have been taken for the engine and boiler, and boys'

Wisconsin Industrial School for Boys, at Waukesha.

warming room, and play room in bad weather. There should be a building for carpenter and paint shop, two stories high, to which a shaft could be run, and a turning lathe and other machinery as might be needed attached. To put up a sufficient building of stone and furnish the necessary machinery, we estimate would cost $4,500, and we ask for that amount. Such a building is a necessity to this institution.

We want an appropriation of five hundred dollars to build stone walks between our buildings, and six hundred dollars to purchase paints and do the painting necessary at once. There can be no difference of opinion as to the benefit to be derived by these expenditures.

Our water supply is not sufficient. When the steam pump is used vigorously for a few minutes, it exhausts the water in our well. It fills up again, it is true; but should we be so unfortunate as to have a fire, serious consequences would result. We want to dig such a well as will always insure us good water, and for the same and fixtures ask for $1,000.

Our laundry wants a brass machine similar to those at the hospitals for the insane, in which to boil clothes. We estimate that $1,000 for that, and other things connected with our laundry, will be needed.

The chairs in assembly room are beginning to be shaky, and we ask for $250 to reseat said room.

The greater part of our fences must soon be rebuilt, and a good share of those on the farm, at once. We ask an appropriation for that purpose of $800.

We ask for more special appropriations than ever before. We desire to obey the law passed last winter. We are obliged to receive and care for all the boys legally committed to this institution. We intend to do our duty. We have asked for no more than we believe is absolutely necessary, and in so doing, only perform what the law requires of us.

Wisconsin Industrial School for Boys, at Waukesha.

(From Superintendent's Report.)

HEALTH.

I take pleasure in stating that at the date of this report the health of the inmates is exceptionally good, and there has been but little sickness in the institution during the greater portion of the year. At the commencement of the fiscal year, considerable sickness of the nature of typho-malarial fever existed, from which two deaths occurred. In addition to these, one has died of heart disease, and one of meningitis, but there have been no deaths since December last.

The physician's report appended will show the number of cases having received treatment.

The sanitary affairs of the institution have received constant attention; much time and care having been devoted to keeping the out-buildings and other places about the premises in a neat and cleanly condition.

Upon the recommendation of the State Board of Health to your honorable body, and instructions received from you, the deposits from the old privy vaults were removed early in the spring and the same placed upon the land as a fertilizer, and we have sufficient reasons for believing that by removing the contents of these vaults, we have contributed in some degree to the general healthfulness of all.

The old vaults have been filled in, and the "dry earth system" is now in use throughout the entire institution.

DISCIPLINE.

The discipline, in an institution of this character, is a matter of prime importance, and worthy of the most careful consideration of those who are engaged or interested in the reformation of its subjects. Under this head, I would respectfully state that we aim to make the discipline as mild as possible, and at the same time maintain that order and decorum which is indispensable to the proper government of the school, and essential to the best interests of the boys after their release. We believe that by having a carefully

Wisconsin Industrial School for Boys, at Waukesha.

prepared system of government, with such rules and penalties as are at once necessary and wholesome, which shall be judiciously and conscientiously administered by those having the care of boys, great good may be attained.

In all matters pertaining to discipline, the end for which the institution was established should be kept constantly in mind, viz., "To aid and encourage the boys in doing right."

A system of discipline built upon this as a corner stone, and justly and kindly administered, will do much toward securing good behavior on the part of the inmates, and will, to a great extent, dispense with what is termed "rigid discipline."

Our system of advancing or retarding a boy in his grade every two weeks, according as his behavior has been good or bad, incites in most cases the desire to do well, as a boy by good conduct and proper advancement may shorten materially the period of his detention in the institution; while by repeated offenses, and inattention to his duties, he necessarily prolongs his stay here.

A boy is thus stimulated to do his best to attain that standing which will justify the managers in releasing him, on a "ticket of leave," as early as may be consistent with the rules of the institution and the best interests of the boy. Having thus been induced to make an effort toward right action, he realizes the improvement in his condition, and the fact that good conduct, here as well as elsewhere, merits and meets with its reward, and that bad conduct must necessarily meet with its punishment. Let this become a settled conviction in his mind, and the boy grows into a useful and law-abiding citizen.

It should be more fully understood by all that this institution is not a prison, nor simply a place of confinement, but a refuge for erring boys, where they may be sheltered from associations which would lead them on to greater crimes and to the incurring of still greater punishments, and where they may be educated and aided in the formation of habits of industry and sobriety.

LABOR AND INDUSTRIES.

The boot and shoe factory is in a prosperous condition. In this department one hundred and twenty-three of our boys are employed. Sixty dozen pairs of boots are manufactured each week. The class of goods manufactured here finds ready sale at liberal prices throughout our State.

The Wisconsin sock and mitten factory gives employment to about the same number as the boot factory. Here we knit on machines and by hand about sixty dozen pairs of socks (principally cotton) per week. For these goods we can always find an open market, with a fair compensation in return for the small amount of capital invested, and the labor of the smaller class of boys, to whom this work is best adapted.

TAILOR SHOP AND MENDING ROOM.

In the former department several of our boys are employed, under the supervision of the tailor, in the making of all outer garments worn by the boys.

Each boy, upon entering the school, is provided with a new suit of uniform clothes, also with suitable working clothes, and all boys when released are furnished with a good suit of citizen's clothes.

In the mending-room (a new feature with us), under the supervision of a lady overseer, some eight of the boys are employed in repairing the clothing of the boys made in the tailor shop. In addition to the repairing done, some of the smaller boys are engaged in cutting and preparing such rags as may be unfit for other purposes, yet are suitable to be woven into rag carpets, of which one hundred and twenty yards have been made since the commencement of this work.

Considering the large number here to be provided for with clothing and the usual amount required for each boy (pants, jackets, vests, overalls, blouses, caps, etc.), together with all of the necessary repairs, the observing will not fail to see that much is required from these departments.

In addition to the large number of boys employed in the shops, many are engaged in doing various kinds of outdoor work: The cultivation of the farm and garden, keeping the lawns, walks, roads, etc., in proper order. In the bakery, kitchen, laundry, and in doing general house work, all of which are indispensable to the requirements of the institution.

Wisconsin Industrial School for Boys, at Waukesha.

FARM AND GARDEN.

The crops of the farm and garden have been good. In addition to the land owned by the State, we have cultivated fifty acres more, and the products of the same have well repaid us for the rent and labor.

It will be clearly seen, by referring to the table of farm and garden products, and also that of live stock, that a large portion of our subsistence is obtained by the labor of the boys, together with that of employed help, from the cultivation of the farm and garden; while the farm does not produce any portion of the breadstuffs consumed, it furnishes large quantities of the various kinds of vegetables for our tables, together with corn, oats, hay, etc., all of which are consumed by the stock. The milk from thirty cows is principally consumed by the boys. All of the pork used is raised and fattened on the premises.

SCHOOL.

Our schools have been conducted with energy, and the scholars have made fair progress.

Every boy is required to attend school four hours each day. This time is divided into two sessions, one in each half day. The teachers' report will show the working of the various departments.

LIBRARY AND READING ROOM.

The library has been replenished this year with a large number of new books. Special care has been exercised in selecting such as are most suitable and interesting for boys. For the reading room it would be desirable to receive, in addition to those now contributed, more of our best and most exceptional newspapers and magazines, to be put on file where those boys who are desirous of keeping themselves posted in regard to the news of the day, will have opportunity to read them. I believe this suggestion from me will not be considered by any presumptuous.

W. H. SLEEP,
Superintendent.

Wisconsin Industrial School for Boys, at Waukesha.

(From the Teachers' Report.)

I herewith present the annual report of the schools for the year ending September 30, 1880:

Number under instruction at the commencement of the year	431
newly committed during the year	108
returned during the year	10
Number under instruction during the year	549

Number left during the year	119
now in attendance	430
	549

Of the one hundred and eight received:

Could not write	43

Commenced reading from Chart	23
First Reader	33
Second Reader	33
Third Reader	16
Fourth Reader	4
	108

Entered one of the Primary Departments	88
Intermediate Departments	16
the Grammar Department	4
	108

The boys are divided into two classes, which alternately work and attend school. In each session of the school there are five departments. The course of study for each session is the same, and has not been materially changed from that which has been pursued for the past year.

There are in each of the departments three classes, and boys who are ambitious and studious are allowed to work faster than their class, and thus advance more rapidly in the school. This is necessitated by the great disparity in the age and natural ability of the boys who come here.

Classes are promoted from one department to another every six months by passing a written examination, prepared by the principal. And in order to insure thoroughness and lead to frequent reviews, each teacher, except in the lowest primary, gives his pupils

Industrial School for Girls, at Milwaukee.

a written examination every six weeks upon the ground gone over in that time.

As will be seen by the statistical part of this report, more than seven-ninths of the boys entering the school go into one of the primary departments; hence it may become necessary to devise some means to prevent the overcrowding of these rooms.

In addition to these departments there is a school in the Correction House, taught by J. H. Whitcher, for two hours each day. In this there are usually from thirty to forty boys, who, on account of bad conduct, are kept there for various periods of time. They are from the various departments of the school, and necessarily ungraded, and in this report are classed with the departments in which they belong.

We have not as yet been able to bring all of the departments up to the requirements of the course marked out, but will undoubtedly be able to attain it soon.

Respectfully submitted,

G. H. REED,
Principal.

INDUSTRIAL SCHOOL FOR GIRLS, AT MILWAUKEE.

SCHOOL ROOM STATISTICS.

Whole number in school November 1, 1879	70
Received during the year	77
Whole number taught during the year	147
Dismissed	88
Remaining in school November 1, 1880	109

The pupils received were classified as follows:

Division 1	12
2	28
3	88
Too young to be classified	4
Total	77

Industrial School for Girls, at Milwaukee.

Pupils dismissed were from:

Division 1... 14
         2....................... 9
         3................... 13
Too young for classification................. 2

          Total... 38

Present classification:

Division 1. 18
         2......................... 64
         3....... 23

          Total...................................... 105

Number of children in school........................... 109
Boys................... 23
Girls.. 86

Number of children in Fifth Reader......................... 19
                     Fourth Reader........... 24
                     Third Reader.............................. 18
                     Second Reader............................. 24
                     First Reader.............................. 14
                     Learning to read from chart................. 6

          Total.............................. 105

Number of children in " A " Arithmetic..................... 6
                     " B " Arithmetic..................... 17
                     " C " Arithmetic..................... 45
                     Tables and Numeration................. 37

          Total.............................. 105

Number of children in " A " Geography.................... 16
                     " B " Geography.................... 16
                     " C " Geography.................... 39
                     Oral Geography 34

          Total................................ 105

Number of children in oral Grammar....................... 78
Studying Spelling aside from definitions in Reading Lessons 20
Alphabet class....................... 7
United States History............... 18
Number of school books................................. 250
Number of books in Library. 276

Industrial School for Girls, at Milwaukee.

SCHOOL EXERCISES.

Monday, Wednesday, and Friday, in writing, reading, arithmetic, history, geography, and spelling.

Tuesday and Thursday, in reading, spelling, arithmetic, geography, and language lessons.

Saturday, in literary entertainments, reading aloud, etc.

The morning session of two and one-half hours for the smaller children, is mostly spent in Kindergarten work. All inmates are in school from 2:30 to 5 o'clock P. M., and the First and Second Departments have an additional session from 6:15 to 7:45 o'clock P. M.

(From Report of School Committee.)

Realizing that the efficiency of labor depends not only upon natural ability, but also upon thorough training and general intelligence, we feel that it should be made possible for each child to receive a good general education, so directed as to invigorate the body, strengthen the mental powers, and elevate the moral faculties. The difference which education makes in instructions comprehended, the quickness with which facts are noted, the suggestions for the improvement of the work which are made, the lessened amount of superintendence required, and the saving of waste from blunders, untrustworthiness, and misdirected labor, are thoroughly appreciated by the School Committee, and considered by them in all of their plans for the conduct of the school proper of the Institution.

The deportment of the scholars, and the assiduity with which they have applied themselves to their studies, are commendable. During the erection of the new building, the doors of the old school rooms were enlarged, so they can now be virtually thrown into one room.

A pleasant feature in the home instruction has been introduced by the superintendent, who devotes one hour every Saturday evening in giving familiar "talks" or lectures to the older girls on household matters of interest.

INSTITUTION FOR THE EDUCATION OF THE BLIND, AT JANESVILLE.

(From the Superintendent's Report.)

In any well-established school, the routine of successive years can vary but little. Any changes are usually matters of growth, and come about so imperceptibly as scarcely to be noted as changes. Our aim is to develop every faculty of our pupils, and to train their powers so that they may be always ready for most efficient use. That the highest degree of success is not attained in every case, should not cause surprise, nor afford sufficient reason for discouragement.

Each year brings new faces among us, and each year some leave the school rooms and enter upon the wider experiences of life. Some of these, having completed a course of study, take up life's duties and responsibilities with intelligent minds, well stored with information, possessing habits of industry and hands accustomed to useful occupation. Others leave prematurely, having become eager to assume life's burdens before they were fully prepared for them, or, perhaps, impatient of the restraints of school. Still others, who have made commendable efforts to improve, and who have gained much in knowledge and skill during their pupilage, being scantily endowed by nature, have yet fallen short of many desirable attainments. Representatives of each of these classes have left school during this year.

Misapprehension as to the degree of blindness which a child must suffer in order to be received as a pupil in this school, is so frequent that it may not be amiss again to call attention to the fact that this Institution is considered supplementary to the common school system of the State, and is designed to provide means of education to all youth of suitable age and capacity, who cannot see well enough to study from an ordinary school book.

When considerable useful vision exists, it has been thought necessary to require a physician's certificate as to the amount of sight and the condition of the eyes. While the work of the school must be planned chiefly with reference to the requirements of those who

Institution for the Education of the Blind, at Janesville.

are totally blind, we aim, as far as practicable, to adapt it to individual necessities.

The total number of names on the roll for the past year is eighty-nine — forty-eight girls and forty-one boys,— of whom eleven have entered since the date of the last report, and twelve have left school not expecting to return.

I regret to say that there has been less regularity in attendance than in some previous years. Some pupils and their parents seem to appreciate the importance of prompt and continuous presence at school; while others allow trivial reasons to delay their return to school after the summer vacation, or to call them away during the progress of the term.

Irregularity in attendance is a serious evil in any school, but in a school for the blind, where instruction is chiefly oral, the attending evils are very greatly increased, and damage results not alone to the absent or tardy pupil, but also to his classmates, who must delay their progress while he makes up lost time. It would be well if parents could understand that they cannot keep their children at home after the opening of the term, or call them away for even a few days during the session, without serious detriment, not only to the interests of their child, but to the remainder of the school.

The health of the pupils has been exceptionally good during the year. While due credit should be given to the watchful care of the matron, and to the skill of the attending physician, it is undoubtedly true that much benefit has resulted from the increased attention to open air exercise, which the sidewalk built a year ago has done much to facilitate and encourage.

The work of all American schools for the blind is conducted in three departments, literary, musical, and industrial. Training in each of these is necessary to give symmetrical development, and a fair opportunity for such preparation as shall fit our pupils for useful and happy lives.

Reading, spelling, arithmetic, geography, and grammar must always have the largest share in the school programme; but each term we have several classes in higher branches. During last term classes were instructed in rhetoric, United States history, geometry, and chemistry. This term we have classes in physical geography, English history, geology, and English literature.

In this department, thorough instruction and faithful study have borne their legitimate fruits.

Three vocal classes, a class in harmony, and the orchestra meet daily for instruction and drill. Forty pupils have received lessons upon the piano, nineteen upon the organ, eleven upon the violin, four upon other instruments, and ten have received individual vocal training. We have frequently had pupils with better voices and more natural musical ability than at present; but rarely, if ever, has better work been done, or more manifest improvement been made, than under the present organization of the musical department.

Each pupil is expected to spend at least one hour daily in some industrial occupation. The younger ones continue to find in bead-work profitable training for muscles and the sense of touch. The older girls have done an unusual variety of plain and fancy work, and a number of them have improved very much in their ability to do useful service in keeping in order and making their own clothing.

For several years past, the results of the broom shop have been unsatisfactory, and the obstacles in the way of blind broom-makers have been increasingly formidable. At present, the number of our graduates who are known to be following this trade successfully, is very small. Some persons who, during a number of years, made a comfortable living by broom-making, have found themselves unable to compete with the cheap factory-made brooms with which most of the markets of the State are now supplied, and have been obliged to seek some other occupation. It is encouraging to know that such persons, as a rule, have proved the value of the education they had received, by their ability to turn to some other occupation when one resource had failed.

We have now four looms, and have had, to this date, enough custom work brought in to keep them all busy. An experienced weaver, Mrs. Hanson, is in charge, and her pupils make rapid im-

Institute for the Deaf and Dumb, at Delavan.

provement. The work done bears comparison with that of sighted weavers, and has been our only advertisement. The success of those who have attempted to follow this business at their homes, gives great cause for encouragement.

Cane-seating furnishes preparatory training of decided value, and these classes are now doing excellent work.

A good library in ordinary print is one of the most important agents in the successful education of the blind. The supply of books of reference and text-books should be ample, and should keep pace with the progress of the art of teaching and the development of science. By the arrangement of the school programme, our pupils listen to general literature, read by teachers, at least one hour daily. Books for this purpose should be carefully selected, and should include history, biography, travel, poetry, some standard fiction, and at least samples of the works of all leading literary writers. There should be a good supply of juvenile literature, and also enough moral and religious books of a non-sectarian character to provide for considerable reading upon the Sabbath.

MRS. SARAH F. C. LITTLE,
Superintendent.

INSTITUTE FOR THE DEAF AND DUMB, AT DELAVAN.

(From the Trustees' Report.)

The work of the Institution during the past year has been carried on under many embarrassments on account of the very imperfect accommodations which were provided in great haste after the burning of the former building. The inmates were subjected to more than ordinary exposure to the weather, involving serious risk to health. But the winter was unusually mild, and the danger itself probably led to special watchfulness and care. Thus, in the good providence of God, the family has been remarkably exempt from serious sickness or physical ailments of any kind.

Though the teachers have had many and great inconveniences to contend with, the work of instruction has not been interrupted or seriously impaired. The Board cannot too highly commend the cheerfulness and earnest zeal with which the officers and employes of the Institution rallied to meet the exigency of a great calamity, and they are gratified with the evident proficiency and intellectual growth of the pupils of all the classes. They are happy also to report favorably of the conduct of the pupils. In circumstances which rendered the maintenance of discipline more than ordinarily difficult, their deportment was in an extraordinary degree marked by good order and fidelity to duty. The pressure of necessity, felt by all, was more effective than the mere force of executive authority to restrain evil impulses, and to prompt all to willing subjection and self-sacrifice for the common good. The standard of scholarship has been well sustained, and the way is prepared for a decided advance, as the classes come now into new school rooms, provided with better facilities than the Institution has ever before possessed. The opening of the school for the current year was delayed two weeks that the new school-house might be ready for occupation by the classes at the outset.

At the end of the school year in June last, Prof. J. W. Swiler, for many years an efficient and successful teacher in the Illinois Institution for the Deaf and Dumb, was elected to the office of superintendent, and has entered upon its duties with energy and devotion. The office of matron, made vacant by the resignation of Mrs. Broadrup, has been filled by the appointment of Miss Julia A. Taylor, who comes to the service with the advantage of a long and successful experience in similar positions in Indiana and Illinois. A large increase in the number of pupils has necessitated the employment of an additional teacher, and Mrs. Belle Tallman, a former teacher in our Institution, has been appointed. With these exceptions, the corps of instructors and other officers is continued the same as last year. Dr. De Motte, released from duty here, has been called to the charge of a similar institution in the State of Kansas, whither the best wishes of this Board follow him.

As soon as possible after the action of the last legislature, contracts were made for the erection of new buildings according to the plans adopted by the legislature, and at a cost coming within the

Institute for the Deaf and Dumb, at Delavan.

amount of money designated and appropriated. The work has been pushed on with energy and rapidity, hindered only by the difficulty, almost impossibility, of securing the full force of mechanics needed; since the general revival of business enterprise, after years of depression, has created a demand for labor in building quite beyond the supply.

The plans adopted contemplated the erection of four buildings in place of the one consumed. On the 30th of September, two of these, the chapel and dining room and the school-house were in use, though not quite completed in all parts; the dormitory for boys was advanced, so that it will no doubt be ready for occupancy in November; and the main, central building, which is to provide offices, rooms for the Superintendent's family and female teachers, and a study room and dormitory for girls, was in a fair way to be fully completed soon after the first of January next.

The architect has kept an assistant from his office constantly on the ground to superintend the work, and the executive committee of the Board have exercised a general oversight of the whole. The Board believe the contractors have been true and faithful to their agreements, except as to time of completion, so that at a very moderate expense these accommodations will be secured, adapted to their purpose, with as much architectural beauty, perhaps, as the case demands. While rejoicing in facilities for carrying on the work of the Institution, thus restored and improved, the Board have felt sincere and deep regret that the appropriation was not made sufficient to provide for some substantial qualities now wanting in the buildings, especially such as might guard more effectually against the danger from fire.

The special appropriations of the last legislature were limited to $65,000 for buildings, and $5,000 for new boilers and furniture. The lowest bid for erecting the buildings came only just within the sum named, leaving a sum insufficient to pay architect's fees, nothing for changes and repairs in the old laundry building to adjust it to the new dining room and chapel, nothing for cleaning and grading the grounds, putting in sewers and new cisterns, nothing for carrying steam from the boilers to the buildings, nor for making necessary plank walks. In setting the boilers, it was also found necessary to make excavation, to strengthen the foundation of existing walls and to build a portion of wall anew; also to provide steam traps for bringing condensed steam back to the boilers, and to put on non-conducting covering to the system of steam pipes in the boiler room. These unanticipated expenses more than exhausted the amount appropriated for boilers and furniture, leaving the furnishing of the new buildings wholly unprovided for. Yet the adjustments named must be made while the work of building was going on, and new furniture will be required before further appropriations from the legislature can be obtained. To meet this exigency, the Board, in conformity with the statute, called on your Excellency, the Secretary of State and the Attorney General to consider the case, and received your approval for incurring expenses to the amount of $7,000 beyond the appropriations made. The certificate of approval accompanies this report.

The Board commend to your attention and consideration the accompanying report of the Superintendent. The changes recently introduced in the grading and arrangements for the instruction of the classes are in the line of progress, and conformed to the methods best approved in our modern systems of public education. The two teachers of articulation are meeting with a measure of success in their efforts, fully equal, it is believed, to that achieved in any institution in our land where that method of instruction is made exclusive.

The Board regard the corps of instructors, as now constituted, with great satisfaction. It embraces men and women of good capacity, high character, noble aims, and sincere devotion to the best welfare of those placed under their charge, to whose care parents and friends may, with all confidence, commit the children and youth of our State, whose physical infirmity precludes them from other schools and institutions of education. This institution should be regarded not as a charity, an asylum, a house of refuge, but rather as an important branch of that system of public education, through which the State seeks to make of its entire people intelligent, industrious, virtuous, and patriotic citizens. As such

Institute for the Deaf and Dumb, at Delavan.

it is again heartily commended to the fostering care of our legislature and executive officers, and to the beneficent good will of all who, in the spirit of true patriotism and broad philanthropy, would promote the stability of the commonwealth and the highest well-being of their fellow-men.

A. L. CHAPIN,
President.

(From the Superintendent's Report.)

Fifty-eight pupils are in the primary department, at the completion of which they are able to write and read simple sentences, using verbs, nouns, adjectives, and adverbs to a limited extent, and also have some knowledge of addition. Fifty-three are connected with the intermediate department, which gives them instruction in composition, introduces them to history and geography, and carries them through the fundamental rules of arithmetic. Forty-six are in the academic classes, in which they are taught the ordinary branches of a common school education, with some of the studies that pertain to high schools and academies. Fifty-five pupils are in the articulation classes.

Upon application, all deaf persons of lawful age, not imbecile or idiotic, have been admitted to the privileges of the school. Efforts are being made to secure the attendance of other children still kept at home.

The new school-house, now in daily use, is a substantial two-story brick building, 122 by 66 feet, surmounting a basement of heavy stone. Two principal entrances are connected by separate walks with the buildings used by boys and girls. The school-house is heated by steam, and supplied with water. There are eight rooms on each floor, twelve of them in use; the others will be occupied during the current year. These rooms are pleasant, light, and airy, so constructed that direct sunshine may be admitted to each during some portion of the day. Increased attendance has made the employment of an additional teacher necessary. Mrs. C. B. Tallman, formerly a teacher here, has re-enlisted in the work, and now has in charge the B class of new pupils. The A class of new pupils, under Miss Mary Hunter's training, is making rapid progress in reading, writing, and spelling. Effective work is done in the primary and intermediate classes. The attendance this term is 30 per cent. advance on last term, so that the beginning classes are larger than usual. The order of recitations in these classes remains unchanged.

In a school for the deaf and dumb where the pupils are wholly dependent upon their instructors for what they learn, having little communication with, and no intelligent means of instruction from, other persons, it is thought best to provide for advanced classes the means of a more complete development by bringing them under the direct personal influence of the thoughts and methods of different teachers. Accordingly recitations of the advanced classes have been arranged, with hourly changes from room to room, giving each teacher a special department of the work and commensurate responsibility. Prof. Cochrane has classes in language and composition; Prof. Schilling, in arithmetic; and Prof. Fuller, in geography, history, and natural science.

ARTICULATION.

Special attention is given to articulation and lip-reading. Two teachers of experience, thoroughly familiar with the work, devote all their time to this department.

Ten of the new pupils recite to Miss Eddy in articulation, and are already making marked improvement.

As soon as pupils are found to be susceptible of vocal culture, they are placed in some one of these speaking classes. It is not expedient to give all deaf children vocal training. Some are unable and others unwilling to learn; however, since 55 pupils in a school of 156 are in speaking classes, the importance of this department is evident, and its perpetuity secured. Daily experiments, carefully and persistently made with the Audiphone, during a period of several months, indicate that but few of the pupils use it with advantage. It is of service to a limited number of the semi-deaf; but its utility as an instrument of instruction has not yet been proven.

The need of special instruction in writing and drawing is felt,

Institute for the Deaf and Dumb, at Delavan.

and as soon as the arrangement and equipment of buildings is completed, a teacher will be employed to develop this important department. The foundations of good penmanship must be early laid, and drawing is the only accomplishment the deaf and dumb can acquire. Its importance as a useful art is daily increasing, and its practical value in designing, painting, and wood-carving is more generally recognized than ever before.

JOHN W. SWILER,

Superintendent.

16 — St. Sup.

EXAMINATION

OF

TEACHERS FOR STATE CERTIFICATES.

Held at Madison, August 10–13, 1880.

HISTORY OF THE UNITED STATES.

1. How were the various English charter and proprietary rights severally extinguished ?
2. Describe and draw plan of the battle of Bunker Hill.
3. State what seem Providential interpositions in favor of Americans during the Revolution, and why so regarded?
4. Write of the " Virginia and Kentucky Resolutions."
5. What public acts of Gen. Jackson were of debatable propriety, and why?
6. State the various acts of the general government promotive of education; and those in the interest of the laboring poor.
7. Enumerate and locate the several battles in which Gen. Grant commanded, stating opposing commanders and particulars.
8. What were the terms of Gen. Johnston's capitulation to Gen. Sherman in North Carolina, and why so obnoxious to the authorities?
9. In what were the ratifications of the last three amendments to the United States Constitution peculiar; and how do some consequently regard them, and why?
10. Sketch life of Alexander Hamilton, or of Aaron Burr.

Examination of Teachers for State Certificates.

ARITHMETIC.

1. Write in decimal notation, five thousand three hundred seventy-five hundredths.
2. Find the quotient of 4,334 by 122, on the supposition that both dividend and divisior are written on the scale *eight.*
3. Find what part 2 A. 16½ R. are of 16 A. 12¾ R.
4. Reduce $\frac{15}{17}$ to thirds.
5. Write the principles that underly the reduction of fractions.
6. Find .01¼ per cent. of 48,240.
7. A cistern 6 ft. by 8 ft. contains 80 bbls.; what is its depth?
8. What sum of money at 8 per cent., simple interest, amounts to $355.20, in 2 yr. 3 mo. 18 da.?
9. An agent receives a remittance with which to purchase flour after deducting his commission, 1¼ per cent. for purchasing; his commission is $45, what is the cost of the flour?
10. If ⅛ of a lot of goods be destroyed, at what per cent. above cost must the remainder be sold that a gain of 20 per cent. on the cost of the whole may be realized?

GEOGRAPHY.

1. What are the principal agencies now at work in producing changes upon the earth's crust?
2. Explain the formation of coral reefs.
3. What conditions determine the climate of any country?
4. Describe the Mississippi system of drainage.
5. Describe the mountain system of North America.
6. What is the northern boundary of the Pacific Ocean? Of the the Atlantic Ocean?
7. Bound Lake Michigan. Lake Huron.
8. What are the trade winds, and how are they caused?
9. What are tidal waves? Upon what does their height depend?
10. Explain the formation of springs.
11. Explain the formation of dew.

CIVIL GOVERNMENT.

1. How was the United States Constitution ratified, and why in that peculiar manner?
2. What says the United States Constitution respecting war, military and related topics?
3. By what provision does a nickel coin circulate for five cents, while it does not contain two cents worth of metal?
4. If our State so appreciated a President as to vote him a thousand dollars, could he accept it; and why?
5. A census having been taken, what must now be done; and when, how, and why?
6. Give a synopsis of the XIV amendment.
7. Female suffrage being now proposed in Wisconsin, what yet remains to determine whether it be granted?
8. Which State courts do, and which do not, have jury trial; and why?
9. Give a synopsis of what the State shall print and publish.
10. Distinguish republic from democracy; sovereignty from jurisdiction; quorum from majority; law from equity; presentment from indictment.

PHYSIOLOGY.

1. Classify foodstuffs. Where and by what agencies is each kind digested?
2. Explain the sounds of the heart; the mechanism of the valves.
3. What is the cause of the pulse? Why is there none in the capillaries? In the veins?
4. Explain the action of any inhibitory nerve.
5. What is blood? Tell all that you can of its coagulation.
6. What are the respiratory changes in lungs, blood, and tissues?
7. How is the hepatic glycogen formed? For what is it used?
8. What is the action of the spinal cord as a conductor? As a center?

Examination of Teachers for State Certificates.

9. What are the functions of the cerebrum?   Of the cerebellum?
10. What is the source of the energy of the body?
11. Describe the ear, and explain its action.
12. What is the muscular sense?

ALGEBRA.

1. Explain what is meant by *known* and *unknown*, *positive* and *negative*.

2. Distinguish between $\frac{3}{4}a$ and $a^{\frac{3}{4}}$.

3. What is the value of the reciprocal of $\dfrac{1}{x^{-\frac{3}{4}}}$, when $x=16$?

4. Change $\dfrac{a^{\frac{2}{3}}b^{\frac{1}{2}}}{x^{-2}y^{\frac{1}{2}}}$ to an equivalent, which involves neither fractional nor negative exponents.

5. Resolve $a^{\frac{2n}{3}}x^{\frac{2m}{5}}$ into two binomial factors, and write the general formula which applies.

6. Given $2x-\sqrt{\dfrac{x^2+15}{4}}=10$, to find the value of x.

7. State the axioms which underly the transformation of equations.

8. Change $\dfrac{c\sqrt{a}}{x^{\frac{1}{3}}}$ to an equivalent having a rational denominator.

9. Given $\begin{cases}(x+z)^2=a\\x^2+z^2=c\end{cases}$, to find x and z.

10. Given $x^{\frac{3}{t}}=\left[(c+d)^3\right]^{\frac{1}{a}}$, to find x.

Examination of Teachers for State Certificates.

READING,

1. What contributes most to pleasant, effective reading, and how attained?
2. State the office of punctuation in composition, and the relation of pauses thereto.
3. Write about *inflection.*
4. Write about *monotone.*
5. Write about *posture* of reader.
6. To what extent should the memory of pupils be exercised on the lessons of the usual school readers, and why?
7. By some tabular outline indicate what is embraced in expression.

　　Oral reading of selected articles.

GRAMMAR AND ANALYSIS.

1. What is meant by parts of speech? Illustrate.
2. Copy the following, underline and classify the pronouns: He gave me this, on the condition that I should remain?
3. What do you understand by *grammatical property, government, agreement?*
4. How do you determine the case of a noun?
5. Write the principal parts of the following: dive, drink, lay, fall, sit.
6. Make a list of the auxiliary verbs and illustrate the use of each.
7. Write a synopsis of the word *run* in the progressive form, third person, singular number.
8. Write a sentence containing the word *what* used as a relative.
9. Parse the italicised words in the following: The *youth who* has acquired a habit of *reading* instructive *books*, has a *pleasing* occupation for his leisure hours.
10. Write sentences illustrating the different constructions of the infinitive.

11. Give a complete classification of sentences and elements of sentences according to your system of analysis.

12. Analyze the following:

> " I see before me the gladiator lie;
> He leans upon his hand — his manly brow
> Consents to death, but conquers agony,
> And his drooped head sinks gradually low,
> And through his side the last drops, ebbing slow
> From the red gash fall heavy, one by one,
> Like the first of a thunder shower."

PENMANSHIP.

1. Can every (sound) person become a *good, systematic* writer, habitually; and why?

2. Give a series of figures or diagrams, as movement exercises preliminary to writing; and state value of each.

3. State a series of signals wherewith to open and to close writing exercies.

4. Is one uniform position desirable in an entire school, and why?

5. Should the teacher set copies, and why?

6. State horizontal spacing to observe between letters, words, and sentences.

7. Make letters, each illustrating a different shading, stating what.

8. Make, and state proportions of each capital principle.

9. By using numbers to designate principles, analyze *Teaching.*

10. As specimen of best copy-hand, write,— Penmanship is the product of trained eye and trained muscles.

GEOMETRY.

1. What is the subject-matter of pure geometry?

2. To what practical purposes is geometry applied?

3. Define and illustrate the different kinds of triangles.

4. Name and illustrate the different kinds of quadrilaterals.

5. Define and give an example of an axiom, a postulate, and a problem.
6. Demonstrate, "that the sum of the interior angles of a triangle is equal to two right angles."
7. On a given line, as one side, construct an obtuse-angled triangle, having a given area, and demonstrate the correctness of your construction.
8. State and demonstrate a theorem, involving the parallelism of planes.
9. Demonstrate "that an angle at the circumference is measured by one-half the subtended arc."
10. Give your method of bisecting an angle, and outline the demonstration of its correctness.

NATURAL PHILOSOPHY.

1. Name the universal properties of matter.
2. Define and give examples of *adhesion, cohesion.*
3. How far will a stone fall in seven seconds?
4. At the equator, what must be the length of a pendulum that vibrates once in five minutes?
5. State the general law of the lever, and show its application by an example of each class.
6. If the air supported a column of water 50 feet in hight, what would be the pressure of the atmosphere per square inch?
7. Give reasons in support of the Dynamic Theory of heat.
8. Explain the ways in which heat is diffused.
9. Give the philosophy of the bent appearance of a straight stick partially submerged in water.
10. Explain the construction of the microscope.

ORTHOGRAPHY.

1. By tabular outline, indicate the items included in Orthography.
2. Classify a number of suffixes by the part of speech represented, and state to what part of speech each affixes.

Examination of Teachers for State Certificates.

3. What of punctuation is necessary in Orthography, and for what purposes?
4. Make list of compound words whose spelling is not like the original component words, and account for each deviation.
5. Give a list of pure foreign words and phrases which our language has adopted, and state meaning of each.
6. From either root, mit (mis), or finis, form a list of derivatives.
7. Draught a letter to a book house, ordering six text-books of unlike kinds and prices.
8, 9, and 10. Spell and otherwise dispose of a list of words dictated.

ORTHOEPY.

1. Classify the *occasional* vowels as *long* and *short*, by cognate or correlative pairs.
2. If all vowels originate in the larynx, why are they not alike in sound? What are their differences, and how produced?
3. For which distinct sounds, recognized by Webster, has he no distinguishing representative characters; and why?
4. Which consonants are nearest related to vowels, and which vowels nearest related to consonants; and why this relation?
5. Which class of consonants form syllables in which there is *said* to be no vowel sound? Explain.
6. Write of the sounds of $\bar{a}$, $\bar{i}$, $\bar{o}$, and $\bar{u}$.
7. By some tabular outline, state the anatomical organs employed in pronunciation, and function of each.
8, 9, and 10. Mark sounds of letters, and state rules of pronunciation therefor, as dictated.

ENGLISH LITERATURE.

1. Into what periods is the history of our language clearly separated.
2. Why should the writings of Chaucer be assigned a prominent place in English Literature?

Examination of Teachers for State Certificates.

3. State the character of Spenser's writings.
4. Classify Shakespeare's plays and mention an example of each class.
5. Mention the principal prose writers of the Elizabethan Age, and state the character of their writings.
6. Give an analysis of one of Milton's works.
7. What is the character of the writings of Pope, Addison, and Swift?
8. In what century was novel writing introduced, and who were among the early novelists?
9. Compare the writings of Dickens and Thackeray.
10. Give the names and the chief works of three historians of the eighteenth century.

MENTAL PHILOSOPHY.

1. What are the differences between physiology and mental philosophy?
2. What is a visual sensation? A visual perception? A visual judgment?
3. Explain the theory of association?
4. How would you explain the origin of ideas?
5. How do emotions and sensations differ?
6. What is unconscious cerebration?
7. What are the important differences between the two leading schools of philosophy?
8. Define cause; hypothesis; theory.

GENERAL HISTORY.

1. Into what epochs is history usually divided, and why?
2. Write of the most decisive battle of each epoch, stating why each is so estimated.
3. Write of Xenophon and his ten thousand.

Examination of Teachers for State Certificates.

4. Write of the origin and status of Roman Pontifical jurisdiction.

5. Write of the wars between England and France in the four-
teenth century.

6. Write of the common people of Europe of 400 to 800 years
ago.

7. Write about the Tulip Mania, or of the Mississippi Scheme, or
of the South Sea Bubble.

8. Write of the Covenanters.

9. Which of Napoleon's marshals long survived as king; and how
did he attain and retain such rank?

10. Write of Louis Kossuth.

GEOLOGY.

1. What explanation does the evolution theory offer of the origin
of the earth?

2. What are the divisions of the age of reptiles?

3. Describe the Devonian Age.

4. What was the plant life of the Triassic and Jurassic Ages?

5. What minerals enter most largely into the composition of rocks?

6. What is the distribution of glacial drift in North America?

7. Give a method of measuring the rate of subaerial denudation?

8. How was coal formed?

9. Describe the Stone Age.   The Bronze Age.

POLITICAL ECONOMY.

1. What are the objections to the greenback currency?

2. What is rent?

3. What effect would a great increase of the population have
upon the wages of the people of America?

What is the effect if two currencies of unequal value are put
into circulation in the same country?

5. What is the effect of usury laws?

6. What is wealth?
7. Can there be a general rise in values?
8. Can there be a general rise in prices?
9. Why, as a rule, do women get lower wages than men for the same work?
10. What are the disadvantages of the division of labor?

BOTANY.

1. Into what series are plants divided? Into what classes?
2. How is the germinating plantlet nourished?
3. What are buds? When and where do they appear?
4. What is the structure and action of the roots? How does their mode of growth differ from that of the stem?
5. What are the functions of the leaves? Name five variations and adaptations in their forms.
6. What is a bulb? How does it grow?
7. What is the flower? Name its parts and explain their functions.
8. What is cross-fertilization?
9. What is the fruit? Define simple and multiple fruits.
10. What is a cell? How are vegetable cells put together? In what way does sap pass from one to another? Why does it ascend to the leaves?
11. In what way does the vegetable world prepare food for the animal world?
12. What is the source of vegetable energy?

THEORY OF TEACHING.

1. What branches of study do you consider of greatest value in elementary instruction?
2. Mention the characteristics of a successful school?
3. Mention the principal causes of disorder in schools?

Examination of Teachers for State Certificates.

4. What authority has the teacher in matters of organization and discipline? From whom is the authority obtained?

5. What means do you employ to secure a full, prompt, and regular attendance?

6. At what minimum age do you judge, pupils might profitably enter your school?

7. State briefly your method of dealing with pupils at the beginning of their school experience?

8. In what ways would you assist pupils in their school work?

9. Name the educational works that you have read.

10. State your theory in regard to compositions, declamations, and school exhibitions.

Apportionment of School Fund Income in 1880.

STATISTICAL TABLES.

The following apportionment was made in June last, on the returns reported for the school year ending August 31, 1879. The rate was forty cents per scholar.

The amount received by the independent cities is included.

Table No. I.

APPORTIONMENT OF SCHOOL FUND INCOME IN 1880.

COUNTIES.	Number of Children.	Apportionment.
Adams	2,588	$1,035 20
Ashland	307	122 80
Barron	1,862	744 80
Bayfield	271	108 40
Brown...	12,753	5,101 20
Buffalo	6,001	2,400 40
Burnett...	677	270 80
Calumet...	6,216	2,544 00
Chippewa	4,501	1,800 40
Clark..	3,132	1,252 80
Columbia..	10,996	4,398 40
Crawford..	6,237	2,494 80
Dane	20,150	8,060 00
Dodge	18,888	7,855 20
Door	3,893	1,557 20
Douglas...	250	100 00
Dunn	5,862	2,344 80
Eau Claire	5,540	2,216 00
Fond du Lac	19,398	7,759 20
Grant	15,016	6,006 40
Green...	8,366	3,346 40
Green Lake..	5,399	2,159 60
Iowa..	9,508	3,803 20
Jackson...	4,575	1,830 00
Jefferson	13,158	5,263 20
Juneau	5,781	2,312 40
Kenosha...	5,179	2,071 60
Kewaunee...	6,625	2,650 00
La Crosse	8,937	3,574 80
La Fayette	8,477	3,390 80
Lincoln	468	187 20
Manitowoc	16,320	6,528 00
Marathon..	5,160	2,064 00
Marinette	2,087	834 80

Apportionment of School Fund Income in 1880.

Apportionment of School Fund Income in 1881 — Continued.

COUNTIES.	Number of children.	Apportion- ment.
Marquette	3,748	$1,499 20
Milwaukee	45,804	18,121 60
Monroe	8,119	3,247 60
Oconto	2,656	1,062 40
Outagamie	10,728	4,291 20
Ozaukee	6,660	2,664 00
Pepin	2,314	925 60
Pierce	6,517	2,606 80
Polk	3,216	1,286 40
Portage	6,216	2,496 40
Price	91	....
Racine	11,036	4,414 40
Richland	7,019	2,807 60
Rock	13,308	5,323 20
St. Croix	6,089	2,435 60
Sauk	10,247	4,098 80
Shawano	3,045	1,218 00
Sheboygan	13,973	5,589 20
Taylor	516	206 40
Trempealeau	6,471	2,588 40
Vernon	9,006	3,602 40
Walworth	9,190	3,676 00
Washington	9,499	3,799 60
Waukesha	10,609	4,243 60
Waupaca	7,774	3,109 60
Waushara	4,921	1,968 40
Winnebago	15,051	6,020 40
Wood	2,340	936 00
Totals	479,741	$191,917 60

Districts, Children, and School Attendance.

Table No. II.

DISTRICTS, CHILDREN, AND SCHOOL ATTENDANCE.

Counties.	Number of regular school-districts in the county.	Number of such districts which have reported.	Number of parts of districts in the county.	Number of parts which have reported.	Number of joint districts with school-houses or sites in the county.	Number of male children over four and under twenty years of age.	Number of female children over four and under twenty years of age.	Whole number of children over four and under twenty years of age in the county.	Number over four and under twenty years in those districts which maintained school five or more months.	Number of days a school was taught by a qualified teacher.	Number over four and under twenty years, who have attended school.	Number under four years of age, who have attended school.	Number over twenty years of age, who have attended school.	Total number of different pupils who have attended school during the year.
Adams	50	50	38	37	17	1,368	1,165	2,533	2,514	11,181	2,004	8	15	2,027
Ashland	6	6	..	..	8	233	245	478	463	960	267	6	4	267
Barron	59	55	15	15	..	1,154	1,084	2,238	2,047	472	1,570	..	..	1,580
Bayfield	1	1	..	..	5	118	142	260	260	200	93	3	4	93
Brown	83	83	11	11	16	5,007	4,715	9,722	9,722	18,715	5,174	1	28	5,181
Buffalo	64	63	37	37	..	3,241	3,073	6,314	6,314	18,049	3,949	..	7	3,978
Burnett	12	12	1	1	..	411	378	789	745	1,230	479	1	16	486
Calumet	55	55	23	23	11	3,369	3,102	6,531	6,531	11,189	3,511	2	11	3,527
Chippewa	96	89	1	1	6	2,562	2,425	4,987	3,952	11,639	2,555	5	4	3,568
Clark	67	67	27	27	11	1,846	1,675	3,521	3,463	13,203	2,418	17	60	2,422
Columbia	110	110	40	48	86	4,254	4,250	8,518	8,478	26,878	6,612	5	86	6,689
Crawford	71	69	46	46	20	2,731	2,482	5,203	5,203	15,045	3,621	8	28	3,663
Dane, 1st district	82	82	102	100	45	4,165	3,802	7,967	7,887	24,324	5,118	10	20	5,144
Dane, 2d district	89	89	61	61	83	3,981	3,813	7,794	7,689	19,914	5,259	7	67	5,288
Dodge	136	136	111	111	60	7,932	7,556	15,488	14,888	34,894	9,558	..	..	9,632

Districts, Children, and School Attendance.

County													
Door	43	43				2,173	1,086	4,159	4,069	6,849	2,416	20	2	2,438
Douglas	2	2				144	118	203	202	340	165			165
Dunn	81	80	34	17	15	3,038	2,889	5,927	5,900	14,195	4,152	12	37	4,201
Eau Claire	69	60	10	10	3	3,088	2,917	6,005	6,002	8,021	4,058	2	35	4,005
Fond du Lac	124	124	53	53	44	6,670	6,399	13,069	13,069	32,275	7,940	22	32	8,044
Green	155	155	108	108	55	7,567	7,280	14,847	14,847	33,165	11,053	5	55	11,113
Green Lake	100	100	53	53	29	4,291	3,983	8,274	8,274	24,814	6,542	10	50	6,602
Iowa	48	48	49	47	23	2,121	1,953	4,074	4,021	12,165	2,721	2	20	2,743
Jackson	102	102	45	44	20	4,205	4,006	8,211	8,211	18,920	6,193	14	31	6,338
Jefferson	58	58	38	38	20	2,497	2,244	4,741	4,741	11,929	3,430	10	24	3,464
Juneau	82	82	91	91	49	5,226	4,900	10,126	10,126	24,258	6,490	11	28	6,529
Kenosha	76	76	39	37	19	3,018	2,912	5,930	5,917	13,896	4,329	6	13	4,348
Kewaunee	39	39	46	46	21	1,617	1,481	3,098	3,098	9,412	1,942		11	1,953
La Crosse	45	47	16	16	16	3,528	3,290	6,818	6,818	8,559	3,279	36	7	3,322
La Fayette	66	66	17	16	10	2,370	2,231	4,601	4,601	11,076	3,027		15	3,042
Langlade	102	102	52	52	25	4,098	4,054	8,153	8,151	22,796	5,798	8	24	5,830
Lincoln	13	13				260	267	527	527	1,848	469	3	3	475
Manitowoc	86	86	46	44	22	8,034	7,885	15,919		18,342	8,403	4	21	8,428
Marathon	83	83	8	8	3	2,353	2,093	4,446	4,375	10,683	2,563			2,562
Marinette	12	12				1,318	1,216	2,534	2,534	1,900	1,210	1	24	1,213
Marquette	43	43	39	39	19	1,807	1,547	4,604	3,354	9,071	2,379	31	1	2,437
Milw., 1st dist.	30	30	14	14	5	2,343	2,261	3,670	3,670	5,610	1,576		2	2,219
Milw., 2d dist.	32	32	2	2	2	1,850	1,820	8,243		5,605	5,723		30	1,578
Monroe	85	85	81	80	38	4,302	3,941	8,243	8,81	20,463	5,723	3	2	5,756
Oconto	33	33	4	4	2	1,021	968	1,989	1,974	1,300	1,239	1	2	1,242
Outagamie	106	106	26	26	14	4,175	3,985	8,160	8,160	16,637	5,114	25	4	5,143
Ozaukee	52	52	10	10	7	3,268	3,297	6,565	6,565	9,132	3,298	7	6	3,311
Pepin	31	31	14	14	7	1,200	1,137	2,337	2,337	5,924	1,737	1	22	1,760
Pierce	88	87	42	41	16	3,381	3,150	6,531	6,339	15,841	4,451	10	28	4,489
Polk	59	59	20	23	13	1,833	1,691	3,523	3,465	9,545	2,472	4	16	2,492
Portage	67	66	18	18	19	2,002	2,418	5,020	4,916	10,902	3,013	6	10	3,029
Price	5	5				98	73	171	159	898	63		9	63
Racine	56	56	48	47	20	2,857	2,657	5,514	5,514	15,086	2,723	4	9	2,736
Richland	101	101	44	44	18	3,503	3,420	7,013	6,913	18,251	5,502	10	45	5,557
Rock, 1st dist.	60	60	52	52	23	2,25.	2,49	4,402	4,405	17,009	3,439	5	28	3,472
Rock, 2d dist.	55	55	65	65	32	1,963	1,849	3,812	3,812	18,485	2,831		17	2,848

17—ST. SUP.

Districts, Children, and School Attendance.

TABLE No. II.—DISTRICTS, CHILDREN, AND SCHOOL ATTENDANCE.—Continued.

COUNTIES.	Number of regular school districts in the county.	Number of such districts which have reported.	Number of parts of districts in the county.	Number of parts which have reported.	Number of joint districts with school-houses or sites in the county.	Number of male children over four and under twenty years of age.	Number of female children over four and under twenty years of age.	Whole number of children over four and under twenty years of age in the county.	Number over four and under twenty years in those districts which maintain school five or more months.	Number of days a school was taught by a qualified teacher.	Number over four and under twenty years of age, who have attend school.	Number under four years of age, who have attended school.	Number over twenty years of age, who have attended school.	Total number of different pupils who have attended school during the year.
St. Croix	86	77	33	22	18	3,120	2,808	5,928	5,878	15,625	3,888	2	25	8,015
Sauk	120	120	86	86	45	5,251	5,079	10,380	10,324	21,102	7,273	3	51	7,826
⬛	67	67	7	7	6	1,948	1,708	3,656	3,656	7,947	1,864	10	2	1,876
Sheboygan	90	90	56	54	23	5,504	5,248	10,752	10,752	21,164	6,415	4	25	6,444
Mor.	17	17	.	.	.	358	283	641	626	2,280	355	2	.	357
Trempenleau	65	65	34	34	19	3,449	3,145	6,594	6,443	12,415	4,063	8	32	4,103
Vernon	113	113	71	71	33	4,766	4,488	9,254	9,106	24,976	7,217	22	84	7,323
Walworth	87	87	83	79	39	4,372	4,263	9,285	8,359	24,897	5,937	5	10	5,958
Washington	127	127	48	48	39	4,787	4,498	8,634	8,285	18,870	4,911	8	9	4,928
Waukesha	70	76	106	106	42	5,165	4,907	10,072	10,072	19,256	6,757	20	33	6,810
Waupaca	84	84	51	51	24	4,053	3,751	7,804	7,763	17,803	5,358	8	9	5,375
Waushara	46	46	91	91	48	2,560	2,442	5,008	5,008	18,709	3,451	28	28	3,512
Winnebago	66	66	79	79	33	3,695	3,315	7,010	7,010	20,416	4,909	18	12	4,909
Wood	41	39	.	.	4	1,177	1,182	2,359	2,359	5,179	1,588	6	6	1,000
Totals	4,347	4,329	2,452	2,402	1,256	198,734	187,554	386,288	383,283	399,154	251,224	482	1,285	252,991

Table No. III.
GRADED SCHOOLS, TEACHERS, WAGES, ETC.

Graded Schools, Teachers, Wages, Etc.

COUNTIES.	No. of schools with two departments.	No. of schools with three departments.	No. of schools with four or more departments.	No. of districts that have adopted a course of study.	No. of teachers required to teach the schools.	No. of male teachers employed during the year.	No. of female teachers employed during the year.	No. of different persons employed during the year.	Average wages of male teachers per month.	Average wages of female teachers per month.	Highest wages paid.	Number of schools visited by the county superintendent during the year.
Adams	3				69	26	92	118	$24 00	$17 70	$33 70	67
Ashland					6	2	5	7	70 00	41 25	110 00	5
Barron			1	1	53	31	65	96	28 78	25 58	40 00	59
B'y'd	1				2	1	1	2	95 00	40 00	95 00	1
Brown	4	1	3	1	98	45	75	120	39 75	25 26	100 00	101
Bo.	1			2	88	58	62	120	39 37	25 37	93 75	87
Burnett		1	1	5	12	7	15	22	28 83	28 49	35 00	
Calumet	3				75	33	65	98	36 24	25 04	60 00	59
Chippewa	1	1	2	3	109	47	110	157	37 22	29 73	75 00	76
Clk		1	1		85	34	114	148	33 06	25 83	88 89	62
Columbia	6	1	2	6	165	78	190	268	36 14	20 47	111 11	150
rd	1		1	2	91	49	116	165	26 09	18 93	50 00	90
Dane, 1st district	3	1	1	9	136	68	170	238	35 02	25 73	88 87	127
Dane, 2d dist	2	2	1	15	131	54	145	199	37 27	23 94	100 00	
Dodge	5	3	4	20	218	104	214	318	33 50	21 19	80 00	187

Graded Schools, Teachers, Wages, Etc.

TABLE No. III.— GRADED SCHOOLS, TEACHERS, WAGES, ETC.— Continued.

COUNTIES.	GRADED SCHOOLS.				TEACHERS.				WAGES.			
	No. of schools with two departments.	No. of schools with three departments.	No. of schools with four or more departments.	No. of districts that have adopted a course of study.	No. of teachers required to teach the schools.	No. of male teachers employed during the year.	No. of female teachers employed during the year.	No. of different persons employed during the year.	Average wages of male teachers per month.	Average wages of female teachers per month.	Highest wages paid.	No. a schools visited by the county superintendent during the year.
Door	3	1		14	55	23	49	72	$33 17	$25 83	$70 00	75
Douglas	5		1		4	2	4	6	60 00	32 50	70 00	2
Du'n	1	1	4	12	108	54	127	181	32 90	27 31	107 50	85
Eau Claire	4	2	3	5	95	28	120	148	46 47	28 25	160 00	65
Fond du Lac	8	4	6	7	191	86	217	303	32 69	21 70	100 00	191
Grant	5	1	2	26	250	94	257	361	36 47	21 87	111 10	
Green	6			14	156	84	190	274	31 85	21 17	122 23	120
Green Lake	2	2	2		75	36	87	123	30 95	20 70	50 00	75
Iowa	1	1	1	25	130	63	188	201	29 83	21 38	45 00	
Jackson	3	3	8	17	91	30	107	137	30 57	24 20	150 00	82
Jefferson	1	1	8	16	159	74	149	223	34 61	21 00	150 00	84
Juneau	1			5	111	87	129	166	37 90	19 54	100 00	96
Kenosha	1	1	1	1	62	89	58	97	32 15	27 94	55 00	61
Kewaunee	1	1	2	1	55	88	26	84	34 75	23 94	75 00	46
La Crosse	2	1		2	74	50	65	115	38 66	23 86	80 00	66
La Fayette	4	1		18	146	84	151	235	36 57	23 76	115 00	126
Lincoln				1	15	4	18	17	48 50	32 60	80 00	13

Graded Schools, Teachers, Wages, Etc.

County									Av.	Av.	Max	
Manitowoc	1	1	4	18	135	84	65	149	$44 18	$30 15	$140 00	81
Marathon	4			11	85	46	72	118	33 66	25 54	50 00	21
Me......	2	1	1	1	27	6	35	41	61 25	32 74	100 00	
...te......												
Milwaukee, 1st district	2	1	1		63	18	54	72	27 60	17 37	65 00	61
Milwaukee, 2d dist	5		2		44	21	33	54	41 48	27 37	120 00	35
Monroe	5	1		6	35	21	24	45	45 85	31 35	88 89	62
Oconto	4	1		4	144	43	181	223	34 96	20 73	120 00	104
Outagamie	1		1	9	33	11	36	47	35 66	26 98	50 00	31
Ozaukee	3		1	1	113	37	132	169	33 23	22 48	52 50	106
Pepin	2		2	4	70	49	27	76	41 00	21 59	122 28	50
Pierce	3			24	40	14	44	58	30 90	24 56	38 57	37
Polk			1	8	120	63	123	186	35 15	25 19	80 00	102
Portage		1	1	7	73	33	82	115	34 03	28 80	55 00	60
Price	1		1		88	29	105	134	31 42	21 09	50 00	90
...ae......	3			11	5	1	5	0	40 00	36 87	40 00	5
Richland	2	1	1	12	82	27	88	115	38 06	25 28	100 00	73
Rock, 1st dist	6		1	12	130	50	151	201	28 47	20 47	77 78	285
Rock, 2d district	2		3	22	93	40	124	164	32 91	21 68	90 00	83
St.	6			3	96	32	139	171	27 63	22 83	77 77	
Sauk	1	3	1	36	105	59	110	160	38 28	28 75	70 00	104
Shawano	2	1	1	1	179	79	201	250	36 50	23 94	133 33	157
Sheboygan	1			6	67	26	64	90	30 75	21 22	94 44	67
Taylor		2	2	5	125	70	120	199	41 06	22 71	80 00	125
Trempealeau	1	2	1	4	18	1	26	27	40 00	27 39	40 00	17
Vernon	1	3	1	21	92	53	91	143	34 57	25 63	100 00	123
Walworth	4	3	4	21	149	87	170	257	26 80	18 27	60 00	152
Washington	5	3		5	163	69	183	252	38 52	24 54	111 11	126
...ha......	9	1	2	15	135	69	66	135	36 81	20 90	80 00	98
Waupaca	8	2	1	8	130	58	161	219	44 09	26 00	121 50	118
Waushara	4			11	128	43	162	205	36 05	23 13	100 00	197
Winnebago					98	81	135	166	25 94	17 64	40 00	104
Wood	2		7	7	113	41	144	185	32 32	21 84	62 00	104
					41	14	36	50	35 18	25 16	60 00	36
Totals	165	54	75	537	6,133	2,781	6,525	9,306	$37 14	$24 91	$160 00	4,916

Table No. IV.
SCHOOL-HOUSES AND SITES.

School-Houses and Sites.

COUNTIES.	No. of new ones built during year.	Whole number of school-houses in the county.	No. pupils school-houses will accommodate.	No. of school-houses of stone or brick.	No. of school-houses in good condition.	No. of school-houses properly ventilated.	Highest valuation of school-house and site in the county.	Cash value of all school-houses in the county.	Cash value of all the sites.	Cash value of apparatus, etc.	No. of sites containing less than one acre.	No. of sites well enclosed.
Adams	1	67	2,600		51	42	$3,000 00	$16,075 00	$1,723 00	$330 00	38	9
Ashland	1	5	200		5	5	1,500 00	4,500 00	800 00	150 00	5	8
Barron	3	63	2,107		59		925 30	17,306 81	1,361 00	1,482 00	18	7
Bayfield			125	9	1	1	3,500 00	3,000 00	500 00	200 00	1	1
Brown	3	85	6,512	5	63	51	11,100 00	43,553 00	6,200 50	2,782 75	49	37
Buffalo	6	80	4,666		63	59	7,600 00	43,260 00	4,020 00	1,916 00	40	23
Burnet		11	518		10	11	945 00	3,250 00	225 00	316 00		4
Calumet	2	67	4,360	12	57	53	5,000 00	36,635 00	4,051 00	1,919 00	52	35
Chippewa	4	101	4,129	1	80	47	5,000 00	37,280 50	3,829 00	2,439 78	60	33
Clark	6	76	3,475	1	65	53	14,500 00	47,696 50	2,693 00	3,022 00	80	27
Columbia	1	147	8,614	14	111	93	13,500 00	70,796 00	7,400 00	2,781 00	114	32
Crawford	4	91	4,043	8	57	65	2,750 00	21,110 50	1,703 50	2,336 50	53	19
Dane, 1st dist.	2	127	6,307	33	96	66	10,000 00	66,020 00	7,623 00	2,220 00	90	51
Dane, 2d dist.	2	118	6,288	33	94	89	4,000 00	58,915 00	5,470 00	2,213 00	69	36
Dodge	2	191	12,411	40	161	147	10,700 00	78,310 00	9,880 00	3,848 00	163	82
Door	6	49	2,734		37	35	4,500 00	16,810 00	2,771 00	1,779 00	21	15
Douglas		8	300		2	2	2,000 00	4,500 00	400 00	100 00		
Dunn	4	100	4,676	1	79	80	10,000 00	49,937 06	7,027 00	3,850 75	47	24

School-Houses and Sites.

County											
Eau Claire	5	68	4,155	3	58	4	$18,000 00	$57,225 00	$7,959 00	$2,972 30	43	24
Fond du Lac	1	171	11,116	22	127	83	9,000 00	88,950 00	12,350 10	3,744 10	139	70
Grant	3	215	13,930	38	175	181	20,800 00	169,263 00	9,089 50	5,790 00	125	77
[ ]en	3	131	7,168	26	94	90	27,500 00	87,305 00	5,803 00	1,546 00	94	41
[ ]en Lake	1	70	3,411	8	63	51	3,075 00	31,270 00	2,267 20	564 00	49	22
Iowa	1	135	7,307	11	93	80	5,800 00	44,580 99	3,918 00	1,902 00	80	33
Jackson	5	75	3,682	2	56	56	27,000 00	50,661 00	2,815 00	1,167 00	40	19
Jefferson	1	131	9,397	79	111	98	27,400 00	160,971 00	10,908 00	3,650 00	99	69
Juneau	3	94	5,016	1	60	64	7,000 00	35,333 00	3,418 75	1,550 00	81	23
Kenosha	2	60	2,615	3	48	42	3,500 00	29,940 90	3,330 00	1,227 00	48	31
Kewaunee	4	53	4,484	1	49	18	6,800 00	26,555 00	6,752 00	2,890 00	35	30
La Crosse	3	66	3,941	12	51	49	4,000 00	32,740 00	3,055 00	2,272 00	49	33
La Fayette	4	128	8,200	22	92	97	33,000 00	110,749 00	8,438 49	5,607 85	77	65
[ ]		13	675		11	7	6,164 00	11,650 00	707 00		11	2
[ ]	6	108	9,901	18	90	74	40,000 00	104,366 00	12,437 00	6,043 00	87	41
Marathon	7	77	3,629		62	49	2,500 00	29,070 00	2,313 00	2,551 01	48	21
Marinette	6	23	1,185	2	23	18	6,000 00	20,825 00	3,693 00	600 00	14	5
[ ]ate		59	3,328		43	40	2,200 00	18,785 00	1,180 00	598 50	36	8
Milw., 1st dist.	4	35	2,841	14	28	32	12,500 00	35,200 00	5,429 00	1,233 00	32	17
Milw., 2d dist.	8	32	2,044	14	26	27	6,450 00	27,418 00	3,315 75	1,412 00	28	19
[ ]ne	3	126	7,190	4	89	82	19,375 00	37,882 00	5,144 00	1,812 00	92	42
Oconto	3	33	1,944	2	28	21	1,700 00	18,565 00	1,301 00	2,200 00	18	16
Outagamie	1	106	6,967	6	88	81	3,000 00	37,259 00	8,274 00	2,829 35	94	52
[ ]e	6	60	4,854	37	53	37	7,000 00	38,825 00	4,608 50	2,844 00	53	29
Pepin	4	37	2,178	3	31	23	7,410 00	20,520 00	1,278 00	775 00	18	7
Pierce	5	105	4,729	4	83	34	15,000 00	43,721 00	1,900 00	1,967 00	87	25
Polk		71	3,019	1	58		1,400 00	26,398 00	1,408 00	2,819 00	20	19
Portage		85	3,691		67	50	2,159 00	22,868 00	1,586 50	1,264 50	48	20
Price		5		7	5	5	1,000 00	3,350 00	700 00		7	
Racine	3	76	4,130	25	61	43	7,235 00	44,615 00	5,030 00	1,801 75	68	37
[ ]d	8	121	6,286	2	90	102	2,000 00	38,728 15	3,733 00	2,473 70	102	39
[ ], 1st dist.	1	83	4,110	85	62	53	18,400 00	61,366 00	4,102 00	1,538 50	48	33
Rock, 2d dist.		86	3,954	13	67	63	5,755 00	49,760 00	7,630 00	2,067 50	65	45
St. Croix	3	103	3,793	4	60	20	8,500 00	36,069 00	3,499 00	3,261 00	45	29
Sauk	5	165	9,162	13	102	95	20,000 00	87,495 00	9,223 00	3,566 25	119	50
Shawano	6	67	8,189	1	49	47	2,000 00	13,106 76	1,605 00	940 00	40	16

School-Houses and Sites.

TABLE No. IV.—SCHOOL-HOUSES AND SITES—Continued.

SCHOOL-HOUSES AND VALUATION.

COUNTIES.	No. of new ones built during year.	Whole number of school-houses in the county.	No. pupils school-houses will accommodate.	No. of school-houses of stone or brick.	No. of school-houses in good condition.	No. of school-houses properly ventilated.	Highest valuation of school-house and site in the county.	Cash value of all school houses in the county.	Cash value of all the sites.	Cash value of apparatus, etc.	No. of sites containing less than one acre.	No. of sites well enclosed.
Sheboygan	2	111	7,899	6	90	85	$10,000 00	$56,020 00	$5,280 00	$3,503 00	98	44
Taylor	5	17	667	....	17	17	1,850 00	5,743 25	695 00	686 00	3	2
Trempealeau	8	86	4,532	7	63	17	6,500 00	53,618 00	3,074 00	1,830 00	48	26
Vernon	5	148	8,252	8	99	98	10,000 00	53,902 50	4,702 00	2,434 00	124	28
Walworth	....	126	7,685	26	103	79	19,000 00	105,089 00	11,133 00	1,698 00	92	53
Washington	4	100	8,465	54	91	70	7,000 00	77,223 00	6,760 00	6,280 00	92	22
Waukesha	....	118	6,808	45	98	93	20,000 00	104,433 40	11,988 00	3,804 00	85	52
Waupaca	8	108	4,480	3	93	87	6,000 00	51,112 00	6,215 00	2,379 00	88	45
Waushara	1	94	5,896	8	76	77	1,400 00	28,177 00	2,532 25	2,061 00	65	13
Winnebago	1	101	1,564	13	91	85	8,000 00	65,193 00	5,994 00	2,515 00	83	53
Wood	4	88		1	30	25	8,500 00	18,673 20	1,655 00	855 00	15	15
Totals....	191	5,495	315,728	745	4,295	8,561	$40,000 00	$2,992,184 63	$298,795 04	$141,348 58	3,782	1,894

School Appliances, Children Classified, and Text-Books.

Table No. V.

SCHOOL APPLIANCES, CHILDREN CLASSIFIED, AND TEXT-BOOKS.

COUNTIES	APPLIANCES				CHILDREN CLASSIFIED								TEXT-BOOKS				
	No. of districts having blackboards.	No. having a map of Wisconsin.	No. having a map of the United States.	No. having a Webster's Unabr'd Dictionary.	No. of children between 4 and 7 years of age in the county.	No. between 4 and 7 yrs of age, who have attended public schools.	No. of children between 7 and 15 years of age in the county.	No. between 7 and 15 years of age, who have attended public school.	No. of children between 15 and 20 years of age in the county.	No. between 15 and 20 years of age, who have attended public school.	Percentage of enrollment on No. of children in the co. only.	Percentage of attendance on No. enrolled in the public schools.	No. of districts which have adopted a list of text-books.	No. which use only text-books adopted.	No. of districts which purchase text-books.	No. which loan them to pupils.	No. which sell them to pupils.
Adams	67	6	16	57	544	361	1,323	1,203	606	440	79	69	42	30	22	18	10
Ashland	6			5	130	65	242	163	106	36	55.8	57					
Barron	55	5	22	53	492	286	959	844	787	450	70	68	55	43	44	30	11
Bayfield	1	1	1		104	20	118	52	38	21	36	77	1	1	1	1	0
Brown	83	50	45	61	2,573	987	4,702	3,459	2,721	928	53	56	25	13	10	1	54
Buffalo	69	20	37	69	1,450	710	3,263	2,675	1,601	561	60	57.8	61	58	56	2	4
Burnett	12	8	6	11	257	109	518	292		86	60	58.1	9	8	10	8	20
Calumet	62	23	40	61	1,687	845	3,200	2,306	1,644	359	53.7	59.5	52	39	27	8	4
Chippewa	88	23	39	79	2,216	695	2,202	1,799	1,479	1,544	71	62	65	63	50	52	18
Clark	71	26	42	72	946	517	1,734	1,257	841	618	67	76.5	58	56	55	38	17
Columbia	142	63	49	130	1,590	1,064	4,547	3,782	2,376	1,700	77.6	66.3	73	49	18	1	8
Crawford	75	23	29	72	1,050	706	2,358	2,186	1,795	720	60	66.5	49	30	12	3	56
Dane, 1st dist.	121	46	71	115	1,658	925	3,942	3,453	2,367	735	64.2	64	87	71	58	3	88
Dane, 2d dist.	105	38	56	99	1,538	944	3,700	2,909	2,451	1,429	67.8	60	71	51	89	7	88
Dodge	190	80	83	181	8,586	1,835	7,235	5,475	4,657	2,948	61.7	65	105	65	43		
Door	39	19	21	39	1,151	618	2,002	1,552	1,016	502	57	53	40	87	33	15	10

School Appliances, Children Classified, and Text-Books.

TABLE No. V.—SCHOOL APPLIANCES, CHILDREN CLASSIFIED, AND TEXT-BOOKS.

COUNTIES.	No. of districts having blackboards	No. having a map of Wisconsin	No. having a map of the United States	No. having a Webster's Unabr'd Dictionary	No. of children between 4 and 7 years of age in the county	No. between 4 and 7 years of age, who have attended public school	No. of children between 7 and 15 years of age in the county	No. between 7 and 15 years of age, who have attended public school	No. of children between 15 and 20 years of age in the county	No. between 15 and 20 years, who have attended public school	Percentage of enrollment on No. of children in the county	Percentage of attendance on No. enrolled in the public schools	No. of districts which have adopted a list of text-books	No. which use only text-books adopted	No. of districts which purchase text-books	No. which loan them to pupils	No. which sell them to pupils
Douglas	2		2	2	60	81	120	107	82	27	63	71		51	45	28	17
Dunn	91	28	44	75	1,448	814	2,886	2,461	1,614	877	70	55.2	04	87	82	20	12
Eau Claire	62	23	34	57	1,610	892	2,998	2,490	1,394	676	67.5	69	44	38	19	8	20
Fond du Lac	155	59	76	189	2,783	1,530	5,800	4,591	4,486	1,869	74.4	61	84	75	54	6	44
Grant	203	78	92	189	3,284	1,964	7,178	6,288	4,385	2,801	70	68	95	80	22	3	17
Green	180	31	64	111	1,744	1,102	3,080	3,408	3,086	2,406	66.8	76.7	89	17	22	4	19
Green Lake	68	11	11	52	845	478	1,956	1,495	1,273	748	75.4	64.8	89	49	80	8	28
Iowa	100	33	40	105	1,718	1,197	3,866	3,449	2,637	1,547	72.3	62.5	39	38	43	7	36
Jackson	71	21	22	62	1,078	555	2,151	1,927	1,512	948	64	62.5	55	76	38	4	28
Jefferson	127	46	46	118	2,153	1,24?	5,025	4,129	2,948	1,112	73	63.5	89	31	17	5	12
Juneau	89	18	30	60	1,231	774	2,735	2,523	1,964	1,032	63.7	69.4	49	25	16	3	18
Kenosha	60	20	25	52	419	276	1,312	977	1,367	689	48.2	75	48	17	15	4	13
Kewaunee	51	81	41	38	1,435	1,006	3,161	2,034	1,722	239	66	47	20	23	25	6	13
La —e	62	26	57	57	1,270	675	2,254	1,801	1,077	551	72	60.9	30	48	25	41	10
La Fayette	114	55	9	91	1,738	1,065	3,909	3,848	2,504	1,885	80	64	69	13	13	13	9
Lincoln	13	8	75	18	167	153	193	192	167	130	52.2	80.4	13	43	35	1	81
Manitowoc	103	65	75	88	4,091	1,702	7,910	5,758	3,928	943	57.4	60.3	59	43	35	44	8
Marathon	76	36	49	71	1,259	567	2,200	1,698	987	307			42	41	52		

School Appliances, Children Classified, and Text-Books.

County / District																	
Marinette	12	12	12	9	706	851	1,814	829	514	30	47.7	48	12	7	7	2	5
Marquette	60	20	22	51	637	518	1,315	1,084	1,402	777	71	67.4	27	27	5	1	4
Milw., 1st dist.	35	25	33	82	1,055	434	1,974	1,365	1,575	419	48.2	00	24	20			
Milw., 2d dist.	30	26	27	29	947	292	1,894	1,148	829	136	43	58.3	16	11	3	1	2
Monroe	120	30	31	118	1,878	1,236	3,886	3,276	3,451	2,103	62.3	71	68	38	16	2	24
Oconto	31	21	18	26	600	320	938	734	451	185	62.7	52.5	26	26	26	16	10
Outagamie	102	54	64	91	2,035	1,385	3,519	2,963	2,606	766	50.4	58	54	40	37	4	32
Ozaukee	59	40	44	51	1,636	803	3,352	2,486	1,577		74	56.6	36	35	29		22
Pepin	37	18	17	34	580	350	1,122	1,009	635	378	68	64.3	21	17	13	10	8
Pierce	102	56	49	92	1,549	837	3,204	2,815	1,778	800	75.5	73	90	58	55	15	31
Polk	69	28	38	66	942	414	1,815	1,559	766	500	60	50.5	54	52	50	23	27
Portage	78	26	26	60	989	554	2,368	1,882	1,663	612	42.7	58.7	58	49	43	4	42
Price	5	16		5	52	25	98	42	9		50.3	68.5	5	5	5	5	
Racine	72	53	32	50	1,182	602	2,599	1,957	1,783	164	78.4	63	33	26	10	2	13
Richland	119	20	52	108	1,271	975	3,111	2,867	2,531	1,660	78	68	69	88	9	4	20
Rock, 1st dist.	81	25	41	67	903	567	2,097	1,828	1,405	1,044	74.2	69	44	34	12	1	11
Rock, 2d dist.	78	40	27	70	806	514	2,370	1,918	1,088	585	65.6	74	55	45	17	6	14
St. Croix	97	54	43	81	1,233	725	5,085	2,189	2,317	1,050	70.4	55.5	59	39	29	9	18
Sauk	145	31	97	138	2,436	1,208	1,744	4,410	2,809	1,655	51	65	111	79	5	18	40
Shawano	53	86	18	54	1,212	470	5,257	1,261	700	198	59	60.4	52	49	50	20	18
Sheboygan	109	9	91	101	2,331	1,293	292	4,272	3,164	850	55.4	67.3	54	37	25		24
Taylor	16	53	5	16	196	132	2,944	242	203		62	69.2	15	13	11	9	4
Trempealeau	84	26	32	68	1,515	1,294	4,610	2,299	2,177	514	78	46.3	50	42	41	8	29
Vernon	135	59	45	125	1,903	1,222	3,701	4,198	2,593	1,797	68.7	60	76	60	40	9	30
Walworth	122	46	61	101	1,623	918	4,103	3,399	3,393	1,620	52.8	65.9	37	19	8	2	4
Washington	102	63	55	88	2,228	963	4,778	3,014	2,954	934	67	63	59	52	34	7	28
Waukesha	118	58	70	108	2,158	1,388	3,652	4,002	3,136	1,367	68.8	78	80	74	62	4	59
Waupaca	101	27	74	102	1,910	1,179	2,294	3,161	2,242	1,035	69	60	65	57	61	9	52
Waushara	93	73	50	82	1,030	640	3,229	2,051	1,684	760	70.9	66	59	48	62	33	34
Winnebago	98	1	59	83	1,496	823	702	2,906	2,285	1,240	67.3	60	68	49	20		24
Wood	35		1	27	390	183		700	1,267	705		63.2	22	21	20	15	5
Totals	5,161	2,116	2,541	4,631	88,174	49,235	183,054	149,723	116,659	54,665	av.64	av.63.5	3,234	2,470	1,951	619	1,253

Libraries, Town Schools, and State Tax.

Table No. VI.
LIBRARIES, TOWN SCHOOLS, AND STATE TAX.

COUNTIES.	No. of districts in the county having libraries.	No. of volumes added during the year.	Amount expended for the libraries during the year.	No. of volumes now in the libraries.	Cash value of all the libraries.	How many town libraries in the county.	No. of towns in county favorable to town system.	No. of towns which have voted on the question.	No. of towns favorable to a town high school.	No. of towns which have voted on the question.	No. of towns favorable to a State school tax.
Adams	1			38	$40 00	2	2	2	2		4
Ashland							2	8		1	2
Barron	1										12
Bayfield	2			0	9 00						
Brown	3	60	$109 53	20	245 00	1	1		1	1	1
Buffalo	1	87	83 10	62	285 00		3	8	1	1	19
Burnett				62	48 00						3
Calumet	23										2
Chippewa		19	35 00	48	95 00	1	3	3			11
Clark	5										
Columbia	2			30	165 00		2		2	1	9
Crawford	4			42	40 00			4	2		4
Dane, 1st dist	8	18	20 00	08	70 00				1		4
Dane, 2d dist		32	25 00	87	111 00						2
Dodge	27			81	901 50		2	2			
Door		27	39 50	87	105 00			18		3	

Libraries, Town Schools, and State Tax.

County					
Douglas	2	26	$19 50	—	—
Dunn	4	2	15 00	64	$300 00
Eau Claire	8	6	20 50	261	302 50
Fond du Lac	11	—	40 00	417	629 00
Kent	6	5	125 00	611	1,194 00
Green	7	238	—	1,332	142 50
Green lake	1	—	—	192	—
Iowa	—	4	51 40	8	—
Jackson	18	1	8 00	374	587 00
Jefferson	12	2	—	503	340 60
Juneau	3	—	10 00	628	455 00
Kenosha	2	—	31 00	74	40 00
Kewaunee	1	—	—	50	57 00
La Crosse	1	—	—	25	25 00
La Fayette	—	—	—	—	—
Lincoln	—	—	—	—	—
Manitowoc	8	26	31 00	387	385 00
Marathon	3	59	103 97	189	479 15
Marinette	1	—	—	75	125 00
Marquette	—	6	—	—	5 00
Milwaukee, 1st dist	4	—	10 00	439	216 00
Milwaukee, 2d dist	2	86	—	150	188 00
Monroe	1	16	10 00	—	30 00
Ozaukee	2	2	—	60	30 00
Pepin	2	7	6 60	778	658 00
Pierce	1	434	279 76	70	36 20
Polk	5	84	—	930	801 53
Portage	2	—	25 00	4	84 00
Price	2	—	—	—	41 00
Racine	16	85	5 00	583	568 45
Rock, 1st dist	3	—	71 40	530	310 00
Rock, 2d dist	15	—	10 00	881	315 00
St. Croix	3	142	46 75	360	152 50

Libraries, Town Schools, and State Tax.

TABLE No. VI. — LIBRARIES, TOWN SCHOOLS, AND STATE TAX — Continued,

COUNTIES.	LIBRARIES. No. of districts in the county having libraries.	No. of volumes added during the year.	Amount expended for the libraries during the year.	No. of volumes now in the libraries.	Cash value of all the libraries.	How many town libraries in the county.	TOWN SCHOOLS. No. of towns in county favorable to town system.	No. of towns which have voted on the question.	No. of towns favorable to a town high school.	No. of towns which have voted on the question.	STATE TAX. No. of towns favorable to a State school tax.
Sauk	14	4	$2 00	797	$857 00		1	3	1	1	6
Shawano	15			517	400 00		1	1	1		1
Sheboygan	1	8	2 80	38	18 00		1	1	2		2
Klor									1		2
Trempealeau	5	105	42 65	149	122 05	1			1	3	2
Vernon	5	2		432	390 00	2	3	2	3		9
Walworth	5			145	296 00						
Washington			7 00	311	207 00	4	1		2		18
Waukesha				30	75 00					1	1
Wanpaca										1	2
Mra							1				
Winnebago	4	6		136	190 00						
Wood							1	3			3
Totals	273	1,549	$1,287 40	15,850	$13,141 98	26	87	47	83	26	180

Private Schools not Incorporated.

Table No. VII.

PRIVATE SCHOOLS NOT INCORPORATED.

COUNTIES.	No. of such schools in the county	No. of teachers engaged in such schools	Av. number of days such sch'ls have been taught	No. of pupils registered in them, that have not attended public school	Average number in daily attendance	No. between 4 and 7 years of age in attendance	No. between 7 and 15 years of age in attendance	From tuition	From donations	From a other sources	Total receipts	For teachers' wages	For building and repairs	For all other purposes
Adams														
Ashland														
Barron														
Bayfield	1	2	200	340	115	18	59	$100 00	$170 00	$300 00	$470 00	$770 00		$20 00
Brown	5	2	130	89	28				65 00		65 00	40 00		
Buffalo	5	7				70	39							
Burnett														
Calumet	8	9	150	148	31	40	273	1,439 25	1,390 00	58 35	2,887 60	1,370 00	$25 00	35 00
Chippewa	2	3	200	75	74		41	60 00	300 00		360 00	360 00	1,540 00	
Clark			69	28	30			75 00		270 00	345 00	345 00		
Columbia	5	10	120	199	40	83	185	100 0.	210 00	165 00	310 00	302 00	8 00	
Crawford	8	13	100	165	40	44	213	700 00	378 00		1,243 00	1,088 00	87 50	60 00
Dane, 1st dist.	13	13	146	263	233									
Dane, 2d dist.	12	12	113											
Dodge	25	26		1,370	37	56	570	524 00	1,320 00	2,563 60	4,407 60	4,144 00	69 04	153 60

Private Schools not Incorporated.

TABLE No. VII.—PRIVATE SCHOOLS NOT INCORPORATED — Continued.

COUNTIES.	No. of such schools in the county.	No. of teachers engaged in such schools.	Av. number of days such sch'ls have been taught.	No. of pupils registered in them, that have not attended public school.	Average number in daily attendance.	No. between 4 and 7 years of age in attendance.	No. between 7 and 15 years of age in attendance.	From tuition.	From donations.	Fr'm all other sources.	Total receipts.	For teachers' wages.	For building and repairs.	For all other purposes.
Door	1	1			10									
Douglas	2	2	40											
Dunn														
Eau ꝏ														
Fond du Ꝃ	22	31	143	1,038	86	73	241	$3,678 00	$1,000 00	$6,639 38	$10,287 38	$7,827 45	$465 65	$949 66
Grant	12	12	129	288	47	63	119	805 37	300 00	24 00	1,105 37	835 37	250 00	20 00
Ꝃen Ꝃe	6	3	37	3	19	11	50	49 00	161 00		234 00	228 00		6 00
Green Ꝃke	6	6	180	100	52	27	84			510 00	510 00	500 00		10 00
Ꝃwa	2	3	180		80	15	81	1,220 00	30 00	61 00	30 00	250 00	1 00	10 00
Jackson	5	6	54	451	68	130	273	1,220 00	2,913 00	363 00	4,194 00	1,300 00	2,806 00	247 50
Jefferson	16	16	162	92	22	40	70		50 00	120 00	413 00	385 00	15 00	48 00
Juneau	6	6	106	114	85	3	93	600 00	170 00		720 00	650 00		90 00
Kenosha	4	5	206	120	46	72	24		95 00		471 00	401 00		70 00
Ꝃne	8	8	197	61	34	18	91	301 00		90 00	526 25	436 00	65 00	25 25
La Ꝃase	7	8	125	142	120	12	130	341 25			500 00	425 00	10 00	65 00
La Fayette	1	2	180						500 00					
Lincoln														

Private Schools not Incorporated.

County														
Manitowoc	19	22	164	673	58	137	479	$1,203 00	$450 00	$270 00	$1,923 00	$1,615 00	$70 00	$90 00
M.														
Marinette	1	8	200	176	125	50	90							
Marquette	1	1	100		64	48	88	510 00	500 00	100 00	1,110 00	1,350 00		20 00
Milw., 1st dist	11	14	152	325	65	55	95	942 00		347 45	1,289 45	1,40 00		57 45
Milw., 2d dist	4	4	175	202	20	10	15	72 00	350 00	250 00	672 00	622 00		50 00
Monroe	7	10	98	239	37	73	134							
Oconto	7	8	108	200	28	86	93	578 90	300 00		878 90	388 00	300 00	
Outagamie	10	11	153	611	127	27	370	595 00	130 00	15 00	790 00	735 00	15 00	40 00
...ee														
Pepin	4	5	70	24	75									
Pierce	2	8	75		12	12	34							
Polk	2	4	151	161	44									
Portage														
Price														
Racine	9	17	169	346	89	30	100	830 00	43 00		373 00	343 00	30 00	
...d														
Rock, 1st dist	2	2	105	9	8	6	3	120 00			120 00	120 00		
Rock, 2d dist														
St. Croix	10	9	167	115	31	15	5	378 00	350 00	11 89	739 89	728 00		11 89
Sauk	8	8	145	105	87	9	78	120 00						
Shawano	17	19	174	449	70	57	271	1,277 20		16 00	1,293 20	1,277 20	16 00	
Sheboygan														
Taylor	1	1		18		16								
...nleau														
Vernon	16	16	91	14	47	16	166	318 00	211 30		529 30	529 30	3 25	
Walworth	6	7	157	133	47	35	95	480 75	125 00		605 75	640 75		50 00
Washington	22	28	184	305	48	259	556	1,022 65	108 00	930 00	2,660 65	3,212 40	95 23	276 54
Waukesha	6	10	191	194	94				145 00		145 00	720 00		
...cs	11	7	620	144	95			850 00	300 00	250 00	900 00	900 00		
Waushara	8	8	235	126	62	26	223							
Winnebago	8						110							
Wood														
Totals and av.	851	411	136.4	9,659	2,521	1,685	5,047	$17,770 87	$12,114 30	$13,224 67	$43,109 34	$35,977 47	$5,871 67	$2,405 39

Financial Statistics — Receipts.

Table No. VIII.

FINANCIAL STATISTICS — RECEIPTS.

Counties.	From money on hand, August 31, 1879.	From taxes levied for building and repairing.	From taxes levied for teachers' wages.	From taxes levied for apparatus and library.	From taxes levied at annual town meeting.	From taxes levied by county supervisors.	From income of school fund.	From all other sources.	Total amount received during the year.
ashs	$1,752 01	$604 27	$5,662 89	$18 75	$54 37	$1,018 37	$1,031 52	$1,771 90	$11,908 01
Ashland	1,281 47				2,321 70	1,800 00	188 80	44 65	4,365 15
Barron	1,056 78	474 50	3,697 42	66 48	3,458 95	313 46	534 99	2,902 31	12,504 89
Bayfield	329 24	150 00	1,500 00	200 00		116 00	115 14	353 42	2,763 80
Brown	7,488 79	2,671 59	15,140 21	263 88	2,468 49	3,474 68	3,88 13	2,051 53	38,723 17
Buffalo	5,703 61	1,431 71	16,123 87	110 15		3,690 9?	2,412 61	4,450 98	33,823 85
Burnett	1,748 45	15 00	50 00	25 00	1,378 76	466 26	224 92	668 98	4,102 75
Calumet	4,729 45	2,128 54	11,898 28	170 05		2,370 59	2,600 30	3,607 30	27,504 51
Chippewa	5,649 49	1,420 83	9,089 12	155 00	13,839 24	1,164 00	1,7·3 79	10,751 96	43,713 32
Clark	7,766 93	4,990 75	14,218 91	330 41	356 87	1,378 73	998 19	8,791 80	38,827 59
Mia	5,908 40	1,948 26	23,394 58	319 87	1,532 59	3,080 30	3,·60 68	9,103 82	49,688 19
Crawford	4,585 77	935 35	7,448 10	101 98	987 35	1,9·8 74	907 84	2,057 54	21,502 44
Dane, 1st district	4,323 74	2,685 61	20,057 87	246 23	1,087 36	3,249 27	3,351 57	4,837 32	40,196 26
Dane, 2d dist	4,588 95	1,255 42	12,803 88	106 50	504 33	4,067 8?	3,204 74	5,034 29	37,567 03
Dodge	15,072 05	4,404 89	20,223 35	150 30	1,850 75	5,733 96	6,070 21	10.887 36	73,392 87
Door	5,280 22	2,473 80	9,296 11	239 00	546 07	978 56	1,460 54	2,748 31	23,193 98
Douglas	767 68		645 61					495 75	1,909 04
Dunn	8,749 34	8,294 17	17,519 12	476 30	1,653 54	2,115 99	2,248 26	5,145 61	43,843 36
Eau Claire	12,694 91	3,219 98	22,186 38	380 91	4,998 44	1,055 84	2,072 24	8,382 49	55,791 64

Financial Statistics — Receipts.

County									
Ford du Lac	$8,952 74	$2,082 97	$27,928 42	$133 80	$565 42	$4,410 56	$5,450 74	$5,450 70	$54,975 35
Grant	13,784 00	8,449 30	35,026 74	489 66	4,391 58	5,591 96	5,308 73	7,817 33	75,879 30
Geen	7,485 09	3,712 39	240 67	137 47	303 82	3,013 73	8,380 28	6,207 84	48,881 12
Green Lake	2,654 57	1,284 50	9,531 08			1,512 04	1,530 56	2,380 03	18,947 84
Iowa	4,425 04	2,127 29	19,087 41	253 91	416 60	2,876 41	3,132 15	3,230 54	34,546 25
Jackson	4,638 76	1,442 64	14,281 07	414 82	657 58	1,448 20	1,585 63	3,110 79	27,635 02
Jefferson	6,232 60	2,144 52	23,098 82	20 00	226 42	3,832 07	4,722 01	8,7?9 25	48,733 77
Juneau	5,319 87	1,085 72	11,093 97	1?7 07	5,418 70	1,918 36	2,046 00	3,264 88	29,552 91
Kenosha	2,925 09	1,044 88	0,001 77	49 70		2,072 14	1,263 16	2,561 10	21,939 39
Kewaunee	3,070 73	1,447 92	7,195 18	2 00	1,496 98	2,383 13	2,770 13	2,021 66	21,944 98
La Crosse	4,465 08	2,344 51	11,354 13	61 20	228 73	1,815 22	1,863 52	1,863 60	26,091 99
La Fayette	5,488 96	2,131 20	25,243 43	44 00	884 87	3,084 22	3,371 46	4,194 11	43,803 50
Zain	733 13	1,146 58	2,860 78		200 00	403 16	223 35	1,630 78	7,186 58
Manitowoc	15,637 91	3,996 61	25,977 84	387 58	1,676 44	12,070 38	6,358 70	7,453 71	73,559 17
Marathon	9,828 76	3,109 69	10,211 37	275 97	2,051 56	2,126 84	1,573 04	6,650 70	34,060 21
Mte	3,684 72	2,944 40	4,144 50		307 96	482 39	892 38	5,700 87	17,647 22
ate	2,124 80	512 20	4,066 90	127 75	162 50	349 84	1,237 83	2,522 91	12,519 14
Milwaukee, 1st d't	5,457 14	652 15	7,633 23		479 58	631 14	1,714 11	2,089 52	23,189 97
Milwaukee, 2d d't	2,181 80	3,788 93	6,984 04	71 25	500 00	3,497 58	1,895 11	2,479 35	21,395 27
Monroe	8,366 51	1,718 77	21,040 45	180 51	4,076 91	2,955 88	3,137 63	4,123 57	45,609 28
Onto	7,448 81	358 33	3,787 27	13 18	1,618 69	393 52	516 84	763 50	15,159 43
Outagamie	6,101 02	2,850 2?	14,477 38	41 13	77 88	3,859 37	3,261 86	4,276 15	34,944 76
Ozaukee	2,646 48	1,306 21	9,539 38	40 30	1,001 14	3,071 48	2,654 86	3,954 97	26,075 08
Pepin	2,403 86	603 28	5,440 60	15 00	134 00	837 21	286 42	1,940 00	1,836 47
Pierce	7,180 30	8,266 11	20,144 82	326 14	351 89	2,077 37	2,213 50	12,503 80	49,982 23
Polk	4,996 44	1,538 55	8,980 64	48 22	1,480 68	1,587 53	1286 40	6,375 36	26,293 82
Portage	3,974 04	992 77	10,538 94	12 50		1,475 46	1,759 55	1,901 00	20,366 62
Price	464 89	435 95	1,800 55	39 25				754 14	1,818 13
Roine	3,801 16	1,794 99	13,147 62	15 00	857 25	2,166 36	2,226 93	2,057 43	25,074 80
Richland	5,909 69	2,724 51	14,478 38	96 60	543 90	3,441 40	2,543 75	4,942 55	34,680 83
Rock, 1st district	5,752 91	1,267 44	15,568 44	216 00		3,103 86	1,792 71	3,248 51	30,949 87
Rock, 2d district	6,154 29	1,253 68	15,069 17	47 00	250 00	3,946 57	1,410 71	2,789 13	30,910 55
St. Croix	7,065 70	5,398 89	21,633 18	665 84	3,907 44	1,072 04	2,018 96	3,937 82	41,600 25
Sauk	8,476 52	3,132 12	29,716 99	204 84		4,286 70	3,981 96	10,706 38	60,504 51
Shawano	5,461 86	386 41	6,378 69	217 56	602 10	1,112 69	1,170 53	2,401 02	12,349 00
Wgan	7,521 80	916 35	15,453 07	283 49	8,551 64	3,757 62	4,664 85	7,197 28	43,089 46

Financial Statistics — Receipts.

TABLE No. VIII. — FINANCIAL STATISTICS — RECEIPTS — Continued.

COUNTIES.	From money on hand, August 31, 1879.	From taxes levied for building and repairing.	From taxes levied for teachers' wages.	From taxes levied for apparatus and library.	From taxes levied at annual town meeting.	From taxes levied by county supervisors.	From income of school fund.	From all other sources.	Total amount received during the year.
Taylor	$1,758 40	$1,023 77	$2,548 25	$132 04	$1,387 51	$747 68	$170 62	$1,639 59	$9,220 81
Trempealeau	6,587 64	2,119 96	15,198 99	377 27	588 60	2,040 81	2,866 06	2,924 08	32,428 15
Vernon	6,187 49	1,957 71	15,869 66	151 59	553 44	3,823 18	3,381 15	7,862 83	39,094 99
Walworth	9,141 14	1,756 75	33,615 54	148 00	531 83	3,316 39	3,624 28	7,319 74	60,375 71
Washington	4,954 94	1,408 71	12,532 98	157 69	2,974 70	5,100 03	3,760 79	5,017 83	35,833 21
Waukesha	6,945 68	5,864 45	28,279 69	297 00	605 90	3,980 20	4,199 94	9,061 98	59,133 65
Waupaca	7,989 65	3,171 88	17,805 11	188 03	946 92	2,758 69	2,989 18	3,828 00	39,627 47
Waushara	2,723 10	1,068 08	10,408 92	88 97	20 00	2,331 21	1,751 94	3,387 06	21,839 28
Winnebago	7,981 80	2,269 34	14,844 13	103 70		4,548 91	2,719 45	3,570 80	35,988 13
Wood	2,178 08	586 93	4,087 54	120 00	179 74	91 00	527 92	3,078 82	13,156 27
Totals	$359,395 27	$130,850 23	$889,918 88	$10,184 01	$84,168 61	$164,881 60	$140,808 35	$289,597 67	$2,007,098 94

Financial Statistics — Disbursements.

Table No. IX.

FINANCIAL STATISTICS — DISBURSEMENTS

COUNTIES.	For building and repairing.	For apparatus and library.	For services of male teachers.	For services of female teachers.	For old indebtedness.	For school furniture, registers, records, etc.	For all other purposes.	Total amount paid out during year.	Money on hand August 31, 1880.
Adams	$815 73	$38 11	$2,347 94	$5,528 10	$487 09	$77 41	$608 77	$9,944 93	$1,964 15
Ashland	30 00		2,280 00	1,327 00		25 00	739 12	3,671 22	683 93
Barron	815 45	60 76	2,118 00	4,356 00	1,745 77	171 46	1,736 15	11,012 59	1,492 28
Bfld	9 12	80 94	1,000 00	426 02			300 41	1,816 49	947 31
Brown	2,033 51	229 93	11,030 17	12,180 77	827 24	708 22	2,836 90	29,025 50	8,797 65
Buffalo	5,920 11	226 06	12,554 00	6,706 00	1,076 41	775 85	8,046 33	27,304 76	6,519 09
Burnett	678 94	154 72	361 00	1,399 0	51 65	43 79	275 49	2,964 60	1,971 46
...net	1,681 71	133 41	7,5?1 0	8,450 00	391 26	423 79	2,194 96	20,776 13	6,728 38
...wa	2,462 46	1,049 67	7,589 83	14,600 10	3,122 17	578 54	3,751 14	33,415 36	10,088 58
Clark	8,910 05	379 70	5,144 4?	11,874 77	2,876 32	456 53	4,?09 19	28,840 96	9,986 63
...bia	1,961 10	265 44	13,128 71	18,260 80	1,797 88	732 67	5?9 38	41,666 88	8,285 91
Crawford	1,534 43	116 69	4,893 09	7,288 16	763 70	301 19	1,472 85	16,928 00	5,113 27
Dane, 1st district	2,286 08	140 32	10,063 50	13,467 70	1,155 90	460 06	3,737 05	33,291 55	7,655 37
Dane, 2d district	2,853 12	87 50	8,403 50	15,034 14	614 16	267 92	3,043 79	30,852 14	7,102 67
Dodge	4,067 45	309 36	17,049 85	22,144 00	2,610 58	258 81	7,?07 03	53,607 07	19,785 80
Door	2,553 56	215 48	3,688 80	6,751 0?	382 72	619 19	1,954 97	15,351 78	6,844 22
Douglas	48 49		660 00	759 75		45 40	268 54	1,782 13	126 91
Dunn	4,5?3 11	169 85	9,747 47	14,324 56	1,118 79	1,004 65	4,096 49	34,002 83	9,927 91
Eau Claire	2,735 78	52 59	8,692 00	18,218 88	3,298 56	401 77	8,374 60	41,734 18	14,057 46
Fond du Lac	1,981 05	111 57	13,904 91	21,195 62	536 02	541 93	4,794 11	43,165 21	11,9:0 14
Grant	3,294 68	330 03	18,115 80	28,241 14	2,289 62	994 99	7 ?0 03	60,552 29	15,327 01
Green	3,460 72	243 21	11,882 25	17,841 75	1,?1 32	729 33	4,870 35	40,518 93	8,312 19

Financial Statistics — Disbursements.

TABLE No. IX. — FINANCIAL STATISTICS — DISBURSEMENTS — Continued.

COUNTIES.	For building and repairing.	For apparatus and library.	For services of male teachers.	For services of female teachers.	For old indebtedness.	For school furniture, registers, records, etc.	For all other purposes.	Total amount paid out during year.	Money on hand August 31, 1880
Green Lake	$1,831 54	$4 44	$3,820 85	$7,395 39	$120 94	$189 23	$1,639 26	$15,857 30	$3,139 24
Iowa	1,065 57	138 85	9,878 83	13,010 15	661 41	824 13	3,308 70	29,317 88	6,288 30
Jackson	1,840 01	224 78	4,778 75	12,051 65	526 66	404 41	2,427 33	22,263 90	5,871 43
Jefferson	2,007 71	103 92	13,713 50	16,935 96	658 60	891 49	6,081 14	40,239 90	9,903 49
Juneau	1,773 81	30 11	6,507 50	11,656 52	210 24	283 98	3,008 24	23,234 72	6,587 04
Kenosha	3,402 33	43 37	5,941 26	7,106 52	485 21	90 14	2,038 42	19,113 86	2,825 45
Kewaunee	2,184 07	75 06	7,999 75	3,653 50	351 50	358 56	2,187 58	17,085 35	5,079 22
La Crosse	2,256 68	129 08	8,837 00	6,895 00	510 46	514 68	1,992 92	20,036 72	5,455 27
La Fayette	2,404 02	537 97	11,735 17	15,422 00	1,506 34	224 22	4,379 43	38,197 39	5,606 11
Lincoln	1,281 53	......	1,472 00	2,388 00	644 36	32 00	317 96	6,185 85	860 03
Manitowoc	5,300 08	185 50	5,509 15	16,762 00	782 38	1,222 97	5,860 91	55,622 99	17,936 18
Marathon	2,792 09	388 40	26,506 51	8,456 95	3,160 16	456 70	2,528 24	23,439 93	13,215 85
Marinette	3,733 14	34 20	710 00	4,590 00	71 00	258 15	6,043 51	15,439 00	2,208 22
Marquette	692 54	11 01	2,970 00	4,842 00	478 50	29 24	1,240 49	7,591 78	4,721 95
Milwaukee, 1st dist	505 27	30 65	6,113 88	6,853 78	343 44	76 82	2,108 87	16,034 83	755 14
Milw., 2d dist	2,693 65	82 51	6,587 75	4,450 25	337 77	479 92	1,887 61	16,156 60	4,875 38
Monroe	2,321 06	144 75	8,301 41	19,778 87	374 69	718 65	3,092 77	35,632 20	9,077 03
Oconto	1,087 59	34 76	2,274 00	4,015 59	215 12	133 99	1,062 83	9,783 37	6,314 41
Outagamie	1,980 15	129 57	6,350 00	13,752 53	1,701 20	482 89	2,701 24	27,097 57	7,847 19
Ozaukee	1,971 66	57 08	13,089 72	4,286 50	534 52	395 63	1,470 19	22,406 71	4,268 37
Pepin	965 96	146 32	2,167 00	5,453 00	319 00	140 41	704 12	9,895 81	2,440 66
Pierce	1,639 18	491 08	8,969 30	12,673 50	788 20	448 91	4,203 59	38,468 55	10,913 68
Polk	1,533 76	184 52	8,635 50	9,021 81	1,408 09	864 82	2,912 36	19,460 30	6,833 46
Portage	1,058 29	48 47	8,675 00	8,730 95	478 75	120 54	1,353 11	15,417 46	4,949 16

Financial Statistics — Disbursements.

Price	$485 95	$39 25	$120 00	$1,390 55	$128 00	.....	$796 38	$8,810 12	$900 00
Racine	2,145 96	82 81	5,012 55	13,117 64	210 51	$1,302 91	3,175 05	23,810 88	4,599 00
Richland	4,428 82	151 17	6,875 86	12,793 60	349 89	500 99	2,512 03	26,603 58	6,780 39
Rock, 1st district	1,070 18	203 86	6,575 45	11,821 50	07 01	396 87	2,048 34	24,073 21	6,876 06
Rk, 2d district	1,036 15	57 12	4,368 50	13,055 16	302 33	107 78	2,741 40	22,568 50	8,343 05
St. Croix	4,752 28	322 03	10,075 80	14,021 82	3,230 46	526 08	3,841 60	36,704 23	7,637 06
Sauk	3,832 80	152 52	14,877 05	22,863 09	1,825 00	753 85	5,163 08	49,465 89	11,068 63
Shawano	735 70	177 18	3,334 36	5,492 75	280 81	305 15	1,658 24	11,984 19	6,099 43
Sheboygan	1,133 05	45 63	13,650 82	12,562 88	420 40	241 04	3,5 6 7	32,242 04	10,817 42
Taylor	1,370 87	72 04	180 00	2,824 99	836 16	302 96	893 97	6,286 35	2,834 46
Trempealeau	1,048 23	72 74	8,951 70	11,363 12	704 02	647 43	2,985 27	25,221 13	7,268 05
Vernon	2,556 05	239 93	9,726 41	11,939 0	568 70	448 78	3,276 55	20,141 02	9,053 37
Walworth	1,700 35	61 42	13,314 37	24,782 00	2,112 11	347 17	5,822 08	49,854 45	9,565 25
Washington	2,038 81	185 32	12,140 50	6,667 90	672 21	660 47	2,514 84	27,632 20	8,201 01
Waukesha	5,046 60	197 07	14,448 42	19,644 50	754 46	1,218 18	5,719 62	43,240 33	10,763 78
Waupaca	8,189 92	281 24	8,003 50	14,222 51	687 87	406 05	3,778 56	30,569 65	9,057 82
Waushara	1,571 11	1,537 17	3,545 00	9,314 31	497 50	217 89	2,219 08	17,402 00	4,437 22
Winnebago	2,585 87	100 40	13,444 60	6,703 00	1,126 29	265 40	2,980 44	27,205 50	8,782 63
Wood	570 22	103 66	1,488 00	3,588 96	656 79	117 35	1,132 13	10,700 97	2,618 01
Totals	$149,970 26	$11,020 20	$492,132 43	$690,585 31	$58,656 31	$28,017 41	$195,541 83	$1,636,172 11	$447,634 61

Teachers' Certificates and Normal School Teachers.

Table No. X.
TEACHERS' CERTIFICATES AND NORMAL SCHOOL TEACHERS.

COUNTIES.	Number of Teachers holding State Certificates.	NUMBER CERTIFICATES ISSUED. MALE. 1st Grade	MALE. 2d Grade	MALE. 3d Grade	FEMALE. 1st Grade	FEMALE. 2d Grade	FEMALE. 3d Grade	Total.	NUMBER CERTIFICATES REFUSED. MALE. 1st Grade	MALE. 2d Grade	MALE. 3d Grade	FEMALE. 1st Grade	FEMALE. 2d Grade	FEMALE. 3d Grade	Total.	Number of Teachers who are graduates of Normal Schools.	Number of other Teachers who have attended Normal Schools.
Adams		1	3	14		1	71	89			5			20	25		5
Ashland	1			1		3	4	8									
Barron	4		2	84		1	69	106	1	1	6			24	32		8
Bayfield							1	1									
Brown		8	8	86	2	4	55	104		1	20		2	35	56		25
Buffalo	8	2	16	50		5	65	141		2	17			24	45		11
Burnett	1							14								2	
Calumet	8		8	30	3	5	68	107			6			13	10	3	20
Chippewa	1	1		50	2	7	111	170			2			23	25	2	11
Clark	8	1	3	28	1	6	83	116			11			62	73	4	16
Columbia	2	3		75		9	234	331			40			90	130		20
Crawford		4	11	21		19	84	125			10			12	22	2	12
Dane, 1st dist.	10	4	5	61	2	8	144	240			26			78	104	4	20
Dane, 2d dist.	2	6	19	35	1	19	87	139		11	45	8	18	145	190	7	10
Dodge		1	6	71	1		120	234	3		72			124	230		70
Door			17	24			59	84			3			13	16	1	16
Douglas							8	6									
Dunn	5		1	40		8	90	140	1	1	12	2	2	26	44	4	12

Teachers' Certificates and Normal School Teachers.

County	1	2	3	4	5	6	7	8	9	10	11	12	13	14	15	16	17
Eau Claire	10	7	20	15			5			129	95	6	7	15	1	5	3
Fond du Lac	52	8	116	95			21	4		253	184	9	1	56	3	5	2
Grant	90	22	336	243	11	2	76	4	3	396	267	14	4	85	14		28
Green	20		53	32		2	21			218	163	5		38	10	12	
Green Lake	15	1	50	29	9	1	15	8	1	90	59	4	3	15	7	2	1
Iowa	46	9	302	255		2	31	4	1	188	123	7	5	41	8	2	
Jackson	4	2	44	41	3		3			140	100	9	2	25	3	4	2
Jefferson		2	213	153	4		53	3	2	215	130	22		52	8	1	6
Juneau	28		87	50			25	4		163	107	6	4	44	4	3	2
Kenosha	7	2	46	38			3			82	38	5		26	8	2	1
Kewaunee	19		37	13	12	5	23	1		60	21	4	2	29	6	1	
La Crosse	50	2	67	41			26		2	134	72	4	4	41	13	2	1
La Fayette		5	112	59			28			201	117	11		57	12		
Lincoln	4		75	49	2		26	1	2	15	10			3		1	2
Manitowoc	3	2	8	5	10		3	6		152	74	1		66	6	3	
Monroe	20		4	2						102	63	3		27	8		1
Marinette	8		120	60			50			39	30	4		5	1	2	
Milwaukee, 1st dist	10	1	10	10				1		102	81	1		11		1	
Milwaukee, 2d dist	9	1	7	5			1			52	32	6		9	3	3	
Oconto	7		85	77	1		8	1		53	30	8	1	14	8	5	2
Outagamie	5	2	8	8						258	187	1		42	13	4	1
Ozaukee	27	1	72	62		1	10	1		47	28	1		9	4	2	1
Pepin	5		5	3		2	1	2		143	111	6	4	27	3	3	
Pierce	4	2	42	35			7			64	29		3	26	5	5	1
Polk	106	1	87	73			10	1		57	34	11		8	1	4	
Portage	12		33	32			1	2	1	160	106	6		22	13	2	1
Price	15		74	70	1		4			85	51			21	2	4	
Racine	7	2	76	63			11	1	1	113	79	11	1	16	8	4	1
Richland	5		134	92	1		38	2	2	11	9	12	2	2			
Rock, 1st dist	12	1	46	33	2		13			124	76	15	4	28	9	2	1
Rock, 2d dist	13	3	24	23			1			33	50	18	1	23	5	5	2
St. Croix	30		43	26			17			188	115	19		41	10	6	
Sauk	40	6	71	54			17			207	150	2		23	7	1	2
Shawano	30	8	18	11			7			156	85	3		39	6	2	13

Teachers' Certificates and Normal School Teachers.

TABLE No. X.—TEACHERS' CERTIFICATES AND NORMAL SCHOOL TEACHERS—Continued.

COUNTIES.	Number of Teachers holding State Certificates.	Number Certificates Issued.							Number Certificates Refused.							Number of Teachers who are graduates of Normal Schools.	Number of other teachers who have attended Normal Schools.
		MALE.			FEMALE.			Total.	MALE.			FEMALE.			Total.		
		1st Grade.	2d Grade.	3d Grade.	1st Grade.	2d Grade.	3d Grade.		1st Grade.	2d Grade.	3d Grade.	1st Grade.	2d Grade.	3d Grade.			
Sheboygan	2	1	..	59	..	..	101	161	2	..	47	..	..	87	136	1	16
Taylor	..	..	..	1	..	1	27	29	..	..	..	..	..	5	5	..	..
Trempealeau	1	7	10	39	3	4	75	138	1	3	8	..	5	86	45	..	9
Vernon	3	4	14	48	2	6	102	176	2	1	21	1	5	87	69	1	4
Walworth	..	8	7	65	..	7	165	247	..	4	19	..	..	64	84	8	58
Washington	1	5	8	40	..	..	59	107	5	8	11	..	..	35	55	2	35
Waukesha	10	8	5	32	3	5	162	209	3	..	22	8	6	88	125	8	30
Waupaca	..	8	8	39	..	..	125	170	..	3	20	..	..	100	120	2	25
Waushara	..	..	6	27	..	9	109	151	..	..	25	..	..	92	117	5	..
Winnebago	1	8	8	17	..	1	129	158	..	..	8	..	..	50	61	15	60
Wood	1	2	1	9	..	..	61	73	..	..	1	..	..	23	24	2	4
Totals	121	148	350	2,025	68	380	5,602	8,593	27	67	1,017	21	88	3,157	4,377	169	1,211

Text-Books.

Table No. XI.
TEXT-BOOKS.

COUNTIES.	READING.												SPELLING.										
	Webb's Model.	Sanders's Union.	Sanders.	National.	McGuffey.	Independent.	Harvey.	Wilson.	Sheldon.	American Educational.	Appleton.	New American.	Wilson.	Webster.	Webb.	Town.	Swinton.	Sanders's Union.	Sanders's.	National.	McGuffey.	Independent.	Harvey.
Adams		48		3		4	1		4	6	8			16			12	30		2	1		12
Ashland											2						5						
Barron		12	1				10	17		10			18				1	10			20		
Bayfield										1							1						
Brown	1									21	42						19	13		53			2
Buffalo		3		25	35		3	1		4	1	28	1	7			1		7	4			22
Burnett		2		2			2	4		25			2				11			12			
Calumet		9		16		2	24			15	1		6				49			23			
Chippewa																							
Clark			39	45			17	9	4	8			9				17	18	58	1	13	1	11
Columbia		13	15	11		4	1	83		16	3	3	34				11	17	20	4	1		3
Crawford		19	39	2	12		13	13		11	51		19		14		14	33	81	2	5	4	10
...e, 1st dist...		35	28	4	6	4	39	6		9	13		2				13	8	55	6	8		38
...e, 2d dist...		6	61	4	2		2	1		18	52		2				13		100				
Dodge			15	8	3			17		17			20				9						
Door									2								1	27					

Text-Books.

TABLE No. XI.—TEXT-BOOKS— Continued.

COUNTIES.	READING												SPELLING										
	Webb's Model.	Sander's Union.	Sanders.	National.	McGuffey.	Independent.	Harvey.	Wilson.	Sheldon.	American Educational.	Appleton.	New American.	Wilson.	Webster.	Webb.	Town.	Swinton.	Sander's Union.	Sanders.	National.	McGuffey.	Independent.	Harvey.
Douglas				7		9		14		16			14		1					4		3	
Dunn		11	29					5		44	3		5		1		32		31		2	1	21
Eau Claire	1	5	91		70		25	3		9	8		1	1		20	42	1	103	17	68	7	49
Fond du Lac			10	27	12	31	25	18		24	2					1	14	8	8		22		7
Grant	4	9		2	1	7	49	6		55	28		4				44	20	25	8			5
Geen		11					8	2		10							77	30	24	8	6		
Green Lake		24	18	2	35	5	7	10		21	4		4		6	1	25		21	8	8		4
Iowa			26	14		4		7		12	12		3	3			11	6	48	1	2	1	
Jackson		6	7	4	3		16	1		9	31		11				13	3	23	5	12		7
Jefferson		2		1	1	2				8	4	8	8	1		1	19	31	21	12	16		
Juneau		89	27	7	6		8	1		23	2						23	4	20	4	19		10
Kenosha	2	3	25	5	2	11				5	2		1				2	7		1	3	1	2
Kewaunee		5	5	10	8	19	9	4		17	42	8	4			12	22		45		1	7	11
La Crosse			16		2	6		5					2				1	10	3	27		1	
La Fayette		8			4	2				21		9					22	7	58			2	
Lincoln													17				7		13			4	
Manitowoc	8	14	54	28	4		8	20		21		9											
Mon			12							10													

Text–Books.

County	Totals
Marinette	342
Marquette	43
[ ] 1st dist	386
[ ]ee 2d dist	299
[ ]oe	1,404
Oconto	552
Outagamie	1,009
Ozaukee	54
Pepin	38
Pierce	82
Polk	342
Portage	73
Price	735
Racine	795
[ ]nd	25
[ ]k, 1st dist	394
Rock, 2d dist	307
St. Croix	178
Sauk	385
Shawano	345
Sheboygan	965
Taylor	599
Trempealeau	20
Vernon	
Walworth	
[ ]hington	
[ ] [ ]sha	
Waupaca	
Waushara	
[ ]go	
Wood	
Totals	

Table No. XI.
TEXT-BOOKS.—Continued.

Text-Books.

COUNTIES	Davies	French	Quackenbos	Ray	Robinson	Thompson	White	Davies	Loomis	Olney	Ray	Robinson	Schuyler	Cornell	Eclectic	Guyot	Harper	McNally	Mitchell	Monteith	Swinton	Warren
					ARITHMETIC					ALGEBRA							GEOGRAPHY					
Adams		1	19	1	45						3			20		1	11		5	11	18	
Ashland				3	3										5						4	
Barron	3	17			23									10	5		18			5	12	
Bayfield					1															1	1	
Brown	23	4	88	58	19	2	9			2	1	1		11	1	2	4	3	39	18	18	
Buffalo	19	6			9		8	1		1				39	2		6			3	5	
Burnett	26				1		2	1									7					
Calumet	26	4	3		25	2	19					2			20	1	10	8	16	14	26	
Chippewa	5	19			49		2					1		2			35	3	24	19	41	
Clark	1	8		4	36		9		3			8	1		10		49	2	5	15	15	1
Columbia					97							12		2	1	1			2	16	7	1
Crawford	4	1	2	42	45	9	9	1			5	7		86	9		6			8	29	
Dane, 1st dist			29	34	37	14	2			14	2	2		9	1		23	15		10	18	
Dane, 2d dist	10		11	41	29	24	3	1	2		2	6		10			9	5	5	34	7	
Dodge	20		6	58	47		37		2			21		40	64		81	6	2	44	9	
Door				17	6									8			5		3			
Douglas											1										1	1
Dunn	9	15		14	39	3	1				1	8		13	1		23			9	84	
Eau Claire				3	50	8						4		11			14				20	1
Fond du Lac	27		2	1	53	55	30	10		1	8	18		33	25	2	12		1	22	88	18

Text-Books.

County																			
Grant	11	2		106		89	1	1	4	19	2	7	7	43	4	26	10	35	87	30	4
Green		8	3	39	3	5		1		4		14		5		46		3		54	
Green Lake	3	3	1	1	1	9		1		14		12		2	1	15	12	6	45	14	2
Iowa	5			50	11	7	2			12		9		3		10		5	9	36	1
Jackson	16	10		15	24	12		1		2	1	8		1		14	6		20	21	
Jefferson		8		30	10	4	14			6		49		16	5	14	4	2	20	5	
Juneau	1					1				2		8				16	4	31	12	20	
Kenosha	5	1				13		1		6						24	2		7		
Kewaunee	14	1		22	1	6				1		11		9		2		24	24	8	
La Crosse	5			10	4	2		3		2		3		11	2	2	13		25	13	
La Fayette	9			70	16	3	1		1	6		18		6		18		8		18	
Lincoln	9			1			6	4	3	1				1		11	3	33	18	30	1
Manitowoc	51	9		35		64				2				3		12		5	30	14	
Marion	6	2		8	3	2	5			6		8				20			6		
Marinette		1		1		3	1		1	1				1		2	1			9	
Marquette	2			14		4	2			1						4	6	3	10	7	
Milwaukee, 1st dist.	5	2		22		26	1			7				24		3	2	3	9	6	
Milwaukee, 2d dist.	2	2		15		1	2			1						5	17	12	20	21	1
Monroe	5	8		45		3			1	2		8				8	1			6	
Oconto	28			8		1	1			3		2		6		17		19	29	4	
Outagamie	2			4		3	6					11				11			31	10	
Ozaukee		3		1	2		1						1			7			6	13	
Pepin	6					4								6		4	8		21	63	
Pierce	1			1		5				12		3		5	1	14	13	4	17	20	1
Polk	26	4	14	6		4	5			3		15				7		61	6	7	
Portage	8	17	8			5	3			3		14				25		4		5	
Price	5			6	6	4	3			2				5	1				7	4	4
Racine	4	1	6			1	1	2	1	2		16		1		11	8	4	5	8	5
Richland	2		14	19	14	6		1	1	3	1		3	8		41	13	61	3	13	3
Rock, 1st dist.	21	7	11	16	11		6		2	5		21	2	1		42	1	4	21	11	
Rock, 2d dist.	4		11			28	1		1	9		17	1	8		30	29		28	37	
St. Croix	36	9		5		2			2	2		16		30		31			1	7	
Sauk	8	1		2					1							11	18	9	23	36	1
Shawano	56	1				2		1		8			1	2		14		9		10	
Sheboygan	1															13		1			
Taylor																1					

Text-Books.

TABLE No. XI. TEXT-BOOKS.—Continued.

COUNTIES.	ARITHMETIC.							ALGEBRA.						GEOGRAPHY.								
	Davies.	French.	Quackenbos.	Ray.	Robinson.	Thompson.	White.	Davies.	Loomis.	Olney.	Ray.	Robinson.	Schuyler.	Cornell.	Eclectic.	Guyot.	Harper.	McNally.	Mitchell.	Monteith.	Swinton.	Warren.
Trempealeau	15	1	27	...	27	...	1	...	...	...	...	3	1	28	2	...	3	...	...	18	34	...
Vernon	1	...	...	91	27	...	6	...	...	...	10	3	1	...	21	18	10	12	...	41	30	...
Walworth	2	1	...	...	92	8	15	1	...	...	...	15	...	1	17	18	17	2	12	2	37	...
Washington	17	...	30	73	7	...	...	...	...	...	...	...	...	37	13	1	13	13	...	51	...	...
Waukesha	4	6	38	5	27	21	3	3	...	...	...	12	...	38	4	4	28	...	11	6	...	...
Waupaca	18	17	...	2	47	16	3	2	8	...	...	4	...	2	5	...	47	...	...	6	9	...
Waushara	...	...	24	2	57	...	...	...	...	...	...	7	...	...	...	3	...	...	6	5	22	...
Winnebago	10	...	...	7	70	...	8	...	...	...	...	6	...	...	14	...	1	10	...	25	44	4
Wood	5	...	11	...	9	...	...	...	...	...	...	...	...	14	...	...	2	...	...	9	35	...
Totals	550	215	381	1,011	2,057	190	342	52	19	24	41	246	12	597	407	57	908	224	394	860	1,092	38

Text–Books.

TABLE NO. XI.
TEXT–BOOKS—Continued.

COUNTIES	Geometry: Robinson	Geometry: Olney	Geometry: Loomis	Geometry: Davies	Physiology: Steele	Physiology: Hitchcock	Physiology: Dalton	Physiology: Cutter	Physiology: Brown	U.S. Hist.: Venable	U.S. Hist.: Swinton	U.S. Hist.: Scott	U.S. Hist.: Quackenbos	U.S. Hist.: Goodrich	U.S. Hist.: Barnes	U.S. Hist.: Anderson	Grammar: Swinton	Grammar: Quackenbos	Grammar: Pinneo	Grammar: Kerl	Grammar: Harvey	Grammar: Green	Grammar: Clark
Adams											24		18	3	17		18	16		23	8	2	
Ashland														8			3	1	1	23	8		
Barron											37				4		14			19	9		4
Bayfield											1		4	7			1						
Brown										8	27	6	33		7		16	32	11	17	1		17
Buffalo	2	2			2			1	1						15		10			2		5	3
Burnett										2	2				2		8				26		1
Calumet					1		1			1	2		2	1	1	3						1	
Chippewa					2		1		2		25			6	4		15			14	25		2
Clark	1		1		1	1	1	1		9	56	4	3		13	1	9	3		19	3	1	10
Columbia											18	8		7	52	1	37		8	19	20		2
Crawford									1		18			5	3		48	1		46			
Dane, 1st dist	1				1	1				10	38		32	9	12		16	33	1	31	10		3
Dane, 2d dist	1							3	4		31	8	6	19	11		18	6	7	34	17		6
Dodge							1	6	4		29	10	2	48	72		11	5		34	42		60
Door		3				1		1		1	23			4			56			14			2
Douglas								1		5	8		1				1						
Dunn	1				1					33	39	10	2	2	6		38			20	3	1	2
Eau Claire	4				1				1		17	1			6		34			3	4		
Fond du Lac	2	1		1	4	2		2	2	14	40			26	15		3			83	48	1	4

Text-Books.

TABLE No XI.—TEXT-BOOKS—Continued.

COUNTIES.	GRAMMAR.							UNITED STATES HISTORY.							PHYSIOLOGY.					GEOMETRY.			
	Clark.	Green.	Harvey.	Kerl.	Pinneo.	Quackenbos.	Swinton.	Anderson.	Barnes.	Goodrich.	Quackenbos.	Scott.	Swinton.	Venable.	Brown.	Cutter.	Dalton.	Hitchcock.	Steele.	Davies.	Loomis.	Olney.	Robinson.
Grant	10	2	58	47	17		37	25	22	8	2	10	42	25	7	4		4	2		6		2
Gr..n	3		33	20		3	49	1		9			78	5	2	1			1			1	1
Green Lake	9		5	40		5	9	1	2	8	4	2	24	2	1		1						1
Iowa	5	1	18	23	4		55		10	4	3	3	40	3		3		1	2	1	1		1
Jackson	9	8	2	19		10	16	2	8	1		3	29		1	1	1			1	1	2	
Jefferson	8		14			42	16		7	9	33	2	7	5			1		1				
Juneau	7	24		24		9	17		43		9		10		1	1		1					1
Kenosha	1	1	7	8			10		5	4		1	14	1	2	1		2			1		1
Kewaunee	1			22					4	6	1		14		1								
La ..e	9		17				10				7		22	6		1			1		1		1
La Fayette			33	21	7	5	27	1	21	19	14	9	15		2								
Lincoln	3		10		2	11		4	7					5								1	
Manitowoc	2	5	8	59			9		9	10			48	3				1					
Marathon	8		26	7	3		12		8			11	15	5				1	4				
Marinette	2		1	1			2		3			6	1		2	2	1	2					
Marquette							1	1		1	1		1						1				
Milw., 1st dist	1	8	3	4	7		4		4	11	4	1	10	1									
Milw., 2d dist.	2	3	3	4	6		6		34	4	2	2	7			4	1		4		1		1
Monroe	7	11	29	16	8	4	15		2	10	5	5	19	16	1		1					1	1
Oconto	1	2	2	7			8		13	23			5			2							
Outagamie			16	8	15	7	8		7	7			7		2	4			1		1		
Ozaukee	14			18			14	8					24			1		1	1				1

Text-Books.

County									Totals
Pepin									36
Pierce									10
Polk									21
Portage									13
Price									45
Racine									18
Richland									13
Rock, 1st dist.									67
Rock, 2d dist.									48
St. Croix									240
Sauk									1,466
Shawano									163
Sheboygan									408
Taylor									417
Trempealeau									615
Vernon									106
Walworth									1,128
Washington									392
Waukesha									114
Waupaca									1,294
Waushara									680
Winnebago									120
Wood									324
Totals									

Teachers' Institutes.

Table No. XII.

TEACHERS' INSTITUTES.

COUNTIES.	WHERE HELD.	BY WHOM CONDUCTED.	WHEN HELD.
Adams	White Creek.....	A. J. Hutton..............	Sept. 27
Brown	Depere	A. A. Miller and J. M. Rait	Aug. 16
Buffalo.....	Alma	J. B Thayer	Sept. 13
Calumet ...	Chilton ....;	Robert Graham	Sept. 20
Chippewa ..	Chippewa Falls ..	J B. Thayer	April 5
Chippewa ..	Chippewa Falls .	T. B. Pray and Miss A. Hosford.	Aug. 23
Clark	Unity	J. B. Thayer ....…...	April 12
Clark	Neillsville	J. B. Thayer ....·	Sept. 26
Columbia ..	Portage	A. J. Hutton....................	Mar. 22
Columbia ..	Lodi	Albert Salisbury	Oct. 11
Columbia ..	Cambria	Albert Salisbury	Oct. 18
Crawford...	Wauzeka	A. J. Hutton	Sept. 13
Dane,—			
1st dist...	Sun Prairie.....	A. J. Hutton	Oct. 18
2d dist...	Oregon	A. J Hutton	Oct. 11
Dodge	Beaver Dam.....	J Q. Emery	Sept. 20
Door	Sturgeon Bay....	Robert Graham	Oct. 4
Dunn	Menomonie	A. R Sprague and G. T. Foster .	Aug. 80
Eau Claire..	Augusta.........	J. B. Thayer	Oct. 11
Fond du Lac	Fond du Lac	Robert Graham	Mar. 22
Grant	Platteville.......	A. J. Hutton	Aug. 2
Grant	Fennimore......	George Beck......	Aug. 16
Green	Monroe	Albert Salisbury	Aug. 23
Green Lake.	Princeton	Albert Salisbury	Sept. 20
Iowa	Dodgeville......	D. McGregor and Miss A. White	Aug. 23
Jackson	Black River Falls	J. B. Thayer	Aug. 30
Jefferson ..	Fort Atkinson ...	Albert Salisbury	Mar. 29
Juneau	Mauston	A. J. Hutton	Aug. 16
Kenosha ...	Salem...........	Albert Salisbury	Sept. 6
Kewaunee ..	Kewaunee	Robert Graham	Oct. 11
La Crosse...	West Salem	Hosea Barns and Miss Hosford .	Sept. 6
La Fayette .	Darlington	Hosea Barns and C. A. Burlew..	Aug. 23
Manitowoc .	Manitowoc	J. Q Emery and C. F. Viebahn .	July 26
Marathon...	Wausau	Robert Graham	Sept. 6
Marinette ..	Marinette	Ed. McLoughlin	Aug. 30
Marquette..	Montello	C. A. Burlew and J. H. Gould...	Sept. 6
Milwaukee,			
1st dist...	Hale's Corners ..	Albert Salisbury	Oct. 4
2d dist...	Wauwatosa......	J. Q. Emery	Sept. 6
Monroe	Sparta	A. J. Hutton	Mar. 29
Oconto.....	Oconto	L. D. Harvey....................	Aug. 9
Outagamie .	Appleton	B. R. Grogan................ ...	Sept. 6
Ozaukee ...	Cedarburgh	Ed. McLoughlin	Aug. 16
Pepin	Pepin	B. M. Reynolds and J. H. Gould	Aug. 16
Polk	Osceola Mills....	W. D. Parker and Miss M. Kelly.	Aug. 9
Portage	Plover	Albert Salisbury	Mar. 15
Pierce	Maiden Rock....	Jas. T. Lunn	Sept. 13
Racine	Rochester	Albert Salisbury and E. R. Smith	Aug. 9

Teachers' Institutes.

TABLE No. XII— TEACHERS' INSTITUTES — Continued.

COUNTIES.	WHERE HELD.	BY WHOM CONDUCTED.	WHEN HELD.
Richland ..	Richland Center .	A. J. Hutton	April 12
Richland ...	Richland Center .	W. S. Johnson ....,.......	Aug. 16
Rock,—			
1st dist ...	Evansville.......	Albert Salisbury	April 5
2d dist....	Milton	J. Q. Emery	Aug. 23
Sauk......	Prairie du Sac...	Chas. H. Nye	Aug. 16
Shawano ...	Shawano	Alex. F. North.............	Sept. 6
Sheboygan..	Sheboygan Falls	L. D. Harvey	Aug. 23
St. Croix ...	Hammond......	J. B. Thayer	Mar. 22
Trempealeau	Blair	J. B. Thayer	Aug. 16
Vernon	Viroqua	A. J. Hutton	Aug. 30
Walworth ..	Elkhorn.......	J. Q. Emery	Aug. 9
Washington	West Bend	A. R. Sprague and G. T. Foster .	Aug. 16
Waukesha..	Waukesha.......	George Beck and J. M. Rait.....	Aug. 30
Waupaca...	Waupaca........	A. A. Miller....................	Aug. 30
Waushara .	Pine River	Robert Graham ....•.......	April 5
Winnebago.	Omro	Robert Graham	Aug. 23
Winnebago	Neenah	Robert Graham	Aug. 30
Wood	Centralia	J. Q. Emery	Oct. 4

Teachers' Institutes — Special Reports.

Table No. XIII.

TEACHERS' INSTITUTES — SPECIAL REPORTS.

Counties	No. of teachers required to teach the schools in county	No. Attending Institute — Male	No. Attending Institute — Female	No. Attending Institute — Total	Number of days institute was in session	Average daily attendance	First grade	Second grade	Third grade	Average age of members	Average experience in months in teaching of those having taught	Not having taught, but intending to teach	Number having previously attended institutes	Colleges and Universities	Academies	Normal Schools	High Schools	Common schools only	No. of schools in county, or superintendent district	No. of evening lectures
Adams	69	8	53	61	9	52	1	1	42	20.2	15.7	17	47	4	8		8	50	67	1
Brown	98	19	55	74	10	56	1	8	41	21.1	29	26	53			12	45	13	87	
Buffalo	88	24	23	47	10	29	2	15	25	23	19.7	9	35	3	8	11	19	9	89	4
Calumet	75	24	49	73	10	64	2	2	57	21.3	26.3	19	55	8	3	20	41	5	67	
Chippewa	109	20	56	76	4½	66.7	2	16	48	21.7	21	15	53	8	4		41	23	108	2
Chippewa		10	47	57	9	38.4	1	10	40	21.3	19	4	44			3	40	9		
Clark	85	14	24	38	5	34.4	5	4	22	21.5	19.7	9	32	6	2	3	16	11	79	1
Clark		13	54	67	9	45.6	6	15	35	21	24.6	19	56	9	2	5	44	10		
Columbia	165	32	98	130	5	116	2	18	70	21.7	20	13	83	9	19	4	83	20	146	
Columbia		13	28	41	5	35.8	2	3	34	23.6	22.4	2	31	2	4	3	17	8		1
Columbia		15	21	36	9	28	1		23	23.4	8.3	6	16		2	5	24	6	92	1
Crawford	91	10	27	37	10	28.3		9	27	20.4	20.1	9	19	14	15	4	42	15		
Dane, 1st dist.	186	16	65	81	10	63.9	2	19	46	21.7	14.6	16	55	10	2	1	8	6	136	2
Dane, 3d dist.	181	7	18	25	5	24.2	1	8	19	20.8	10.5	6	17	20	4	11	38	4	131	
Dodge	218	30	78	108	10	52	7	30	58	22	26	12	77	10	1	2	88	46	191	
Door	55	5	19	24	8	20	1	1	15	20.5	20.8	4	18	1	2	2	17	1	52	
Dunn	108	12	56	68	10	55	2	12	40	20	28	18	4	4	1	9	29	25	103	1

Teachers' Institutes — Special Reports.

County																												
Eau Claire	64	1	15	4	1	1	18	3	18	20.5	15	2	2	18	5	22	19	8	95
Fond du Lac	191	81	89	23	1	5	109	8	23	21.3	96	9	9	111	9	139	115	24	191
Grant	264	6	7	60	1	3	49	14	24.5	22.9	43	9	17	54.5	10	77	60	17	250
Green		22	27	20	4	2	48	24	23.8	23.3	41	8	5	65.2	10	78	53	25	156
Green Lake	105	42	51	20	1	6	58	42	17	19.7	52	6	2	63	10	100	50	50	75
Iowa	68	32	10		1	12	44	11	11.5	20	38	9		48		58	42	16	130
Jackson	129	20	44	3	2	7	75	54	23	21.5	72	15	5	103	8½	124	102	22	91
Jefferson	87	9	29	20	14	8	33	1	26.6	20	35	7	9	39.6	9	51	44	7	159
dau	130	13	66	3	4	6	51		19.8	21.2	42	13	2	87	4½	98	80	18	111
Kenosha	107	30	65	10	5	4	75	18	17.5	20	72	14	5	76.8	9	26	80	16	62
Kewaunee	61	2	14			2	45	11	26	23	36	8	2	57	4	67	46	21	55
La Crosse	54	11	15	16	1	5	21	8	26	24.6	17	6	3	26	9	28	12	16	74
La ... te	76	16	25	1	1	6	45	1	22.8	22.5	36	12	3	31	9	52	30	22	146
... Mc	126	40	49	2	5	5	54	23	27.6	20.1	49	14	3	43.2	10	82	61	21	135
... Mon	138	15	53	7	3	3	77	37	20.5	20.5	62	8	4	72.5	5	107	64	43	85
Marinette	77	3	18	11	1	1	32	7	30.7	21.7	30	3		30	10	40	34	6	27
Marquette	30	83	10	5	1		12	3	12.5		7	4	3	14	5	17	13	4	33
Milw., 1st dist.	59	11	26	6		3	47	25	26		86	5	1	54	10	67	52	15	63
... 2d dist.	36	15	2	8	1	2	13	7	59		15	1	1	14	5	22	16	6	44
Monroe	34	29	9	10	5	15	34	15	41.1	24.5	30	6	1	35.3	10	44	29	15	35
Oconto	123	8	77	8	3	9	65	51	18.2	24.1	67	9	6	88.1	10	120	96	24	144
Outagamie	41	18	11	3	1		21	2	40.1	20.1	7	10	9	13	5	25	19	6	33
Ozaukee	106	18	28	10	5	2	53	8	46.3	22	53	8		52	10	71	48	23	113
Pepin	59	34		10	5	15	43	19	19.6	24.8	38	6	5	42.5	5	55	25	30	70
Pierce	37	2	36	4		9	29	8	21	19	13	12	2	31.7	10	46	33	13	40
Polk	105	13	11	5	2		17	9	22	22	13	7	3	15.6	11	31	19	12	120
Portage	65	26	7	13	4	8	37	9	25.3	20.3	35	13	8	40.6	10	49	42	7	73
Racine	84	57	24	13	8	3	70	43	25.2	20	47	10	3	63.2	10	100	78	28	88
Richland	75	21	23	25	25	3	52	29	17.5	20	44	9	2	66	9	76	68	8	82
Richland	129	25	70	2	2	4	67	57	19.7	21	50	14	1	73	9½	114	85	29	130
Rock, 1st dist.		16	50			9	64	17	18.1		32	12		64	9	77	57	20	93
Rock, 2d dist.	92	18	37	9	3	28	61	26	32	20.8	45	7		50	9	84	70	14	96
St. Croix	95	18	16	6	11	3	43	12	24	22.9	35	6	4	32	9½	58	43	15	105
Sauk	105	12	40	25	9	6	55	16	28.6	20	52	1	2	56	10	90	62	28	179
Shawano	165	15	40	4	4	4	53	11	26	21.3	54	6		57.1	5	69	53	16	67
	72	6	13	2	2	4	20	2		22	18	1		25.4		28	25	3	

Teachers' Institutes — Special Reports.

TABLE No. XIII. — TEACHERS' INSTITUTES — SPECIAL REPORTS — Continued.

Counties.	No. of teachers required to teach the schools in county.	No. Attending Institute — Male.	No. Attending Institute — Female.	No. Attending Institute — Total.	Number of days institute was in session.	Average daily attendance.	No. Holding Certificates — First grade.	No. Holding Certificates — Second grade.	No. Holding Certificates — Third grade.	Average age of members.	Average experience in months in teaching of those having taught.	Not having taught, but intending to teach.	Number having previously attended institutes.	Number Having Attended — Colleges and Universities.	Number Having Attended — Academies.	Number Having Attended — Normal Schools.	Number Having Attended — High Schools.	Number Having Attended — Common schools Only.	No. of schools in county, or superintendent district.	No. of evening lectures.
Sheboygan	125	38	85	123	9	84	0	4	98	22.3	29.9	28	93	4		9	84	26	126	
Trempealeau	92	27	61	88	10	65	6	10	56	22	23.4	25	6?	26	1	4	44	13	99	4
hon	149	45	77	122	10	84.7	5	13	77	20	12.8	36	85	10	16	1	54	41	153	
Walworth	162	18	76	94	9	66	7	14	63	22.5	34.3	17	68	2	23	25	27	13	124	
Washington	135	16	41	57	9	47	5	3	41	22	21	11	18			16	38	7	106	
Waukesha	130	21	95	116	5	90	4	20	83	21.8	25	20	90	37		6	14	18	118	2
ca	128	22	90	112	10	89	3	8	79	20	15.5	16	91	4	42	7	46	52	108	
Waushara	98	19	65	84	9	74		4	41	19	17	40	60	4	3	2	8	70	101	
o.	113	9	41	50	8	44		6	88	23	22.5	12	29	33	2	12	38		101	1
go		5	39	44	8	84	1	8	81	21	13	12	41	2		8	31	1		
Wood	41	5	43	48	9	37	1	4	26	19.5	21.8	18	27	1		8	33	10	46	2
Wis.	6,018	1,184	3,309	4,443	527½	A.52.14	189	552	2,697	A.21.3	A.22.96	1,06	2,083	382	305	521	1,937	1,178	5,072	48

School Children and Attendance.

Table No. XIV.

SCHOOL CHILDREN AND ATTENDANCE.

Cities.	No. of male children over four and under twenty years of age.	No. female children over four and under twenty years of age.	Whole No. children over four and under twenty years of age in city.	No. of male children over four and under twenty years of age, who have attended public school during the year.	No. of female children over four and under twenty years of age, who have attended public school during year.	Whole No. of children over four and under twenty years of age, who have attended public school during year.	No. under four years, who have attended public school.	No. over twenty years, who have attended public school.	Total No. different pupils who have attended public school during the year.	No. days school has been taught by qualified teachers.	Percentage of enrollment on No. of children in the city.	Percentage of attendance on No. enrolled in public schools.
Appleton	1,880	1,517	2,897	843	786	1,629		9	1,638	178	57.	91.
Beaver Dam	798	892	1,690	362	439	801			801	194	49.	90.
Beloit	819	770	1,589	571	481	1,052		8	1,060	200	66.	92.5
Berlin	555	564	1,119	365	398	763		4	763	200	67.3	69.
Columbus	323	338	661	245	256	501			505	178	85.	94.
Fond du Lac	2,596	2,886	5,482	1,102	1,219	2,321		2	2,321	200	43.	79.
Fort Howard	551	600	1,151	483	463	891		5	891	200	77.4	91.4
Grand Rapids	281	235	466	155	196	351		1	353	180	75.	91.
Green Bay	1,123	1,179	2,801	504	678	1,182			1,182	180	51.	09.
Hudson	855	823	678	807	283	590			595	185	85.	66.
Janesville	1,582	1,804	3,386	777	950	1,727			1,728	187	51.	76.3
Kenosha	992	971	1,963	454	410	964		11	984	190	85.	70.
La Crosse	2,013	2,058	4,070	1,297	1,251	2,548		4	2,559	199	63.	97.
Madison	1,643	1,874	3,517	910	1,025	1,935			1,939	185	55.	90.
Menasha	556	597	1,153	174	211	385			385	198	83.4	72.
Milwaukee	18,443	19,299	37,742	8,649	8,104	16,753			16,753	200	44.	68.

School Children and Attendance

TABLE No. XIV.— SCHOOL CHILDREN AND ATTENDANCE — Continued.

CITIES.	No. of male children over four and under twenty years of age.	No. female children over four and under twenty years of age.	Whole No. children over four and under twenty years of age in city.	No. of male children over four and under twenty years of age, who have attended public school during the year.	No. of female children over four and under twenty years of age, who have attended public school during year.	Whole No. of children over four and under twenty years of age, who have attended public school during year.	No. under four years, who have attended public school.	No. over twenty years, who attended public school.	Total No. different pupils who have attended public school during the year.	No. days school has been taught by qualified teachers.	Percentage of enrollment on No. of children in the city.	Percentage of attendance on No. enrolled in public schools.
Mal Point	511	582	1,093	302	320	622	...	...	622	180	57.7	70.
Neenah	654	678	1,332	368	373	741	...	...	741	200	55.7	90.
Oconto	670	569	1,239	347	331	678	...	1	679	200	54.7	53.5
Oshkosh	2,857	3,017	5,874	1,094	1,123	2,217	...	...	2,217	200	41.	91.
Portage	780	781	1,51	541	452	993	...	10	1,004	198	64.	61.
Prairie du Chien	495	530	1,025	263	222	485	1	1	486	200	48.3	62.5
Racine	2,840	3,018	5,858	1,086	1,216	2,302	...	...	2,302	200	40.	69.
Sheboygan	1,553	1,520	8,073	562	552	1,114	...	...	1,114	200	43.	90.
Stevens Point	677	731	1,408	419	451	870	...	7	877	179	62.	86.
Watertown	1,744	1,739	3,483	576	560	1,136	...	2	1,138	200	31.	89.
	610	520	1,130	405	345	750	...	...	750	180	66.3	87.
Bls	47,349	49,592	96,941	28,104	28,097	46,201	1	65	46,267	5,181	55.5	79.8

Teachers, Salaries, Graded and Night Schools.

Table No. XV.
TEACHERS, SALARIES, GRADED AND NIGHT SCHOOLS.

Cities	No. male teachers required	No. female teachers required	No. teachers required to teach the schools	No. male teachers employed during year	No. female teachers employed during year	Whole No. teachers employed during year	Highest salary paid to male teachers (per annum)	Average salary paid to male teachers (per annum)	Highest salary paid to female teachers (per annum)	Average salary paid to female teachers (per annum)	Average age of male teachers employed	Average age of female teachers employed	No. of schools in city with four or more departm'ts	No. schools with three departments	No. schools with two departments	No. mixed or ungraded schools	No. night schools	No. teachers employed in the same	No. pupils attending same
Appleton	5	23	28	5	23	28	$1,400 00	$630 00	$600 00	$400 00	32	29	4	3	3				
Beaver Dam	1	12	13	1	12	18	800 00	800 00	500 00	280 00	32	27	2	2	4				
Beloit	1	18	19	1	18	19	1,500 00	1,500 00	600 00	394 44	44	27	2	2	3				
Berlin	2	12	14	2	12	14	1,200 00	750 00	40 00	300 00	32	27	1	1	1				
Columbus	2	6	8	2	7	9	1,200 00	850 00	60 00	330 00	28	26	6		4	2			
Fond du Lac	8	38	46	8	38	46	1,300 00	550 00	50 00	80 00	36	25	1			6			
Fort Howard	3	10	13	3	10	13	900 00	600 00	80 00	83 00	27	23	1						
Grand Rapids	1	4	5	1	4	5		900 00	40 00	87 00	25	28	2						
Green Bay	2	17	19	2	18	20	900 00	850 00	61 00	82 00	49	26	1	6	1	1	1		
Hudson	1	7	8	1	7	8	800 00	800 00	40 00	87 00	28	31	6						
Janesville	1	35	36	1	44	45	1,500 00	1,500 00	40 00	34 00	46	24	3	1	1	3			
Kenosha	2	13	15	2	14	16	1,400 00	900 00	50 00	81 00	27	30	5	1	2	2	1	2	75
La Crosse	7	33	40	7	34	41	1,650 00	1,135 75	50 00	41 00	37	26	5						
Madison	5	29	34	5	29	34	900 00	900 00	40 00				1	1	5				
Menasha	1	8	9	1	8	9	2,200 00	528 90	1,200 00	82 50	32	30	20		5				
Milwaukee	56	244	300	56	207	263	2,200 00		1,200 00			30							

Teachers, Salaries, Graded and Night Schools.

TABLE No. XV.—TEACHERS, SALARIES, GRADED AND NIGHT SCHOOLS—Continued.

CITIES.	No. male teachers required.	No. female teachers required.	No. teachers required to teach the schools.	No. male teachers employed during year.	No. female teachers employed during year.	Whole No. teachers employed during year.	Highest salary paid to male teachers (per annum).	Average salary paid to male teachers (per annum).	Highest salary paid to female teachers (per annum).	Average salary paid to female teachers (per annum).	Average age of male teachers employed.	Average age of female teachers employed.	No. schools in city with four or more departmts.	No. schools with three departments.	No. schools with two departments.	No. mixed or ungraded schools.	No. night schools.	No. teachers employed in the same.	No. pupils attending same.
Mineral Point..	3	8	11	3	8	11	$1,600 00	$1,010 00	$420 00	$390 00	40	32	1	1	2	1			
Neenah	1	12	13	1	13	14	1,000 00	1,000 00	500 00	329 16	39	30	1		2	1			
Oconto.........	4	6	10	4	6	10	700 00	525 00	300 00	300 00	24	22	1		2				
Oshkosh...... "	7	46	53	7	46	53	1,750 00	791 66	450 00	332 60	38		6	1		2			
Portage .... "	2	14	16	2	14	16	1,200 00	900 00	450 00	314 28	28	28	3		1				
Prairie du Kien	1	7	8	1	7	8	750 00	750 00	350 00	343 00	35	21	1	7	1				
Racine.........	7	38	45	7	39	45	1,900 00	1,007 14	550 00	390 00	33	24	7			2			40
Sheboygan.....	3	16	19	3	16	19	500 00	450 00	400 00	347 00	28	22	2			1			
Stevens Point..	3	9	11	4	10	14	990 00	594 00	400 00	286 65	39	27		2	2	3	2	2	
Watertown	4	18	22	4	18	22	1,200 00	725 00	500 00	338 33	39	28	2	2	2		1	2	84
Wausau	2	11	13	3	11	14	1,000 00	620 00	360 00	237 27	24	22	2	1	1	1			
Totals......	134	694	828	187	679	809	$2,200 00	av$829 32	$1,200 00	av$386 85	av33	av26¾	88	33	36	26	4	6	199

School-Houses, Sites, and Valuation.

Table No. XVI.

SCHOOL-HOUSES, SITES, AND VALUATION.

CITIES.	No. public school-houses in the city.	No. school-houses yet required.	No. school-houses built during the year.	Whole No. school children resident in city.	Whole No. pupils school-houses will accommodate.	No. of school-house sites owned by city.	No. sites containing only one lot.	No. sites containing more than one lot.	No. of sites suitably enclosed.	No. school-houses built of stone or brick.	Highest valuation of school-house and site.	Cash value of all public school-houses in the city.	Cash value of sites.	No. of school-houses properly ventilated.	No. of school-houses with separate outhouses for the sexes.	No. of school-houses in good condition.
Appleton	8	2	1	2,897	1,800	7		7	7	4	$12,000 00	$45,000 00	$15,000 00	1	7	7
Beaver Dam	4			1,690	850	5		5	4	4	12,000 00	30,000 00	5,000 00	3	4	4
Beloit	3	1		1,589	1,000	3		3		3	35,000 00	65,000 00	8,000 00	2	3	3
Berlin	3		1	1,119	900	2		2	2	3	35,000 00	47,000 00	7,000 00	3	3	3
Columbus	2			661	420				1	1	6,000 00	5,000 00	3,000 00	2	2	2
Fond du Lac	19			5,482	2,800	17	1	15	17	2	50,000 00	98,700 00	22,000 00	4	19	19
Fort Howard	1			1,151	890	5	2		1	1	14,000 00	20,000 00	3,000 00		2	3
Grand Rapids	1	1		466	600	1		1	1	1	30,000 00	25,000 00	2,000 00		1	1
Green Bay	8	6		2,301	1,020	5		5	5	3	30,000 00	55,000 00	9,000 00		6	6
Hudson	3			678	576	3		3	2	3	7,000 00	12,000 00	2,000 00	3	3	3
Janesville	6			3,386	1,801	6		6	6	5	33,000 00	85,000 00	11,000 00	3	6	6
Kenosha	4	1		1,963	750	6		6	6	5	10,000 00	23,000 00	3,600 00	4	4	4
La Crosse	9			4,070	2,100	9	3	6	3	5	24,300 00	68,000 00	17,125 00	2	4	4
Madison	9	9		8,517	1,750	8	2	8		8	27,000 00	90,000 00	10,000 00	9	9	9

School-Houses, Sites, and Valuation.

TABLE NO. XVI.—SCHOOL-HOUSES, SITES, AND VALUATION.—Continued.

CITIES.	No. public school-houses in the city.	No. school-houses yet required.	No. school-houses built during the year.	Whole No. school children resident in city.	Whole No. pupils school-houses will accommodate.	No. of school-house sites owned by city.	No. sites containing only one lot.	No. sites containing more than one lot.	No. of sites suitably enclosed.	No. of school-houses built of stone or brick.	Highest valuation of school-house and site.	Cash value of all public school-houses in the city.	Cash value of sites.	No. of school-houses properly ventilated.	No. of school-houses with separate outhouses for the sexes.	No. of school-houses with outhouses in good condition.
M omha	5	...	...	1,153	410	4	...	5	5	4	$6,000 00	$7,500 00	$2,500 00	5	5	5
M lwaukee	25	...	...	37,742	13,648	24	...	24	24	21	52,000 00	440,500 00	202,300 00	...	25	25
Mineral Point	2	...	1	1,093	900	2	...	2	2	2	10,000 00	15,000 00	4,000 00	2	2	2
Neenah	5	...	1	1,332	1,200	5	...	5	4	3	30,000 00	36,000 00	5,000 00	1	5	5
Oconto	5	...	1	1,289	750	5	...	5	5	1	5,500 00	6,900 00	1,600 00	1	5	5
Oshkosh	10	1	...	5,874	8,500	12	...	12	11	5	50,000 00	100,000 00	28,000 00	10	10	10
Portage	4	...	...	1,025	1,050	4	...	4	4	3	10,000 00	25,000 00	6,000 00	4	3	4
Prairie du Chien	5	...	...	...	...	5	2	3	5	3	15,000 00	20,000 00	1,500 00	5	5	4
I ne	8	...	1	5,858	2,500	3	...	7	7	7	15,000 00	50,000 00	15,000 00	8	8	8
Sheboygan	6	2	...	3,078	1,400	4	2	1	4	3	7,000 00	12,000 00	8,000 00	3	6	4
Stevens Point	4	3	...	1,405	900	5	...	5	2	3	5,700 00	18,000 00	2,500 00	5	4	4
Watertown	5	...	...	3,488	1,200	3	2	5	5	3	10,000 00	32,000 00	12,000 00	5	5	5
W usau	3	...	1	1,180	1,000	...	...	3	...	2	20,000 00	25,000 00	2,500 00	2	3	8
Totals	170	18		96,941	45,405	159	14	145	133	107	$52,000 00	$1,441,600 00	$403,625 00	85	154	158

Table No. XVII.

SCHOOL ROOMS, APPARATUS, LIBRARIES, KINDERGARTENS, ETC.

School Rooms, Apparatus, Libraries, Kindergartens, Etc.

Cities	Number of members of Board of Education	KINDERGARTENS — No. of pupils that have attended during year	KINDERGARTENS — Number of teachers employed	KINDERGARTENS — Number of Kindergartens in the city	LIBRARIES — Cash value of all the libraries	LIBRARIES — Whole number volumes in all the libraries	LIBRARIES — Total amount expended for library books during the year	LIBRARIES — Total number volumes added during the year	SCHOOL ROOMS AND APPARATUS — Cash value of all apparatus, including maps and globes	SCHOOL ROOMS AND APPARATUS — Whole No. adequately supplied with apparatus	SCHOOL ROOMS AND APPARATUS — Whole number supplied with other apparatus	SCHOOL ROOMS AND APPARATUS — Whole number supplied with a globe	SCHOOL ROOMS AND APPARATUS — Whole number supplied with outline maps	SCHOOL ROOMS AND APPARATUS — Whole number supplied with illustrative charts	SCHOOL ROOMS AND APPARATUS — Number sufficiently supplied with blackboards	SCHOOL ROOMS AND APPARATUS — Whole number of school rooms occupied
Appleton	10				$800 00	400	$150 00	75	$800 00	1	3	7	10	20	27	28
Beaver Dam	9				600 00				250 00		18	12	12	18	13	13
Beloit	6				500 00	400	15 00	148	300 00	1	20	20	20	20	20	20
Berlin	6				150 00	579	82 00	33	600 00		14	3	14	14	14	14
Columbus	3				400 00	50			350 00	20	1	4	6	2	8	8
Fond du Lac	8					174	100 00	46	600 00	1	4	5	80		46	46
Fort Howard	7				20 00				75 00	4		2	1	1	13	18
Grand Rapids	7				50 00	30		30	100 00		8	5	5	1	5	5
Green Bay	7				50 00	100	15 00		680 00		1	8	15	10	16	16
Hudson	7				50 00	100		1	25 00		1	1	6	2	8	8
Janesville	6				350 00	102			600 00	30	38	33	38	6	38	38
Kenosha	9	40	2	1	200 00	300	60 00	10	500 00	27	27	4	4	38	14	14
La Crosse	6	125	2	2		70			1,100 00	1	1	8	20		38	33
Madison	8	40	1	1	50 00				1,500 00			27	27	20	27	27
Menasha	5					64			550 00			2	4	27	8	8
Milwaukee	26	60	7	1					5,890 00	25	25	25	25	8	25	217

School Rooms, Apparatus, Libraries, Kindergartens, Etc.

TABLE No. XVII.—SCHOOL ROOMS, APPARATUS, LIBRARIES, KINDERGARTENS, ETC — Continued.

CITIES.	Whole number of school rooms occupied.	Number sufficiently supplied with blackboards.	Whole number supplied with illustrative charts.	Whole number supplied with outline maps.	Whole number supplied with a globe.	Whole number supplied with other apparatus.	Whole No. adequately supplied with apparatus.	Cash value of all apparatus, including maps and globes.	Total number volumes added during the year.	Total amount expended for library books during the year.	Whole number volumes in all libraries.	Cash value of all the libraries.	Number of Kindergartens in the city.	Number of teachers employed.	No. of pupils that have attended during year.	Number of members of Board of Education.
Mineral Point	9	9	9	9	5	2	1	$250 00			200	$150 00				8
Neenah	18	18	8	8	4	4	4	875 00								5
Oconto	9	9	5	5	6			200 00			180	100 00				4
Oshkosh	59	50	36	36	10	15	59	2,600 00								7
Portage	16	16	10	10	5	10		400 00			1,580	500 00				6
Prairie du Chien	8	8	6	8	4	4	8	200 00			270	225 00				5
Racine	45	45	1	5	6	1		700 00	16	$25 00	183	200 00	1	2	40	6
Sheboygan	19	19	10	6	5	2		400 00	4	4 00	710	1,100 00				8
Stevens Point	11	11		2	1	1		80 00			40	125 00	1	2	40	8
Watertown	21	21	21	21	17	1	21	1,500 00								7
Wausau	12	12	8	1	1	1	1	50 00								6
Totals	725	528	296	339	228	187	204	$20,175 00	863	$401 00	5,482	$5,020 00	7	16	345	190

Children Classified, Text-Books, and Course of Study.

Table No. XVIII.
CHILDREN CLASSIFIED, TEXT-BOOKS, AND COURSE OF STUDY.

CITIES.	No. of children between four and seven in the city.	No. of such children in attendance at public schools.	No. of children between seven and fifteen in the city.	No. of such children in attendance at public schools.	No. of children between fifteen and twenty in the city.	No. of such children in attendance at public schools.	Has a list of text-books been adopted?	Are these the only books used as regular text-books?	Are text-books purchased by the city?	Are they sold or loaned to pupils?	Has a course of study been adopted?	Into how many grades divided?	Through how many years extending?	Does any course include ancient languages?	Does it propose to fit pupils for college?	What per cent. finish the course of study?
Appleton	691	303	1,374	1,183	882	152	Yes.	Yes.	No.	Sold.	Yes.	10	10	Yes.	Yes.	66
Beaver Dam	800	375	480	305	410	121	"	No.	"		"	12	12	"	"	6
Beloit	254	84	738	645	572	831	"	Yes.	Yes.	Loaned	"	14	14	"	"	
Berlin	243	132	598	526	279	95	"	"	No.		"	13	13	"	"	10
Columbus	107	165	395	327	69	13	"	"			"	12	12	"	"	10
Fond du Lac	1,371	400	2,219	1,596	1,892	816	"	"			"	12	12	No.	"	10
Fort Howard	107	212	491	440	377	239	"	"			"	11	11	Yes.	"	5
Grand Rapids	691	71	252	234	107	48	"	No.	Yes.	Sold.	"	11	11	No.	No.	10
Green Bay	185	454	1,071	644	600	84	"	"	No.		"	13	13	"	"	1
Hudson	546	170	320	300	173	125	"	"			"	12	12	Yes.	"	
Janesville	540	247	1,433	1,257	1,407	224	"	"			"	12	12	"	"	
Kenosha	161	161	938	703	485		"	"			"	13	13	"	Yes.	1
La Crosse	983	514	3,175	1,832	913	218	"	Yes.		Sold.	"	11	11	"	Yes.	
Madison	687	600	1,587	1,400	1,293		"	No.			"	13	12	Yes.	No.	33
Menasha	241	122	547	256	365	7	"	Yes.			"	12	12	No.	No.	10

Children Classified, Text-Books, and Course of Study.

TABLE No. XVIII.—CHILDREN CLASSIFIED, TEXT-BOOKS, AND COURSE OF STUDY—Continued.

CITIES.	CHILDREN CLASSIFIED.						TEXT-BOOKS.				COURSE OF STUDY.					
	No. of children between four and seven in the city.	No. of such children in attendance at public schools.	No. of children between seven and fifteen in the city.	No. of such children in attendance at public schools.	No. of children between fifteen and twenty in the city.	No. of such children in attendance at public schools.	Has a list of text-books been adopted?	Are these the only books used as regular text-books?	Are text-books purchased by the city?	Are they sold or loaned to pupils?	Has a course of study been adopted?	Into how many grades divided?	Through how many years extending?	Does any course include ancient languages?	Does it propose to fit pupils for college?	What per cent. finish the course of study?
Milwaukee	9,341	5,489	19,350	10,921	9,051	393	Yes.	Yes.	Yes.		Yes.	4	4	Yes.	Yes.	
Mineral Point	180	86	568	543	350	44	"	No.	No.		"	9	9	No.	No.	10
Neh	184	108	946	534	212	104	"	Yes.	Yes.	Sold.	"	11	11	"	"	
Oconto	464	245	565	420	210	14	"	"	No.		"	6	8	Yes.	Yes.	10
Oshkosh	1,352	576	3,250	1,878	2,272	269	"	No.			"	7	12	"	No.	
Portage	331	167	746	608	494	134	"	Yes.	Yes.	Loaned.	"	6	11	No.	Yes.	
Prairie du Chien	233	161	494	295	300	80	"	"	No		"	3	10	Yes.	"	
Racine	1,488	288	2,771	1,764	1,604	256	"	"			"	12	12	"	"	20
Sheboygan	1,100	167	1,505	947	468		"	"	"		"	10	10	"	"	25
Stevens Point	348	285	714	513	346	80	"	"	"		"	12	12	"	"	
Watertown	873	272	1,443	795	1,168	171	"	"	Yes.	Loaned.	"	10	10	"	"	5
Wausau	396	237	563	396	171	187	"	"	No.		"	12	12	No.	"	
Totals	24,001	11,969	46,522	20,679	26,499	8,750						av. 10	av. 11.1			14.5

Table No. XIX.

PRIVATE SCHOOLS NOT INCORPORATED.

Private Schools not Incorporated.

Cities.	No. of such schools in the city.	No. of male teachers engaged in such schools.	No. of female teachers engaged in such schools.	Average number of days such schools have been taught.	No. of pupils in them that have not attended public school.	Average number in daily attendance.	No. bet. four and seven years in attendance.	No. bet. seven and fifteen years in attendance.	No. bet. fifteen and twenty years in attendance.	From tuition.	From donations.	From all other sources.	Total receipts.	For teachers' wages.	For building and repairs.	For all other purposes.	Total expenditures.
Appleton	4	2	6	200	816	268	42	287		$718	$100		$818	$761	$20,185	$90	$21,686
Beaver Dam	3	1	2	200	150	125											
Beloit	2		3	200	40	47											
Berlin	3	3		100	65	40											
Columbus	2	1	1	160	45	50											
Fond du Lac	11	6	10		450												
Fort Howard																	
Grand Rapids	5	1		200	450												
Green Bay																	
Hudson	4		10														
Janesville	5	2	5	180	250	225	195	181		1,900		1,000	2,900	2,000	50	500	2,550
Kenosha	4	3	7	175	375	350	90	200									
La Crosse	8	6	10		600	100	195										
Madison	6		10	180	650												
Menasha	2		6	200	350	300											

Private Schools not Incorporated.

TABLE No. XIX — PRIVATE SCHOOLS NOT INCORPORATED — Continued.

CITIES.	No. of such schools in the city.	No. of male teachers engaged in such schools.	No. of female teachers engaged in such schools.	Average number of days such schools have been taught.	No. of pupils in them that have not attended public school.	Average number in daily attendance.	No. bet. four and seven years in attendance.	No. bet. seven and fifteen years in attendance.	No. bet. fifteen and twenty years in attendance.	From tuition.	From donation.	From all other sources.	Total receipts.	For teachers' wages.	For building and repairs.	For all other purposes.	Total expenditures.
Milwaukee	48	78	133	226	7,901	7,410	1,616	6,157	868	$500	$500		$1,000	$1,000			$1,000
Mineral Point	3		6	180	100	80	80	80									
Neenah	4	1	4	100	125	100											
Oconto	1		5	200	320	140											
Oshkosh	6				1,000	164	7	118									
Portage	1		2	195	147	112	40	215									
Prairie du Chien	2		4	215	255	180				334			334				
Racine	9		26	200	1,034	94	165										
Sheboygan	4	9	1	161	665	140	165	501		615		$1,915	2,530	2,700		$21	2,721
Stevens Point	3	5	5	180	220	197	90	174		1,040			1,040	900		140	1,040
Watertown	5	6	9	213	770	100											
Wausau	2	1	1	140													
Totals	138	127	266	av.181	16,279	10,222	2,352	7,863	868	$5,107	$600	$2,915	$8,622	$7,361	$20,235	$751	$28,347

Financial Statistics — Receipts.

Table No. XX.
FINANCIAL STATISTICS — RECEIPTS.

CITIES.	Money on hand Aug. 31, 1879.	From taxes levied for building, repairing.	From taxes levied for teachers' wages.	From taxes levied for apparat's library.	From taxes levied at annual meeting.	From taxes levied by county pervis's	From income State school fund.	From all other sources.	Total am't received during the year.
Appleton	$5,776 55	$1,043 00	$11,725 00	$350 00	$991 00	$902 53	$952 48	$1,055 15	$22,885 71
Beaver Dam	1,617 85	....	4,000 00	....	2,000 00	640 30	640 30	796 93	9,694 88
Beloit	6,746 32	....	8,585 00	....	5,138 57	1,169 29	342 23	1,020 73	23,062 14
Berlin	2,577 14	....	....	....	5,500 00	440 42	781 73	208 69	9,567 98
Ills.	363 65	500 00	....	....	8,000 00	267 52	278 80	723 13	5,133 10
Fond du Lac	186 50	....	....	....	20,503 12	....	2,170 94	502 08	23,362 64
Fort Howard	1,635 97	....	....	....	4,930 00	465 20	445 36	....	7,496 53
Grand Rapids	406 12	....	....	....	2,810 00	....	....	583 87	3,499 99
Green Bay	4,491 57	360 00	....	....	8,000 00	785 84	858 60	334 18	14,830 19
Hudson	2,022 08	....	....	....	4,004 38	229 90	250 40	....	6,506 76
Ele.	1,302 90	....	....	....	15,000 00	2,318 75	1,423 20	....	20,959 78
Kenosha	107 01	....	....	....	8,000 00	1,500 00	784 80	91998	10,649 78
La Crosse	11,034 38	....	....	....	25,950 00	1,507 84	1,671 60	257 97	40,657 05
Mon.	6,476 04	260 00	....	....	18,842 99	1,604 40	328 93	493 23	27,704 77
Min.	2,861 98	....	....	....	3,590 01	600 00	456 00	452 41	8,051 53
Milwaukee	11,527 90	....	....	....	124,324 03	51,774 14	14,806 40	283 55	190,904 57
Mineral Point	4,762 56	....	....	....	5,000 00	412 30	453 60	421 81	10,050 27
Jah	10,894 87	....	....	....	6,120 95	700 00	....	12,463 99	29,679 81
Oconto	......	....	....	....	6,000 00	....	476 90	....	6,476 90
Oshkosh	15,047 07	....	....	....	12,414 19	12,585 81	2,607 33	398 00	48,052 40
Portage	595 56	....	....	....	5,500 00	634 60	699 60	1,022 22	8,451 98
Prairie du Chien	3,132 00	8,000 00	....	....	2,200 00	650 00	398 40	323 79	6,703 19
Racine	680 89	....	....	....	22,000 00	2,025 00	2,182 40	917 23	35,805 52
Sheboygan	7,542 09	....	....	....	4,000 00	1,017 22	1,917 22	1,071 43	14,647 96
Pans Point	478 98	....	....	....	4,546 96	527 44	850 29	6 00	6,928 74
Witown	4,533 46	....	....	....	7,754 27	1,395 36	1,424 80	1,203 94	16,310 73
Hau	561 17	1,281 84	....	....	3,415 51	418 81	398 40	....	6,073 73
Ills	$106,884 11	$11,444 84	$24,310 00	$350 00	$331,535 97	$84,657 67	$37,600 71	$25,213 16	$609,087 63

Financial Statistics — Disbursements.

Table No. XXI.

FINANCIAL STATISTICS — DISBURSEMENTS.

CITIES.	For building and repairing.	For apparatus and libraries.	For services of male teachers.	For services of female teachers.	For old indebtedness.	For furniture, reg. ist's, & rec.	For all other purposes.	Tot. am't p'd out during the year.	Money on hand Aug. 31, 1880.
Appleton	$731 46	$384 13	$4,226 90	$7,700 00	$1,055 41	$292 27	$2,103 83	$16,592 00	$6,293 71
Beaver Dam	249 94		800 00	3,263 50	2,267 55	113 76	1,349 95	8,043 70	1,651 18
Beloit	353 16	41 00	1,500 00	7,085 00	5,831 99	86 25	2,549 14	15,946 58	7,055 56
Berlin			1,500 00	3,600 00			1,717 87	6,817 96	2,750 02
Columbus	576 84	100 00	1,200 00	2,298 50			346 81	4,522 15	610 00
Fond du Lac	1,300 00	175 00	4,155 00	12,670 00		595 82	3,603 63	22,499 45	863 19
Fort Howard	100 14		1,800 00	2,900 00			729 25	5,529 34	1,966 19
Grand Rapids	22 35	38 00		1,350 00		23 70	466 00	2,800 05	699 94
Green Bay	510 26	61 20	1,700 00	6,209 99			2,022 62	10,504 07	4,326 12
Hudson			800 00	2,410 00		120 00	1,323 98	4,653 98	1,852 78
Janesville	1,350 00		1,500 00	11,043 00		125 00	4,025 80	18,043 80	2,914 98
Kenosha	139 58		1,800 00	4,957 76		164 33	2,538 47	9,600 14	1,049 64
La Crosse			7,950 00	13,625 60			5,620 07	26,195 67	14,461 38
Madison	1,345 61	60 00	2,835 00	12,508 50			3,880 40	20,689 51	7,015 26
Manitowoc	88 72		900 00	2,500 00		193 69	484 79	4,167 20	3,884 33
Milwaukee		602 04	53,900 00	116,431 73			30,812 41	201,746 18	100,686 29
Mineral Point	1,363 02		1,830 00	1,960 00	1,420 00	435 15	1,028 80	6,616 97	3,493 30
Neenah	17,616 66	215 00	1,000 00	4,125 00		321 00	1,178 58	25,876 24	3,808 57
Oconto	3,800 00		2,100 00	1,800 00		450 00		8,150 00	
Oshkosh	10,375 67		4,955 00	15,300 00	285 75	23 50	5,131 28	35,784 45	7,267 95
Portage			1,800 00	4,280 00			2,225 11	8,580 86	
Prairie du Chien			750 00	2,391 25	8 26	2,538 38	893 84	4,035 09	2,668 10
Racine	5,931 68	50	7,050 00	14,200 00			2,846 08	32,574 85	3,230 67
Sheboygan	291 20	25 00	2,100 00	5,580 00			1,196 61	9,192 81	5,455 15
Stevens Point	255 00		1,564 00	2,397 00			568 77	4,784 77	2,143 97
Watertown	344 83	57 65	2,900 00	6,152 85		567 38	1,761 95	11,784 66	4,526 07
Wausau	1,281 84		1,220 00	2,440 00		97 89	1,034 00	6,073 73	
Totals	$48,027 96	$1,759 52	$114,785 90	$271,238 68	$10,868 96	$6,147 12	$81,439 99	$531,806 21	$190,609 35

Teachers' Certificates, Normal School Teachers, and Experience.

Table No. XXII.
TEACHERS' CERTIFICATES, NORMAL SCHOOL TEACHERS, AND AVERAGE EXPERIENCE.

Cities.	No. of State certificates.	Certificates Granted — Male Teachers 1st grade	2d grade	3d grade	Female Teachers 1st grade	2d grade	3d grade	Total.	Certificates Refused — Male Teachers 1st grade	2d grade	3d grade	Female Teachers 1st grade	2d grade	3d grade	Totals.	No. of graduates of Normal Schools.	No. attended Normal Schools.	Avg. time in yrs. male teachers remain.	Avg. time in yrs. female teachers remain.	Avg. experience in years of male teachers.	Avg. experience in years of female teachers.
Appleton	8	4		2			21	27									3	4	6	8	8
Beaver Dam	1	1			1	3	8	13								2		5	6	10	4
Beloit	2		2	5		8	4	17			5		8	3	5	1	2	3	4	15	5
Berlin	2		4	6		1	6	15						26	26	1	3	3	4	10	4
Columbus	1			3			38	45								1	4	4	6	10	7
Fond du Lac		1		1	1		10	18								1		4	5	6	
Fort Howard	1					2	4	4								1	2	3	4	4	8
Grand Rapids	1	1			1		14	18							2	1	2	3	3	8	6
Green Bay							4	4									2	3	7	4	7
Hudson			1	4			4	18								2	1	2	4	4	
Janesville	8		2	3		12	33	40								3	3	5	5	14	6
Kenosha	8	1				1	31	34								6	12	2	5	7	6
La Crosse			4	3		5	12	89							2	2	2	5	5	12	5
Madison	11		2		6	1	7	11								96	2	3	2	10	
Menasha		9	4				11	13								1		4	4	9	8
Milwaukee		1	2	3											129		8	5	5		6
Mineral Point														8	8			3	4		7
Neenah	1		1															7	7	10	

Teachers' Certificates, Normal School Teachers, and Experience.

TABLE No. XXII.—TEACHERS' CERTIFICATES, NORMAL SCHOOL TEACHERS, AND AVERAGE EXPERIENCE.

Cities	No. of State certificates	Certificates Granted — Male Teachers 1st grade	Male 2d grade	Male 3d grade	Female Teachers 1st grade	Female 2d grade	Female 3d grade	Total	Certificates Refused — Male 1st grade	Male 2d grade	Male 3d grade	Female 1st grade	Female 2d grade	Female 3d grade	Totals	No. of graduates of Normal schools	No. attended Normal Schools	Avg. time in yrs. male teachers remain	Avg. time in yrs. female teachers remain	Avg. experience in years of male teachers	Avg. experience in years of female teachers
Oconto			1	1		4	6	12						2	2		1	8	8	4	8
Oshkosh		2						60													
Portage			1			2	18	17								1	1	5	6	5	6
Pr du Chien						6		6								4		4	2	9	
Racine						18		14						14	14	8		8	4	11	6
Sheboygan																		9	8		
Stevens Point		2	1		7	9	9	14			1				1		2	2	8	6	7
Watertown	3	1			1	9	5	22						4	4			10	2	7	6
Wausau		2		1		1	10	15							5	1	1	4			
Totals	31	25	20	29	17	68	235	481			6		3	54	182	128	50	4	av. 8.5		55

Text-Books.

Table No. XXIII.
TEXT-BOOKS.

Cities.	Spelling.	Reading.	Mental Arithmetic.	Written Arithmetic.	Grammar.	Geography.
Appleton		Harvey		Wite	Harvey	Eclectic.
Beer Dam	Swinton & Pat'n	Harvey	White	White & Robin'n	Harv. & Swint.	Eclectic.
Beloit	Am. Ed. Series.	Am. Ed. Series.	Robinson	Robinson	Wn., Gn, Cl'k	Eclectic.
Berlin	Swinton	Union	Robinson	Robinson	Fowler	Harper.
Whs	Sanders	Educational	Robinson	Robi son	Swinton	Harper.
Fond du Lac		Independent	White	White	Harvey	Monteith.
Fort Howard	Sanders's Union.	Sa's Union	Robinson	Robinson	Kerl	Guyot.
Grand Rapids	Swinton	Appleton	Davies	Davies	Harvey	Swinton.
Green Bay	. & Henkle	Union Series		Robi son	Kerl	Swinton.
Hudson	Towndsends	A bn	Davies	Davies	Swinton & Greene	Harper.
Janesville	Union	Union	White	Robinson	Swint. & Greene	Harper.
Kenosha	Harvey	Harvey		White	Harvey	Swinton.
La Crosse	Harvey	H rvey	Robinson	White	Harvey	Wn.
Madison		Independent	Robinson	Robinson	Swinton	Ecl etc.
Oha	Harvey	Harvey		Robinson	Swinton	Ecl etc.
Milwaukee	Swinton	Harvey	White	Ray	Geen	
Mineral Point	Swi. & McGuffey	Appleton	Robinson	Wite	Harvey & S. L. L.	Eclectic.
ah	Swinton	Willson	Robinson	Robinson	Swinton	Eclectic.
Oconto	Willson	Sanders		Robinson	Swinton	Cornell.
Oshkosh	Swinton	Harvey	Robi son	Olney	Swinton	Swinton.
Portage	Henkle	Appleton	Robinson	Wite	Harvey	Harper.
Prairie du Chien	National	Appleton	Robinson	Robinson	Kerl & Swinton	Eclectic.
Racine	Swin's W'rd B'k	I dnt	Robi son	Robi son	Green & Swinton	Eclectic.
Sheboygan	Sanders's h.	Harvey & Rand'l	Rob'son & Stod.		bn	Swinton.
Stevens Point		Ap. & Douai G.		Fish	Harvey	Swint. & Harper.
Watertown	Swint. & DeWolf	Harvey	Olney	Ray & Mod, K&B	Swint. & Whtn'y	Swint. & Harper.
Wausau	Harvey			Key	Harvey	Harper.
						Harp., Corn., Guy.
						Eclectic.

Table No. XXIII.
TEXT-BOOKS—Continued.

Text-Books.

CITIES.	United States History.	Physiology.	Algebra.	Geometry.	Latin Grammar and Reader.	Natural Philosophy.
...	Barnes	Cutter	...	Bon	...	N ...
Beaver ...	elle	Cutter	Olney	loey	El etc	N ...
...	...	Cutter	Robins n	Hn	Harkness	...
Berlin	Swinton	dler	Robinson	...	Allen	Steele.
...	Barnes	Hut hinson	lbi nen	Hn	Al'n & Gre'nou.	N ...
... du Lac	...	Hut ...	loey	...	Al'n & Gre'nou.	...
Fort	Swinton	...	...	...	...	Steele.
Grand Rapids	Anderson	...	Davies	Davies	... & Jones	...
Green ...	Barnes	Steele	lbi bon	Robinson	An & Gre'nou	...
...	Q ...	...	Davies	this	...	...
Janesville	Barnes	Ger ...	Mon	Mon	A ...	Steele.
...	Barnes & Ven	... Hn	Mer	Mer	M, G'n, Barth	Norton.
La ...	Barnes	...	...	this	Harkness	...
Madison	Barnes	Hn	Mon	this	Allen	Sele.
...	Barnes	Hn	Fish & Robinson	...	...	...
...	Barnes	Ger ...	this	this	Al'n & Gre'nou.	Hir & Stew't
...	Barnes	loey	Hn	Hn	...	...
Mil Pint	... Han	Hn	...	Hn	...	Wills.
...	...	Sele Hk	Mon	Robi son	...	Sele.
...	Scott	...	Olney	loey	Bar'ol & Bi'ham	N ...
...	Lossing	Brown	Mon	Robinson	Harkness	N r tn.
Portage	...	Brown	Hn	...	...	Avery.
... du Chien	...	Mer	this	eDk	Harkness	...
...	...	Winson	sels	...	...	Avery.
Sheboygan	Swinton	...	... Cmp	this	Al'n & Gre'nou.	Avery.
Stevens Point	Barnes ... Qk'bos	telle ...	...	... & Loomis	Smith	Applet'n's Sci.
Watertown	Swin. ...	... n Sci. Pr.	Hn	...	Harkness	Norton.
...	... Hn	Ger	loey	loey	...	

Statistics of Free High Schools.

Table No. XXIV.

STATISTICS OF FREE HIGH SCHOOLS.

1	2	3	4	5	6	7	8	9	10	11	12	13	14
LOCATION.	NAMES OF PRINCIPAL.	Year when the school was established as a free high school.	Number of male teachers.	Number of female teachers.	Number of male pupils not over twenty years of age.	Number of female pupils not over twenty years of age.	Whole number not over twenty years.	Number registered over twenty years of age.	Whole number of pupils registered.	Average daily att'n'dance.	Number of days of high school.	Number of pupils in common branches only.	Number of pupils in algebra or geometry.
Md	Lois Ostenson	1878	1		16	9	25		25	20	80	20	5
Appleton	R. H. Schmidt	1876	2	1	50	74	124	6	130	118	178	40	27
Avoca	R. J. Porter	1876	1	2	14	25	39		39	29	175	4	11
Baraboo	W. A. Wis	1877	1	1	21	36	57	7	64	36	176		40
ʌder Dam	G. o. H. ther	1875	1		36	58	94	4	98	60	194	25	20
Belt	Wm. H. Bach	1877	1	2	51	73	124	10	134	102	200	18	95
Berlin	I. N. Stewart	1878	2	3	49	53	102		102	72	200	26	36
Black River Falls	A. R. Sprague	1875	2	1	22	36	58	2	60	83	180	10	51
Boscobel	S. R. Willoughby	1875	1	9	15	20	35	2	37	29	200	38	85
Brandon	Kirk Sp or	1877	1	1	29	42	71		71	41	200	47	24
Brodhead	T. C. Richmond	1877	1		31	50	81	7	88	38.5	180	78	34
Burlington	Edwin R. nith	1877	1	1	43	51	94		94	56	200	40	45
Chilton	J. E. h	1875	2	1	39	18	47		47	80	195	30	12
Chippewa Falls	F. P. Secor	1877	1	1	18	11	24		24	23	181		7

Statistics of Free High Schools.

TABLE No. XXIV.—STATISTICS OF FREE HIGH SCHOOLS—Continued.

1 LOCATION.	2 NAME OF PRINCIPAL.	3 Year when the school was established as a free high school.	4 Number of male teachers.	5 Number of female teachers.	6 Number of male pupils not over twenty years of age.	7 Number of female pupils not over twenty years of age.	8 Whole number not over twenty years.	9 Number registered over twenty years of age.	10 Whole number of pupils registered.	11 Average daily attendance.	12 Number of days of high school.	13 Number of pupils in common branches only.	14 Number of pupils in algebra or geometry.
…lus	G. M. Bowen	1876	2	…	88	50	88	4	93	65	198	57	65
Darlington	Dwight Kinney	1876	1	1	33	65	98	5	103	66	200	37	44
Delavan	Elias Dewey	1877	1	1	48	50	98	…	98	60	180	13	85
…re	L. K. Strong	1879	1	1	10	24	34	8	34	30	180	21	18
Durand	Frank H. Plumb	1876	1	…	20	22	42	5	50	30	177	42	5
Eau Claire	J. K. McGregor	1877	1	2	17	25	42	…	47	28	170	4	43
Elkhorn	A. I. Sherman	1876	1	1	43	41	84	5	84	56	180	50	80
Evansville	Charles W. Merriman	1877	1	1	38	33	71	…	76	41	180	10	30
Fond du Lac	C. A. Hutchins	1877	3	2	87	101	188	6	188	104	200	…	114
Fort Atkinson	J. Q. Emery	1877	1	2	51	82	183	1	139	96.5	177	…	83
Geneva	Walter Allen	1877	1	1	30	37	67	…	68	35	180	87	15
Glenbeulah	J. F. Morin	1878	1	…	27	25	52	2	52	39	176	80	12
Grand Rapids	J. Rosholt	1875	1	…	16	28	44	…	46	29.4	180	21	11
Green Bay	Alfred Thomas	1879	1	2	22	51	73	…	73	48	180	15	52
Hazel Green	S. A. Harper	1876	1	…	19	26	45	5	50	36	188	10	18
Highland	H. A. Terrill	1880	1	…	9	11	20	6	26	14.1	120	21	…

Statistics of Free High Schools.

Town	Principal	Year												
Hillsborough	John Cowsy	1876	1		15	22	87	4	41	20	154	84	7
Horicon	L. H. Clark	1878	1		47	52	99	2	101	84	200	40	31
Janesville	R. W. Burton	1878	1	3	50	110	160		161	106	185		71
Kenosha	...W. Hubbard	1875	1	2	34	47	81	1	82	70	187	31	25
Kewaunce	Michael ...	1875	1		19	15	34	1	35	20	200	20	6
La Case	...O. Durkee	1878	3	1	43	72	115	10	125	87	196		80
Lake Mills	J. H. ...	1876	1				40		48	80	180	17	21
	J. G. ...	1876	1	1	57	77	134	3	137	80	188	100	8
	W. E. ...	1875	1		37	54	91	3	93	56.8	176	41	51
Lone Rock	T. C. Morrow	1876	1		12	17	29	2	34	21	119	15	14
Madison	S. ...	1875	5				240	5	244	92	185	112	99
Marinette	J. C. Crawford	1877	1	6	5	14	19	4	19	12	200		19
Mauston	John A. Anderson	1876	1	1	42	47	89		90	61	187	37	19
Mayville	W R St. John	1876	3		30	26	56	1	56	35	200	32	24
	H. D Kinney	1876	1		31	33	64		67		176	23	14
	Geo. L. ...	1878	1	1	25	19	44	3	46	24	140	38	15
Mineral Point	J. H. Terry	1875	1		10	31	41	2	41	32	180	13	29
Monroe	N. C. Twining	1878	3		58	74	132	11	143	110	180		50
	Jas. Melville	1877	1	1	25	26	51		51	27	180	22	18
Mount Hope	J. F. Burgess	1877	1		23	16	39	7	46	34	68	46	
Muscoda	H. R. Smith	1877	1	1	32	36	68		68	55	180	63	5
	Ole N Wagley	1877	1	1			66		66	39	160	39	17
Neenah	H. A. Hobert	1875	1	1	24	51	75		75	68	200	75	32
	H. W. Deming	1875	1	1			56	2	58	30	180	45	7
New Lisbon	...T. Foster	1876	1	1	24	34	94	2	60	40	180	20	18
	H. W. Rood	1876	1		38	56	94		94	50	180	51	33
Oregon	E. S. Richmond	1879	1		15	19	84		34	31	80	7	7
Oshkosh	E. ...Wood	1877	1	8			320	12	320	210	200		
Pepin	W. E. Barker	1875	1		18	35	53	4	65	34.5	175	31	5
Pewaukee	John Steel	1875	1				60	7	64	89	100	52	17
Plymouth	W. J. Brier	1877	1		29	21	50	10	57	33.2	177	13	3
Portage	W. G. Clough	1877	2		60	66	126		136	75	193	38	26
Port Andrew	P. H. Fay	1876	1		16	15	31		46	20	120	21	40
Racine	O. S. Westcott	1877	2	3	59	83	141	2	(141)	105.8	200		2
Reedsburg	J. H. Byde	1879	1		28	42	70	4	74	46	176	43	78
Richland Center	W. S. Sweet	1875	1	1	20	24	44	5	49	87	180	27	16

Statistics of Free High Schools.

TABLE No. XXIV.—STATISTICS OF FREE HIGH SCHOOLS—Continued.

1	2	3	4	5	6	7	8	9	10	11	12	13	14
LOCATION.	NAME OF PRINCIPAL.	Year when the school was established as a free high school.	No. of male teachers.	No. of female teachers.	Number of male pupils not over twenty years of age.	Number of female pupils not over twenty years of age.	Whole number not over twenty years.	Number registered over twenty years of age.	Whole number of pupils registered.	Average daily attendance.	Number of days of high school.	Number of pupils in common branches only.	Number of pupils in algebra or geometry.
Ripon, 1st ward	James M. Craig	1877	1	1	17	18	35	1	36	34	180	17	18
Ripon, 2d ward	J. P. Haber	1877	1	1	10	32	42	1	43	33	179	18	18
Sauk City	Elvin C. Wiswall	1877	1	.	28	43	71	.	71	33	196	51	12
Sextonville	E. E. Fowler	1878	1	.	20	27	47	14	61	35	185	98	27
Shawano	L. D. Roberts	1879	1	.	15	18	33	.	33	28	60	28	5
Sheboygan	L. D. Harvey	1877	1	1	26	26	52	3	54	36	196	30	15
Sheboygan Falls	B. F. Anderson	1877	1	1	30	33	63	.	63	54	191	33	25
Shullsburg	A. L. Knight	1877	1	1	16	28	44	2	46	89.9	200	36	17
Sparta	J. H. Cummings	1876	1	3	39	77	116	6	122	94.8	200	.	54
Stevens Point	Frank L. Green	1877	1	1	32	58	90	5	95	48.2	179	25	34
Spring Green	W. A. De La Matyr	1876	1	1	38	31	69	7	76	53	180	16	53
Stockbridge	James C. Hall	1875	1	.	25	16	41	2	43	27.2	160	48	.
Stoughton	J. S. Maxson, & A. R. Ames	1876	2	1	23	27	50	.	50	29	180	.	10
Sturgeon Bay	C. M. Smith	1878	1	1	12	26	38	2	40	33.2	180	26	12
Tomah	T. B. Pray	1876	1	1	38	28	66	2	68	.	180	18	.
Two Rivers	J. M. Rait	1877	1	.	33	20	53	.	53	30	200	19	17

Statistics of Free High Schools.

Viroqua	M. L. Holt	1875	1		18	27	45	7	52	25.5	173	16	19
Watertown	W. E. Stroetzel	1876	2	1	51	71	122	2	124	54	200	25	99
Waupaca	C. M. Gates	1876	1	2	36	53	88	1	89	62	172	17	13
Waupun (Dodge Co.)	Orin F. Hall	1877	1		27	27	54		55	30	180	31	14
Waupun (F. d. L. Co.)	J. A. Kelly	1878	1	1	26	18	44		44	30	195	25	15
Wauwatosa	A. W. Smith	1877	1		10	21	31		31	24.4	180	15	16
West Depere	Geo. Clithero	1878	1	1	21	18	39		39	27	180	2	14
West Salem	E. D. Wood	1875	1	1			41		41	28	180	15	14
Wonewoc	I. A. Sabin	1877	1	1	30	34	64	1	65	43.5	180	50	5
Totals			111	96	2,419	3,241	6,483	247	6,730	av 48.9	16,003	2,535	2,449

Statistics of Free High Schools.

Table No. XXIV. — Continued.

STATISTICS OF FREE HIGH SCHOOLS—Continued.

1	15	16	17	18	19	20	21	22	23	24	25	26	27
LOCATION.	Number of pupils in natural sciences, including physical, geography and physiology.	Number of pupils in modern languages.	Number of pupils in ancient languages.	Average age of pupils on entering the high school.	Average age of pupils at leaving the high school.	Number of male graduates past year.	Number of female graduates past year.	Total number of male graduates.	Total number of female graduates.	Salary paid to principal.	Whole amount paid for instruction.	Amount received for tuition.	Amount of aid received from the State.
Almond	3			17						$200 00	$200 00	$27 00	$67 66
Appleton	60	20	20	16	19	8	2	24	2	1,400 00	2,985 00	375 00	338 45
ws.	85	7		15	9					630 00	1,035 00	51 90	213 21
Baraboo	24	9	9	15	20	4		4		1,170 00	1,580 00	200 00	338 45
Beaver Dam	30	25		16	18		5	12	31	800 00	1,375 00	22 00	338 45
Beloit	58	29	85	13.5	18	4	6	44	94	1,500 00	3,000 00	536 50	338 45
Berlin	45		20	14	18	2		2	9	1,00 00	1,850 00	154 00	338 45
Elk River Falls	80	15	6	15				19	23	1,50 00	2,250 00	240 87	338 45
Boscobel	85	34	1	16	19		4				1,350 00	97 85	
Brandon	24			14	17			8	5	90 00	700 00	121 50	236 91
Brodhead	29		8	4.8	18.8	8		7	18		1,260 00	133 00	338 45
Burlington	54	42	9	13	18		8	6	19	90 00	1,350 00	140 61	338 45
Chilton	13	13	5	14	17	8	2	5	4	80 00	900 00	870 90	304 60
Chippewa Falls	16		4							75 00	775 00		262 80

Statistics of Free High Schools.

Col...tus	78		18		15.5	18.5	1	3	3	16	$1,90 00	$1,450 00	$261 00	38 45
Dixon	44	24	10		16	17	3	6	10	20	1,55 00	1,550 00	130 00	38 45
...han	35		20		15	18	4	8	17	35	1,00 00	1,80 00	124 75	38 45
...le	15		7		15						60 00	87 50	80 00	34 04
...uld	8					21	2				6 0 00	60 00	26 50	03 06
Eau Claire	88		19		15	20	1	3	5	19	1,300 00	1,62 50		38 45
Elkhorn	44	8	13		15	17	2	3			800 00	1,160 00	97 12	38 45
Emile	55		18		15.7	18	1	3	8	5	90 00	1,260 00	34 00	338 45
Fond du Lac	188		40		14	18	2	16	51	152	1,200 00	3,90 00	25 00	38 45
Fort ...Mon.	77	28	15		14.3	18.3	4	6	16	29	90 00	2,160 00	38 28	38 45
Geneva	25				14.5	18	1		7	8	90 00	1,55 00	31 25	93 06
...th					12						60 00	1,600 00	30 00	04 60
Grand Rapids	18		10		15	18		4		23	90 00	90 00		38 45
Green Bay	56		20		14	18	8	10	3	12	1,300 00	2,90 00	24 00	82 75
...el Green	35		5		16	19		4	4		30 00	50 00		86 27
Highland	6				16						85 00	35 00		89 52
Hill	7				15.5	17.5	1	4	1	4	60 00	560 00	36 00	38 45
...gh	28		7		14	16	4	5	24	92	60 00	1,200 00	96 00	38 45
...cin	84	19	92		15.2	18.7	2	3	1		90 00	98 75	120 00	33 84
...alle	11		25		13	19	1	4	30	4	50 00	30 00	27 55	38 45
...ca					13	16		1	8		60 00	50 00	58 50	38 45
...le	8	6			14.7	18		5			50 00	4,60 00	60 00	23 06
La ...se	95	63	60		15.1	18.8	3	3	18	11	60 00	95 00	14 97	38 45
Lake ...ls	24				15	17.5	3	4	5	5	50 00	1,300 00		89 06
...lar	13		6		14	19	6	1	43	62	1,000 00	1,85 00	250 58	38 45
Lodi	51	28	15		15	18	2	9	1	4	90 00	40 00	15 00	92 29
Lone ...ok	19	80	6		13	16.2	8	4	8	3	450 00	84 95	400 00	38 45
...aton	24		120		13	17.5	1	8			1,000 00	86 00		38 45
Marinette	19	40	19		13	16	8	4			1,200 00	50 00	96 25	89 91
...h	30	10	13		13	17		8		2	50 00	850 00	69 38	87 67
...he	26	13			13	14	2	3	2	3	800 00	1,20 00	35 50	38 45
...le	21		8		14	19	1	2	2	15	420 00	420 00		12 13
...n	14		35		14	17	3	5	22	2	1,200 00	1,80 00	71 10	38 45
...l Point	29	29			15						1,100 00	2,000 00	55 00	97 99
Montello	105	6			17						85 00	85 00	14 00	38 45
...nt ...le	13										22 50	22 50		41 43

Statistics of Free High Schools.

TABLE No. XXIV.—STATISTICS OF FREE HIGH SCHOOLS—Continued.

1 LOCATION.	15 Number of pupils in natural sciences, including physical geography and physiology.	16 Number of pupils in modern languages.	17 Number of pupils in ancient languages.	18 Average age of pupils on entering the high school.	19 Average age of pupils at leaving the high school.	20 Number of male graduates past year.	21 Number of female graduates past year.	22 Total number of male graduates.	23 Total number of female graduates.	24 Salary paid to principal.	25 Whole amount paid for instruction.	26 Amount received for tuition.	27 Amount of aid received from the State.
…la	5		8	14	17	1	1	1	1	$600 00	$825 00	23 20	279 21
…ah	85	16	8	14	18					639 00	1,120 00		338 45
Neenah	23			15		4	24			1,000 00	1,500 00	23 00	338 45
Neillsville	10	23	11	15	18		5		1	800 00	825 00	129 25	279 21
New …lin	14			13.7	18		1			1,000 00	1,270 00	69 75	338 45
…bo	39		8	15		3		40	98	630 00	900 00	6 00	304 60
Oregon	20									240 00	360 00	71 00	121 82
…kh			2				11	11	1	1,750 00	5,250 00		338 45
Pepin	20	28	9	16	19	5	1		18	630 00	630 00	42 50	213 20
Pewaukee	9	2	8	14	17	2	2	15		375 00	375 00	17 00	126 90
…bgh	44	49	71	18				65	100	900 00	900 00	326 69	304 60
Portage	98	12	8	14	18.	4	9			1,200 00	1,800 00	203 69	338 45
Port Andrew	6			14	17.5					270 00	270 00	92 00	91 52
Racine	79			17.2	18.5		3	7	4	1,900 00	3,450 00	371 75	338 45
Reedsburg	25									800 00	1,160 00	111 65	289 92
…ald …er	18									700 00	760 00	179 49	257 22

Statistics of Free High Schools.

School													
Ripon, 2d dist	23		6	14	16.7	1	8		5	$600 00	$900 00	$2 80	$304 60
...k City	21		10	14	17			3	5	900 00	1,305 00	49 60	338 45
Sextonville	12	60		12	17		1		4	800 00	800 00	17 00	270 75
Shawano	24			14	17	1		1	1	350 03	350 00	45 00	118 44
Sheb... yn	10	18								283 33	283 33		95 87
Sheboygan Falls	25		11	13	16		6	1	8	1,250 00	1,750 00	25 00	338 45
Shullsburg	30	16	14	15	18		6	11	17	78 00	1,225 50	170 00	338 45
Sparta	32	34	26		18	2	8	4	10	800 00	1,100 00	39 20	338 45
Spring Green	81		4	14.1	19.1			15	22	1,200 00	2,600 00	154 20	338 45
...s Point	6		25	17	19		2	6	8	1,100 00	1,370 00	537 75	338 45
	49	43		14.8	17	4				900 00	1,300 00	2 50	338 45
				15						480 00	480 00	21 86	162 44
S...n Bay	40			14	17					800 00	800 00	41 00	236 05
Tomah	12	8	20	15.9					34	630 00	697 50	36 25	338 45
Two Rivers	30			14.5	17					1,000 00	1,360 00	161 00	338 45
	53	3	13	14	17			12		1,000 00	1,000 00	5 00	270 75
Waupaca	6	110	99	13	16					800 00	800 00	110 00	338 45
W... (Dodge Co)	99	16		15						1,200 00	2,087 00	81 75	338 45
W... (F du L Co)	5		14	14	16					800 00	1,328 00	250 00	338 45
W...a	14	42	2	14	16		7	1	11	750 00	750 00	41 00	228 45
West Depere	8			14	17.3		2		2	450 00	500 00	63 00	169 20
West Salem	15		8	15	18		2		2	800 00	800 00	213 07	270 75
Wonewoc	27			14	17					800 00	990 00		335 07
	41			16						675 00	845 00	123 00	285 98
	9									720 00	805 00	24 25	272 44
Totals	3,065	1,023	1,128	av.14.6	av.17.8	4	237	615	1,087	$78,023 83	$116,683 53	$9,862 05	$25,000 00

Colleges and Universities.

Table No. XXV.

COLLEGES AND UNIVERSITIES.

	INSTITUTION.	Location.	President of Board of Trustees.	President of Faculty.	Year of foundation.	Religious Denomination.	No. of instructors.
	1	2	3	4	5	6	7
	Beloit [?]ge	Beloit	Aaron L. [?]in	Aaron L. Chapin	1847	Cong'l and Presbyterian	11
	Carroll College	Waukesha	Vernon Tichenor	[?]ge H Reid	1841	Presbyterian	8
	College of the Sacred Heart	Prairie du Chien	William Becl er	William Becker	1865	Roman Catholic	..
	Galesville University	[?]le	J. W. McLaury	J. W. McLaury	1854	[?]n	8
	[?]le [?]sity	[?]al ton	Phi [?]as [?] [?]	E. D. [?]y	1847	Methodist Epal	11
	Milton College	Milton	W. C. Whitford	Albert Whitford	1867	Seventh-day [?]ist	9
	Mil[?] le College	[?]le	M. P. [?]tt	C. S. Farrar	1851	Unsectarian	18
	Mi[?]en House School	Franklin	H. A. [?]	H. A. [?]	1862	[?]n Reformed	6
	Northwestern University	Watertown	Augustus F. Ernst	[?]s F. Ernst	1865	Lutheran	6
	[?]le College	Racine	Stevens Parl er	[?]ens [?]arr	1852	[?]nt Epal	6
	Ripon College	Ripon	Edward H. Merrell	Edward H. Merrell	1863	Cong'l and Presbyterian	12
	St. [?] le College	[?]Mt [?]lvary	Peter Ennsdorf	[?]s Halsband	1863	Roman [?]ic	11
	University of the Sacred Heart	Watertown	C. Kelly	C. Kelly	1872	Roman [?]ic	7
	University of Wisconsin	Madison	George H. Paul	John Bascom	1848	State [?]on	88
	Wayland [?]arsity	Beaver Dam	[?]an E. Wood	Nathan E. Wood	1855	Baptist	6
	[?]in [?]le College	Fox Lake	W. J. Dawes	A. O. V[?]ht	1855	Congregational	5
						Total	152

Colleges and Universities.

TABLE No XXV.—COLLEGES AND UNIVERSITIES—Continued

Institution (1)	Freshman Male	Freshman Fem	Sophomore Male	Sophomore Fem	Junior Male	Junior Fem	Senior Male	Senior Fem	No. students not in regular classes Male (9)	Fem	No. students in preparatory classes Male (10)	Fem	Whole no. students Male (11)	Fem	Total	A.B. Male (12)	Fem	B.S. Male (13)	Fem	2d degree Male (14)	Fem	Honorary (15)	Grads last comm. (16)	Whole grads since foundation (17)	Yrs prep (18)	Yrs other aca. (19)	Yrs each coll. (20)
Beit College	21	..	15	..	12	..	15	..	10	..	94	..	142	..	142	13	..	2	..	8	..	2	15	287	8	..	4
Carroll College	8	..	..	..	..	..	..	..	..	12	10	15	20	34	54	..	..	..	..	..	..	..	7	26	2	3	..
College of the Sacred Heart	22	..	13	..	13	..	10	..	..	..	81	27	89	30	119	..	..	..	..	..	3	3	..	27	8	3	4
Galesville University	9	14	4	5	13	3	6	4	2	..	29	18	116	80	196	2	1	4	5	5	3	..	15	237	3	4	4
Milton College	7	14	5	5	3	5	5	7	..	67	63	39	82	64	146	2	7	1	..	4	..	..	10	142	2	4	4
Milw..ute College	9	..	..	..	..	..	..	..	..	..	..	127	220	220	220	..	..	..	..	..	..	..	7	150	5	..	3
Northwestern University	9	..	11	..	15	..	11	..	5	4	56	..	59	..	59	6	..	1	..	3	1	..	12	90	2	5	4
...le College	8	..	10	..	8	5	6	4	9	..	110	89	154	146	154	..	..	1	..	..	..	..	6	50	3	..	4
Ripon College	15	..	11	4	8	5	5	1	30	..	32	86	156	..	156	2	..	1	..	..	..	..	6	136	6	3	3
St. Laurence College	13	..	9	..	28	..	8	..	54	37	40	..	105	139	285	4	..	5	9	10	12	4	4	97	3	5	2
Univ'ity of the Sacred Heart	15	..	11	..	12	..	8	12	..	..	67	38	98	135	98	14	..	9	..	1	1	1	6	162	2	..	4
Wayland University	62	22	51	13	35	13	27	..	..	..	..	..	346	..	481	..	..	..	..	..	..	..	71	69	2	4	4
Wi..nein Female College	..	..	..	..	..	..	..	..	..	..	..	..	..	..	101	..	..	..	..	..	..	..	4	647	3	..	4
	..	..	..	..	..	..	..	..	..	..	..	..	..	..	..	..	..	..	..	..	..	..	..	56	..	..	..
Totals	189	68	146	29	147	31	98	31	110	120	671	350	1,506	709	2,211	143	9	26	9	27	4	10	169	2,177			

Colleges and Universities.

TABLE No. XXV.—COLLEGES AND UNIVERSITIES—Continued.

Institution	No. of weeks in scholastic year.	No. of volumes in college library.	No. of volumes added during year.	No. of volumes in society libraries.	No. of scholarships used the past year.	No. of acres occupied by site.	No. acres owned, not including site.	Cash value of site.	Cash value of acres owned not including site.	Cash value of buildings.	Cash value of apparatus, cabinets, and furniture.	Amount of endowment and other funds.	Amount of contributions the past year.	Amount of income from endowment and other funds.
	21	22	23	24	25	26	27	28	29	30	31	32	33	34
Beloit College	39	10,000	182	1,000	21	24	1,200	$15,000	$9,000	$55,000	$10,000	$143,700.00	$13,700.00	$10,000.00
Carroll College	40	300				14		8,000		3,000	300	2,000.00		140.00
College of the Sacred Heart	43					40								
Galesville University	40	4,000	100	1,000	5	12	267	5,000	10,000	20,000	1,500	4,000.00	3,500.00	
Lawrence University	38	8,770	200	700	156	2 2/5	2,000	20,000	11,650	31,000	6,600	85,465.38	12,000.00	5,765.15
Milton College	39	1,200	100				100	2,000	800	20,000	5,000	7,974.93	3,364.50	443.62
Milwaukee College	40	3,000				90		10,000			1,700	800.00		200.00
Mission House School	38					28		7,000		37,000			4,000.00	
Northwestern University	40	1,800	200		4	90	870	80,000		70,000	2,000	5,000.00	3,000.00	
Racine College	38	7,000	250	900	58	12		5,000	6,500	60,000	3,000	65,000.00	18,100.00	8,480.56
Ripon College	39	5,000		493		40		1,200		9,000	1,450			
St. Laurence College	43	560	48			235		30,000		30,000				
Univ'ity of the Sacred Heart	40	250					28,569	50,000	41,000	300,000				
University of Wisconsin	39	10,000	800			20				30,000	50,000	449,091.64		29,727.12
Wayland University	38	1,850			10	3	80	6,000				19,000.00		
Wisconsin Female College		800						2,000			500	10,190.00		
Totals		54,530	1,880	4,093	264	616 2/3	32,586	241,200	78,950	665,000	82,050	$842,221.95	$57,664.50	$54,756.45

Colleges and Universities.

TABLE No. XXV.—COLLEGES AND UNIVERSITIES—Continued.

INSTITUTION.	Amount of income from tuition and incidental fees.	Whole amount of income.	Tuition in collegiate department for year.	Tuition in preparatory department for year.	Cost of board and lodging per year.	Amount paid for instruction the past year.	Amount paid for building aid repairs the past year.	Amount paid for incidental expenses the past year.	Whole amount of expenses the past year.	Date of next commencement.
1	35	36	37	38	39	40	41	42	43	44
Beit College	$5,000 00	$15,000 00	$36	$26	$200 00	$14,800 00	$3,750 00	$2,250 00	$20,800 00	June 29, '81
Carroll College	1,600 00	1,740 00	32	24	100 00	1,550 00	10 00	180 00	1,740 00	Junc 24, '81
...ge of the ...d Heart			50	25	175 00					June 22, '81
Galesville University	2,468 00	8,233 27	40	32	100 00				12,825 26	June 30, '81
Lawrence University	2,365 50	6,163 62	21	15	142 00	7,300 00	4,000 00	1,087 24	6,148 37	Iue 29, '81
Milton College			33	27	97 50	4,067 32	818 50	362 55		Iune 21, '81
Milwaukee College	500 00	4,500 00	60	50	300 00		2,600 00			Sept. 7, '81
Mi ... House School	1,480 00	8,480 00	100	30	100 00	2,210 00	2,000 00	500 00	4,500 00	Iune 29, '81
...rn Uni versity	52,406 20		30	400		4,340 00	250 00		57,000 00	June 28, '81
Racine College	7,300 98	15,781 51	850	24	117 00	8,026 16	1,0'9 77	6,073 46	15,719 39	June 24, '81
Ripon College	48 00	48 00	24	24	130 00		240 00	1,200 00	1,440 00	Sept. 3, '81
St. Laurence College			24		100 00					June 28, '81
...y of the Sacred Heart										
University of ... Win	4,381 30	80,106 24	100	80	133 00	49,502 40	25,186 14	20,421 50	97,060 04	June 21, '81
Wayland University					88 00					June 23, '81
Wisconsin ... College			26	26	124 00					June 15, '81
Totals	$77,549 98	$140,053 67				$93,205 88	$39,824 88	$41,074 75	$217,823 06	

Theological Seminaries.

Table No. XXVI.

THEOLOGICAL SEMINARIES.

INSTITUTION.	Location.	President of Faculty.	Year of foundation.	Religious Denomination.	No. of instructors.	No. students in regular classes.	No. students in preparatory classes.	Whole No. students past year.	No. of graduates at last commencement.	Whole No. of graduates since foundation.	No. of years in theological course.	No. of years in preparatory course.	No. of weeks in scholastic year.	No. of volumes in library.
1	2	3	4	5	6	7	8	9	10	11	12	13	14	15
Luther Seminary	Madison	F. A. Schmidt.	1876	Nor. Ev. Luth'n	3	23	20	43	3	15	3			300
Mission House School	Franklin	HA Muehlmeier	1862	German Ref'm'd	3	7	6	13			3		38	2,221
Nashotah House	Nashota Miss'n	Azel P. Cole	1842	Prot. Episcopal	4	16		16	8	212	3		42	7,000
Norwegian Seminary	Marshall	David Lysnes	1874	Nor. Lutheran	1	3	11	14		8	3		34	475
St. Francis de Sales	St. Francis	Killian C. Flasch	1856	Roman Catholic	13	105	140	245	28	325	3	7	42	7,000
Totals					24	154	177	331	39	560				16,996

Theological Seminaries.

TABLE No. XXVI.—THEOLOGICAL SEMINARIES—Continued.

INSTITUTION.	Number of volumes added during the year.	Number acres of land occupied by site.	Number acres land owned, not including site.	Cash value of site.	Cash value of buildings.	Amount of endowment and other funds.	Amount of contributions the past year.	Income from endowment and other funds.	Whole amount of income the past year.	Tuition in regular department for the year.	Tuition in preparatory department for the year.	Cost of board and lodging for the year.	Amount paid for instruction the past year.	Amount paid for building and repairs the past year.	Amount paid for incidental expenses the past year.	Date of next commencement.
	16	17	18	19	20	21	22		24	25	26	27	28	29	30	31
Luther Seminary	20	3		$4,000	$15,000			$4,000	$4,000	Free.	Free.	$80	$4,000	$200	$50	Sept. 1, '81
Mission House School	87	90	410	10,000		$5,000	$4,000	200		Free.	Free.	Free.				Sept. 7, '81
Nashotah House		40			90,000	52,000	6,000	4,000	10,000	Free.	Free.	Free.				June 29, '81
Norwegian Seminary	5					15,000										Sept. 11, '81
St. Francis De Sales		160		100,000												Sept. 7, '81
Totals	112	293	410	$114,000	$105,000	$72,000	$10,000	$8,200	$14,000				$4,000	$200	$50	

Table No. XXVII.
ACADEMIES.

Academies.

INSTITUTION.	Location.	President of Board of Trustees.	Principal.	Year of Foundation.	Religious Denomination.	Number of instructors.
1	2	3	4	5	6	7
Big F..ot Academy	Walworth	O. U. Whitford	O E .t Min	1857	Seventh-day Baptist	2
German & English Acad..my	Milwaukee	I. Keller	I Keller	1849	Unsectarian	12
Janesville Engl sh Acad	Janesville	J. B Silsbee	J. B. .afe	1880	Unsectarian	7
Ken per Hall	Pleasant Prairie	Sr. Edith	L. C. .nc	1872	Prot nt Episcopal	7
Lake Geneva Seminary	Geneva	Julia A. Warner	Julia A. ..Wir	1869	..ian	7
Markl am ..my	Milwaul .te		Albert Markham	1864	..ian	4
Marshall Ad my	Ma shall	O. J. Hallestad	F. W. Denison	1869	Norwegian Lutheran	4
Mo..	Madison		J. J. Anc. rsn	1876	Evang-lical .tan	6
National German Seminary	Milwaukee		I. Keller	1878	..atian	8
..ac Seminary	..ac	John G. McMynn	Grace P. Jones	1856	Prot Episcopal	5
Racine Academy	Rochester	G. H. Hub'ard	Irn G. NcMynn	1875	Unsectarian	4
Rocl ester Seminary	Racine	M. Hyacintha	R. M. Burrus	1867	Free Will B.. tst	4
St. Gtherine's .tale Acad	Sinsinawa M'nd.	M. Emilie	M. Hyacintha	1860	Roman Catholic	
St. Era Academy	Prairle du Chien	M. Emilie	M. Emilie	1852	.an Catholic	8
St. Mary's Institute	Sharon	Sr. M. Seraphia	Sr. M. Seraphia	1872	.an Catholic	12
Sharon .aly	Racine	John L.ndon	O. W. .nk	1866	..arian	1
.e Home School		Mary S. M ..thy	Mry S. .. Mrphy	1877	P.t Epi ..pal	10
					Total....	161

Academies.

TABLE No. XXVIII.— ACADEMIES — Continued.

Institution.	No. of students in academic classes. — Male	Fem.	No. of students not in regular classes. — Male	Fem.	No. of students in preparatory classes. — Male	Fem.	Whole No. of students the past year.	No. students who graduated past yr. — Male	Fem.	No. of Graduates since foundation. — Male	Fem.	No. of students in English course.	No. of students in classical course.	No. of students in modern languages.	No. of students in natural sciences.	No. of students preparing to enter college.	No. of years in academic course.	No. of weeks in scholastic year.	No. of volumes in academic library.	No. of volumes added the past year.	No. of volumes in society libraries.	No. of scholarships used the past year.	No. of acres of land occupied by site.	No. acres of land owned, not including site.
	8		9		10		11	12		13		14	15	16	17	18	19	20	21	22	23	24	25	26
Big Foot Academy	69				90		72					259	52		160			39					2	
German & English Academy	27	33			7	57	259					32		250	15			14	500					
Janesville English Academy		29	6	7		13	32				12	20	11		29	6	4	36	1,000		50	12	6½	
Kemper Hall	8	24		8	20	9	36			65		67	26	28	43		4	88	1,000	20	50		6	
Lake Geneva Seminary	8	29	5	5	24	28	116	4		2		88	42	6	40	88	4	88						
Markham Academy	52						80					14	11	37		8	4	40	800					
Marshall Academy	18	14			33	43	32		2	25	14	96		7			4	32		29				
Monona Academy	10						76			4	1			26	26		3	38	800					
National German Seminary		5					26	8			55						3	44	250					
Oconomowoc Seminary					30	35	88		5	4	23	72	7	60	12			40	50	50			11¾	
Racine Academy			69	19		22	65		4					12	50		4	38	2,050				1	100
Rochester Seminary	57				25	10	106				5			75	110			44	925	350			3½	800
St. Catharine's Male and							72					35	6					46	1,000				40	
St. Clara Acad.	120						145							7	13		4	40					10	
St. Mary's Institute	30		4		43		63					57						30	3,000	20			2	
Wharton Academy																								
The Home School																		40						
Totals	184	342	87	92	229	259	1,808	14	22	96	139	620	155	517	498	42			9,075	469	50	12	12.82¾	400

Academies.

TABLE No. XXVII. — ACADEMIES — Continued.

INSTITUTION.	Cash value of site.	Cash value of land owned, not including site.	Cash value of buildings.	Cash value of apparatus and cabinets.	Amount of endowment and other funds.	Income from tuition and incidental fees.	Whole amount of income the past year.
	27	28	29	30	31	32	33
Big Foot Academy	$250 00		1,500 00			$10,000 00	$13,000 00
German and English Academy			25,000 00	5,000 00		1,000 00	1,000 00
Janesville High Academy				150 00		10,800 00	10,800 00
Kemper Hall	26,144 00		50,000 00	2,000 00			9,200 00
Lake Geneva Seminary	8,000 00		43,000 00	1,000 00			
Markham Academy	6,000 00		6,000 00	1,000 00			18,000 00
Marshall Academy							
Monona Academy					$18,000 00		
German Seminary			15,000 00	1,000 00	35,000 00		35,000 00
Oconomowoc Seminary	10,000 00		4,000 00			5,100 00	5,100 00
Racine day	2,500 00		5,000 00			1,000 00	1,000 00
Rochester day	100 00		16,000 00				
St. Female Academy	10,000 00	$3,000 00	40,000 00	750 00		10,000 00	10,000 00
St. day		15,000 00	45,000 00			7,172 35	7,172 35
St. Mary's Institute	5,000 00					210 00	210 00
Sharon day	800 00	1,000 00	7,000 00			4,000 00	4,000 00
The Home School	800 00						
Totals	$69,594 00	$19,000 00	$263,500 00	$10,900 00	$53,000 00	$49,282 35	$114,482 35

Academies.

TABLE No. XXVII. — ACADEMIES — Continued.

INSTITUTION.	Tuition and incidental fees for the year.	Cost of board and lodging for the year.	Amount paid for instruction the past year.	Amount paid for building and repairs the past year.	Amount paid for incidental expenses the past year.	Whole amount of expenses the past year.	Date of next closing exercises.
	34	35	36	37	38	39	40
Big Foot Academy	$24 00		$10,000 00	$35 00	$500 00	$12,500 00	July 8, '81
German and English Academy	60 00	$120 00		2,000 00	45 00		July 1, '81
Janesville English Academy	15 00	120 00		10 00	300 00	11,000 00	June 24, '81
Kemper Hall	150 00	150 00	3,660 00	2,585 00	5,270 00		June 23, '81
Lake Geneva Seminary	32 00	270 00	1,000 00	300 0:			June 23, '81
Markham Academy	120 00						June 1, '81
Marshall Academy	18 00						
Monona Academy	29 00	82 00					
National German Seminary		120 00	3,000 00		150 00	3,150 00	July 8, '81
Oconomowoc Seminary	50 00	300 00					
Racine Academy	100 00	256 00	2,600 00	175 00	200 00	2,975 00	June 25, '81
Rochester Seminary	24 00	95 00		500 00			
St. Catherine's Female Academy		140 00					June 80, '81
St. Clara Academy	165 00						July 1, '81
St. Mary's Institute		150 00					June 30, '81
Sharon Academy			210 00	1,800 00	5,422 20	6,722 20	
The Home School	100 00	300 00					June 29, '81
Totals			$20,470 00	$6,905 00	$11,887 20	$43,717 20	

Business Colleges.

Table No. XXVIII.
BUSINESS COLLEGES.

INSTITUTION.	LOCATION.	PRINCIPAL.	Year of foundation.	No. of instructors.	No. of students the past year.	No. of graduates the past year.	Whole No. of graduates since foundation.	No. of weeks in scholastic year.
1	2	3.	4	5	6	7	8	9
Green Bay Business College	Green Bay	C. A. Murch	1868	2	150	15	...	52
La Crosse Business College	La Crosse	J. L. Wallace	1808	2	176	12	...	52
North Western Business College	Madison	R. G. Deming	1865	5	190	...	...	40
Oshkosh Business College	Oshkosh	W. W. Daggett	1867	4	120	...	455	52
Silsbee Commercial College	Janesville	J. B. ...ie	1877	3	107	12	50	40
Spencerian Business College	Milwaukee	Robert C. Spencer	1863	5	212	...	94	52
		...s	...	21	955	39	599	...

Business Colleges.

TABLE No. XXVIII.— BUSINESS COLLEGES — Continued.

INSTITUTION.	No. of volumes in library.	No. of volumes added the past year.	No. of scholarships used the past year.	Cash value of apparatus and other appurtenances.	Income from tuition and incidental fees.	Tuition for the year.	Cost of board and lodging for the year.	Amount paid for instruction the past year.	Amount paid for incidental expenses the past year.	Whole amount of expenses the past year.	Date of the close of the year.
1	10	11	12	13	14	15	16	17	18	19	20
Green Bay Bus. College	150	6	16	$200	$1,300 00	$40			$300 00	$1,300	
La Crosse Bus. College	300	21	176					$250	700 00	950	June 24, 1881
Northwestern Bus. College					3,225 00	36	$150	300	310 00	610	
Oshkosh Bus. College	100	15	85	1,000	200 00	50	120	150	240 00	390	
Silsbee Com. College			110	350	2,571 50		2C0		2,048 68	2,048	
Spencerian Bus. College	260				6,840 00	85					
Totals	810	42	387	$3,350	$14,096 50			$700	$3,598 68	$5,498	

Table No. XXIX.

DISTRIBUTION OF DICTIONARIES.

STATEMENT *showing the counties, towns, and districts, which have been supplied with dictionaries during the year ending December 10, 1880.*

COUNTIES.	TOWNS.	Depart-ments.	No. of district.	No. of copies.
Adams	Big Flats	.....	8	1
Barron	Clinton	......	2	1
	Dallas, and Sheridan, Dunn county	.. ...	1	1
	Shetek	......	11	1
Brown	Depere, village...................	2	1	2
	Eaton....	......	8	1
	Fort Howard, city....	8	2	8
	Preble	......	1	1
	West Depere, village	2	....	2
	Wrightstown	2	1	2
Buffalo.......	Dover	......	4	1
	Montana..........................	......	4	1
Burnett	Bashan	......	1	1
	Grantsburg	......	8	1
	Trade Lake.................. ...	......	4, 5	2
Calumet......	Chilton	......	7	1
Chippewa	Bloomer....	.....	9, 11	2
	Chippewa Falls, city	2	2	2
	Lafayette, & Seymour, Eau Claire Co.	......	8	1
	Sigel	......	18	1
	Wheaton.........................	......	5, 7	2
Clark	Eaton and Loyal	......	1	1
	Grant............................	......	5	1
	Hixton	......	4, 5	2
	Pine Valley......................	2	4	2
	Unity............................	......	2, 4	2
	Warner	......	4, 5	2
	Weston and York	......	2	1
	York	......	2, 3, 4	8
Columbia	Arlington, and Vienna, Dane Co....	......	1	1
	Courtland..	......	1	1
	Courtland and Randolph, joint with Fox Lake and Westport, Dodge Co.	1	9	1
	Randolph, Scott, and Kingston....	......	7	1
Dane.........	Dane and Vienna..................	......	4	1
	Madison, city	1	....	1
	Madison and Fitchburg....	......	1	1
	Stoughton, village.	4	8	4
	Vienna and Windsor, joint with Leeds, Columbia Co.............	......	5	1
	Westport	1	1	1
Dodge	Beaver Dam	......	7	1
	Burnett and Oak Grove............	......	2	1
	Elba.............................	......	2	1
	Westport.........................	......	7	1

Distribution of Dictionaries.

TABLE No. XXIX.— DISTRIBUTION OF DICTIONARIES — Continued.

COUNTIES.	TOWNS.	Departments.	No. of districts.	No. of copies.
Door	Bailey's Harbor..............	.....	2	1
	Gardner	.....	3	1
	Gibraltar	1	1	1
	Gibraltar	.....	3	1
Dunn	Dunn.......................	1	2	1
	Lucas	.....	4	1
	Menomonie.................	6	1	6
	Sand Creek, Sheridan, etc.	.....	1	1
	Sheridan...................	.....	5	1
	Sherman...	6	8	2
	Stanton	.....	2	1
	Taintor.................	.....	1	1
	Tiffany	.....	5	1
Eau Claire ...	Bridge Creek...............	.....	2	1
	Bridge Creek	1	3	1
	Eau Claire............	2	3	2
	Fairchild	.....	8	1
	Ludington	.....	5,6	2
	Otter Creek.................	.....	6	1
	Pleasant Valley.................	.....	9	1
	Washington	.....	5	1
Fond du Lac .	Metomen....................	1	12	1
	Ripon	2	2	2
Grant	Beetown...	.....	10	1
	Fennimore..................	1	2	1
Green	Monroe..................	3	1	3
Green Lake..	Manchester	.....	7	7
Iowa	Eden and Highland.................	.....	2	1
	Highland.....................	3	8	3
	Pulaski..................	1	1	1
Jackson	Franklin	.....	2	1
	Melrose....	.....	8	1
	Sullivan	.....	1,2,3	3
Jefferson	Jefferson, city.................	2	1	2
Juneau........	Armenia.................	.....	4	1
	Necedah	1	1	1
Kenosha	Brighton and Paris	.....	6	1
	Randall and Salem.................	1	9	1
Kewaunee....	Krok	.....	1	1
	Montpelier..................	.....	4	1
La Crosse	La Crosse, city...	2	....	2
La Fayette ...	Gratiot	1	1	1
Langlade	Langlade..................	.....	2,3,6	3
	Spring Brook	.....	1 to 6	6
Lincoln	Pine River..................	.....	4	1
Manitowoc ...	Cato, Eaton, and Rockland	.....	4	1
	Kossuth	.....	2	1
Marathon	Brighton....	.....	6	1
	Holeton	.....	8,4	2

Distribution of Dictionaries.

TABLE No. XXIX.— DISTRIBUTION OF DICTIONARIES — Continued.

COUNTIES.	TOWNS.	Departments.	No. of districts.	No. of copies.
Marathon--con	Hull	......	5	1
	Marathon.........................	......	5,6	2
	Mosinee	1	1	1
	Rietbrock	......	2	1
	Weston	......	5	1
Marinette	Marinette....................	5	1	5
	Peshtigo......	2	1	2
	Peshtigo.........................	......	9, 11,12	8
Milwaukee ...	Greenfield	......	4	1
	Lake	......	1	1
	Milwaukee, city................	9	....	9
Monroe	Clifton	......	5	1
	Wells.........................	......	8	1
Oconto	Gillett.......................	......	5	1
	Little River..................	......	8	1
	Pensaukee	1	2	1
Outagamie ...	Appleton, city	1	1	1
	Appleton, city	2	2	2
	Bovina	......	6	1
	Buchanan	......	2	1
	Kaukauna	......	5	1
	Kaukauna, & Wrightst'n, Brown Co	......	1	1
	Liberty	......	8	1
	Maine	......	8	1
	Seymour	......	6,7	2
Ozaukee	Port Washington................	4	1	4
	Saukville	......	8	1
Pepin	Pepin	......	7	1
	Waterville	......	6	1
Pierce........	Ellsworth.....................	... .	7,8	2
	Hartland	1	1	1
	Salem	......	4	1
	Trimbelle.....................	......	2	1
Polk..........	Alden	......	6	1
	Laketown	......	4	1
	Luck	......	8	1
	Osceola.......................	8	9	2
Portage	Alban	......	2	1
	Carson	......	4	1
	Grant.........................	......	8	1
	Hull..........................	......	4	1
	Sharon	......	6	1
	Stevens Point.................	......	2,8	2
	Stockton......................	......	18	1
Price	Brannan.......................	......	1,2	2
Racine	Racine, city..................	5	....	5
	Raymond	......	8	1
Richland	Orion	......	5	1
	Richwood	1	9	1

TABLE No. XXIX. — DISTRIBUTION OF DICTIONARIES — Continued.

COUNTIES.	TOWNS.	Departments.	No. of districts.	No. of copies.
St. Croix	Baldwin	......	1,2	2
	Cylon	......	2	1
	Emerald.............................	......	4	1
	Richmond and Star Prairie	1	1	1
	St. Joseph..........................	......	3	1
	Somerset	......	6	1
	Warren.............................	......	6	1
Sauk	Freedom	......	6	1
	Prairie du Sac	1	5	1
	Reedsburg..........................	1	1	1
Shawano	Angelica	......	2	2
	Fairbanks	......	1	1
	Green Valley	......	2	1
	Milltown	......	4,6	2
	Washington.........................	......	8	1
Sheboygan ...	Lyndon.............................	......	9	1
	Sheboygan, city....................	1	....	1
Taylor	Medford	......	1,2	2
	Medford	......	4 to 7	4
Trempealeau .	Lincoln.............................	......	3	1
	Pigeon	......	2	1
	Preston.............................	......	1,5	2
Vernon	Forest	......	3	1
Walworth	East Troy..	......	3	1
Washington ..	Barton and West Bend	......	13	1
	Farmington........	1	5	1
Waukesha....	Lisbon	......	5	1
	Lisbon	1	10	1
	Muskego and New Berlin	......	1	1
	Pewaukee	1	3	1
Waupaca.....	Helvetia	......	2	1
	Little Wolf	......	6	1
	Little Wolf, Mukwa, etc............	2	2	2
	Union	......	5	1
Waushara....	Hancock	......	9,10	2
	Leon and Saxville.............. .	1	1	1
Winnebago...	Nepeuskun, Omro, etc..............	2	1	2
Wood	Auburndale.........................	......	3	1
	Centralia, city	1	1	1
	Lincoln	......	4	1
	Marshfield	......	2,3	2
	Sigel	......	5	1
	Wood	.....	4	1
	Total number copies	......	....	267

Dictionaries Sold.

Table No. XXX.

DICTIONARIES SOLD.

STATEMENT *showing the districts to which dictionaries have been sold during the year ending December 10, 1880.*

COUNTIES.	TOWNS.	Departments.	No. of district.	No. of copies.
Adams	New Haven	......	5	1
	Quincy.............................	......	4	1
Ashland......	Ashland............................	......	1	1
Brown	Howard...	......	4	1
Buffalo.......	Maxville	......	2	1
Calumet......	Brothertown.......	......	9	1
	Chilton	......	4	1
	Stockbridge	......	4	1
Chippewa ...	Chippewa Falls, city.......	1	1	1
Clark	Beaver	......	1	1
Columbia	Arlington	......	5	1
	Caledonia...........	......	2, 7	2
	Columbus	......	1	1
	Fountain Prairie and Otsego	......	6	1
	Hampden	......	3, 6	2
	Lodi	1	1	1
	Lowville	......	5	1
	Newport, and Dell Prairie, Sauk Co	......	6	1
	Scott	......	2	1
	West Point	......	4	1
Crawford	Eastman	... ..	2, 5	2
	Seneca.............................	......	2	1
	Utica	......	1	1
Dane....	Blooming Grove, (Jt.)	......	1	1
	Bristol and York..................	......	5	1
	Madison.........	......	7	1
	Madison, city......................	4	....	4
	Middleton	......	3, 8, 9	3
	Oregon	......	9	1
	York	......	1	1
Dodge	Burnett and Chester	......	1	1
	Calamus	......	1	1
	Chester and Waupun	......	7	1
	Hebron	......	1	1
	Hubbard............................	2	1	2
Door	Gibraltar ·	......	1	1
Dunn	Lucas, Menomonie, and Weston....	......	4	1
Eau Claire ...	Fairchild	......	3	1
	Union	......	5	1
Fond du Lac .	Eldorado	......	6	1
	Osceola............................	......	2	1
	Rosendale and Springvale	......	7	1·
	Taycheedah	......	6	1

Dictionaries Sold.

TABLE No. XXX.— DICTIONARIES SOLD — Continued.

COUNTIES.	TOWNS.	Depart-ments.	No. of districts.	No. of copies.
Grant	Boscobel............................	1	1	1
	Glen Haven..........................	......	4	1
	Lancaster............................	......	1, 3	2
	Smelser.............................	......	2, 4	2
	Woodman	......	1	1
Green	Albany	......	8	1
	Brooklyn	.....	10	1
	Jordan, and Wiota, La Fayette Co..	......	4	1
	Spring Grove	......	4, 7, 9	3
	Washington.........................	......	1	1
Jackson	Melrose	......	5	1
Jefferson	Cold Spring	......	4	1
	Farmington.........................	......	1	1
	Waterloo, village...................	......	1	1
	Watertown..	......	2	1
Juneau	Germantown........................	......	3	1
	Lemonweir and Lisbon.	......	12	1
	Plymouth...........................	......	8	1
	Wonewoc...........................	......	8	1
Kenosha	Bristol.............................	......	11	1
	Prairie	......	4	1
	Somers	......	1	1
La Crosse	Bangor	......	4	1
La Fayette ...	Belmont	......	1	1
	Darlington	......	7	1
Manitowoc ...	Cato................................	......	7, 10	2
	Manitowoc	......	8	1
Marathon	Mosinee	......	1	1
Marinette	Peshtigo............................	1	1	1
Marquette ...	Montello and Shields...............	... ..	3	1
	Oxford	......	8	1
Milwaukee ...	Wauwatosa	......	7	1
Monroe	Leon and Wells.....................	......	1	1
	Sparta..............................	... ..	2	1
	Tomah	......	8	1
Outagamie ...	Appleton, city......................	2	2	2
	Appleton, city......................	2	4	2
	Bovina	......	3	1
Pierce	Clifton. Oak Grove, and Prescott ...	......	1	1
	River Falls....	......	6	1
Polk	Eureka	......	1	1
	Farmington	......	2	1
	Osceola............................	......	5	1
Portage	Almond	......	6	2
	Amherst............................	2	2	2
Racine	Burlington, Dover, and Rochester .	......	1	1
	Caledonia...........................	......	16	1
	Dover..............................	......	1	1
	Rochester	......	2	1
	Yorkville...........................	......	8	1

Dictionaries Sold.

TABLE No. XXX.— DICTIONARIES SOLD — Continued.

COUNTIES.	TOWNS.	Departments.	No. of districts.	No. of copies.
Richland.....	Dayton	......	1	1
	Eagle...	......	1, 2	2
	Forest	......	2	1
	Marshall and Rockbridge	......	1	1
	Richwood	......	2	1
Rock	Beloit and Rock	......	1	1
	Clinton ,.........................	1	2	1
	Clinton	......	3	1
	Fulton	2	8	2
	Harmony...	......	5	1
	Johnstown..........................	......	2	1
	Newark	.....	5	1
	Porter.................................	......	8	1
St. Croix.....	Richmond	......	2, 3	2
Sauk	Delton............................	......	7	1
	Excelsior	......	8	1
	Fairfield	......	6	1
	Franklin...........................	......	3	1
	Greenfield	......	3	1
	Merrimack	......	1	1
	Prairie du Sac	... .	5	1
	Reedsburg........................	1	1	1
	Washington......................	......	4	1
	Westfield	......	7	1
	Woodland & Westford, Richland Co.	......	7	1
Sheboygan ...	Holland	......	10	1
	Lima...............................	......	5	1
	Mitchell (Jt.)	......	11	1
	Mitchell & Osceola, Fond du Lac Co.	.....	1	1
	Mosel	......	1, 2, 3	3
	Scott	......	1	1
	Wilson	......	6	2
Trempealeau .	Arcadia	......	2, 5	2
	Lincoln and Pigeon	......	1	1
Vernon.......	Greenwood and Hillsborough.......	.. ..	3	1
	Sterling and Freeman, Crawford Co.	......	12	1
	Union	......	4	1
Walworth	Bloomfield.........................	......	1	1
	Delavan	......	6, 7	2
	Geneva	.....	8	1
	Lyons	1	2	1
	Spring Prairie (Jt.)..............	......	1	1
	Sugar Creek	......	5	1
	Whitewater	......	5	1
	Whitewater and Richmond	......	9	1
Washington ..	Hartford...........................	......	7	1
	Kewaskum	......	8	1
Waukesha	Delafield and Merton..............	......	2	1
	Delafield, Pewaukee, etc	......	10	1
	Genesee	......	3, 4	2

Dictionaries Sold.

TABLE No. XXX. — DICTIONARIES SOLD — Continued.

COUNTIES.	TOWNS.	Departments.	No. of districts.	No. of copies.
Waukesha...	Genesee and Mukwonago...........	......	8	1
	Pewaukee	2	1	2
	Summit	......	1	1
	Waukesha	......	7	1
	Waukesha (Jt.)	......	12	1
Waupaca.....	Lebanon........................	......	4	1
	Weyauwega	......	3	1
Waushara....	Marion	......	2	1
	Wautoma........................	......	5	1
Winnebago...	Algoma and Omro	......	2	1
	Clayton, Menasha, and Neenah.....	......	4	1
	Menasha........................	......	1	1
	Neenah, city...................	1	....	1
	Nepeuskun	......	2, 9	2
	Omro and Winneconne............	......	5	1
	Oshkosh and Vinland	......	4	1
	Total number copies	....		187

City Superintendents.

Table No. XXXI.

CITY SUPERINTENDENTS.

In Commission, December, 1880.

CITY.	NAME.	No. of schools in city.	Salary.	Expenses for printing, postage, and stationery.
Appleton	A. H. Conkey	8	$275	$25 00
Beaver Dam	James J. Dick	8	200	150 00
Beloit	T. C. Chamberlin	7	100	....
Berlin	D. P. Blackstone	2	100	5 00
Columbus	John S. Maxwell	5	50	30 00
Fond du Lac	C. A. Hutchins	16	500	200 00
Fort Howard	George Richardson	2	250	20 90
Grand Rapids	J. Rosholt	1	100	10 00
Green Bay	J. H. Leonard	5	300	50 00
Hudson	Simon Hunt	2	180	....
Janesville	R. W. Burton	12	1,500	100 00
Kenosha	John W. Hayes	6	200	100 00
La Crosse	J. J. Fruit	11	800	125 00
Madison	S. Shaw	8	2,000	30 00
Menasha	Chas. R. Smith	1	50	5 00
Milwaukee	James Mac Alister	25	2,750	1,159 28
Mineral Point	H. Van Dusen	5	100	10 00
Neenah	John B. Russell	4	200	25 00
Oconto	Hamilton Allen	5	150	25 00
Oshkosh	George H. Read	3	600	295 90
Portage	A. C. Kellogg	14	300	5 00
Prairie du Chien	A. C. Wallin	4	100	20 00
Racine	E. B. Gray	8	1,500	....
Sheboygan	James Bell	11	150	30 00
Stevens Point	Frank L. Green	4	100	....
Watertown	William H. Rohr	5	300	35 72
Wausau	B. W. James	5	100	25 00
	Totals	187	$12,955	$2,480 00

County Superintendents.

Table No. XXXII.

COUNTY SUPERINTENDENTS.

In Commission, December, 1880.

COUNTY.	NAME.	POST OFFICE.	No. of schools in county.	Salary.	Printing, postage, and stationery.
Adams	Jesse M. Higbee...	Plainville	67	$500	$51 00
Ashland......	E. C. Smith.......	Ashland........	6	100	25 00
Barron	H. J. White........	Sumner	63	500	100 00
Bayfield......	John McCord	Bayfield.......	2	100	....
Brown	Minnie H. Kelleher	Depere........	87	800	100 00
Buffalo.......	J. C. Rathbun......	Alma	89	800	175 00
Burnett	E. M. Wilson......	Grantsburg	12	100	10 00
Calumet.....	M. B. Minaghan...	Chilton	67	800	100 00
Chippewa	C. D. Tillinghast...	Bloomer	101	1,000	200 00
Clark	John S. Dore	Neillsville. ...	79	800	200 00
Columbia	Henry Neill.......	Portage	146	1,000	200 00
Crawford.....	J. H. McDonald ...	Eastman	92	800	176 14
Dane, 1st dist..	C. E. Buell	Sun Prairie....	136	800	200 00
Dane, 2d dist..	E. E. Fitz Gibbons.	Waunakee	131	800	146 50
Dodge	John T. Flavin	Watertown	191	1,200	150 00
Door.........	Chris Daniels......	Sturgeon Bay..	52	500	75 00
Douglas	Irvin W. Gates	Superior	5	50	....
Dunn	Florence Tickner..	Menomonie....	103	800	155 01
Eau Claire ...	Agnes Hosford	Eau Claire	64	800	150 00
Fond du Lac .	Ed. McLoughlin...	Eldorado Mills	191	1,100	163 00
Grant........	Charles L. Harper .	Hazel Green ..	264	1,000	216 00
Green........	D. H. Morgan	Albany	165	800	200 00
Green Lake. .	A. W. Millard	Manchester ...	68	800	150 00
Iowa.........	Wm. A. Jones	Mineral Point.	129	800	150 00
Jackson	T. P. Marsh	Sechlerville...	87	800	150 00
Jefferson	C. L. Hubbs.......	Fort Atkinson.	130	800	135 57
Juncau	W. G. Spence......	Mauston	107	800	200 00
Kenosha	Daniel A. Mahoney	Salem........	61	750	150 00
Kewaunee ...	W. H. Timlin	Kewaunee.....	54	800	100 00
La Crosse.....	C. S. Stockwell	Onalaska......	76	800	150 00
La Fayette ...	C. G Thomas......	Darlington	126	900	200 00
Lincoln.	David Finn........	Jenny.........	15	300	50 00
Manitowoc...	C F. Viebahn	Manitowoc	138	1,200	....
Marathon	Thomas Greene....	Wausau.......	77	800	69 75
Marinette	L. W. Winslow	Peshtigo	30	500	10 00
Marquette ...	Rich. G. O'Connor.	Montello	59	500	150 00
Milw., 1st dist.	James A. R an ...	Oak Creek	36	500	59 25
Milw., 2d dist.	Geo. H. Fowler....	Wauwatosa....	34	800	65 00
Monroe	A. F Brand	Sparta	123	800	72 72
Oconto.......	Hamilton Allen...	Oconto........	41	500	100 00
Outagamie ...	John A. Leith	Mackville.....	106	800	200 00
Ozaukee	W. F. Scott	Cedarburg. ...	59	800	75 00
Pepin	W. E. Barker......	Pepin.........	37	500	68 85
Pierce........	Jas. T. McCleary ..	River Falls....	105	800	140 00
Polk.........	Henry P. Dike ...	Osceola Mills .	65	500	150 00
Portage	Andrew P. Een....	Amherst.......	84	800	44 23

County Superintendents.

TABLE No. XXXII. — COUNTY SUPERINTENDENTS — Continued.

COUNTY.	NAME.	POST OFFICE.	No. schools in county.	Salary.	Expenses for printing, postage, and stationery.
Price	J. D. Wyatt........	Phillips........	5	$150	$100 00
Racine	Charles A. Morse..	Racine	75	800	99 42
Richland	David D. Parsons..	Richland Center	129	800	100 00
Rock, 1st dist.	John W. West	Evansville......	92	800	150 00
Rock, 2d dist.	William Jones	Clinton.........	95	800	108 44
St. Croix.....	Betsey M. Clapp...	New Richmond.	105	800	201 00
Sauk.........	James T. Lunn	Ironton	165	1,000	86 00
Shawano	William Sommers .	Shawano	71	500	75 00
Sheboygan ...	B. R. Grogan	Elkhart Lake...	126	800	·200 00
Taylor	John B. Anderson .	Chelsea	18	200	25 00
Trempealeau .	Stephen Richmond	Arcadia	99	800	130 48
Vernon	William Haughton	Viroqua	153	800	115 00
Walworth	W. R. Taylor	Whitewater.....	124	800	180 00
Washington ..	James Finnegan ..	Kewaskum	106	800	45 00
Waukesha....	John Howitt	Waukesha......	118	850	185 00
Waupaca	L. L. Wright	Waupaca........	108	1,000	200 00
Waushara ...	Jas. H. Tobin......	Auroraville.....	101	800	21 00
Winnebago...	W. W. Kimball....	Eureka	101	800	110 00
Wood	T. E. Nash	Centralia.......	46	600	....
		Totals	5,779	$46,400	$7,564 81

Lightning Source UK Ltd.
Milton Keynes UK
UKHW01f1000180918
329097UK00014B/1409/P